THE ENGLISH NOVEL
IN HISTORY
1895–1920

Written specifically for students and assuming no prior knowledge of the subject, David Trotter's *The English Novel in History 1895–1920* provides the first detailed and fully comprehensive analysis of early twentieth-century English fiction.

Whereas all previous studies have been rigorously selective, Trotter looks at over 140 novelists across the whole spectrum of fiction: from the innovations of Joyce's *Ulysses* through to popular mass-market genres such as detective stories and spy-thrillers.

By examining the novels in both stylistic and historical terms, David Trotter looks at the ways in which writers responded to contemporary preoccupations such as the spectacle of consumption and the growth of suburbia, or to anxieties about the decline of Empire, racial 'degeneration' and 'sexual anarchy'. He also challenges the view that literature of the period can be interpreted as a neat procession from realism to Modernism.

The English Novel in History 1895–1920 is a stunning and thought-provoking study, and one that will redefine our understanding of literary Modernism. It will rapidly establish itself as the most comprehensive introduction to the subject and will be essential reading for all students of modern English literature.

David Trotter is Quain Professor of English Language and Literature at University College London.

THE NOVEL IN HISTORY
Edited by Gillian Beer
Girton College, Cambridge

Informed by recent narrative theory, each volume in this series will provide an authoritative yet lively and energetic account of the English novel in context. Looking at the whole spectrum of fiction, at elite, popular and mass-market genres, the series will consider the ways in which fiction not only reflects, but also helps shape contemporary opinion. Incisive and interdisciplinary, the series as a whole will radically challenge the development model of English literature, and enable each period – from the eighteenth century to the present day – to be assessed on its own terms.

THE ENGLISH NOVEL IN HISTORY 1895–1920

David Trotter

London and New York

Front cover illustration (paperback): 'The Lord of the Dynamos' by Alvin Langdon Coburn, from H.G. Wells's *The Door in the Wall* (1911), courtesy of the International Museum of Photography, George Eastman House.

First published 1993
by Routledge
11 New Fetter Lane, London EC4P 4EE

Simultaneously published in the USA and Canada
by Routledge
29 West 35th Street, New York, NY 10001

Reprinted 1998. 2001

© 1993 David Trotter

Routledge is an imprint of the Taylor & Francis Group
Typeset in Baskerville by Selwood Systems, Midsomer Norton
Printed and bound in Great Britain by
LSL Press Ltd. Bedford. Bedfordshire

British Library Cataloguing in Publication Data
A catalogue record for this book is available from the British Library

Library of Congress Cataloging in Publication Data
A catalog record for this book is available from the Library of Congress

ISBN 0–415–01501–4 (hbk)
ISBN 0–415–01502–2 (pbk)

CONTENTS

CONTENTS

INTRODUCTION

In 1899, Henry James envisaged a profitable future for the novel. Popular taste had established it as a universal form, 'the book *par excellence*'. 'In the flare of railway bookstalls, in the shop-fronts of most booksellers, especially the provincial, in the advertisements of the weekly newspapers, and in fifty places besides, this testimony to the general preference triumphs, yielding a good-natured corner at most to a bunch of treatises on athletics or sport, or a patch of theology old and new' (James 1984a, p. 101). What James witnessed in the flare of the bookstalls and advertisements was a dramatic expansion and diversification of the market for fiction (Cross 1985, ch. 6; Bowlby 1985, ch. 6; Keating 1989, ch. 1 and 7).

James was fascinated by the sway the novel appeared to hold over its readers. 'It is not too much to say of many of these that they live in a great measure by the immediate aid of the novel' (1984a, p. 101). The novel's uncanny penetrativeness, its ability to arouse and resolve an array of anxieties and aspirations, made it the great 'anodyne' of the age.

The 'immediate aid' given by the novel was a function, to some extent, of sheer presence, sheer visibility, 'mass and bulk' (p. 100). The most common critical response to this mass and bulk has been a rigid demarcation between highbrow (James, Conrad, Lawrence, Joyce, Woolf), middlebrow (Wells, Bennett, Galsworthy, Forster) and lowbrow (names too numerous and repellent to mention). There are scrupulous and imaginative histories available which assess the first group critically, summarize the second sympathetically, and ignore the third (Hewitt 1988). But it seems to me that if we are to address the issues raised by James, about the novel's diffusion and penetrativeness,

1

we must be prepared to think about all manner of fictions. My aim is to provide a more comprehensive account of the fiction of the period than has hitherto been available.

This does not mean that we should cease to make distinctions between different kinds and qualities of writing. The secure appeal of the novel, broadly understood, was to James's mind a cause for modest optimism. But he did not by any means endorse the banality on which that appeal had largely come to depend. Instead, he drew attention to two factors which in his view had prevented the novel from achieving variety and interest as well as popularity. The first was the prohibition on certain kinds of subject-matter; the second was the related assumption that safety lay in recycling 'forms at once ready-made and sadly the worse for wear' (p. 109).

James knew that the prohibition could not last for ever, and that the novel would be reshaped fundamentally by social changes such as 'the revolution taking place in the position and outlook of women' (p. 109). Some of these changes – increasing secularization, the revolt against Victorianism, the end of reticence – have been chronicled authoritatively (Hynes 1968; Rose 1986; Keating 1989). My account will differ in three ways. First, I have shifted the emphasis from social and intellectual to economic and political history, in order to concentrate on a number of developments whose consequences can still be felt today: the demise of an ideology of production, and its replacement by an ideology of consumption; the biologizing of social theory which put into play the concepts of degeneration and regeneration; the emergence of nationalism. Secondly, I have concerned myself in this book not only with attitudes but with anxieties, phobias, aspirations, fantasies. Thirdly, I have not confined myself to pioneering writers, but have explored the emergence of new (or newly aligned) subject-matters in all manner of fictions.

With respect to prohibitions, James need not have worried. Of course, a great deal was still prohibited; or, if not prohibited, then considered of no account. But I hope that a sufficiently catholic survey of the fiction of the period will uncover enough pockets of interest to suggest a versatile, adventurous literary culture. Reviewing Elinor Mordaunt's *The Park Wall* (1916), a novel of little account at the time or since, Woolf observed that in one scene at least the author was 'attempting something that the Victorians never thought of, feeling and finding expression for an emotion that escaped them entirely' (1986–8, II, p. 44). The scene in question (Mordaunt 1916, pp. 174–88) concerns a daughter's declaration that she will not return to her husband, and her family's appalled reaction. It is the absurdity of that reaction, its expression in 'scarcely articulate cries and curses', which struck Woolf, I think, as a feeling newly apprehended. Such newly apprehended feelings will be an important subject of this book.

James's second stricture, concerning the thinness of literary forms, is harder to controvert, and it exercised him greatly. The vitality of the novelist's 'first-hand impression, the effort to penetrate,' he said, would only be sustained by an 'architecture, distribution, proportion' sadly lacking in the great mass of contemporary fiction (1984a, p. 110).

This message comes across rather more clearly in a later essay on 'The new novel', published in 1914. There James contrasts Conrad, a 'votary of the way to do a thing that shall make it undergo most doing', with the younger generation of novelists who merely 'saturate' themselves in their (often fascinating) material (1984a, p. 147). We have here, in the opposition between technique and data, art and journalism, the substance of the major contemporary debates about the nature and role of fiction (James and Wells 1958, Woolf 1919, 1924). James and Woolf, with their fondness for complexity, their insistence that consciousness should be represented from within rather than without, herald the emergence of a writing which we would now term Modernist: a literature characterized by the rejection of the existing consensus between writer and reader and an investment in innovatory techniques.

The concept of Modernism encourages us to think of literary experiment not as a constant focus of creativity and self-definition throughout history, but as the product of a specific crisis. It encourages us to think of our modernity as somehow more modern than other people's: a 'revolution of the word'. The standard view of Modernism as a literary response to a breakdown in social order and continuity (Hough 1960, Ellmann and Feidelson 1965, Bradbury 1971, Bergonzi 1986, Brown 1990) anticipates, and has been reinforced by, the apocalyptic tenor of contemporary critical theory, its fondness for dramatic ruptures and displacements. The concept of postmodernism has thickened the brew even further, since it encourages us to believe that we differ from Modernism only in the degree of our modernity, our distance from 'traditional' habits of mind. Its advocates don't just want apocalypse. They want apocalypse squared.

The idea of Modernism has an important descriptive function. It allows us to characterize certain writers by, say, their difficulty and their self-consciousness. It allows us to discriminate between them and their immediate predecessors. We can suggest, for example, that one part of the Modernism of Joyce, Lewis and Pound was to renounce renunciation: the paths taken by Lambert Strether, Merton Densher and Emilia Gould would not be taken by the paganized protagonists of a fully Modernist fiction, by Miriam Henderson or Stephen Dedalus. Recognizing the importance of this descriptive function, some critics have tried to refine it. But the refinements have never caught on, because for many people accuracy of description is not really the point. The point is to fashion a slogan.

Modernism has consequently acquired an explanatory, or causative, function. It has come to signify a cultural event or force which, at a particular 'moment', in Europe and the Americas, determined the way writers wrote. To write in a Modernist fashion was to write in the conscious or unconscious knowledge that things had changed utterly – in 1910, or 1914, or whenever. The problem with this explanatory function is that it is a blatant mystification, for nobody has been able to say exactly what the event or force *was* which caused writers to write in a certain way. The recent concern with politics and gender in Modernism, while in some respects a welcome demystification, has only reinforced the lofty notion of a world-historical march from realism to Modernism and then on into postmodernism. The more accurate a politicized or gendered understanding, the more likely it is to dissolve such world-historical schemes.

Modernism has acquired another, equally enduring function, as a criterion of value. Writers who didn't respond to its promptings can be said to have blinded themselves not only to history, but to the sources of their own creativity. Writers who did can be seen as prophets, without honour in their own age, but the creators of our own. This tendency is evident in revaluations of the 'Modernist women' – H. D., Bryher, Gertrude Stein, Dorothy Richardson, Djuna Barnes, Harriet Monroe and many others – who experimented not only in their writing, but also in their lives, by rejecting conventional sexual roles and by estab-

4

lishing networks of support and patronage. Unfortunately, however, the concept of Modernism is still used to evaluate rather than describe: to distinguish between those writers who are considered innovatory, and thus worthy of study, and those who aren't. The implication is that a rejection of 'male' realism was the necessary condition of personal and political freedom. Women writers who led 'unconventional' lives, but wrote in a 'conventional' manner, get short shrift, even from feminist critics.

My intention here is to abandon the explanatory and evaluative functions of the concept of Modernism, and to refine its descriptive function. We do need to be able to say what writers were doing differently, from the turn of the century onwards, even if we do not regard that difference as an abrupt departure. This will involve, as I have already suggested, a more wide-ranging account of the prohibitions they broke, the subject-matters they addressed. I believe that the kind of 'realism/modernism/post-modernism trajectory' outlined by Fredric Jameson (1990, p. 156) will have to be (re)traced *through*, rather than across or over, the specific differences which constitute the history of English fiction in the High Modernist period.

We need to be able to establish those differences in the domain of style, of literary language. Here a large, and on the whole unacknowledged, obstacle confronts us: the model of communication almost invariably adopted by literary and cultural historians. According to this model, communication requires no more than the encoding of a message into a signal, and the subsequent decoding of the signal back into a message. The problem with this is that the process of encoding and decoding is rarely if ever sufficient to ensure communication. In order to understand not only what is said but *why* it is said, we must first decode the linguistic content of an utterance, and then use that decoded content as the basis for inferring what the speaker means to communicate. Decoding is merely a necessary, automatic preliminary to the interpretation of an utterance like 'He's taken the collection.' Our grammatical competence tells us that a man has done something involving a collection; but no more. It is left to our central cognitive system to fix a referent for the pronoun 'he' and to disambiguate the words 'take' and 'collection'; to work out whether the churchwarden has completed his rounds or a burglar has absconded with the Meissen. The meaning of the utterance will be the construal which makes most sense, is most relevant, in a particular context (Smith 1989, p. 9).

Literary texts appear to create their own contexts. Perhaps that is why literary criticism, from Aristotle to Roland Barthes and beyond, has been preoccupied with the encoding and decoding of messages. It has been based on a code model of communication. Although the problem of inference – of what readers *do* with the output of decoding, and why, of what writers might reasonably or unreasonably expect them to do – confronts it at every turn, it lacks an inferential model of communication, and is therefore perpetually forced to turn back either to the text, to signs, to codes, or to a cultural context which has itself been redefined as a system of codes, a set of discourses 'in' which subjectivity is constructed. The Saussurean model of communication, on which all forms of contemporary 'theory' are based, is emphatically a code model, and has in this respect nothing new to offer. The dominance of the Saussurean model has been criticized (Sperber 1975; Fabb 1988); and efforts have been made to take account of the part played in literary interpretation by context (Fish 1980; Culler 1981; Jauss 1982) and by the central cognitive processes (Hobbs 1990). What many of these attempts have lacked, however, is a model of communication capable of establishing a relation between the non-linguistic process of inference and linguistic form.

Theory has often been accorded the status of an intellectual revolution. But it is conceivable that the real revolution took place while the theorists were looking the other way, in work which laid the foundations for an inferential model of communication (Grice 1975). The study of utterance interpretation, of language use, has subsequently evolved into a separate discipline, or sub-discipline, pragmatics (Leech 1983; Levinson 1983). At the heart of the version I shall adopt here, Relevance Theory, is a 'Principle of Relevance' which, in guaranteeing that an utterance deserves attention, also guarantees that the cost of processing that utterance will always be more than offset by the contextual effects (the cognitive benefits) gained (Sperber and Wilson 1986). Relevance Theory is highly controversial, and I do not mean to invoke it as a *deux ex machina*. But it does enable us to think in terms other than those provided by the code model of communication, and, specifically, to pursue connections between linguistic form and pragmatic interpretation. Where Roland Barthes used the structure of syntax as a metaphor for the structure of narrative, I shall use Relevance Theory's account of the processing of utterances as a metaphor for the processing of literary texts.

This book is intended to provide ways of thinking about English fiction published between 1895 (the date, roughly, of the demise of the three-volume novel, and the literary and commercial contracts sustaining it) and 1920 (by which time High Modernism had set in with a vengeance). It will do so, first, by mingling canonical with non-canonical writers; secondly, by recording the emergence not only of 'new' attitudes, but of 'new' feelings (anxieties, phobias, aspirations); and thirdly, by developing an inferential model of literary communication. I am aware that it does not bring these projects to a conclusion. But I hope that it will encourage a less restrictive discussion of the writing of the period.

Part I

ECONOMIES AND STYLES

1

CONSUMING PASSIONS

Age of demand, economy of abundance, democratization of luxury, retail revolution, consumer capitalism: such are the terms in which the period between the 1870s and the 1920s has been described by economic and social historians. The terms indicate a shift of emphasis, in economic theory and practice, from production to consumption, and from the satisfaction of stable needs to the creation of new desires. My interest lies in the cultural implications of that shift.

Something approaching 'consumer capitalism' had of course been around, in Europe and America, for a long time – in Britain, at least since the eighteenth century (Brewer et al. 1982; Brewer and Porter 1992). But the late Victorian version existed on a much larger scale; it was systematic, irreversible, pervasive. Stuart Chase, writing in the early 1930s, argued that between 1880 and 1920 America had made the transition from an 'economy of scarcity' to an 'economy of abundance' (1971, pp. 10–12). The American economy was the most *spectacularly* abundant in the world, and therefore the most written about, then and now (e.g. Potter 1954; Douglas 1977; Birken 1988). But the other industrialized nations can also be said to have made the transition, more hesitantly perhaps, to an 'economy of abundance'.

The late nineteenth century saw a genuine improvement in living standards. 'For the first time people had a *choice* of how and where to spend their money' (Fraser 1981, p. ix). Terrible poverty persisted, of course, and the 'democratization of luxury' did not extend all that far down the social scale. Even so, the years between 1880 and 1895 saw an improvement in working-class living standards as well, despite rising unemployment

(Hobsbawm 1969, p. 162). It is the element of choice – barely existing at the lower end of the social scale, seized eagerly and with mounting confidence by the lower-middle and middle classes, taken for granted by the elite – which made the difference.

THE LAWS OF HUMAN ENJOYMENT

Simon Patten, Professor of Economics at the University of Pennsylvania from 1887 to 1917, could claim to be the first theorist of economic abundance. His most popular work, *The New Basis of Civilization*, was published in 1907, and went through eight editions in the next sixteen years. Before the nineteenth century, Patten argued, all civilizations had been 'realms of pain and deficit' (1968, p. 10). But modern technology and modern management were converting pain into pleasure, deficit into surplus. Patten celebrated the minutiae of the new abundance. Canned peas aroused in him a Kiplingesque enthusiasm for modernity. 'The preservation of food by canning is to time what transportation is to space. One opens an indefinite territory and the other secures an indefinite time in which to consume what has been quickly perishable' (p. 20). Patten, like Chase, was describing an American abundance. But he did recognize similiar developments in Britain (1899, pp. 379–409).

From the beginning of his career, Patten had attempted to theorize the 'new order'. 'The theory of consumption,' he wrote, 'rests upon the laws of pleasure and pain, modified by the social environment in which men live.' That theory would subordinate political economy to psychology, to 'the laws of human enjoyment'. 'Men,' he concluded, 'do not always have the same desire for a commodity' (1889, pp. v–vii). He distinguished desire, 'intensity of feeling', from need (p. 14); and argued that desires change as the quality of life improves. For example, the nutritional value of a varied diet had reduced the strength of modern appetites, ensuring that the point of satiety was reached more rapidly. It was important that men and women should be able to choose among pleasures, but also that their choice should be guided, and perhaps regulated, by scientific laws. Sexuality, for example, should be controlled by the laws of eugenics.

In *The Theory of the Leisure Class* (1899), Thorstein Veblen characterized consumption as a display of power and status (1925, p. 84). In traditional societies, leisure constituted the most effective 'signature' of power and status. But the anonymity and transience of modern life had heightened the effectiveness of conspicuous consumption (p. 87). Veblen's most significant emphasis was on the theatricality of consumption. Desire is fuelled by spectacle.

Recent attempts to define an economy and a social psychology of abundance echo Patten and Veblen, even when they do not refer to them explicitly. The most illuminating of these attempts, to my mind, is Lawrence Birken's account of the replacement of a productivist by a consumerist ideology in the final decades of the nineteenth century (Birken 1988). Birken argues that the ideological dominance of political economy between 1750 and 1870 revalued work, making it, for the first time in history, an activity as prestigious as fighting or praying. With the demise of classical political economy in the 1870s, however, a new value emerged: consumption. Birken's interest is in the social psychology of consumption, in the way desire began to replace property as the 'symbolic badge of individualism' at the turn of the century (p. 12). But the terms of his analysis derive from the so-called 'marginalist revolution' which transformed economic theory during the 1870s.

Within a generation, working independently of each other, a group of writers – Leon Walras in France, Karl Menger in Austria, W. Stanley Jevons and Alfred Marshall in Britain, J. B. Clark in America – converted economics from a theory of production to a theory of consumption, and thus broke decisively with the productivist ideology of Adam Smith, Ricardo, Mill and Marx. The 'problem' of economic theory, Jevons wrote, was not to increase the wealth of nations, but to 'maximise pleasure' (1888, pp. 39–40). Production, no longer regarded as the essential economic activity, became a kind of detour, something the consumer had to undertake in order to ensure further consumption.

Classical political economy had emphasized, on the one hand, the productivity, and, on the other hand, the neediness of human beings. The British tradition stressed the creative power of labour; labour was the measure of value. But there were problems it could not resolve. David Ricardo noted the existence of certain commodities (diamonds, for example) whose value is determined by their scarcity, not by the labour required to produce them. 'The mere fact,' Jevons observed, 'that there are many things, such as rare ancient books, coins, antiquities, etc., which have high values, and which are absolutely incapable of production now, disperses the notion that value depends on labour' (1888, p. 163).

According to the continental tradition, value depended on a need or utility conceived in universal terms: water is more useful than cake for everyone everywhere. These writers assumed that the things which are absolutely necessary for human life (air, sunlight, water) have the greatest value. But some of them cost nothing. 'The inability of Say and his followers to explain why some necessary things were free, like Ricardo's inability to explain the price of exceptional scarce commodities,' Birken concludes, 'was a result of these economists' adherence, well into the nineteenth century, to the Enlightenment vision of productive and needy human beings' (1988, p. 30).

The solution proposed by Jevons was a theory of marginal utility: the value of a commodity should be measured by the utility to the consumer of one additional unit. In normal circumstances a diamond will be worth more than a pint of water, not so much because it is necessary or because its production requires an enormous amount of labour, but because it is relatively scarce. An additional diamond will normally have a greater value than an additional pint of water. The late nineteenth-century economy of abundance gave rise to an economic theory based on scarcity.

'Only with the gradual recognition of the distinction between utility and marginal utility,' Birken argues, 'do we see the beginnings of a systematic ideology of individualistic desire' (p. 30). Jevons suggested that the sole criterion of what is or is not useful should be the 'will or inclination of the person concerned'. Utility, he added, is not an 'inherent quality', but 'a circumstance of things arising out of their relation to man's requirements' (1888, pp. 39, 43). It is the laws of human enjoyment, as Patten would have said, which determine economic value. The effect of these developments was to subordinate political economy, previously the most authoritative of all the social sciences, to psychology. Birken relates them to the more or less contemporary emergence of sexology. 'If the marginalists were ready to concede that the entire economic system as they saw it was but a means to satisfy the desires of individual consumers, sexual scientists such as Krafft-Ebing and Freud were intent upon finding the laws that governed those desires.' He points out that the two sciences of human enjoyment both stressed scarcity and idiosyncratic consumption (Birken 1988, p. 30). They made intelligible a whole range of preferences and aspirations that to some extent had been masked by the ideology of production.

SCARCE COMMODITIES

In Rider Haggard's *King Solomon's Mines* (1885), the adventurers find themselves trapped in a cave containing a fortune in gold and precious stones. It dawns on them that in these circumstances a diamond is worth considerably less than a sip of water. Even so, they each take a pocketful with them when they escape: enough to make them wealthy men (1951, pp. 397–401). There was nothing new about treasure caves, treasure islands; or indeed about the presence of consumer durables, scarce or plentiful, in fiction (Altick 1991). However, a new kind of scarcity, a new embodiment of economic and social value, became increasingly prominent.

The final decades of the nineteenth century saw the introduction or popularization of technologies which significantly altered the pattern of life (Giedion 1948; Briggs 1988): the phonograph, the wireless, moving pictures, the bicycle, the telephone (Pool 1977), the motor car and the aeroplane (Overy 1990). Addressing the Institute of Electrical Engineers in 1889, Lord Salisbury argued that scientific discoveries had made a greater impact on daily life than 'the careers of the greatest conquerors or the services of the greatest statesmen' (quoted in Briggs 1988, p. 373). Salisbury, Britain's last Victorian prime minister and the epitome of aristocratic conservatism, dabbled in chemistry, and installed electricity in his mansion at Hatfield.

In 'A Telephone Conversation' (1880), Mark Twain had described the new protocols (prolonged goodbyes, for example) which a particular technology had brought into being. British writers were slow to follow his example. In *A Call* (1910) and *Marriage* (1912), telephones merely further the plot; they don't reveal identity (Hueffer 1984, pp. 47–8; Wells 1986a, p. 120). The only Edwardian writer known to me who made a passably inventive use of them was the author of a pornographic novel in which a courtesan rides her lover while he is speaking on the phone to his valet. 'Suits he asked for, collars, shirts, etc., boots and ties, and at the hats he spent violently' (Anon 1909a, p. 23).

No doubt he had 'spent' pretty violently *on* the hats: the scene neatly combines two forms of idiosyncratic consumption. Courtenay Youghal in *The Unbearable Bassington* (1912) and Blazes Boylan in *Ulysses* (1922) are both marked as cardboard seducers by their easy expenditure and confident telephone manner (Saki 1963, pp. 382, 471; Joyce 1960, p. 292). But it was not until *Vile Bodies* (1930) and *A Handful of Dust* (1934) that a novelist was able to show how the telephone had altered the very form of relationships (Waugh 1938, pp. 183–4; 1951, pp. 59, 151).

For the most part, technology became an item in a programmatic dispute between ancients and moderns. Wells's enthusiasm for machines encouraged him to regard aviation as a new and rather startling method of courtship. The planes flown by Ponderevo in *Tono-Bungay* (1909) and Trafford in *Marriage* (1912) exemplify the protagonists' fitness not only as technocrats but as lovers; as the planes swoop down, the heroines submit (1964, pp. 250–1; 1986a, pp. 80–2). Again, though, it was not until Woolf's *Mrs Dalloway* (1925) that a novelist was able to show how aviation might alter consciousness (Beer 1990).

Forster, by contrast, an ancient by temperament, regarded another innovation, the motor car, with unqualified distaste. On two occasions in *Howards End* (1910) – Mrs Munt's rescue mission in Chapter 3 and the Honiton wedding in Chapter 25 – motor cars provide an arena for conflict between modernity and tradition, the male principle and the female principle. Handbooks like Dorothy Levitt's *The Woman and the Car* (1906) made it clear that motoring was regarded by many women as an opportunity for self-expression. In *Howards End*, on the other hand, the motor car merely enforces the will of bourgeois males on the lower classes, by blinding and choking them as they tramp the roads, and on women. Even the interfering Mrs Munt becomes an attractive character when she resists Charles Wilcox's bullying, which is nowhere more apparent than in his handling of a car. The sterile journey delivers the combatants to Howards End, and Mrs Wilcox, who belongs, of course, not to 'the young people and their motor', but to the house and its overshadowing tree (Forster 1941, p. 22). Later, the Honiton guests arrive at Shrewsbury to find a Wilcoxian fleet of cars awaiting them. The vulgar Myra Warrington changes her smart railway hat for an even smarter motoring hat (p. 196). Dorothy Levitt would have approved; Forster does not. When the vehicle carrying Margaret

Schlegel squashes a cat, she throws herself out in protest.

The impact made by new (and still scarce) technologies on the representation of behaviour can only be measured over the longer term. But it would be a mistake to look only for dramatic connections between the theory of consumption and the theory of consciousness. For the shift of emphasis from production to consumption also generated a new activity, a new practice: shopping. That activity did enter immediately, and potently, into fiction.

THE RETAIL REVOLUTION

British manufacturers found it hard to compete with their American and German rivals in the new, technologically advanced industries: chemicals, machinery, metals. They concentrated instead on older, more labour-intensive industries such as textiles and shipbuilding, or on consumer durables. By the turn of the century the largest industrial enterprises in the world's first industrial nation were the makers of branded packaged products for the retail market: Lever Brothers in soap, Ricketts & Sons in starch and blueing, Distillers Ltd in whisky, Guinness in stout and Cadbury in chocolates (Chandler 1990, pp. 37–8). While the technological revolution faltered, in Britain the 'retail revolution' advanced as rapidly as anywhere in the world outside America (Adburgham 1989).

During the course of the nineteenth century, hawkers and stall-holders gave way to fixed shops. Marked prices replaced haggling, or the shopkeeper's judgement of what a customer would bear. Hearsay gave way to window displays and other forms of advertisement. During the second half of the century, new types of retailing unit became more prominent. Large-scale organization arrived with the multiples, usually specializing in a small number of low-cost items, and with department stores, which offered an unprecedented range of goods under one roof (Fraser 1981, p. 133). These stores, with their grandiose architecture and theatrical lighting and displays, created new exterior and new interior spaces (Miller 1981; Adburgham 1989, ch. 13). Shopping became a new bourgeois leisure activity (Bowlby 1985, p. 14).

Because women assumed responsibility for equipping and provisioning the home, and because more of them had more money to spend, commerce increasingly took the form of a masculine appeal to women. As Bowlby puts it, the making of consumers 'fitted into the available ideological paradigm of a seduction of women by men' (p. 20). The window-shopping, the unflustered survey of abundance, the pause for reflection before purchase: these new habits activated and exploited narcissism (p. 32). To many commentators, consumerism has seemed a form of subjection. But there is some evidence that it might also have provided new opportunities, even a new freedom.

Entering a department store in the 1890s meant leaving, momentarily, the home, and the roles prescribed for women by domesticity. Lady Mary Jeune recalled the misery of shopping with her mother twenty-five years earlier (1895, p. 124). Since then the department stores, with their 'obtrusive fascinations', their brightness and brilliancy, had created an altogether different experience: 'one, more enterprising than the others, is said to supply young men for dancing, and coffins to bury them in' (p. 125). Shopping, once a duty, had become a pleasure. Lady Jeune regarded the stores as a feminine environment, and women assistants as the most insidious votaries of narcissism.

William Leach has argued that consumer capitalism included manipulative and utopian tendencies, and that the latter allowed middle-class women at least to 'reconceive' themselves, by creating new forms of employment (copywriting, designing, modelling, managing) and a new 'public space' (Leach 1984). In America, leading feminists like Lucy Stone and Charlotte Perkins Gilman joined Nationalism, a socialist party founded by Edward Bellamy, which put the department store at the heart of its utopian vision. Stores everywhere offered the women's movement advertising space. Novelists like Theodore Dreiser and Inez Haynes Irwin (best known as the historian of the Woman's Party) portrayed the theatre of conspicuous consumption as a means of self-determination for women.

English writers proceeded more cautiously. Mrs Trenchard, in Hugh Walpole's *The Green Mirror* (1918), is as distressed by the new department stores as Margaret Schlegel by motor cars. She patronizes the resolutely old-fashioned Army and Navy Stores. 'Here were no extravagances, no decadencies, no flowing creations with fair outsides and no heart to them, nothing foreign nor degenerate' (p. 171). She is much moved by the splendid displays of English furniture and English hams. Her daughter,

Millie, who has lived in Paris, thinks the place 'an impossible anachronism' (p. 170). They visit the Stores in search of a hot-water bottle, and are accordingly directed to the 'rubber department' (p. 171).

Wells's *The Wife of Sir Isaac Harman* (1917) was his most ambitious, and most self-critical, attempt to acknowledge the independence of women from men. Ellen Harman uses the public space of the department store to shake off a private detective set on her by her possessive husband. She 'exercises' the poor man upon Peter Robinson's, Debenham and Peabody's, and the recently installed 'moving staircase' at Harrods, leading him a merry dance through 'departments of increasing indelicacy' (Wells 1986c, pp. 406–7). Again, though, the adventure simply confirms Ellen's enterprising stubbornness.

It was Joyce who came closest to understanding the ambiguities of the commodity, at once image (mirror to the soul) and object. In the 'Lotos-Eaters' episode of *Ulysses* (1922), Leopold Bloom buys a bar of lemon-scented soap. He has entered the chemist's shop in order to get some lotion made up for Molly (1960, pp. 103–5), but his thoughts, dissolved by the scent of the soap, begin to drift. 'Do it in the bath. Curious longing I. Water to water. Combine business with pleasure' (p. 105). One faintly luxurious act of expenditure stimulates thoughts of another.

But the bar of soap, purchased in the name of fantasy, soon reverts to objecthood. It becomes a constant angular presence. In 'Hades' Bloom feels it in his hip pocket (p. 108); when the carriage arrives at the cemetery, he transfers it elsewhere (p. 126). At the end of 'Lestrygonians', flustered by the sight of Blazes Boylan, he finds it while looking for something else (p. 234). In 'Nausicaa' it *interrupts* a sexual fantasy (p. 489). The bar of soap is at once a fragmentary mirror to Bloom's desire, and a most inconvenient object. Its odyssey may well constitute consumerism's first epic: appropriately enough, a mock-epic, a shadow-play.

The example of *Ulysses* suggests that there would be little point in cataloguing commodities or shopping-precincts. We should look instead for occasions on which the assimilation of the new activity of shopping significantly alters the activity of writing, and thus conceptions of identity.

SOME SHOPS

Arnold Bennett's Clayhanger tetralogy – *Clayhanger* (1910), *Hilda Lessways* (1911), *These Twain* (1916), *The Roll Call* (1918) – describes the advent of modernity, and the conflict it provokes between generations. The head of the family, Darius, has risen from humble origins to a position of wealth and influence as Bursley's leading printer. His selfless enterprise has soured into a patriarchal despotism which his son, Edwin, must resist in order to create a life of his own. Edwin wants to be an architect, not a printer, and his first declaration of independence is the purchase, at the cost of 17 shillings, of a number of books he does not strictly need. 'He was intoxicated and he was frightened. What a nucleus for a collection of real books, of treasures!' (Bennett 1954, p. 248).

The event is not described as it happens, but on a later occasion, when his father inspects his bedroom (pp. 246–9). That one event should be folded into another, creating a narrative loop, indicates the furtive radicalism of Edwin's self-assertion. The books have little or no value as books; they mean little at the time of their purchase. It is only in retrospect, under Darius's threatening gaze, that their meaning is revealed. In the theatre of consumption, meaning is relative. There is no common ground to which it can be referred. The idiosyncrasy of Edwin's choice, and of its reception, establish it as an act of self-assertion, a modern act, one which scandalizes the ideology of production. (Another tyrannized son, Ernest Pontifex, knows pleasure for the first time when his clergyman father leaves the house to go shopping: Butler 1923, p. 102).

When women consume, when women desire, things are more complicated, but also, in a way, more simple. In *The Old Wives' Tale* (1908), Sophia, the more adventurous of the Baines sisters, elopes with a commercial traveller, Gerald Scales. Arriving in Paris a married woman, 'possessed by the desire for French clothes as by a devil', she tackles her husband on the subject of frocks (1964, p. 299). That desire expresses her, but it does not emancipate her, as the desire for books had emancipated Edwin Clayhanger. Gerald knows better than she what clothes will suit her. Sitting in the fashionable Restaurant Sylvain, she is an exhibit rather than a free woman (p. 303), and the narrative makes no concession at all to any freedom – any viewpoint – she might have gained through the theatre of consumption: it simply absorbs both her beauty and her vulnerability. In the end, she frees herself from Gerald, and from spectacle, by reverting to the Baines values of enterprise, thrift, self-denial (Darius Clay-hanger's values). The free fall of relativity is something Bennett imagines on behalf of men, but not women.

It took a more consciously experimental and feminist writer than Bennett to redress the balance. In *Honeycomb* (1917), the third volume of *Pilgrimage* (1915–35; 1967), Miriam Henderson has half an hour to kill in the West End of London. She spends it in Regent Street, looking at the shops.

> She pulled up sharply in front of a window. The pavement round it was clear, allowing her to stand rooted where she had been walking, in the middle of the pavement, in the midst of the pavement, in the midst of the tide flowing from the clear window, a soft fresh tide of sunlit colours ... clear green glass shelves laden with shapes of fluted glass, glinting transparencies of mauve and amber and green, rose-pearl and milky blue, welded to a flowing tide, freshening and flowing through her blood, a sea rising and falling with her breathing.
>
> (Richardson 1979, I, p. 417)

Observer and observed, exterior and interior, merge. But this absorption in spectacle does not condemn Miriam to passivity. Instead, it inspires her to send a male friend a note announcing her presence in the West End, her occupation of public space, from the local post office (just as Stephen Dedalus in central Dublin will send a telegram to Buck Mulligan in central Dublin). 'She felt her hard self standing there as she wrote, and shifted her feet a little, raising one heel from the ground, trying to feminize her attitude; but her hat was hard against her forehead, her clothes would not flow ...' (p. 419). The window-shopping has given her a 'West End life of her own', a masculine address and presence. The style of the chapter, disjointed and impressionistic to begin with, acquires a 'masculine' self-assurance as Miriam takes her stand.

One might expect the West End stores to make a difference. But less exalted forms of exchange also induced variations in narrative technique. The early chapters of *Sons and Lovers* (1913) are largely concerned with the deteriorating relationship between Walter and Gertrude Morel, and take place for the most part inside the distinctly claustrophobic family home. On market nights Gertrude escapes into a more various, if no less quarrelsome, world. She argues with the lace woman, laughs with the fish man and, attracted by the cornflowers on a little dish, becomes coldly polite to the crockery man.

> 'I wondered how much that little dish was,' she said.
> 'Sevenpence to you.'
> 'Thank you.'
> She put the dish down and walked away; but she could not leave the market-place without it. Again she went by where the pots lay coldly on the floor, and she glanced at the dish furtively, pretending not to.
>
> (1948, pp. 94–5)

The purchase satisfies desire rather than need. The attribution of coldness to the pots lying on the floor creates that mirroring of subject in object which will enlarge, in a modest way, her identity. As if recognizing that desire can only be acknowledged obliquely, intermittently, the narrative suddenly becomes preoccupied with the clothes she is wearing. But she won't be deflected, and returns to complete a bargain whose full meaning will only emerge after the event, when she shows the dish to her son (pp. 96–7). Like Bennett, though more subtly, more generously, Lawrence disturbs the smooth flow of narrative time (event and meaning locked into step), and the consistency of point of view, in order to admit a new and complicated feeling, a new experience.

THE ART OF ADVERTISEMENT

As notable a feature of the 'economy of abundance' as the development of new technologies and retailing methods was the increasing pervasiveness of advertising. In his introduction to a book on the subject, Sidney Webb observed that the new industry had achieved an annual turnover of around £100 million in Britain, and five or six times that amount globally (Goodall 1914, p. ix). When Thomas Barratt became a partner in A. and F. Pears Ltd. in 1865, its annual advertising budget was £80; ten years later he was spending well over £100,000 on memorable coups involving Millais's 'Bubbles' and a testimonial from Lillie Langtry (Turner 1965). If shopping encouraged small-scale experiment, advertising had an amplitude, a ruthlessly assimilative ingenuity, which tended to overawe mere novelists.

In 1897 Henry James published a perceptive essay about Queen Victoria's Diamond Jubilee, in which he pointed out that the main purpose of the event was to reinforce the nation's 'passionate feeling for trade' by defacing London with advertisements; the Queen herself was both a victim of and party to this tawdry exhibition. After all, one of her acknowledged functions was to 'make trade roar' (James 1968, pp. 208–12). She was barely in her grave before the new Prince of Wales, the future George V, made his famous 'Wake up, England!' speech at the Guildhall, in which he declared that Britain would only retain its pre-eminence as a trading nation if manufacturers advertised more vigorously.

Advertising reinforced the perception that value could no longer be measured by labour or utility. 'The greatest feeling of worth,' wrote Walter Dill Scott, Director of the Psychological Laboratory at Northwestern University, 'attaches itself to those things which are the objects of our most fundamental instinctive desires' (1909, p. 103). The function of advertising was to arouse, perhaps to create, those desires. 'Successful advertisement writing,' Goodall concluded, 'must, of course, consciously or unconsciously, be based on the laws of psychology. A good advertisement attracts attention, arouses interest, awakens desire and moves the will – to purchase' (1914, p. 62).

James and Wells quarrelled famously about the function of the novel, one insisting on art, the other on utility, but their representations of advertisement are comparable, and comparably defensive. Chad Newsome's manifest destiny, in *The Ambassadors* (1903), is to go home and 'boss the advertising' (1907–9, XXII, p. 84). Jim Pocock wonders why Strether does not press him harder: 'if you've believed so in his making us hum, why have you so prolonged the discussion?' (p. 85). That had, in fact, been Strether's original intention. During their first encounter in Paris, a walk in the streets after the theatre, he recognizes Chad as an 'irreducible young Pagan'. 'They'd be able to do with one – a good one; he'd find an opening – yes; and Strether's imagination even now prefigured and accompanied the first appearance there of the rousing personage' (XXI, pp. 156–7). The point about Chad is that he is easily prefigured, easily advertised. But the sentence announcing this is oddly un-Jamesian. The interjected affirmation touches the pulse of consciousness on the raw in a way that James rarely allows, especially when the consciousness in question is as ruminative as Strether's. The inexperience it reveals in Strether makes one feel almost queasy.

By the time Jim Pocock turns up, Strether has learnt better, or different. He has met Madame de Vionnet and her daughter, and discovered that making things hum is mere barbarism. And yet prolonging the discussion is no answer. Strether's artful delay has encouraged some critics to suppose a degree of complicity between the commercial deception practised in Woollett, the social deception practised in fashionable Paris, and the aesthetic deception practised by the novelist himself (Greenslade 1982; Seltzer 1984, pp. 144–5). But we must also take account of Strether's response to Chad's revelation, towards the end of the novel, that he has been 'getting some news of the art of advertisement', and has decided that it 'really does the thing'.

'I've been finding out a little; though it doubtless doesn't amount to much more than what you originally, so awfully vividly – and all, very nearly, that first night – put before me. It's an art like another, and infinite like all the arts.'

(XXII, p. 316)

Chad's celebration of the art of advertisement is almost parodically Jamesian in its deferential precision. But the reminder that in abandoning Madame de Vionnet he is doing no more than Strether originally advised him to do is artful only in its brutality. If Strether did collude, naïvely, with the art of advertisement, he has paid the price. Now, he feels faint. The faintness represents the eclipse of his way of thinking, and James's. The novel announces that eclipse by an apparently helpless repetition. Chad and Strether are face to face under the street-lamp which witnessed their original encounter, on the night of the theatre.

Tono-Bungay (1909) follows the brilliant careers of the narrator, George Ponderevo, and his uncle, Teddy. Teddy owns a chemist's shop in Wimblehurst, a place which badly wants 'Waking Up!' (Wells 1964, p. 154); it could use a Chad Newsome – or perhaps

Luckworth Crewe, the ruthless advertising agent in Gissing's *In the Year of Jubilee* (1894), for whom the world is a gigantic hoarding (1982b, pp. 66–7, 353–4). But Teddy's 'Wake up, Wimblehurst!' speech has absolutely no effect. He leaves for London, and the manufacture of a patent medicine called Tono-Bungay. George eventually joins him, and a chapter entitled 'How We Made Tono-Bungay Hum' vividly describes the marketing of the drug, a 'nothing coated in advertisements' (p. 184). The drug itself seems remarkably similar to those at the centre of the many patent medicine scandals of the era (Fraser 1981, pp. 138–41).

Where James had been glumly disparaging about the art of advertisement, Wells is exuberantly satirical. But the note of helplessness is not altogether absent from his account. He concludes the chapter on making Tono-Bungay hum by reintroducing Ewart, an aesthete who has just returned from Paris. Ewart is hired to design posters advertising the drug, and becomes appallingly sententious on the subject. 'The old merchant used to tote about commodities; the new one creates values' (p. 131). Wells evidently wants to disparage Ewart. But George Ponderevo is as swiftly incapacitated by the aesthete-consumer's bleak frivolity as Strether was by Chad Newsome. Again, the narrative fetches up against, or in, repetition.

Leopold Bloom is an advertising agent, or canvasser, with a more utopian view of the art than Strether's or Ponderevo's. His conception of a perfect advertisement for Hely's stationery, elaborated in 'Lestrygonians', involves a transparent show cart with two smart girls inside (Joyce 1960, p. 195). Such stunts, or 'novelty work', were generally considered too risky (Spiers 1910, p. 46), as Bloom knows, without being able to act on the knowledge. 'Or the inkbottle I suggested with a false stain of black celluloid. His ideas for ads like Plumtree's potted under the obituaries, cold meat department. You can't lick 'em. What? Our envelopes' (pp. 194–5). Bloom's obsession renders his daft utopianism brilliantly.

But even in *Ulysses*, where the writing sometimes hitches a ride on the art of advertisement, there is a kind of defeat. In 'Ithaca' Bloom solemnly catalogues his inventions, concluding triumphantly with the show cart (pp. 799–800). It is a captivating display, but inconsequential. Stephen drifts off into a fantasy scene from a romantic novel, Bloom into a recollection of his father's death (p. 801). Their eclipse is more explicable, less

25

painful, than Strether's; both are exhausted. But 'Ithaca' mirrors 'Lestrygonians' no less bleakly, and defensively, in the end, than one encounter beneath a street-lamp mirrors another. In both cases, recurrence enacts sterility. If shopping stimulated variations in narrative technique, the art of advertisement seems to have driven writers back towards an emphasis on circularity.

2

LABOUR

Whatever is consumed must once have been, in some measure, produced. Although consumption increasingly became the focus of individual and collective fantasy, production did not disappear altogether from view. Nor did the politics of production.

Production and producers appear frequently enough in the Victorian novel (Keating 1971b; Gallagher 1985). The 'condition of England' fiction of the 1840s responded sharply to the political challenge of Chartism and trade unionism. Middle-class writers found ways of representing the conditions which had provoked that challenge and, less satisfactorily, the awareness it sponsored. In the 1860s, Dickens, Eliot and others wrote about electoral reform, and about the looming presence of an enfranchised working class (Gallagher 1985, ch. 9).

Political commentary remained a feature of middle-class fiction well into the 1880s, when the increasing polarization of capital and labour seemed a cause for concern to many writers (Lucas 1971; Harvie 1991, ch. 6). In his first novel, *Workers in the Dawn* (1880), George Gissing presented himself as a mouthpiece of the 'advanced Radical party'; he meant to attack injustice. But although subsequent novels confronted industrialism and poverty, Gissing soon lost patience with the working class.

Socialism did find more consistent champions. The notorious Trafalgar Square 'riot' of 1887 featured in William Morris's *A Dream of John Ball*, Margaret Harkness's *Out of Work* (Harkness published as John Law) and Constance Howell's *A More Excellent Way*, all published in 1888. By the end of the decade, labour, and the politics of labour, had been reinstated as a subject for fiction – and for painting (Lucie-Smith and Dars 1977). Indeed, some literary historians have gone so far as to claim that the period 1880–1914 witnessed the 'rise of socialist fiction' (Klaus 1987a).

But if we take 1890 (and what had been achieved by 1890) as a baseline, the subsequent development of working-class fiction can be regarded as a 'rise' only of the most intermittent and irregular kind. The period 1890–1914 includes significant, but very isolated, achievements. The 'upper-class rebel', for example, features in a number of novels (Ryan 1987); while the Liberal victory at the general election of 1906 turned attention once more to the 'condition of England' (Lodge 1966, pp. 214–42; Hunter 1982, ch. 15). Overall, though, it is hard not to agree with Keating when he speaks of a failure 'to come to terms in any convincing way with either modern politics or working-class life' (1989, p. 311). This chapter will be concerned with some important exceptions to the rule.

THE VISIBILITY OF LABOUR, 1890–1920

The invisibility of labour in fiction is all the more surprising when one considers its unprecedented visibility in other fields of enquiry. This was the great age of empirical sociology. The first volume of Charles Booth's massive *Life and Labour of the People in London* (1891–1902) deals with a single area, Tower Hamlets. Every street was visited, every family interviewed. Colour-coded maps indicated the distribution of wealth. Subsequent volumes covered the rest of the metropolis, though not in such detail. Five were devoted to 'Industry'. Other investigations (Rowntree 1901; Bell 1907) anatomized working-class life in other parts of the country. In 1906 James Milne noted that sociological studies had begun to replace fiction as the layman's guide to economic and political issues (Keating 1989, p. 305).

Every bit as revealing were the reports of the Select Committee of the House of Lords on the Sweating System (1888–90) and of the various departmental committees of the Home Office on dangerous trades (1893–9) (Pike 1969, pp. 206–42, 254–70). The strike of the matchgirls at Bryant and May's East London factory in 1888 and the dock strike in 1889 both became the focus of intense debate; in both cases, the workers' demands were met.

Another notable feature of the period was the effort made to ensure political representation for working people. A massive advance in trade unionism took membership from 750,000 (5 per cent of the workforce) in 1888 to over 2 million in 1900, and over 4 million (23 per cent of the workforce) in 1913. By 1913 a system of collective bargaining had evolved in most major industries. Furthermore, after extensions of the franchise in 1867 and 1884, the two main political parties were more inclined to court the working-class vote. The interests of organized labour were pursued at first in alliance with the Liberal Party, and then, when the Liberals proved reluctant to endorse working-class candidates and to support the unions in their legal battles with employers, independently.

It was also the 'heroic age' of British socialism. The Social Democratic Federation, Marxist in orientation, was founded in 1881. In 1884 the Socialist League, under William Morris, broke away. In the same year, middle-class intellectuals who believed in reform rather than revolution created the Fabian Society. The Independent Labour Party, founded in 1893, was another militant socialist organization. For many thousands of men and women, socialism became a religion, the gospel of a new life (Yeo 1977). It had an 'expressive function' in the lives of its more active adherents (Harrison 1991, p. 145). None of these groups or societies ever achieved a mass membership. But their rallies, meetings, pamphlets and journals stimulated a debate about the nature of democracy which lasted until the First World War.

For working people, the business of keeping body and soul together was, as Harrison puts it, 'the central experience of life' (1991, p. 67). The experience was often an anxious one. Seasonal unemployment, boom and slump, the prevalence of 'casual' labour, the lack of welfare provision: all these factors threatened to separate body from soul at any moment. The experience we would expect the novel to represent, then, is not simply work, but anxiety about work (or the end of work).

ALLEGIANCE AND IDENTITY

Working-class, popular, industrial, proletarian, radical, socialist: the terms are confused, Raymond Williams observes, because the experience they refer to is confused. I shall concern myself here, as he does, with novels in which 'the majority of the characters and events belong to working-class life' (Williams 1982, pp. 112, 120).

Interpretation of the working-class novel has concentrated on the dilemma of writers who wish to promote an allegiance to anti-bourgeois values by means of a literary genre which has traditionally been regarded as distinctively bourgeois. How could such a genre accommodate a modern industrial working class whose 'deepest human experiences' concern work rather than leisure, communal rather than personal relationships (Hawthorn 1990, p. 68)?

Critics usually want to demonstrate either the differences in narrative technique between 'bourgeois' and 'socialist' portrayals of a particular 'industrial formation' (Holderness 1984; Klaus 1987b, pp. 86–93; Hawthorn 1990 – all on mining novels); or the differences in rhetorical technique between a novel intended to be read in the privacy of a middle-class home, and one serialized in a working-class newspaper (Salveson 1987; Frow and Frow 1987) or read aloud at a union meeting (Miles 1984, p. 3; Mitchell 1987). The aim is to show how the working-class novel has succeeded by differing, or failed by not differing enough.

I am not convinced myself that these differences, where they exist, amount to a subversion of the bourgeois novel. Robert Tressell meant every last didactic word of *The Ragged Trousered Philanthropists* (1914); he also insisted that the book was 'not a treatise or essay, but a novel' (1965, p. 14). It is worth exploring the extent to which working-class fiction was able to represent working-class experience while still resembling bourgeois fiction. There were, after all, advantages to be gained from adopting, without too much subversion, the literary form most likely to attract readers.

A number of writers chose to concentrate not so much on work as on the anxiety generated by the casual and precarious nature of employment in many trades. Sweated labour was a major theme of Margaret Harkness's novels. Allen Clarke's *Driving* (1901) gave it another name (driving was a policy adopted in the Lancashire weaving sheds to increase production). Both terms crop up frequently in *The Ragged Trousered Philanthropists*. Both lost their edge in the years before the First World War, on account of union militancy and the gradual establishment of a welfare state. We are dealing with a particular phase of working-class experience, as represented in fiction.

Tressell (Robert Noonan) was born in Dublin in 1871, and

died of tuberculosis in 1911. He worked in the building trade as a house painter. His novel was written between 1905 and 1910, and published, in a truncated form, in 1914. The first twenty-six chapters describe in intricate detail the refurbishment and decoration of a house belonging to the local capitalist, Mr Sweater. The men are driven ferociously by the foreman, Hunter, whose only concern is profit; they live in constant fear of dismissal. Hunter is driven in turn by his employer, Rushton, who is driven by the pressures of competition. The result is a skimped and botched job.

The solutions proposed by Tressell are class solidarity and socialist policies. Political allegiance will provide a more solid basis for individual identity, combating the fear, and the sense of worthlessness, induced by sweating. Frank Owen, Tressell's spokesman, is so engrossed in socialism that he has no time to dwell on his own poverty (1965, p. 425). But most of the other characters find allegiance hard work. Their anxiety is deep-rooted enough, palpable enough, to make one doubt the ability of political allegiance to reform people or societies.

I don't regard this as Tressell's failure. The anxiety he describes was not the product of the novel's generic individualism, but of a specific historical experience. It was the point at which the polarities critics most often invoke – work and leisure, communal and personal – converged in working-class life at the turn of the century. By addressing this anxiety, writers introduced a new subject-matter into the (still bourgeois) novel. They did so, I think, to disconcerting effect. For they suggested that one antidote to anxiety was the formation of a fantasy-self which actively *prevented* allegiance to work and community.

We first see Nelly Ambrose, in Harkness's *A City Girl* (1887), on her way out of the bleak tenement building where she lives. Soon she is examining herself in a shop window. She can't decide whether to buy a blue or a red feather for her Sunday hat. 'She had but one ambition in dress, that was to wear something "stylish". "To look like a lady," she called it' (Law 1984, p. 16). Bedroom mirror and shop window are the focus of a fantasy-self based on the values of consumption rather than production. The dreariness and uncertainty of Nelly's working life make her seduction by a middle-class admirer inevitable (Goode 1982, p. 53). No mere allegiance – to family, faith, occupation, community, fiancé – can match the power of this narcissistic dream as an

31

expression of identity. There are comparable episodes in *The Ragged Trousered Philanthropists*, and in mainstream bourgeois fiction (Bennett's *Old Wives' Tale*, for example). All three novels record the inroads an ideology of consumption was already beginning to make into allegiances created by an ideology of production.

Tressell recognized a similar division within the ideology of production, between different attitudes to labour. Owen agrees to decorate a drawing-room in 'Moorish' style, even though the preparatory work will have to be done in his own time, with little prospect of financial reward. His 'intense desire' to do the job is fuelled by fear that it may at any moment be abandoned (1965, p. 122). The wholly private satisfaction he derives from it does as much as his commitment to socialism to create, or confirm, an identity; it gives him a status apart from his work-mates. Of course, the pleasure of manual labour conscientiously performed was an article of faith with many British socialists, notably William Morris (Townshend 1912, p. 8). But Tressell's vivid description of everyday driving and skimping make it seem like a fantasy almost as narcissistic as Nelly Ambrose's hesitation between blue and red feathers.

By recognizing the mutual implication of desire and anxiety in working-class experience, Harkness and Tressell dramatized the division between allegiance and identity which socialism would have to surmount if it was to achieve anything. Those writers who did imagine an identity founded exclusively on allegiance, and a language which would express it, rarely advanced beyond theory.

In Emma Brooke's *Transition* (1895), the priggish Honora Kemball finds that she has to make her own way in the world, and becomes a schoolteacher. A fellow teacher, Lucilla Dennison, introduces her to Paul Sheridan, who has evolved, in a somewhat Fabian manner, his own version of parliamentary and legislative socialism: he has read Marx and Proudhon, but prefers statistics. In an interesting passage, which bears little relation to what we see of him in the novel, Brooke characterizes his manner of argument, which is vigorously metaphoric, as a poetics of labour. To him,

> the commonest things told the deepest earth histories. The rhythm of his poetry had in it the fall of hammers, the hum of wheels, the ceaseless tramp of the workers' feet, the rattle

of traffic, and the rush of steam. As the genius of the historian out of broken pottery and scattered shreds revives the palpitating life of the long-dead city, so he out of figures would extract the passionate realities and tragedies of present existence.

'Your truest poetry is found in statistics,' he would say.

(1895, p. 168)

Sheridan combines Walt Whitman with Sidney Webb. But the figure Brooke herself finds to characterize him is the archaeologist, not the mechanic or the Whitmanesque lounging democrat. The writer she foresees is not Tressell, but James Joyce, whose reconstruction of the 'palpitating life' of a city has been compared to Heinrich Schliemann's excavation of Troy (Kenner 1972, pp. 42–5). Joyce was to decipher 'earth histories' from common things, and his prose had the rhythm, if not of workers' feet, then, in 'Aeolus', of the printing-press. But no one would call *Ulysses* the working man's Bible. The new language, when it came, was ushered in by Joyce's denial of allegiance to class, nation and creed.

The only working-class novel of the time which does find an intermittent poetry in working-class speech is Patrick MacGill's *Children of the Dead End* (1914). Even there, though, the poetry derives not from statistics, or the rhythm of machines, but from High Romantic tradition. The novel describes the odyssey of a young Irish labourer, Dermod Flynn, who travels to Scotland to pick potatoes, and subsequently works as a plate-layer and navvy. He starts to read Ruskin and Carlyle, and soon discovers socialism (MacGill 1914, pp. 138–9). He submits stories of navvying life to a London paper, and is eventually taken on to the staff. The poetry, however, is to be found not in Flynn's stories, but in the robust speech of two 'gypsies of labour' he encounters on his travels, Moleskin Joe and Carroty Dan. The term 'gypsy' gives the game away. These are the wise vagrants, the hedgerow prophets, of High Romantic tradition: their nearest contemporary equivalents are Brum and New Haven Baldy in W. H. Davies's *The Autobiography of a Super-Tramp* (1908), or the more pious, and more static, hero of *The Roadmender* (1902), by Michael Fairless (Margaret Fairless Barber).

ARABELLA THE OBSCURE

The division between allegiance and identity took another, equally problematic form. Working-class writers who benefited from new educational opportunities, and moved out of that class, tended to write novels which justified their own displacement by devising voyages of self-discovery. Work creates the allegiance of these writers, and of their protagonists; books create identity. Identity emerges through the rejection of allegiance: a pattern perfectly adapted to autobiography and *Bildungsroman* (novel of development), the two genres most favoured by working-class writers during the period.

Joseph Keating began down the coal mine at the age of twelve; his recruitment to the workforce was the beginning at once of allegiance and identity. 'I wanted to be seen going home with the men from the pit, black, vividly black, so black as to be nearly invisible. My desire to be in the mode was much like the enslaving vanity which makes people wish to be in exclusive society' (1916, p. 153). The coal dust is a fantasy, a 'vanity', as well as a uniform. But Keating found a different, contradictory, focus of desire when he began to study (p. 112). At the same time, he became a dandy, a walking antidote to coal dust (p. 111), and developed a fierce dislike of the mines.

Keating managed to escape. He became a clerk, then a journalist, and began writing novels in 1895. The first, *Son of Judith*, was published in 1900. It is about the mines, but more powerfully about escaping from the mines. Morris, the hero, is singled out by his dress and appearance, and by his intensity, from his zombie-like workmates, who despise him for trying to improve himself (1900, pp. 177–9, 184). He must overcome not only their hostility, but also his mother's efforts to shape him into an instrument of vengeance against his own father (the plot is unfalteringly melodramatic). In doing so, he wins the love of a middle-class girl. The new identity, created by purposeful rather than narcotic fantasy, obliterates both family and class. Keating's autobiography, one might note, ends with a first night at the Royalty Theatre, where 'exclusive society' has gathered to applaud his début as a dramatist (1916, pp. 301–2).

The most celebrated and argued-about examples of displacement are, of course, Hardy (a stonemason's son) and Lawrence (a miner's son). Both succeeded as well as anyone in incorporating labour and labouring community into their fiction. Hardy investigated more fully and perceptively than any other novelist, before or since, the ways in which manual labour creates identity. For him, as Elaine Scarry has pointed out, identity is formed not so much by the development of consciousness as by a 'reciprocal alteration' of man and world. 'Man and world each act on the surface of the other; each alters the other's surface either by adding new layers to it or by subtracting layers from it' (Scarry 1983, p. 91).

In *The Woodlanders* (1887), the lamp used by a woman reading at night leaves a layer of smoke on a ceiling, and card-players leave greasy thumbprints on their cards: these alterations of surface evoke, indeed embody, personality and community. Grace Melbury knows Giles Winterbourne by the layers which his work has subtracted from his person – the nails in his boots, seen from below, 'silver-bright with walking' – or added to it: the fragments of apple-rind on the brim of his hat, the pips clinging to the down on his arms and his beard (Hardy 1981, pp. 140, 228).

These are, as yet, temporary and reversible alterations. But over a lifetime a body is so altered by work that it becomes the history of its alterations, as George Melbury's has. 'That stiffness about the arm, hip, and knee-joint, which was apparent when he walked, was the net product of the divers sprains and over-exertions that had been required of him in handling trees and timber when a young man, for he was of the sort called self-made, and had worked hard.' He knows the origins of every one of his aches: 'that in his left shoulder had come of carrying a pollard, unassisted, from Tutcombe Bottom home; that in one leg was caused by the crash of an elm against it when they were felling; that in the other was from lifting a bole' (p. 70). The 'net product' of these aches and pains is a history, a continuous identity, since the injuries caused by labour remain vividly present in the body of the man who has made himself, become a timber merchant. To live and work is to deteriorate, until you *are* your deteriorations. Wearing down, wearing away: these material effects create identity. Deformation is formation. Human beings wear down differentially, and the differentiation individualizes them.

It is significant that *The Woodlanders* should feature so promi-

35

nently in Scarry's account. The later novels tell a different story, about Hardy's preoccupation with marriage and with education. *Jude the Obscure* (1895), in particular, challenges the idea that identity should derive from an allegiance to work and community. Some critics would certainly not agree with this assessment. Terry Eagleton, for example, stresses the 'productive creativity' of Jude's masonry. 'It is in the labour of the Christminster working class that Hardy discovers an alternative to the decayed world of the dons: "For a moment there fell on Jude a true illumination; that here in the stone yard was a centre of effort as worthy as that dignified by the name of scholarly study within the noblest of the colleges"' (Hardy 1974, pp. 12–13). Unfortunately, the illumination falls for a moment only. The sentence after the one quoted by Eagleton reads: 'But he lost it under stress of his old idea.' Jude will only accept employment as 'a provisional thing'. 'This was his form of the modern vice of unrest' (1978b, p. 131). His illumination, his allegiance to work and community, will never be a consistent focus of identity. If *The Woodlanders* fuses allegiance and identity, *Jude the Obscure* separates them.

In the first place, stonemasonry was a nomadic and intermittent trade, as the reminiscences of Henry Broadhurst, who went 'on the tramp' in the 1850s and 1860s, make plain (Burnett 1974, pp 312–19). Jude frequently has to travel in search of work, and his position is not improved by his 'irregular' relationship with Sue Bridehead, or by ill-health. Altogether, there is enough anxiety about to take the edge off his 'productive creativity'. In the second place, and more importantly, Jude is convinced that his 'power', in so far as he has any, lies in another direction. 'I felt I could do one thing if I had the opportunity. I could accumulate ideas, and impart them to others' (1978b, p. 480). That is his fantasy, his equivalent of Morris's books and dandyism.

Unlike Keating, Hardy refuses to regard this fantasy as in any way heroic or singular. He points out that by caring for books Jude does not escape 'commonplace' ideas or gain 'rare' ones, 'every working-man being of that taste now' (1978b, p. 112). Henry Broadhurst became an MP, as did Joseph Arch, who had begun as a farm labourer (Arch 1898). The pursuit of freedom through knowledge was a widespread ambition often expressed in working-class autobiography (Vincent 1981). The identity Jude desires is as ordinary as the allegiance he rejects.

Hardy was equally unsentimental in his depiction of the

one authentically working-class character in the novel, Arabella Donn. When Mary Jacobus wanted to direct critical attention away from its male hero, she wrote about 'Sue the Obscure' (Jacobus 1975). Sue Bridehead has been in the spotlight ever since (e.g. Boumelha 1982, ch. 7). Arabella, however, remains to this day Arabella the Obscure, apparently beyond rehabilitation (though see Morgan 1988, pp. 144–54). And yet her career is as productive of new identities as Jude's.

We first see the pig-breeder's daughter with a bucket of innards in front of her; she has just hurled a piece at the daydreaming Jude (1978b, p. 80). She is comprehensively defined by work, as her supervision of his attempts to kill a pig makes clear.

> 'Make un stop that!' said Arabella. 'Such a noise will bring somebody or other up here, and I don't want people to know we are doing it ourselves.' Picking up the knife from the ground whereon Jude had flung it, she slipped it into the gash, and slit the wind-pipe. The pig was instantly silent, his dying breath coming through the hole.
>
> 'That's better,' she said.
>
> 'It is a hateful business!' said he.
>
> 'Pigs must be killed.'
>
> The animal heaved in a final convulsion, and, despite the rope, kicked out with all his last strength. A tablespoonful of black clot came forth, the trickling of red blood having ceased for some seconds.
>
> 'That's it; now he'll go,' said she. 'Artful creatures – they always keep back a drop like that as long as they can!'
>
> (p. 110)

The scene is curiously respectful to Arabella's pragmatism, and disrespectful to Jude's feeble protests. Jude kicks over a bucket of blood, which stains the snow, 'forming a dismal, sordid, ugly spectacle – to those who saw it as other than an ordinary obtaining of meat' (p. 111). This last qualification is a characteristic knight's move, dislodging Jude's perspective and allowing us to see, not the 'spectacle' prepared for us rhetorically, but an unremarkable event. Not to remark such an ordinary death is Arabella's strength. At the end of the novel she will choose not to remark another ordinary death: Jude's.

The morning after the killing, Arabella clears a space for herself on the table by jettisoning Jude's books. 'In the operation of making lard Arabella's hands had become smeared with the hot grease, and her fingers consequently left very perceptible imprints on the book-covers' (p. 114). In *The Woodlanders*, the card-players leave a trace of themselves, and a trace of community, on their cards. Arabella's imprint, by contrast, is a denial, a gesture of expulsion. It violates an identity she knows to be incompatible with her own.

Arabella takes the initiative, destroying the marriage so that she can emigrate to Australia with her parents. When she returns, it is to a very different scene. Jude encounters her serving behind the bar of an inn in Christminster. The inn has been gutted since he was last there, and refurbished with mahogany fixtures, sofa-benches and ground-glass screens. 'At the back of the barmaids rose bevel-edged mirrors, with glass shelves running along their front, on which stood precious liquids that Jude did not know the name of, in bottles of topaz, sapphire, ruby and amethyst' (p. 236). The bar, with its mirror and unidentifiable liquids, reflects Jude's disorientation. One of the barmaids turns to the mirror to tidy her hair, and he recognizes Arabella. Their subsequent reunion is framed by conversations between Arabella and two faintly grotesque swells, both of whom order newfangled liqueurs: a student called Mr Cockman, and a 'chappie with no chin, and a moustache like a lady's eyebrow' (p. 239). Arabella's social mobility is of a different order from Jude's. It is not a willed transcendence, but a protean adaptability.

There is no sense in which Jude's progress can be measured by the distance he puts between himself and the pig-breeder's daughter, the static embodiment of working-class allegiances. Arabella tracks him through the novel: for example, at the Wessex Agricultural Show (pp. 359–66). She is sometimes credited not only with an interest in Sue and Jude, but with a perceptiveness about their relationship which they themselves lack. That she ends up with the itinerant quack and showman Vilbert is indication enough of her ability to forge temporary identities out of temporary allegiances: something for which Jude has no talent at all. Hardy, I think, should be credited with a very perceptive interest in Arabella and her resilience.

On the whole, however, in the novels of the period, the progress of heroes from humble backgrounds was measured by the distance they put between themselves and their upbringing. The hero of Arnold Bennett's first novel, *A Man from the North*

38

(1898), recapitulates his own escape from the provincial middle class. The hero of *Clayhanger* (1910) founds a frail but enduring identity on an act of consumption which scandalizes his hard-working father. The division between allegiance and identity now runs between rather than within generations. So it is also in *Sons and Lovers* (1913), another novel by a writer who famously left home. Edwin Clayhanger ends up inheriting the print-works. There is no question that Paul Morel will ever follow his father down the mines.

WOMEN AND LABOUR: THE 1890s

There was, however, one area of social life where labour, and the allegiances arising out of it, *did* become the focus of identity, and thus more susceptible to incorporation into the novel as traditionally conceived. A notable feature of late nineteenth-century Britain was the increase in the numbers of middle-class working women. In 1861 nearly 80,000 women were employed as teachers in England and Wales; by 1911 there were 183,000. Over the same period, the number of women employed as clerical workers rose from 279 to 124,000. The proportion of the total workforce holding white-collar jobs increased from 7.6 per cent in 1861 to 14.1 per cent in 1911; the proportion of women workers in those jobs increased from 5 per cent to 16.4 per cent (Holcombe 1973, pp. 204–10, 215). For these women, labour was not only a means of survival, but a focus of identity. They 'believed passionately in the morally redeeming power of work; paid public work would give them dignity and inde-pendence' (Vicinus 1985, p. 6).

In *Woman and Labour* (1911), the Bible of the contemporary women's movement, Olive Schreiner argued that women must gain access to the new opportunities created by social and technological developments; those developments were the 'pro-pelling force' behind the women's movement (1978, pp. 72, 67). Among the new opportunities seized by women were journalism, sociology and literature. Volume VIII (1896) of Booth's *Life and Labour* includes a chapter on journalism. 'A noticeable feature of modern journalism is the number of women who have entered the profession, and this led to the successful establishment in 1894 of the Society of Women Journalists, which has now about 200 members' (Booth 1892–1902, VIII, p. 158). Another favoured profession was sociology. Middle-class women laboured to describe and analyse the labour of working-class women. Clare Collet contributed a chapter on 'Women's work' to Volume IV of Booth's survey. The Fabian sociologist B. L. Hutchins wrote extensively on the same subject (Hutchins 1911, 1915, 1917).

On 11 May 1888 Beatrice Webb (then Beatrice Potter) was interviewed by the Select Committee on the Sweating System; she had spent three weeks working as a tailor in the East End of London (Pike 1969, pp. 211–13). On 30 September 1889 she recorded in her diary that for a month or so she had been 'haunted by a longing to create characters and to move them to and fro among fictitious circumstances – to put the matter plainly, by the vulgar wish to write a novel!' She read George Eliot and Zola with enthusiasm, and was always trying to enlist young writers in the Fabian cause. But sociology seemed to her the more 'worthful' exercise of powers, and she devoted her life to developing the necessary expertise. 'Meanwhile my diary shall serve for those titbits of personal experience which are representative of the special peculiarities of the different phases of society I pass through' (Webb 1986, I, p. 298).

It was no easier for a woman to establish herself as a writer than as a sociologist (Tuchman and Fortin 1989). But many did. Among them was Emily Morse Symonds, niece of John Addington Symonds, who published under the pseudonym of 'George Paston'. By December 1895 she had written three New Woman novels which, if not wildly successful, had at least been reviewed favourably by Arnold Bennett, then literary editor of *Woman*. They met in January 1896, and immediately recognized each other as fellow-professionals, exchanging 'tips' and talking 'shop' for hours on end (Bennett 1966–86, II, pp. 33–4). Bennett told his friend George Sturt that he would 'enjoy the conversation of a *woman* who emphatically knows what is what' (p. 39). It is characteristic of the period that they should meet at the Writers' Club (a club for women writers), and that Bennett should have considered he had learnt from his fellow-professional 'several things worth knowing'. ' "G. P." has just finished her novel. Six months, 2 to $2\frac{1}{2}$ hours per diem. Not excessive, is it?' (p. 42). On 23 December 1896 he took her out to dinner and the theatre. 'Her book is going rather well, & she is half through her next (a tale of literary life) which she says will be her best' (pp. 72–3).

The tale of literary life, *A Writer of Books* (1898), is indeed her best. Like the novel which Bennett himself had completed in May 1896, *A Man from the North*, it is about a writer from the provinces arriving in London to make a name. Cosima Chudleigh, left to fend for herself when her father dies, wants to 'get away from her present surroundings, begin a new existence, and lay the foundations of a career' (Paston 1898, p. 14). The career, not marriage, will provide the new existence. If she fails as a writer, she will become 'a clerk or a shop girl' (p. 13).

Romance, however, intervenes to complicate the picture. Cosima marries a childhood friend, Tom Kingston, just back (suitably bronzed) from the colonies. He turns out to be dull, shallow and hypocritical; no fit companion for an enterprising and imaginative young writer. Cosima falls in love with an older man, Quentin Mallory, of minimum beauty and maximum character. It looks as though romantic convention is about to take over, enabling the heroine to find – through the love of a good man and after much suffering – happiness and self-knowledge. But convention doesn't have things all its own way.

The romantic qualifications of Cosima's two lovers are gauged by their tendency to help or hinder her progress towards artistic maturity. Kingston wants her to write novels which will make money ('a historical romance with lots of fighting in it, or something in the supernatural line with Biblical characters, like Miss – I forget what she calls herself'). He advises her to 'try one of the styles that happen to be in demand' (p. 277). Mallory, on the other hand, is severely critical of her efforts along 'popular lines', and urges her to write books which have psychological depth and convey a personal vision.

Paston challenges romantic convention by separating Cosima, somewhat implausibly, from both her lovers. Cosima realizes that love need no longer be 'a woman's whole existence'; it is likely to prove just as 'episodical' in the life of the 'modern woman' as it is in the life of the modern man. 'It may be eagerly longed for, it may be tenderly cherished, but it has been deposed for ever from its proud position of "lord of all"' (p. 341). For Cosima, work rather than marriage has become the focus of identity. In order to render that new focus, Symonds had to break the link between narrative closure and the social closure represented by marriage.

That link came under increasing pressure, even in the work of well-established middle-of-the-road writers. Adeline Sergeant had supported herself by writing since the mid-1880s. *Esther Dennison* (1889) describes the loneliness of the single working woman in London. *The Work of Oliver Byrd* (1902) concerns two rivals for the affection of a young editor and man about town: the well-to-do Eleanor Denbigh, who takes up writing as a hobby, but is increasingly preoccupied, like Potter, and Sergeant herself, by the plight of the London poor; and Avis Rignold, talented and impoverished, who publishes under a male pseudonym. The devices of conventional domestic melodrama (poison phial, burnt manuscript) are used to highlight the conflicting demands made on women, and the difficulties of independence.

The writer whose name Tom Kingston cannot recall was probably Marie Corelli, who had written bestselling novels in the 'supernatural line'. In 1896 Corelli published *The Murder of Delicia*, which describes the suffering inflicted on a brilliant, popular, not un-Corelli-like lady novelist by her empty-headed, womanizing husband. The novel is unflinchingly sentimental about women and dogs, and scarcely radical in its view of what either should be and do. Even so, it is equally unflinching in its insistence that a society which encourages men to patronize women, and refuses to acknowledge the work women do, is fundamentally unjust and unstable. That the issue of vocation should deflect Corelli momentarily from the supernatural line, and indeed from her literary and political conservatism, indicates its importance at the time.

Vocation was certainly an issue for the Anglo-Irish writers Edith Somerville and 'Martin Ross' (Violet Martin), who devoted the fruits of an increasingly successful collaboration to shoring up their far-from-ascendant Protestant Ascendancy families and family homes; neither married. Somerville and Ross began writing together in 1887. *The Real Charlotte* (1894), their first critical success, concerns the plottings and jealousies of a squat, plain, ruthless forty-year-old woman; Andrew Lang told Violet Martin that it treated of a 'new phase' in relations between the sexes (Somerville and Ross 1989, p. 215).

During the 1890s the 'modern woman' became a popular subject with male writers. Vivie Warren, in Shaw's *Mrs Warren's Profession* (1898), prefers to work in an office rather than live off her mother's immoral earnings and the admiration of her suitors. 'I will never take a holiday again as long as I live,' she staunchly declares (Shaw 1946, p. 270). Rhoda Nunn, in Gissing's *The Odd Women* (1893), has no intention of treading the paths trodden by 'English ladies of the familiar type' (Gissing 1980, p. 3). She is a feminist; with her colleague Mary Barfoot, she runs a school in Great Portland Street which trains unmarried ('odd') women for office work. Her dedication has a sharp ideological edge to it, a real militancy. When Mary Barfoot proposes that they should retrain a woman who has been seduced and abandoned, Rhoda points out sternly that they are not running a 'reformatory', and that they ought not to encourage 'reckless individualism' (pp. 56–7). 'You have hardened your heart with theory,' Mary warns her (p. 132). Even romance, in the shape of Mary's cousin, Everard Barfoot, fails to soften her.

Exponents of hard-heartedness, like exponents of political allegiance, fought a losing battle against the novel's addiction to romance. The heroine of Wells's *Ann Veronica* (1909) achieves independence through education, then happily surrenders it to a likely-looking man. In a series of novels beginning with *Marriage* (1912), Wells sought to redefine social and sexual roles. However, the freedom granted to women in these novels is just that: granted, not won. Wells's self-regard loomed over the women in his life and in his novels, permitting them, by its indifference to convention, a certain room for manoeuvre, but also smothering them in half-concealed vanities, in his own unappeasable longing for social and sexual status. *The Passionate Friends* (1913), for example, obtusely recapitulates the theme of *The New Machiavelli* (1911): a middle-class man's desire for an upper-class woman, and subsequent distraction from a promising political career. Yet Wells was capable of self-criticism. *The Wife of Sir Isaac Harman* (1914) concedes that its heroine will be better off not only without her insensitive husband, but also without her sensitive admirer, a Wellsian novelist called Brumley.

Marriage, a furtive hymn to male guardianship, provoked a violent review from Rebecca West, who insisted that all women 'ought to have a chance of being sifted clean through work' (West 1982, p. 69). Writing to Wells on 7 November 1913, Violet Paget asked him to 'make amends to the poor "neuter", the woman who has left home and is typing or clerking, but always starving herself if not of food then of other human rights often because of her blind, furious wish to independence' (quoted in Smith 1986, p. 378). Some writers did make amends to the poor 'neuter'; and they did so in ways which productively redefine the neuter's supposed neutrality.

PIONEERS, SUFFRAGETTES, LANDGIRLS

Violet Hunt, a socially and intellectually adventurous woman whose current reputation rests unfairly on the fact that she was Ford Madox Hueffer's mistress (Hardwick 1991), made a name for herself with the kind of cynical High Society saga which was popular during the 1890s. The heroine of *A Hard Woman* (1895) is a professional flirt, hardened not so much by theory as by pride and some impressively metallic dresses. One of her flirtations goes disastrously wrong, leaving her penitent and heavily in debt. Her husband forgives her, but he has himself fallen in love with another woman, a 'type-writer girl' and aspiring actress who lives in a slum occupied by 'professional independent women', 'free lances' (Hunt 1896, pp. 135, 138). The result is a stand-off between two types of 'modern woman', each hardened in her own way by modernity, and unhappiness all round.

The Workaday Woman (1906) pairs the narrator, Caroline Courtenay, a hired companion, with Jehane Bruce, a writer. Jehane is 'a worker like myself', and 'one of those women who ought to have been a man' (Hunt 1906, p. 3). Her role, like that of a number of minor characters in contemporary fiction, from Hilda Forester in Olive Birrell's *Love in a Mist* (1900) to Mary Datchet in Virginia Woolf's *Night and Day* (1919), is to embody an unromantic independence, which the heroine admires but does not in the end want for herself. Caroline becomes engaged to charming, feckless Colonel Lisbon. 'Well, well, women must work and men must − play, I suppose' (p. 92). Hunt, however, contrives a particularly ripe form of disgrace for Lisbon, leaving Caroline independent and alone: a poor neuter again.

The workaday women derive their identities from work, and from allegiance: from the communal living which their independence necessitates. Rhoda Nunn has her school for odd women, Mary Datchet her suffrage society. Cosima Chudleigh's boarding-house also contains a woman doctor and a woman journalist. Hilda Forester wants the heroine of *Love in a Mist* to join her and a journalist friend in their Bloomsbury flat, a meeting-place as well as a home (Birrell 1900, pp. 228, 247). Jehane Bruce throws Bohemian parties in *her* Bloomsbury flat at which the relations of the sexes are 'a little altered', and the women gain character at the expense of the men (Hunt 1906, p. 35).

Francis Gribble's *The Pillar of Cloud* (1906) concerns a boarding-house for women who earn their living as clerks, 'typewriters' and daily governesses (1906, p. 1). They form a Way Out Club, where they plot their escape from servitude. Some make it, some don't. Gribble was no feminist. His workaday women seem unable to prosper through their own efforts alone, or through mutual support. But he did insist that they should not rely too much on men, and he did emphasize the idea of female com-munity by tracing the individual destinies of a *group* of women.

In Dolf Wyllarde's *Pathway of the Pioneer* (1906), the group is constituted by an informal society, 'Nous Autres', whose members represent 'the professions open to women of no deliberate training, some education, and too much delicacy for the fight before them' (Wyllarde 1906, p. 8). In the 1890s there had in fact been a 'Pioneer Club' for emancipated women; its emblem was a silver axe, for hewing a path through the thickets of prejudice (Rubinstein 1986, pp. 222–4). Nous Autres include a freelance journalist, an actress, a typist and shorthand clerk, a Post Office clerk, a music teacher and a musician who plays in the Ladies' Catgut Band (a distant relative of Conrad's Lena?). These women, like Gribble's boarders, like Tressell's workmen, have been worn down, numbed, by anxiety (p. 10); some of them experience desires sharpened by anxiety. Like Gribble, Wyllarde switches impartially between the different members of the group. But she seems to have greater faith than he does in the resilience of workaday women, and in their willingness to rely on themselves and on each other.

These collective biographies refigure workaday women as captives in a wilderness of debilitating routine, as pioneers who have sacrificed themselves for a cause whose eventual triumph they will not live to see. They are the material of legend rather than novels, and in this respect anticipate their more notorious successors, the suffragettes. Vicinus points out that the campaign for the vote was the culmination of, as well as a departure from, the Victorian women's movement; the militancy it fostered was as potent a 'new religion' as socialism (1985, pp. 250, 254), and as vivid a spectacle (Tickner 1988).

The career of Evelyn Sharp demonstrates the link between

the bohemianism of the 1890s, the sociological body-counts of the 1900s, and the political fervour of the 1910s. Sharp's family background was middle-class and mildly intellectual. In 1894 she moved to London, to a Bloomsbury hostel, and set about becoming a writer. When one of her stories was accepted by the *Yellow Book*, and one of her novels by the Bodley Head, she moved into the Victorian Club in Sackville Street, which let its top floor to single professional women. She became a protégée of Henry Harland, editor of the *Yellow Book*, and the publisher John Lane. In 1906, inspired by the suffragette playwright and actress Elizabeth Robins, she joined the Women's Social and Political Union. She spoke at meetings, edited *Votes for Women*, demonstrated, went to prison, and on hunger strike. The campaign sketches and stories collected in *Rebel Women* (1910, 1915) were based on first-hand experience (Sharp 1933).

Suffrage made for better plays than novels. But G. Colmore's *Suffragette Sally* (1911) did extend the tradition of collective biography by following the destinies of three representative militants: Lady Geraldine Hill; the provincial, middle-class Edith Carstairs; and the cockney serving maid, Sally Simmonds. The novel reveals an intimate knowledge of the WSPU and its tactics. Lady Geraldine is clearly based on Lady Constance Lytton, who was arrested in Newcastle for throwing a stone at Lloyd George's car. Released immediately because of her rank, she committed another offence, in Liverpool, this time disguised as a working woman, and was subsequently force-fed. The final chapter is left blank, with a note stating that the story cannot be concluded because the issue of votes for women is still in the balance. So much for narrative closure.

And yet there is closure, of an orthodox kind. The inherent bias of the genre towards the middle classes, and particularly the middle classes in love, gradually declares itself. Colmore's attitude towards Lady Geraldine is frankly adulatory, her attitude towards Sally Simmons faintly patronizing. The main thrust of the narrative is provided by Edith Carstairs's conversion to militancy, her deepening commitment measured by changes in the way she feels about her two admirers: Cyril Race, a member of the Liberal Cabinet who puts his own career ahead of support for women, and Robbie Colquhoun, a dull country squire who is won over to the cause and seals his conversion by punching

Race on the nose. *Suffragette Sally* is both collective biography – a new, politicized form – and domestic romance.

The First World War took the political sting out of the suffrage campaign, and provided women with a wide variety of new occupations. Although many women were forced out of their jobs when the men returned, they had shown that they could do those jobs perfectly well. The increasing acceptance of their public contribution is apparent in the ease with which war work was incorporated into orthodox romance in such novels as Berta Ruck's *The Land-Girl's Love Story* (1918) and Mrs Humphry Ward's *Harvest* (1920). The myth of rural England and of a reconstructed 'yeoman' class muffled the singularity of these women's experiences in pious generalization.

The kinds of work that did stimulate inventiveness were the technical and administrative occupations vastly extended by the logistics of the war effort. Sally Richards, the wartime typewriter girl in Violet Tweedale's *The Heart of a Woman*, may have given her woman's heart, in the traditional fashion, to the man who employs her, but she also belongs to a club whose membership consists 'entirely of free lances, unmarried working women of advanced opinions and pronounced celibacy' (Tweedale 1917, p. 225). In 1918 Enid Bagnold, a notably emancipated young woman, published *A Diary without Dates*, a record of her time as a VAD nurse at a hospital in Woolwich, which became sufficiently notorious to get her the sack. Immediately after the war, she went to France as a driver with the First Aid Nursing Yeomanry, an experience which provided the basis for a remarkably bold novel, *The Happy Foreigner* (1920). The heroine, a driver seconded to the French army, does a man's work, and demands equality in every area of life. She selects a lover from among the French officers, and, although infatuated with him, is the first to recognize that he will lose his charm for her the minute he relinquishes his uniform.

E. M. Delafield's *The War-Workers* (1918) eschews romantic interest altogether. The heroine manages a supply depot in the Midlands; we see her from the point of view both of her aristocratic family and of the women who work for her. As in Sarah Grand's *The Heavenly Twins* (1894), a middle-aged doctor offers the heroine authoritative advice; this time, however, he is no more than a single voice in a largely female chorus. The issue explored is whether her supreme dedication does not represent a form of egotism. Delafield, in short, carried on where Gribble and Wyllarde left off. The pathway of the pioneer leads to the Midlands Supply Depot.

By the end of the war, women writers in Britain and America were beginning to experiment with narrative methods designed to render individual consciousness rather than work and community. Richardson's Miriam Henderson certainly has to earn her living, as a teacher, a governess, a dental assistant. But the effect of these experiences is usually to persuade her that she must not allow herself to be defined – limited – by them (Richardson 1979, II, p. 196). Her consciousness exists apart from work and community. The cumulative critical recognition justifiably accorded to Modernist women like Richardson and Woolf, and tailored to their concerns, has had the unjustifiable effect of obscuring their Edwardian predecessors.

Work and community did not altogether disappear from view with the advent of stream-of-consciousness techniques. After the war, Constance Holme, whose previous novels had tended to feature ancient Westmorland families of high standing, began to write about elderly working people. *The Trumpet in the Dust* (1921), like *Mrs Dalloway* (1925), concerns the events of a single day in a woman's life; an ordinary day whose placid surface is disturbed by strange undercurrents of passion, and by the aftermath of war. Holme's technique, like Woolf's, is episodic, lyric, choral. And yet her heroine could not be more different. Mrs Dalloway, a sophisticated society hostess, exists in her shifting moods and recollections, in her hospitality. Mrs Clapham, a charwoman, knows no reality, no identity, outside work.

I have concentrated here on middle-class working women; but I don't want to give the impression that their preoccupations found no echo in the experience of working-class women. The lengthy correspondence between Ruth Slate, a clerk in a City grocery firm, and Eva Slawson, a legal secretary, turns on their perception of themselves as 'odd women' (Thompson 1987, p. 152), and on their voracious appetite for literature: George Eliot, Schreiner, Allen, Wells, Robins, Carey and many others. Slate's declaration of 'obstinacy and independence' (p. 101) could well serve as the manifesto of the poor neuter. It is one of the reasons we have for supposing that work, and solidarity among workers, did not go altogether unnoticed in the age of idiosyncratic consumption.

3

GOLD STANDARDS

The development of consumer capitalism posed questions about value, and about personal worth, which no reassertion of social or political allegiances could answer. Nelly Ambrose's identity rests, equivocally, but to a significant degree, on the choice between red and blue feathers; Leopold Bloom's on an ideal advertisement. How could a sense of worth so subjective, so whimsical, ever be acknowledged, measured, endorsed or denied?

Economic value was measured by money, of course. But there were doubts about the ability of an increasingly complex financial and monetary system to provide an authentic criterion of value: to measure justly. Identities determined by that system, or merely reflected in it, did not always seem secure. Monetary metaphors in the fiction of the period therefore tell us a lot not only about the ways in which personal worth was measured, but also about the unreliability of the criteria of measurement.

THE MEANING OF MONEY

One thing which really bothers the time-travelling Alien in Grant Allen's *The British Barbarians* is the distinction between a pound and a sovereign. ' "Why, a pound *is* a sovereign, of course," Philip answered briskly, smiling the genuine British smile of unfeigned astonishment that anybody should be ignorant of a minor detail in the kind of life he had always lived among' (1895b, p. 12). Sovereign and pound were different names for a unit of account equivalent to 20 shillings or 240 pence. They were also something more than that: a symbol, a unit of sovereignty, the reason for genuine British smiles.

'Every Englishman should be proud of the system of coinage

which has given him stable value,' insisted the *Harmsworth Maga-zine*. 'All the world over the English sovereign is a talisman that unlocks the hearts of the hardest men, on whom shillings would make no impression' (Horner 1899, p. 594). Englishmen in English fiction use this talisman to unlock the hearts of informants, bureaucrats and waiters. Hueffer's Edward Ashburnham makes his presence felt in the Hotel Excelsior at Nauheim with the aid of 'a solid, sound, golden English sovereign' (1972, p. 35): about the only thing in his life which *is* unequivocally solid and sound. Buchan's Richard Hannay, as solid and sound as they come, finds that 'English gold' will procure food and shelter in Bavaria, even in wartime, and a bottle of whisky in Istanbul (1956a, pp. 99, 124, 129–30).

Few of Hannay's compatriots would have been able to lay their hands on English gold. With the outbreak of war, and consequent restrictions on the shipment of bullion, sovereigns became very scarce indeed. The small hoard amassed by Henry Earlforward, in Bennett's *Riceyman Steps* (1923), impresses his wife deeply (1928, pp. 167, 249). In the 1920s other units of account took the sovereign's place, and assumed a little of its aura. The heroine of a short story by Michael Arlen regards £10 notes as symbols of Englishness. 'A Bank of England note is the cleanest expression money has ever acquired' (Arlen 1923, p. 114). In the Edwardian era, however, the sovereign was sovereign.

If British society at the end of the nineteenth century was felt to be on the 'money standard', as Marie Corelli put it in *The Sorrows of Satan* (1895), then British money was on the gold standard. The standard stabilized exchange rates, and prevented the depreciation of currency by tying the issue of notes to the reserves of bullion held by the central bank. The value of money derived from the internationally accepted value of gold, rather than from the sometimes fluctuating authority of the government which issued and stamped coins and notes. Britain had adhered to the standard longer, and more consistently, than its main trading rivals. The standard thus became a symbol of economic sovereignty. It made British money seem 'more genuine', as the economist Hartley Withers remarked: 'money, in the real sense of the word, gold or its equivalents, is only to be had, always and without question, and to any amount, in London' (1909, p. 91).

The system of coins and notes articulated by the gold standard could be seen as a hierarchy of signs. The sovereign seemed the most reliable sign of all because it was what it expressed. In 1869 Sir John Herschel had described it as 'a cosmopolitan coin, really containing what it purports to contain, a fixed quantity of gold' (Powell 1915, p. 493). Value and the mark of value, referent and sign, bullion and government stamp, were independently verifiable and yet stood in direct relation to each other. In its original state, gold has intrinsic value. The processes of moulding and signification which convert raw material into coin do not create a commodity whose value is largely extrinsic (a function of the market). Instead, they preserve its original use-value intact within its new exchange-value. The gold sovereign thus appears to be that rare phenomenon in advanced capitalism: a product which has not effaced its origin, a sign which has not effaced its referent.

Further down the hierarchy of monetary signs is the charmless shilling, a mere 'token' whose value derives almost entirely from the stamp impressed on it by the Mint. The shilling does not even pretend to contain its own worth in silver bullion. Already the relation between sign and referent has become more problematic. Further down still is the banknote, which has no intrinsic value at all, no referent. Rather, its referent is another sign, another appearance: the stability of the central bank in the eyes of the trading community. Sovereigns have a past. The coin preserves the original value of the bullion it incorporates. Banknotes, on the other hand, represent a promise to pay; they have no past, only a rather uncertain future.

Economic civilization has come to rest increasingly on imaginary money: banknotes, cheques, bills of exchange, bonds, and all the other instruments of credit. Each successive sophistication of the means of exchange has produced widespread anxiety about the ways in which value can be known and represented. Thus the 'financial revolution' of the 1690s, which saw the establishment of the Bank of England and the National Debt, and the increasing use of instruments of credit, altered the language of politics (Pocock 1975, 1985). By the beginning of the twentieth century trade and credit had expanded yet further, and the gold standard came to be regarded by some as a defence against irresponsible expansions of credit: against imaginary money.

There were sporadic panics (Cross 1907; Crammond 1908), and not without cause. In the popular invasion-fantasies of the era, the first hint of catastrophe is usually the suspension of payment in specie (Le Queux 1906, p. 21), or the disappearance of gold (Wells 1941, p. 232). Thereafter, anarchy and imaginary money stalk the world. In 1914 the conversion of banknotes into gold was suspended in Russia on 27 July, in Germany on 4 August, in France on 5 August. Britain and the United States abandoned the gold standard in practice, while maintaining its outward, legal form. In the 1920s anarchy and imaginary money did indeed stalk Germany, if not the world. The mark lost its primary function of 'measuring prosaic values in goods and services', and became 'a political barometer, a fluctuating index to political emotions' (Angel 1930, p. 339).

The hierarchy of monetary signs articulated by the gold standard could be seen as a scale against which to measure the reliability of particular representations of value. The representations which will concern me here are representations of 'individual' worth. How did Edwardians assess a person's reliability? How did they live up to, or down to, the images of identity generated by the various expressions of money, clean or unclean? 'Sovereigns in a stocking wouldn't bother her; cheques do,' Margaret Schlegel says of her sister Helen in *Howards End* (1910). What bothers Helen – and Anna Tellwright (Bennett 1936, p. 110) – is not wealth itself, but the 'technique of wealth': the new and often troubling forms taken by money in the Edwardian era (Forster 1941, p. 169).

FINANCE

Virginia Woolf imagined 'great financial magnates' laying 'cheques and bonds' under the foundations of King's College Chapel where charitable monarchs had once laid 'ingots and rough lumps of gold' (1977, p. 20). A new and in some ways more fantastic technique of wealth was now running the world, and it found its embodiment in the financial magnate. Over the course of centuries, land had ceded power to trade; now trade was ceding to finance. This perception created the Edwardian novel of finance: Morley Roberts's *The Colossus* (1899), Harold Frederic's *The Market-Place* (1899), E. Phillips Oppenheim's *A Millionaire of Yesterday* (1900), Hueffer and Conrad's *The Inheritors* (1901), Arnold Bennett's *Grand Babylon Hotel* (1902), Barry Pain's *Deals* (1904), Hilaire Belloc's *Mr Clutterbuck's Election* (1908), Wells's *Tono-Bungay* (1909), Conrad's *Chance* (1913), Oliver Onions's *The*

Debit Account (1913). All these books either concentrate on the figure of the financier, or assume that finance is remaking the modern world in its image.

The scandal of imaginary money is that it does not represent an original intrinsic value; it makes itself out of nothing. Trade, and especially that form of trade which aimed to create new desires rather than to satisfy basic needs, was already scandalous, as Teddy Ponderevo admits. ' "We mint faith, George," said my uncle one day. "That's what we do" ' (Wells 1964, p. 185). To market a drug like Tono-Bungay is to become your own mint: to impress an extrinsic value on a product that has no intrinsic value whatsoever. When the manufacturer becomes a financier, as Teddy Ponderevo does, he begins to impress his forged marks on something even more fantastic than Tono-Bungay: on fantasy itself. The financier Sir George Bontine, in *The Colossus*, is a man who 'made money, until money made itself' (Roberts 1899a, p. 66).

Joel Thorpe, in *The Market-Place*, floats a company to work a redundant rubber plantation, but soon abandons even the pretence of production. ' "There's no money in rubber. I'm entirely in finance – in the Stock Exchange – dealing in differences" ' (Frederic 1899, p. 197). The financier hopes to profit from the difference between the value a share now represents and the value it will represent at some moment in the future. He deals in the difference between signs, rather than the identity of sign and referent. The only substance involved, the only 'commodity', is time. A share certificate has no past, no origin: just a future even more uncertain than that of a banknote.

There is little patriotism about money, someone says in *The Colossus* (p. 137). The money which buys and sells shares is international money, offshore money, money without a home. It poses as great a threat to national sovereignty as it does to historical continuity. The men who handle it are also conceived to be homeless. They are Jews, or foreigners. Sapper's arch-villain, Carl Petersen, is supremely cosmopolitan, and the capitalists he usually conspires with are certainly not British. In *The Inheritors*, it is the state's implication in international finance, an activity already mortgaged to the future and controlled by foreigners, which renders it vulnerable to the ruthless utilitarianism of the new politics (Conrad and Hueffer 1901).

Some consolation is to be found, however, in the vulnerability of the financiers themselves. Money without origin or reference produces a life without origin or reference. Like their cheques and bonds, the millionaires become signs which refer only to other signs. Their wealth has excluded them from the social narratives which certify value and status, from tradition, from homeland. So they attempt to secure a place for themselves in those narratives, and an origin for their nomadic fortunes, by purchasing land. They become lords of the manor. They acquire a tradition. But their attempts to convert imaginary identities into the 'specie' of land and blood usually fail. They clearly don't belong, and soon lapse into boredom and depression.

Scarlett Trent, in *A Millionaire of Yesterday*, floats a company to exploit a dubious mining concession. He is interviewed by a young reporter, and falls in love with her. She becomes his 'standard' of worth, leaving him to marvel at a passion which 'had leaped up like a forest tree in a world of magic, a live, fully-grown thing, mighty and immovable, in a single night' (Oppenheim 1900, pp. 118–19). As the tree leaps, he heads for Africa and his gold mine. He has followed his wealth back to its origin and made the extrinsic value of his cheques and bonds represent the intrinsic value of gold ore. This journey to the frontier reveals the moral 'specie' within him and, paradoxically, refines it to gentility, just as his ore will be refined to ingots (pp. 193, 204–5). *A Millionaire of Yesterday* reveals the lengths to which it sometimes seemed necessary to go in order to redeem yourself from the new technique of wealth.

MINTED SUPERSCRIPTIONS

George Ponderevo concludes that the bank reserve or a policeman keeping order in a crowd are 'only slightly less impudent bluffs' than his uncle's prospectuses (Wells 1964, p. 185). It wasn't just the world of trade and finance, but society in general, which appeared to survive by minting or coining faith. Many Edwardian writers saw the impudent bluffs of moral and social identity mirrored in the hierarchy of monetary signs.

People resemble coins in that they may derive their identity from the stuff they are made of, or from the marks that social orderings have impressed upon them. Not to be marked at all is to be beyond identification, like the patrons of the Italian restaurant visited by the Assistant Commissioner in *The Secret*

Agent (1907), whose personalities are not 'stamped' in any way, professionally, socially or racially (Conrad 1990, p. 115). Such unstamped respectability is a void, a blank space on the map where the less respectable featurelessness of anarchism may also proliferate. But on the whole the unmarked seemed to Edwardian writers less worrying, or at least less pervasive, than the *over-marked*: than those who amounted to no more than their professional, social and racial superscriptions. 'All individuals who have class marked on them strongly resemble each other,' Wyndham Lewis's Tarr remarks scornfully. 'A typical duchess is much more like a typical nurserymaid than she is like anybody not standardised' (1973, p. 23).

Standardization was the price of social and political stability. 'We are stamped, my dear, when we are born,' one socialite tells another in *The Fruitful Vine*, 'just as the new money is, and it is useless to try to get rid of our stamp' (Hichens 1911, p. 23). Lady Walderhurst, in *The Making of a Marchioness*, is evidently to. be trusted, even in suspicious circumstances, because she bears the 'stamp of respectable British matrimony' (Burnett 1901, p. 279). In *The Way of All Flesh* (1903), Dr Skinner, the Headmaster of Roughborough Grammar School, is famous as a man who has moulded his pupils' minds after his own and 'stamped an impression upon them which was indelible in afterlife' (Butler 1923, p. 112).

Some people found this degree of uniformity reassuring, others did not. In *Fraternity* (1909), Hilary and Stephen Dallison, educated at public school and Cambridge, seem as though they have been 'turned out of mint with something of the same outward stamp on them' (Galsworthy 1922, p. 30). They have no intrinsic value, and make no effort to disown or transform the outward stamp impressed on them by their upbringing. D. H. Lawrence objected to Galsworthy's complicity with this failure, but he himself used the same metaphor to criticize the same kind of falsification. In *The Rainbow* (1915), Ursula Brangwen's hatred of war leads her to challenge the 'minted superscription of romance and honour' which has been impressed on it (Lawrence 1989, p. 303). She feels that romance and honour are signs that refer only to other signs, and not to the essential human nature of those marked by them. T. E. Lawrence claimed that military discipline is a kind of minted superscription, a 'character or stamp', as he put it in *Seven Pillars of Wisdom* (1926), which marks off soldiers from complete men (1962, p. 522). He called the book he wrote about his years in the RAF *The Mint* (1936).

Henry James sometimes took a less censorious view of the bourgeois mint. His middle-class characters are capable of transcending, through sheer exuberance or newness, the marks that define and constrict them. He likes Mrs Worthingham, in 'Crapy Cornelia' (1909), whose house has for the distinctly fogeyish Scott-Mason 'that gloss of new money ... which seems to claim for it, in any transaction, something more than the "face" value' (1962–4, XII, p. 338). In James's novels, the encounter between experience and innocence is an encounter between the marked and the unmarked. Merton Densher, in *The Wings of the Dove*, occupies 'that wondrous state of youth in which the elements, the metal more or less precious, are so in fusion and fermentation that the question of the final stamp, the pressure that fixes the value, must wait for comparative coolness' (1907–9, XIX, p. 49).

For other writers, the question of identity seemed even more problematic. Dowell, the narrator of Hueffer's *The Good Soldier* (1915), believes that his wife Florence represents a real human being 'only as a banknote represents a certain quantity of gold' (Hueffer 1972, p. 114). In theory, her actions could be converted into generally recognized values and meanings. In practice, they never are. This particular central bank seems to have suspended payment in specie. Florence amounts to no more than the superscriptions stamped upon her paper qualities, 'a mass of talk out of guide-books, of drawings out of fashion-plates' (p. 114). She is a moral financier, a dealer in emotional differences.

STERLING METAL

The answer to the financiers was a stricter observance of traditional values. Backed by racial gold, the British would always maintain their value: 'the dearer are, on the whole, likely to destroy the cheaper peoples, and ... Saxondom will rise triumphant from the doubtful struggle' (Dilke 1868, II, p. 405). It was the 'ore' of Englishness, not the stamp impressed by an evolving social and political system, which would ensure that triumph. 'By secret and unconscious methods of initiation, ... by the law of nature which gives currency to inherent value no matter whose the superscription, the ideas and aims of the great Elizabethan seamen have become the creed of Empire' (Raleigh

1906, pp. 192–3). Galsworthy's archetypal housewife is no sea-dog, but she regards her own 'sterling nature' as 'the bank in which the national wealth was surely deposited' (1915, p. 152).

If the British race resembled a currency, then the most valuable members of the race ought to resemble its most valuable coin. The splendidly English heroine of *The Call of the Blood* (1906) has a soul 'made of sincerity as a sovereign is made of gold' (Hichens 1930, p. 220). G. A. Henty's friends were, according to his biographer, 'of the more sterling metal, stamped with the brand of solidity' (Fenn 1907, p. 348). The clever but superficial Courtenay Youghal, on the other hand, does not possess the character or the convictions which would give his counsels a 'sterling value' (Saki 1963, p. 433).

The English gentleman was made out of sterling metal, and one way to test his worth was to knock him against something hard and see what he sounded like. The aristocratic Hubert Eldon, in *Demos* (1886), can be recognized by 'the ring of noble metal in his self-assertion' (Gissing 1982a, p. 153). The English gentlewoman apparently sounded much the same. Anne Majendie responds to separation from her husband on a 'pure note'; 'for, tried by courtesy, her breeding rang golden to the test' (Sinclair 1907, p. 234). Breeding was extremely important in the fight against depreciation, but not absolutely essential. Annie Swan's *The Guinea Stamp* (1892), about a wealthy woman who prefers an honest working-man to a dandy, has a self-explanatory epigraph: 'The rank is but the guinea stamp. / The man's the gowd for a' that.' According to Eleanor Denbigh in *The Work of Oliver Byrd*, people of her generation have 'learnt the lesson that "rank is but the guinea stamp"'. She thinks that her lower-middle-class fiancé is 'pure gold', a man who 'rings true' (Sergeant 1902, p. 78).

Metal cannot always be sounded, and in that case the superscription becomes the best indication of quality. Joel Thorpe, in *The Market-Place*, knows that he has arrived in English society when he is invited to stay at Lord Plowden's country home, and meets a pair of 'certificated and hall-marked ladies' (Frederic 1899, p. 63). The hallmark guarantees the origin of an object, and the purity of the metal out of which it has been made. When Tarzan meets Jane Porter, he instinctively kisses her hand; this action is the 'hallmark' of good breeding, which years spent in the most savage of environments has not eradicated (Burroughs 1914, p. 277). Such gentility even transcends race. In *The Gun Runner*, an Englishman down on his luck and a native chieftain meet in a store on the border between Natal and Zululand. The features and bearing of both are 'stamped with the same unmistakable hallmark of birth' (Mitford 1922, p. 11). In popular fiction, nobody ever mistrusts a hallmark. Even Villiers, a second-rate writer who despairs at the banality of his own work, is kept going by 'the knowledge of what he had in him, of what had been hall-marked as containing at least a substantial proportion of gold' (Wales 1906, p. 228).

In serious fiction, things are not quite so simple. In *South Wind* (1917), the Locri Faun, a bronze statue 'stamped' with the 'hallmark' of 'individual distinction', turns out to be a fake (Douglas 1930, p. 343). Madame de Vionnet, in *The Ambassadors*, seems to Strether like 'an old precious medal, some silver coin of the Renaissance' (James 1907–9, XXI, p. 270). Her preciousness enhances her integrity. The same cannot be said of the Prince, in *The Golden Bowl* (1904). 'It was as if he had been some old embossed coin, of a purity of gold no longer used, stamped with glorious arms, medieval, wonderful, of which the "worth" in mere modern change, sovereigns and half-crowns, would be great enough, but as to which, since there were finer ways of using it, such taking to pieces was superfluous' (James 1907–9, XXIII, p. 23). The Prince is a walking disproof of the labour theory of value: his 'worth' is entirely a function of the desires invested in him, and the only currency in which it can be measured is the unstable one of charm.

RESERVES

Sterling qualities so self-evident that they could be recognized by the sound they make or the mark they bear were no doubt rare enough, even among English gentlemen. Such qualities sometimes had to be conceived, therefore, as a reserve of moral 'specie' withheld from daily intercourse, but available in a crisis.

In popular fiction crises abound. Timid youths brought up in a world where their banknotes and their mannerisms are accepted at face value find themselves on rugged frontiers where they must deliver or perish. 'Nature has provided for nearly all contingencies and every man has in him a reserve of strength of which he knows nothing till the moment comes and the call' (Stacpoole 1924, p. 186). Meanwhile timid maidens cultivate a reserve 'like that in the Bank of England, where, besides plenty of currency to meet every ordinary demand at sight, there is a cellar-full for emergencies – all ready to come up, bright, fresh, smiling, sterling' (Greenwood 1893, p. 295).

Allan Quatermain sums up the ideological appeal of the frontier when he reflects that he has always 'handled the raw material, the virgin ore, not the finished ornament that is smelted out of it' (Haggard 1913, p. 1). The frontier converts the finished ornament – the timid youth defined by his superscriptions – back into the ore out of which it was made: the elemental man. Or at least it does in popular fiction.

Lord Jim is certainly a finished ornament. Born in an English parsonage, expertly taught, immaculately dressed, he exhibits the marks of race and gentility. Yet he is a fake. Tested by one of 'those events of the sea that show in the light of day the inner worth of a man', he has no reserves to draw upon. The figure he cuts is not backed by the specie of race, by intrinsic value. Marlow's assessment of him is correspondingly stern. 'He looked as genuine as a new sovereign, but there was some infernal alloy in his metal' (Conrad 1986a, p. 76).

Thus far Jim's fate is the fate of countless wimps and bounders in popular fiction. He fails because he has no reserves of character. But Conrad gives him a second chance. In Patusan, Jim will fabricate character; he will impress on this simulacrum of virgin ore the hallmark of military and political leadership. Beyond the end of the telegraph cables and mail-boat lines, Marlow remarks, 'the haggard utilitarian lies of our civilisation wither and die, to be replaced by pure exercises of imagination' (p. 251). Like a financier, Jim speculates in value. He deals in the difference between what he is worth when he first arrives in Patusan and what he will be worth after the storming of Sherif Ali's stockade. His word is the only measure of his value, and he is finished as soon as it fails on the reputation market.

One sign of Jim's Englishness is his taciturnity. Throughout the period, a reserved manner was taken to be a sign that a man or woman possessed hidden reserves of racial gold. In March 1917, a difficult time for Englishness, Sir Walter Raleigh admitted that there was a certain coldness about the average Englishman which 'repels and intimidates any trivial human being who approaches him'. Trivial human beings – foreigners – are desperate to be liked, and therefore simulate feeling and indulge in exaggeration; they issue 'a very large paper currency' against 'a very small gold reserve' (Raleigh 1918, pp. 69–70). The Englishman's refusal to reveal more of himself than is strictly necessary is proof that any claim he does make will be converted into moral specie on demand.

Conrad and Hueffer put this taciturnity to the test. *The Good Soldier* is the story of the effect that foreign exaggeration and insincerity has on the 'traditional reticence' of those 'proud and reserved people', Edward and Leonora Ashburnham. Edward Ashburnham's reticence derives from the possession of land and an unswerving patriotism (appropriately, he is a member of the National Reserve Committee, and worries constantly about the strength of the Hampshire territorials). Leonora's reticence derives from the 'reservations' of Catholicism. They are confronted by Florence Dowell's vulgarity – her issuing of a large paper currency against a small gold reserve – and give way. Florence makes a sign, a pass at Edward, and the sign forces them to abandon their 'high reserve'.

Another couple forced to abandon their high reserve are Charles and Emilia Gould, in *Nostromo* (1904). The 'indelible' hallmark of breeding survives in Charles, in the way he rides, in his taciturnity. 'His silences, backed by the power of speech, had as many shades of significance as uttered words' (Conrad 1963, p. 175). People learn to trust these silences because they are backed not only by breeding, but by the silver of the San Tomé mine. Handling the first ingot produced, Emilia thinks she has touched an origin, an intrinsic value: 'by her imaginative estimate of its power she endowed that lump of metal with a justificative conception, as though it were not a mere fact, but something far-reaching and impalpable, like the true expression of an emotion or the emergence of a principle' (p. 99). But her 'imaginative estimate' is confounded by the damage the lump of metal does to her marriage. It has no intrinsic value. There is no silver standard. Events force Gould to abandon his taciturnity, to play fast and loose with both his reserve and his reserves. He endorses Decoud's plan for the secession of Sulaco, and uses the San Tomé mine to float a loan. He becomes a financier, a dealer in extrinsic value.

Meanwhile a substantial part of the silver has been withdrawn from circulation, buried by Nostromo on an island. Like Jim, Nostromo mints faith in himself, speculates in the difference his next daring feat will make to his reputation. Like Jim, he is known not by a name but by a title permanently mortgaged to the future. He hopes that the stolen silver will originate a new and more stable reputation. But illicit wealth cannot be expressed as dramatically, as decisively, as courage. Indeed, it forces him to deny or mistrust the very qualities that make him what he is. The treasure becomes a fetish, robbing him of experience, then of life (Simpson 1982, pp. 96–7). For Conrad, there is no such thing as a reserve of character: only a fetish, in Nostromo's case; or an unsustainable and morally destructive strategy, in Gould's; or the desperate fabrication of a badge of courage, in Jim's.

An examination of monetary metaphors reveals the extent of the divergence between popular and serious fiction. In one case, identity is conceived as an intrinsic 'value' which relates to its expression in word and deed as precious metal relates to minted superscription, or as signified relates to signifier; decoding yields instant identification. In the other case, the signs of identity can be decoded easily enough; but they form the basis for a wide range of inferences. The Prince can be identified as the equivalent of an 'old embossed coin'. But it is not at all easy to say what he intends by his air of antique gentility.

The divergence is between attitudes not only to identity, but also to communication. Monetary metaphors had long played their part in debates about language (Shell 1982). Emerson, for one, had no doubt that the corruption of man had corrupted language: 'a paper currency is employed, when there is no bullion in the vaults' (1990, p. 15). Pound gave a new twist to turn-of-the-century demands for a return to the linguistic gold standard when he declared that the genius can pay 'in nugget and in lump gold: it is not necessary that he bring up his knowledge into the mint of consciousness, stamp it into either the coin of conscientiously analysed form-detail knowledge or into the paper money of words, before he transmit it' (quoted in Bush 1976, p. 224). Writing in 1919, Pound had Eliot and Joyce, and the difficulty of their work, very much in mind. His argument takes us beyond the primarily thematic concerns of my first three chapters. It demands an account of the literary 'sign', and of the ways in which Modernist writers sought to complicate that, too.

4

THRESHOLDS

Since I believe that Modernist complexity was made possible, although not *determined*, by changes in the organization of the literary marketplace, I need now to examine those changes, and the phenomenon they produced: the book as scarce commodity.

BUYING NOVELS

From the middle of the nineteenth century onwards, novels often appeared first in serialized form, either in 'numbers' sold separately, or as part of a newspaper or magazine. In either case, they would be cheek by jowl with news items, gossip, puffs and advertisements. Recent studies have placed this process of commodification at the centre of our understanding of the nineteenth-century novel (Sutherland 1976; Bowlby 1985, chs 6 and 7; Cross 1985; Keating 1989, chs 1 and 7). Style is a relation to a reader, and that relation was reshaped fundamentally by changes in the production and distribution of books, magazines and newspapers.

'Between 1880 and 1895,' Cross observes, 'the world of publishing and journalism underwent a radical transformation: the introduction of syndication, the expansion of the popular press, the founding of the Society of Authors, the rise of the literary agent, the relaxing of mid-Victorian pruderies in fiction, the triumph of the adventure story and the gossip column' (1985, pp. 204–5). George Gissing, who had recorded the human cost of these developments in *New Grub Street* (1891), surveyed the mounting tide of print with despair. 'Who in heaven's name *buys* all the books that come forth?' (1961, p. 145).

Not the mass of the population. Keating reckons that at no

time during the period did the weekly surplus of income over expenditure enjoyed by the average family amount to the price of a new novel (1989, p. 408). That surplus was likely to be channelled into the new leisure activities, or into cheap newspapers, magazines and penny novelettes. This was the era of *Tit-Bits* (1881), which offered its readers gossip, competitions and stories; of illustrated 'miscellany' periodicals like the *English Illustrated Magazine* (1883) and the *Strand* (1891); and of W. T. Stead's *Review of Reviews* (1890), each issue of which would contain, he promised, not only a digest of other periodicals but also 'a condensed novel, with its salient features and best scenes intact' (Keating 1989, p. 38). The advent of popular journalism created a huge new market for writers to exploit. Conrad, Joyce and Woolf all submitted work to *Tit-Bits*. Wells wrote anonymous paragraphs, at 2/6d. a time, for several of the new periodicals. But the market for novels, rather than paragraphs, was still a relatively restricted one.

The most significant development within that market was the demise of the three-volume novel in 1895. The three-decker, as it was known, had dominated fiction publishing since the 1820s, kept alive by a cartel of publishers and circulating libraries (notably Mudie's and W. H. Smith's) who depended on its high price for their stable profit margins. Costing 31/6d. in the shop, the three-decker was far too expensive for the average reader to buy. But a publisher could easily realize a profit of £100 on a sale of 500 copies, mostly to the libraries, after paying the author a standard £100 for the copyright (Cross 1985, p. 207). Publishers could sell a small but remunerative quantity of any novel, however bad, provided it filled three volumes and was inoffensive enough to be acceptable to Mudie and W. H. Smith. As a result, John Sutherland points out, 'the new novel, that most speculative of commercial ventures, was the most stably priced and sized commodity in the whole nineteenth-century market place' (1976, p. 12). By the end of the 1880s, the three-decker was an anachronism. Rider Haggard, Hall Caine and R. D. Blackmore began to publish new one-volume novels at the traditional reprint price of 6 shillings. Gissing's friend Morley Roberts declined to publish in any other way; he was able to dispose of five books in six months, Gissing noted enviously (Cross 1985, pp. 207–8). On 27 June 1894 Mudie and Smith announced that from the beginning of 1895 they would not pay more than 4 shillings a volume for fiction, less the usual discounts. Their aim was to force publishers to issue new fiction in single-volume form, and they succeeded. The number of three-volume novels published fell from 184 in 1894 to 52 in 1895, 25 in 1896, and 4 in 1897 (Keating 1989, pp. 26–7). When Mary Braddon, the queen of the circulating libraries, reluctantly abandoned the form in 1895, it effectively ceased to exist.

The circulating and public libraries remained the main purchasers of fiction, but the number of copies sold had to increase at least threefold, and probably more, if the publisher was to make a reasonable profit. A novelist now had to secure library sales, but also attract those individual readers who could afford to buy rather than borrow. It was this situation which produced the modern 'bestseller'. 'The new appeal,' Keating writes, 'would be to the taste and pockets of individual readers' (1989, p. 405). Value was to be measured not by the amount of labour devoted to filling three volumes, or by the standard of utility established by the libraries, but by the idiosyncratic desires of the reader-consumer.

Of course, those writers who were able to identify a substantial sector of the reading public, either by addressing commonplace aspirations and anxieties or by specializing in a particular genre, sold the most copies. In 1907 Ernest Baker surveyed the fiction stocked by public libraries. He classified novelists according to literary quality, and then assessed their popularity. He found that the public libraries held 390 volumes by Meredith, and fewer by James (both Class I novelists), as compared to 2,296 by Mary Braddon, and almost as many by Mrs Henry Wood and Emma Jane Worboise (all Class II novelists). Each library held on average 45 volumes by Guy Boothby and 28 by William Le Queux, among Class III novelists (Keating 1989, p. 418).

I shall have much to say about bestselling novelists in this book, and about those serious writers, from Mary Ward to Wells and Forster, who did manage to secure a large number of readers. But it is also important to recognize a new diversity, made possible by such factors as the reduction in the price of a novel, within the audience for fiction. Somewhere, hidden away, were readers whose idiosyncratic tastes encompassed a feeling for language, or unflustered description, or whatever, and who were ready to pay for the privilege. 'While the new, unusual or experimental writer could not expect to establish himself any more easily under the new system than under the old,' Keating concludes, 'he would at least be able to make direct contact with the portion of the reading-public sympathetic to his work' (1989, p. 405). Studies of James's negotiations with his publishers (Anesko 1986) and the marketing of *The Waste Land* (Rainey 1989) have shown that writers spared no effort to make contact.

The stories James wrote about writers during the 1890s show him imagining not indifference to the marketplace, but a variety of adjustments, or failures to adjust. In 'The Next Time' (1894), Ray Limbert, an 'exquisite failure', decides to improve his fortunes by writing a formulaic bestseller, an 'adventure story on approved lines'. Aiming at a popular bad book, he achieves only another unpopular good book, and retires hurt. In 'The Death of the Lion' (1894), Neil Paraday, another talented though unsuccessful writer, is 'discovered' by a 'big blundering news-paper' and immediately 'proclaimed and anointed'. He succumbs to the temptations of public recognition, and is eventually destroyed by it. In 'John Delavoy' (1898), what the public wishes to recognize is not the writer's work, but the rather uninteresting details of his private life. The biographical approach is 'something the public will stand', an editor tells him, whereas a critical study of his novels would lose the magazine between five and ten thousand readers. Philip Vincent, whose collected works are being illustrated by the unnamed artist in 'The Real Thing' (1890), has enjoyed, late in life, after long neglect, 'the dawn and then the full light of a higher criticism' (James 1962–4, VIII, p. 237).

Keating points out that while the pattern of Vincent's career would have seemed unfamiliar to most major mid-Victorian novelists, it does describe unerringly the experience of many of their successors (1989, p. 380). There was, above all, the example of Meredith, who finally achieved, in the late 1870s, a reputation as an obscure but consequential writer. His books might be too difficult for the 'popular reader', Arabella Shore wrote in 1879, but 'the indirect expressions embody so much wit, or sense or fancy, that we love the work the more for the trouble it has given us' (quoted in Keating 1989, p. 384).

There were many aspiring Merediths. When the publisher A. H. Bullen told Gissing that, while he hoped eventually to make a profit out of his novels, the 'privilege' of publishing them would compensate for any financial loss, Gissing gratefully copied the letter into his diary. David Meldrum, literary adviser to William Blackwood, argued that it would be an honour to publish Conrad and that no consideration should be given to the author's 'popularity' (Keating 1989, pp. 20, 67). J. B. Pinker managed to persuade Henry James that there were firms which would pay for the privilege of publishing a writer of 'the better sort'. 'If the pressure to achieve best-seller status was made more acute by the evolution of a truly mass audience,' Anesko observes, 'the same conditions eventually fostered the recognition that smaller, more discriminating publics existed in tandem with it' (1986, p. 143).

W. D. Howells, James's American mentor and friend, distinguished between two markets, each regulated by a different principle. On one hand, there was the type of fiction which was the equivalent of the circus or the variety theatre, and which seemed 'essential to the spiritual health of the masses'. The demand for such writing was stable, an easily defined need which could be met by an easily defined product. The 'cultivated' classes, on the other hand, demanded a different type of fiction: one regulated by fashion, like the style of clothing (Bowlby 1985, p. 91). Howells felt that the serious writer should decline to enter the fashion parade. But his description of a market regulated by the idiosyncratic desires of individual consumers, rather than by utility or social need, does indicate how a serious writer might compromise with, or be caught up by, fashion – and thus make a living without ever being truly popular.

Veblen believed that William Morris's Kelmscott Press had succeeded by setting aside any concern for utility, or 'serviceability', and publishing rare and costly books which reader-consumers bought in order to acquire 'pecuniary distinction'. The value of such a book was determined not by its intrinsic worth, economic or aesthetic, but by 'the law of conspicuous waste' (1925, pp. 163–4). George Egerton lampooned the kind of society woman whose autographed first editions were 'just adjuncts to herself, trappings to enhance her financial value as a fascinating personality' – like the monogram shaved into the coat of her poodle (1901, p. 148).

The economy of abundance had created a demand not only for loaves of bread, but for diamonds. Henceforth, it would at least be conceivable for a writer incapable of baking bread to facet and polish a single diamond. I want to establish here the consequences of this recognition for the way such a writer might actually write. Modernism, I shall suggest, is the literary equivalent of the theory of marginal utility.

RELEVANCE THEORY

The styles of Modernist fiction have been explained either as a code-violation or as a code-switch. The first explanation is the more popular, and comes in many versions. Modernism, as Bradbury and McFarlane put it, meant not so much a 'new mode or mannerism' as a 'magnificent disaster' for the very idea of mode or mannerism, a 'crisis of culture'. Modernism, they conclude, was less a style than the search for a style (1976, pp. 26, 29). According to the second explanation, the crisis was temporary and the search produced a result: a new mode or mannerism. Fiction continued to represent 'the world', but it now did so with an emphasis on similarity rather than difference. This new purpose was encoded in the text by a syntactic representation which favoured metaphor (the axis of selection) over metonymy (the axis of combination). Readers learnt to recognize a preponderance of metaphor over metonymy as evidence that the writer conceived of human destinies mythically or archetypally (Lodge 1977).

The weakness of both explanations lies in their adherence to a code model of communication. With a few exceptions, such as some of Gertrude Stein's writings, Modernist fiction can be decoded grammatically and semantically without an impossible effort. The problem has always been that the output of decoding, the work done by our knowledge of the grammatical and semantic rules, does not always provide an adequate basis for inferring the writer's intention. We can figure out what the words mean, but not what they mean *in this case*. The code model, which understands language as a single process of encoding and decoding, cannot deal with messages that have been encoded and decoded but still don't 'add up'.

I shall argue here that when Modernist writing stretches the rules, it does so not in order to demonstrate the arbitrariness of all codes, or in order to enact the 'free play' of language, but in order to test our powers of inference. It raises the cost of processing a text in order to make us dig deeper into our mental and emotional resources, to mine our assumptions more extensively, and thus generate richer contextual effects. That, at any rate, is the theory, which, like most theories, doesn't always work in practice. This book is about the practice. I shall argue that, if 'the linguistic structure of an utterance grossly underdetermines its interpretation' (Wilson and Sperber 1988, p. 141), then the linguistic structure of Modernist fiction underdetermines more than most.

In my Introduction I suggested that Relevance Theory, which analyses communication in terms of effort and effect, can help us to understand the ways in which the fiction of the period demands its efforts and produces its effects. People will not pay attention to an utterance unless they expect to obtain information from it without undue effort. Most novels of the period, whether middlebrow or lowbrow, carried an unwritten guarantee that the effort of attention, memory and reasoning required to process them would be kept to an absolute minimum; the cognitive effect, in some cases substantial, being a kind of bonus. The same could not be said of a book by Meredith, James, Conrad, Lawrence, Joyce or Woolf. For these writers, effect was primary, effort secondary. Obscurity was their subject, not a mode or mannerism (White 1981); although one suspects that they were sometimes tempted to measure the effect of their work by the amount of effort it required of the reader. Douglas Hewitt suggests as much when he argues that the complexity of *The Golden Bowl* is meant to intimidate rather than challenge (1988, pp. 22–5).

These are important issues. But we can approach them only by determining how writers balance effort and effect. Processing an utterance involves two kinds of effort: to decode its linguistic structure (identify syntactic functions, etc.); and to combine the output of that decoding with an appropriate context in such a way as to produce an effect which could not have been produced by either operation alone. The set of premises used in interpreting an utterance constitutes its context. A context is 'a psychological construct, a subset of the hearer's assumptions about the world' (Sperber and Wilson 1986, p. 15).

The idea is that there is a small immediately accessible context consisting of the most recently processed propositions, which forms the basis for the interpretation process, and this minimal context is then expanded by reference to

earlier discourse, to encyclopaedic knowledge, or to sense
perception. Each of these extensions of the context will, by
hypothesis, be motivated by the desire to optimize the
relevance of what has been said.

(Smith 1989, p. 75)

A speaker or writer aiming at optimal relevance will try to ensure
that his or her utterance can be interpreted without too great an
expenditure of either kind of effort. However, writers in particular
sometimes go out of their way to make things more difficult. For
example, a periodic sentence structure, which withholds the
main constituent and requires that subordinate or dependent
constituents be held in the mind until its belated appearance,
places a considerable burden on the reader's short-term syntactic
memory, and thus 'achieves its effects at great cost' (Leech and
Short 1981, pp. 225–8). One need look no further than the
complexity of James's syntax for proof that Modernist writers
did not hesitate to test their readers in this way. Some of
the contexts they provided for their writing were even more
strenuous.

Information picked up from the physical environment does
not usually affect the interpretation of literature. Other contexts
do, and the writer can to some extent determine their accessibility.
A reader's interpretation of a passage in a novel will depend on
his or her memory of what has been happening in the previous
ten pages, or the previous hundred. Most writers exploit the
former, a few insist on the latter. Joyce made extraordinary
demands in this respect. In *Ulysses*, when Bloom takes leave of
Molly at the beginning of the day, we do not witness what they
say to each other. The details of this crucial conversation emerge
bit by bit during the course of the novel, some being withheld
until Molly's nocturnal monologue in 'Penelope', the concluding
episode. It is up to us to cross-reference these bulletins, which
no reader could possibly keep in mind, using the book as an
information retrieval system.

Joyce's appeals to encyclopaedic memory are no less exacting.
When Bloom begins to think about the phenomenon of parallax,
in 'Lestrygonians', we must access, as Bloom himself does, the
information stored in encyclopaedic memory at the conceptual
address for 'parallax'. We may well draw a blank; in which
case, as faithful readers, we should consult a dictionary or an

encyclopaedia, or a critical study in which the issue is explored (Kenner 1980, pp. 73–5). *Ulysses* is of course a more punishing novel than most. But the interpretation of Modernist fiction (and poetry) quite often requires the retrieval of information from some pretty inaccessible contexts.

Modernist writers encourage us to access relatively inaccessible contexts by disturbing or neutralizing linguistic form. Normally, the syntactic and phonological organization of an utterance affects the way it is processed and understood. Its 'focus' – the surface constituent which receives the main stress – helps us to assess what it is about (Sperber and Wilson 1986, pp. 202–17; Blakemore 1987, pp. 97–104). Such information status is determined, not by the structure of the discourse, but by the speaker. Even so, there are, if not rules, then at least regularities. It is, for example, a courtesy to the listener to introduce old (given) information before the new information which represents the point of the utterance. This allows the listener to construct a context as he or she processes the utterance, interpreting the new information partly in the context provided by the old. Of course, written statements are not necessarily structured in the same way as spoken utterances. But I believe that the concept of 'focus' can be used metaphorically to illuminate literary practice. Modernist writers went out of their way to complicate the assignment of 'focus'. Again and again, minor disturbances of linguistic structure alert us to the possibility that we may have to work very hard indeed in order to understand what the writer might mean us to infer.

'A CUP OF TEA'

The heroine of Katherine Mansfield's 'A Cup of Tea', Rosemary Fell, a thoroughly 'modern' young woman, visits an antique shop in Curzon Street, Mayfair. She likes the shop, and the shopman, because they repay her patronage with an unobtrusive but comforting deference. On this occasion, she is shown a little enamel box with a glaze so fine 'it looked as though it had been baked in cream'. Hearing that it costs 28 guineas, she decides not to purchase it at once, but asks the shopman to keep it for her.

But the shopman had already bowed as though keeping it

70

for her was all any human being could ask. He would be willing, of course, to keep it for her for ever.

The discreet door shut with a click. She was outside on the step, gazing at the winter afternoon.

(Mansfield 1983, pp. 585–6)

Leech and Short (1981, pp. 126–31) quote this passage and then offer a stylistic analysis of what seems to them its most striking sentence: 'The discreet door shut with a click.' They consider the sentences Mansfield might have written (e.g. 'The door discreetly shut with a click'), and conclude that the sentence she chose creates its effect above all by transferring the shopman's chief attribute to the door he may or may not shut with a click. 'The author makes it seem as if in this euphemistic world, tradesmen, dealers – men of the flesh – have refined themselves out of existence, and have imparted their qualities to the shop itself, its furniture and fittings, in a general ambience of discretion' (p. 129).

The sentence *is* striking, of course, and for the reason Leech and Short suggest. But why exactly does it compel attention? I shall argue that it 'leaps out' of the surrounding passage because it constitutes a threshold, a disturbance of the stylistic norm established by the story's opening. Up until this moment, the story had developed a gossipy conversational style which clearly mimics the idiom and intonations of Rosemary's 'set', and moves fluently into and out of her consciousness. The remark about the door disturbs that style. It places Rosemary and her world with an accuracy, and a quiet irony, of which she herself would not have been capable. Its teasing metaphor (in what sense are doors discreet?) creates a complication. For the first time, we are asked to understand something about the heroine which she herself does not understand, for which she does not have the words. Is it possible to identify anything in the semantic or syntactic structure of the sentence that might have produced this change of emphasis?

'The discreet door shut with a click' (1) is a near-miss for 'The door shut with a discreet click' (2). (2) conveys very roughly the same meaning as (1), but it has a significantly different effect. It seems more natural. We can more readily associate discretion with clicks than with doors. (2), in short, could not be mistaken for a threshold. To grasp why (2) seems natural is to grasp why (1) compels extra attention.

71

Let us imagine what happens as the reader processes the
temporal sequencing of (2). On reaching 'The door', we access
a range of possible referents. The range is immediately and
unambiguously restricted by the definite article, which tells us
that the identity of the door in question has already been
established. We know that Rosemary Fell spends much of her
time entering and leaving shops, and assume that she is in the
habit of doing so by the door rather than the window. We know
that she has just concluded a transaction, and can deduce that
she will now leave the shop she is in. We have no trouble in
identifying the door in question, since it is a part of our knowledge
of the fictional world Mansfield has created. Indeed, it is so much
a part of our knowledge that it can be of no interest in itself. It
is not relevant in its own right. It contributes to the relevance of
the sentence by allowing us access to a context (the behaviour of
doors) which may turn out to be relevant. It raises a question in
the reader's mind – 'What did the door do?' – the answer to
which might well prove relevant. For example, if it turned out
that the door had fallen off its hinges, we might begin to worry
about the heroine's safety. 'The door' is what Sperber and Wilson
call a background implication, because its function is to reduce
processing costs and allow us access to a context which may
carry effects.

As it happens, the door doesn't fall off its hinges. 'The door
shut . . .'. This, too, is a background implication. Our knowledge
of doors tells us that they customarily open and shut, and it
comes as no surprise to find this particular example in the process
of doing so. Again, though, the background implication raises a
relevant question: 'In what manner did the door shut?' There
are several ways in which a door can shut, and the way it does
so can tell us quite a lot about it, or about the state of mind of
people passing through it. This door shuts 'with a discreet click'.
We have arrived at the focus of the sentence: a foreground
implication which is relevant in its own right, and which max-
imizes the contextual effect. Our impression that the shop in
Curzon Street is a discreet place frequented by discreet people
has been significantly reinforced.

So much for what Mansfield might have written. What she
did write produces a comparable, but considerably more powerful, effect. 'The discreet door shut with a click.' The focus of the
sentence is still its final constituent: the new information it has

to give us concerns the manner in which the door shut. But it is harder to process. The initial constituent – 'The discreet door' – must be classed as a background implication. It raises a relevant question, provides access to a context. When we get to the end of the sentence, we already know that this is the kind of door which is likely to shut with a click rather than a bang. And yet that context is relatively large, relatively inaccessible. We have to rummage around in our encyclopaedic entry for 'door' until we discover ways in which a door might be considered discreet. The solution assumed by Leech and Short is that this door is discreet because it is operated by discreet people. But we should surely also consider the possibility that the door is discreet with reference to the street it opens on to: it is unobtrusive, perhaps, recessed, painted an unassuming colour. This interpretation doesn't contradict the one proposed by Leech and Short. But the multiplying of possible interpretations does increase, fractionally, the cost of processing the initial constituent. If the sentence was optimally relevant, we should be able to make up our minds immediately as to the door's discretion, before passing on to the verb phrase 'shut with a click'. To the extent that we have to work at it, the implication does not fulfil its normal function.

There is another factor which needs to be taken into account. As we watch Rosemary hesitate over her little enamel box, we may possibly be reminded, in a vague sort of way, of the scene in *The Golden Bowl* (1904) where the Prince and Charlotte Stant visit a Bloomsbury antique shop (James 1907–9, XXIII, pp. 104–21). There, too, hovers an obliging shopman who is prepared to keep things for the right people, and who lovingly fingers the 'discreet cluster' of objects spread out on the counter. In that scene, discretion is, of course, of the essence. The Prince's fiancée, Maggie Verver, must not find out what they have been up to. It is possible, then, that the puzzling discretion of the door in Mansfield's story may encourage us to access the context provided by another scene, another fictional shop. That context, however, an ambitious, baroque novel about adultery, is a large and relatively inaccessible one. Unless we happen to know *The Golden Bowl* very well indeed, we will probably struggle to connect wimpish Rosemary Fell with James's high-toned lovers. Even so, the possibility of a connection may well strike us as relevant: as likely to enrich the story we are reading. For anyone prepared to recall the details of *The Golden Bowl*, the door's discretion becomes a context not only for the click which confirms it, but for the rest of the heroine's day. One might say that 'The discreet door' is a foreground implication with regard to the sentence that contains it, since it is as relevant as the 'click', but a background implication with regard to the story as a whole. Or we could say that the focus of the sentence is the sentence as a whole, rather than any particular constituent: it's all equally new, equally relevant.

Either way, the sentence draws attention to itself. Its semantic ordering flouts the conventions of normal discourse, conventions which the story has hitherto adhered to. In Relevance Theory terms, it guarantees an increase in contextual effect, but only at the cost of an increase in the effort required to process it. In my terms, it constitutes a threshold. By withholding the kind of relevance we might have expected – a straightforward cumulative 'filling in' of a not unfamiliar fictional world – it invites us to exercise our powers of inference: to access more remote contexts in search of other kinds of relevance. Modernism is another name for that invitation.

The proof that this sentence has significantly raised the stakes lies in the paragraph it initiates. Rosemary Fell finds herself in the street outside the shop. She has crossed a symbolic threshold, exchanging the security of the shop for the insecurity of the street. Dark thoughts assail her, followed shortly by a beggar, a young girl. Rosemary commits the first *in*discretion of the day, perhaps of her life. She invites the girl home with her. Thereafter we are in a different world, where nothing can be taken for granted. We may achieve a richer understanding of that world if we combine our unfolding awareness of it with our recollection of *The Golden Bowl*.

SONS AND LOVERS

A threshold such as that constituted by Mansfield's transposition of 'discreet' can alert readers, without alerting them to anything in particular. Even if we don't access the context provided by *The Golden Bowl*, we may still sense a change of emphasis. Lawrence is not thought of as a writer who left much to chance when it came to alerting his readers. Yet the earlier writing, particularly *Sons and Lovers* and the first half of *The Rainbow*, is wonderfully subtle and unobtrusive in this respect.

Lawrence generally employed a 'loose' sentence structure which avoids anticipatory constituents, enabling us to decode the syntax as we go along. Such a structure makes things easy for the addressee by reducing the amount of syntactic information that has to be stored (Leech and Short 1981, pp. 228–9). A good example is the opening of *Women in Love* (the symbol ˆ marks the boundaries of major constituents).

> Ursula and Gudrun Brangwen sat one morning in the window-bay of their father's house in Beldover,ˆ working and talking.ˆ Ursula was stitching a piece of brightly-coloured embroidery,ˆ and Gudrun was drawingˆ upon a board which she held on her knee.ˆ They were mostly silent,ˆ talking as their thoughts strayed through their minds.ˆ
>
> (Lawrence 1987, p. 7)

There is no anticipatory structure here, either between sentences or between major constituents within sentences. We decode as we go along, holding in our syntactic memory only the immediately preceding grammatical context, a task made even simpler by the cohesiveness of the passage. For example, lexical repetition ensures that we can easily and unambiguously assign a referent to the grammatical subjects of the second sentence.

There is an underlying consistency to Lawrence's style, despite the very different demands he made on it. The features of syntax and cohesion revealed by the opening of *Women in Love* can also be seen in the opening of his first published story, 'Odour of Chrysanthemums'. In the story, furthermore, definite articles link one sentence to another, and text to context: they make believe that the reader is already familiar with the environment described. The text's cohesiveness and intelligibility mirror the cohesiveness and intelligibility of the community Lawrence is writing about. However, Walter Bates's death disrupts both.

> Life with its smoky burning gone from him, had left him apart and utterly alien to her. And she knew what a stranger he was to her. In her womb was ice of fear, because of this separate stranger with whom she had been living as one flesh. Was this what it all meant – utter, intact separateness,

obscured by heat of living? In dread she turned her face away.

(1983, p. 197)

Bates's death forces his wife to recognize that she has been living a lie. The recognition induces a change of stylistic register. A stripped-down poetic language ('ice of fear', 'heat of living') indicates that her feelings exceed the norms both of relationship and of prose description. In addition, three of the five sentences I have quoted include a significant anticipatory constituent: their syntax is fractionally more difficult to decode than the syntax established as a stylistic norm by the bulk of the story. This alteration of linguistic structure constitutes a threshold.

It's a rather clumsy alteration, we might think, too vague, too portentous ('ice of fear'). Lawrence may have thought so. In *Sons and Lovers* he rewrote the scene in such a way as to avoid any hint of clumsiness. Walter Morel is injured in a mining accident; Gertrude, having seen him in hospital, returns home (I have numbered the sentences for ease of reference).

(1) Paul took up his brush again and went on painting. (2) Arthur went outside for some coal. (3) Annie sat looking dismal. (4) And Mrs Morel, in her little rocking-chair that her husband had made for her when the first baby was coming, remained motionless, brooding. (5) She was grieved, and bitterly sorry for the man who was hurt so much. (6) But still, in her heart of hearts, where the love should have burned, there was a blank. (7) Now, when all her woman's pity was roused to its full extent, when she would have slaved herself to death to nurse him and to save him, when she would have taken the pain herself, if she could, somewhere far away inside her, she felt indifferent to him and his suffering. (8) It hurt her most of all, this failure to love him, even when he roused her strong emotions. (9) She brooded awhile.

(1948, p. 110)

The first three sentences are effortlessly decodable. They confirm our familiarity with the fictional world created by the novel. (4) marks a slight change of emphasis by distinguishing Mrs Morel from her children: the use of 'and' as a logical connective, a rarity in modern English prose (Leech and Short 1981, p. 250),

76

spells out a connection which, we may suspect, can no longer be taken for granted. Gertrude's response is different because her relationship with Walter has a history, expounded by the subordinate clause, which stretches back to a time before the birth of her children. Her brooding, like Mrs Bates's, outweighs their anxiety, and her own.

Sentence (5) takes a step back, confirming, in case we might wonder, that she does feel sorry for him. (6), however, pivoting on 'But', begins to tell another story: within the intensity, there is a blankness; within the presence, an absence. (7) attempts to come to terms with this paradoxical lack of feeling; it expands syntactically into an elaborate parallelism which repeatedly defers the main clause. The syntax is complicated, by Lawrence's standards, and hints at a disturbance of the fictional world reestablished so economically by the first three sentences. However, the information structure of (6) and (7) is orthodox enough: a predictable account of what we would expect Gertrude to feel followed by the news that she doesn't feel it. Again, Lawrence holds back from the other, more disturbing story which is gathering way beneath her pity.

That other story emerges in (8). Gertrude's inability to love her husband is not just one feeling among several, but her most powerful. Extraposition moves the subject of the sentence ('this failure to love him') to a place after the verb, and substitutes an anticipatory pronoun or dummy subject ('it'), which requires us to hold a certain amount of syntactic information in our minds. The pronoun could refer back to the indifference previously described. Only when we get past the comma do we realize that the sentence has a second, deferred subject: indifference redefined as 'this failure to love'.

Extraposition also blurs the focus of the sentence. Lawrence could have written: 'This failure to love him, even when he roused her strong emotions, hurt her most of all.' In that case, Gertrude's failure to love her husband, even while pitying him intensely, would have been unambiguously old information; the new information would have been that this failure is what hurts her 'most of all'. End-focus, such a powerful principle in English (Greenbaum and Quirke 1990, pp. 394–5), would have attached maximum relevance to the degree of pain felt. Extraposition throws some at least of that stress forward on to the deferred subject. We are left wondering both about the degree of pain *and* about the nature of the failure which has caused it. This disordering of information structure creates a threshold, which is no sooner announced than dismantled: (9) echoes (4), the last sentence to describe Gertrude Morel from the outside. The text has glimpsed something and then pulled back.

The stylistic threshold does not itself provide access to a context which would explain what is troubling Gertrude. It simply alerts us to a failure which cannot be *easily* explained, which does not belong in the novel's fictional world. Gertrude is not alone in being troubled. Each of the main characters undergoes a comparable experience of failure, rejection or lack. Negativity, a feeling that they don't belong, that family and community have failed them, produces an awakening. In *Sons and Lovers* and the first half of *The Rainbow*, the awakening remains negative; it is an awakening from an old life, rather than to a new life. This emphasis on self-discovery through the gradual emptying out of family and community allegiances survived into Lawrence's later writing, but was increasingly overlaid by a contrary emphasis on apocalyptic severances, and on philosophical or religious paradigms of allegiance. Here, it is subtly and economically indicated by extrapositions which blur the focus of sentences describing a moment of truth for Paul Morel (p. 85) or Miriam Leivers (pp. 195, 271). These stylistic thresholds alert us to a passional change by making it fractionally harder to understand what the change involves. They do not themselves provide a context for it.

In *The Rainbow*, Lydia Lensky, domiciled in England after her husband's death, lives at first in a kind of trance, apparently without a will of her own.

> She was sent to Yorkshire, to nurse an old rector in his rectory by the sea. This was the first shake of the kaleidoscope that brought in front of her eyes something she must see. It hurt her brain, the open country and the moors. It hurt her and hurt her. Yet it forced itself upon her as something living, it roused some potency of her childhood in her, it had some relation to her.
>
> (Lawrence 1989, p. 51)

'It hurt her brain, the open country and the moors': again, extraposition makes manifest Lawrence's intention to make manifest a change in Lydia. Again, the change has no content, but is none the less significant for that. Lydia's 'automatic consciousness' has given way, Lawrence goes on to explain, and its failure frees her (p. 51).

Such gradual, negative awakenings characterize the first two generations chronicled in *The Rainbow*: Tom and Lydia, Anna and Will. Ursula Brangwen is different. Her awakening is apocalyptic, visionary: heralded not by extraposition, a device used less and less, but by symbolism. The book's title provides the context for Ursula's regeneration. 'She saw in the rainbow the earth's new architecture, the old, brittle corruption of houses and factories swept away, the world built up in a living fabric of Truth, fitting to the over-arching heavens' (p. 459). Lawrence's Modernism is generally thought to inhere in his increasing reliance on symbolism: metaphor is the stylistic threshold which makes manifest to us the author's intention that his characters should be regarded as archetypes, his family chronicle as a novel of ideas, himself as a Modernist. But the earlier writing has its own (less emphatic) way of raising the stakes, and its thresholds alert us to passional changes which are all the more vivid for their lack of content.

5

INTERIORS

I have spoken of a 'norm', or a 'normative style', which Mansfield and Lawrence establish and then disrupt, and which can be identified in one case by a particular idiom and point of view, and in the other by a particular syntax. This norm guarantees to minimize the cost of processing and maximize the contextual effect. But the guarantee a text offers does not depend entirely on the shape of its opening sentences. It is something we would expect to identify in generic or narrative as well as stylistic terms. A genre is a criterion of relevance which tells us how to process information, and what kind of contextual effect to anticipate. In this chapter I want to establish the main criteria of relevance which operate in Edwardian fiction.

One of the things that characterizes the Edwardian novel is the density of the detail out of which it constructs a fictional world. This information is structured in such a way that we can combine it with the information stored in memory – including, of course, information about other novels – and so infer an author's intention. Most Edwardian novels supply a surplus, which we sift in different ways, according to different criteria. Most of them, for example, supply a surplus of information about the rooms people occupy, some of which is relevant, and produces a contextual effect, some of which isn't, and doesn't. By examining descriptions of rooms in different kinds of fiction, we can define the various criteria of relevance at work.

POPULAR FICTION

In popular fiction, narrative is paramount; we read to find out what happens. Narrative itself is the criterion of relevance.

Information matters only in so far as it contributes to the solution of an enigma or the overcoming of an obstacle. How is that criterion established?

In 'The Speckled Band', Holmes and Watson enter a room where a woman has died in mysterious circumstances, accompanied by the dead woman's sister, Helen Stoner. 'It was a homely little room,' Watson reports, 'with a low ceiling and a gaping fireplace, after the fashion of old country-houses' (Doyle 1981, p. 267). We are invited to apply to the scene our familiarity with English country houses: a stereotyped, easily accessible context at the time, and indeed ever since. The details which follow (oak panelling, and so on) merely confirm the stereotype. The cost of processing them, with the stereotype in mind, is low; but they hardly yield any effect at all. So much for the Watson view of English country houses.

'Holmes drew one of the chairs into a corner and sat silent, while his eyes travelled round and round and up and down, taking in every detail of the apartment' (p. 267). The detective, not satisfied with stereotype, with easy access, searches for information that stereotype cannot explain, for irrelevance. After combing the floor and the walls, he spots a bell-rope hanging beside the bed, and gives it a brisk tug.

'Why, it's a dummy,' said he.
'Won't it ring?'
'No, it is not even attached to a wire. This is very interesting. You can see now that it is fastened to a hook just above where the little opening for the ventilator is.'
'How very absurd! I never noticed that before.'
'Very strange!' muttered Holmes, pulling at the rope. 'There are one or two very singular points about this room. For example, what a fool a builder must be to open a ventilator into another room, when, with the same trouble, he might have communicated with the outside air!'
'That is also quite modern,' said the lady.

(p. 268)

Watson, content with stereotype, was bound not to notice an irregularity, an irrelevance. Holmes, primed for apparent irrelevance, does. The dummy bell-rope and the ventilator are both modern, incongruous, redundant. The details that do not conform, which Watson fails to notice, are the ones that matter.

81

We know they matter, even if we don't yet know why, because we trust Holmes. We trust Holmes because he has already demonstrated, in one of the preliminary exercises in deduction which open so many of the stories, his eye for what matters. When Helen Stoner first turns up in Baker Street, he immediately deduces that she made an early start, and had a longish drive in a dogcart, along heavy roads, before she reached the station (p. 259). The deduction combines meticulous observation with an encyclopaedic knowledge of the world, including dogcarts.

The story concludes with an account of observations made and contexts accessed. The victim's last words – 'Oh, my God! Helen! It was the band! The speckled band!' (p. 262) – at first led Holmes to suspect a 'band' of gypsies encamped in the neighbourhood. He accessed the wrong context, the wrong information stored at the conceptual address for 'band'. Then the ventilator and the dummy bell-pull suggested an alternative. 'The idea of a snake instantly occurred to me,' he explains, 'and when I coupled it with my knowledge that the doctor was furnished with a supply of creatures from India, I felt that I was probably on the right track' (p. 273). The inference couples observation of the room with a knowledge of its owner and a knowledge of reptiles (the speckled band is, of course, an exotic snake).

Holmes's intervention raises the cost of processing the information supplied. His attentiveness indicates that there is something about the room that a knowledge of English country houses will not explain. But we also know that if we stick with him, noticing what he notices, he will eventually supply the appropriate context, and the desired cognitive effect. Holmes embodies the Principle of Relevance, the guarantee that effort will be adjusted to effect.

Edwardian popular fiction always offers that guarantee in one shape or another; hence its popularity. However, the guarantee was occasionally put to a fairly stringent test. In the concluding chapter of *The Thirty-Nine Steps* (1915), Richard Hannay, hot on the trail of three German spies, tracks them down to a suburban villa on the Kentish coast, where they are masquerading as ordinary, games-playing Englishmen. He decides to overcome his aversion to the middle classes and call on them. The hallway overwhelms him with its banality. 'There were the golf clubs and tennis rackets, the walking sticks, which you will find in ten thousand British homes' (1947, p. 130). Hannay, like Watson, invokes a stereotype which subsequent details – old oak chest, brass warming-pans on the wall – merely confirm. We are in the complacent grip of an easily accessible context.

Hannay, like Holmes, must raise the cost of processing this information by ignoring the stereotype and trying out alternative scenarios. Eventually, one of the men betrays himself by a tiny gesture which recalls a previous manifestation, 'in a moorland farm, with the pistols of his servants behind him'. The spell is broken. 'Some shadow lifted from my brain, and I was looking at the three men with full and absolute recognition' (p. 135). Hannay is closer to the edge than Holmes. At times he has nothing except blind faith to oppose to the complacency of stereotype – supported, in Buchan's view, by the British public's culpable indifference to the threat posed by Germany. The suburban home is a test for us, for our willingness to abandon stereotype, as well as for Hannay. And yet, having accompanied him on so many adventures, we trust him. Popular fiction does raise the cost of processing information, momentarily, in narrative if not in stylistic terms. But it also provides, in the shape of the hero or heroine, a walking, talking Principle of Relevance.

THE CONDITION OF ENGLAND

A number of writers sought to emulate their heavyweight Victorian predecessors by combining a didactic intention with healthy sales figures. For them, the novel was diagnostic. They set out to analyse the 'condition of England'. The criterion of relevance which enables us to sift the information they provide is partly the plot, as in popular fiction, and partly the diagnostic intention. Rooms express the people who occupy them, and both are symptomatic of the condition of England.

In the 1890s the undisputed doyenne of upmarket bestsellerdom was Mary Augusta Ward, better known as Mrs Humphry Ward. *Robert Elsmere* (1888), her account of the devastating effects of loss of faith, was probably the bestselling 'quality' novel of the century. Its runaway success established her as a highly paid author and a public figure (Sutherland 1990). *David Grieve* (1892) and *Marcella* (1894) were as popular as they were earnest, the cheap edition of the latter contributing substantially to the demise of the three-decker. If Mary Ward rejected the arrangement that had sustained George Eliot, and Trollope, and a host of lesser writers, she did nothing to dilute their moral fervour. Her idealism, her desire to serve the whole community, not just novel-readers, made her suspicious of her own success.

David Grieve had drawn on the 'social problem' novels of the 1840s and on the tradition of working-class autobiography. Gissing commented that its method was that of his own *Workers in the Dawn*: 'she is at the very point I had reached, after study of George Eliot, some ten years ago' (1961, p. 145). *Marcella* turns on social and political issues: collectivism, social democracy, the formation of a Labour party, the responsibilities of a landowner. While writing it, she read Gissing's *Demos. A Story of English Socialism* (1886). Both novels feature heroines (Adela Waltham/Marcella Boyce) torn between responsible but unyielding representatives of the landed gentry (Hubert Eldon/Aldous Raeburn) and charismatic socialist agitators who turn out to be brutal frauds (Richard Mutimer/Henry Wharton). In both novels, marriage promises some kind of reconciliation of the possessors and the dispossessed.

Property is the focal point of Mary Ward's diagnosis. In the opening chapter Marcella Boyce, recalled from a bohemian and vaguely socialistic existence in South Kensington, breakfasts in the 'Chinese room' of Mellor Park, a grand if dilapidated mansion recently inherited by her father. The eighteenth-century chinoiserie is described at some length:

> Unluckily, some later Boyce had thrust a crudely Gothic sideboard, with an arched and pillared front, adapted to the purposes of a warming apparatus, into the midst of the mandarins, which disturbed the general effect. But with all its original absurdities, and its modern defacements, the room was a beautiful and stately one. Marcella stepped into it with a slight unconscious straightening of her tall form. It seemed to her that she had never breathed easily till now, in the ample space of these rooms and gardens.
>
> (1984, pp. 18–19)

Marcella feels thoroughly at home. But the heroine's point of view is not, in this kind of novel, the only criterion of relevance. The room, its ancient dilapidation clumsily accommodating the warming apparatus, tells a different story. Beauty and the slight unconscious straightening are not enough. There will be no end of lapses and regenerations before the room and its occupier express each other to the full. The quality bestseller deploys two criteria of relevance: one carried by the plot, as in popular fiction, the other diagnostic.

Marcella's adventures in the East End introduce her to a series of increasingly inappropriate rooms, culminating in a slum tenement where Aldous Raeburn finds her nursing a battered wife.

> Aldous looked round the room – at the miserably filthy garret with its begrimed and peeling wall-paper, its two or three broken chairs, its heap of rags across two boxes that served for a bed, its empty gin-bottles here and there – all the familiar, one might almost say conventionalised, signs of human ruin and damnation – then at this breathing death between himself and her.
>
> (p. 422)

The narrative frankly endorses stereotypes because it has reached its diagnostic limit. Such places exist, and there is little that can be done about them. Raeburn, by this time a reforming MP, responds not to the room – a datum so easily processed that it has no effect at all – but to the incongruity of Marcella's presence (p. 423). That is where the novelist, unlike the sociologist, will demand her effort, and produce her effect.

On her father's death, Marcella inherits Mellor Park, which she means to transform into a 'social centre for all the people about' (p. 537). Ward soon forgets about this project. What matters is that Marcella should marry Raeburn. She summons him, and sits waiting for him in a kind of corridor.

> It was one of the loneliest and oddest places in the house, for it communicated only with her room and the little staircase, which was hardly ever used. ... A flowery paper of last-century date sprawled over the walls, the carpet had many holes in it, and the shallow, traceried windows, set almost flush in the outer surface of the wall, were curtainless now, as they had been two years before.
>
> (p. 553)

The incongruity of this space, which has not been described before, is quite taxing. The effort required to make sense of it is equivalent to Marcella's effort to train herself for Mellor Park and for Raeburn. It is an effort greater than that required to understand any of Ward's social diagnoses. Marcella has finally understood and accepted the incongruities of the 'Chinese room'. 'So, face to face with Nature, the old house, and the night, she took passionate counsel with herself' (p. 553).

WELLS, GALSWORTHY, FORSTER, WALPOLE

The next generation of socially concerned writers had roughly the same aim as Mary Ward: to sell books and influence people. But they had rather less faith in the social efficacy of romantic plots, and rather more faith, or at least interest, in diagnostic technique. If Mary Ward abandoned sociology for romance, they did the reverse. 'They have given us a house in the hope,' Virginia Woolf scornfully remarked, 'that we may be able to deduce the human beings who live there' (1924, pp. 123–4). These deductions depend on our ability to bring to bear a great deal of extraneous sociological knowledge. In order to 'complete' Edwardian novels, Woolf observed, 'it seems necessary to do something – to join a society, or, more desperately, to write a cheque' (p. 119).

In his most complex and powerful Condition of England novel, *Tono-Bungay* (1909), Wells also maintained that the great country houses were the 'clue' to England: modern innovations had merely 'come in as a thing intruded or as a gloss upon this predominant formula, either impertinently or apologetically' (1964, p. 12). But, unlike Mary Ward, he did not want to sustain the 'predominant formula' or to employ it as the background to romantic intrigue. His dilapidated rooms are just that: dilapidated.

A large proportion of Wells's early life was spent below the ground, in a variety of subterranean kitchens and living-rooms (Kemp 1982, pp. 119–20). When he joined the Fabian Society, he was appalled to find that it met regularly in underground apartments in Clement's Inn. In his pamphlet, *The Faults of the Fabian* (1906), he objected as much to the reformers' premises as to their procedures (quoted in Kemp 1982, p. 120). Life would only improve for the majority if their dismal basements were replaced by towers and conservatories.

In the Days of the Comet catalogues the contents of an unimprovable 'old world' room. The wallpaper is faded and disfigured, the tablecloth splashed with ink, the fender a 'misfit'; and so on. The washstand has been 'chipped, kicked, splintered, punched, stained, scorched, hammered, desiccated, damped, and defiled' (Wells 1906, p. 13). As a description, this is remarkably uninformative: a washstand which has suffered that kind of treatment is scarcely a washstand any more. The point, of course, lies in the accumulation, the uninformativeness. This world is not organized according to any criterion of relevance at all; the sentence which describes it therefore has no focus. Wells suspends the criterion of relevance which might make sense of the scene in order to introduce us to a world governed by irrelevance.

The details matter only allegorically. They are 'manifestations' of 'old world disorder'. Thereafter, allegory rules. A comet destroys the old world, and Wells doesn't seem to know much about the new one. The survivors live on a gigantic building site. The hero's mother is transferred from her dismal underground kitchen to an upper room; it is as if Wells's mother, who had once been the housekeeper at Uppark, and who died while he was drafting the book, had been rescued from her basement at last (Kemp 1982, p. 129). The opposite of irrelevance should be relevance. But Wells has invested so much in the irrelevance he deplores that he can't imagine its opposite.

Many of the interiors in *Tono-Bungay* are equally incongruous. Looking back, the narrator, George Ponderevo, wonders why he once found Susan and Teddy Ponderevo's two-room apartment in Camden Town so cheerful. What strikes him now is 'the oddness of solvent, decent people living in a habitation so clearly neither designed nor adapted for their needs, so wasteful of labour and so devoid of beauty' (1964, p. 71). When the success of Tono-Bungay makes Teddy Ponderevo a rich man, he builds himself an 'irrelevant unmeaning palace' on a hill (p. 229). Wells is at his best, his most acutely diagnostic, when he suspends the Principle of Relevance and forces us to confront a surplus of information we cannot make sense of; that, he seems to say, is the condition of England.

John Galsworthy's *The Man of Property* (1906), the first volume of the Forsyte Saga, establishes by its title not only an interest in habitat but a method of reading. The novel is an anatomy of the will-to-possession. Soames Forsyte, the Man of Property, owns an elegant town-house which is designed, above all, to express him. (The closest female equivalent is Saki's Mrs Bassington, who if asked to bare her soul would describe her drawing-room (1963, p. 349). Galsworthy makes damn sure we get the point. 'Could a man own anything prettier than this dining-table with its deep tints, the starry, soft-petalled roses, the ruby-coloured glass, and quaint silver furnishing; could a man own anything prettier than the woman who sat at it?' (p. 70). If Wells was pained by irrelevance, Galsworthy was pained by relevance. Money dominates Soames's life; it is the sole criterion of meaning and value. 'In this house of his there was writing on every wall' (p. 70). Galsworthy's problem, as Lawrence pointed out (1955, pp. 118–30), was that, although his satire was directed against 'social being', he couldn't conceive of any alternative, any underlying individuality. He was so keen to emphasize that Soames thinks only in terms of ownership that he didn't stop to identify the possessions: the roses, the glass, the silverware, the woman.

For Wells, there was writing on every wall, in many languages, none of it comprehensible; the solution was a new set of walls, bright, clean, perfectly engineered. For Galsworthy, the message was written in indelible ink, and so obvious that it scarcely required an interpreter. Forster saw the writing clearly enough, and rather hoped that it didn't mean what he thought it meant. Leonard Bast's south London flat, in *Howards End* (1910), expresses his nature and social status, but cagily, diffidently.

> (1) The sitting-room contained, besides the arm-chair, two other chairs, a piano, a three-legged table, and a cosy corner. (2) Of the walls, one was occupied by the window, the other by a draped mantelshelf bristling with Cupids. (3) Opposite the window was the door, and beside the door a bookcase, while over the piano there extended one of the masterpieces of Maud Goodman. (4) It was an amorous and not unpleasant little hole when the curtains were drawn, and the lights turned on, and the gas-stove unlit. (5) But it struck that shallow makeshift note that is so often heard in the modern dwelling-place. (6) It had been too easily gained, and could be relinquished too easily.
>
> (pp. 46–7)

At first, this looks like Wellsian irrelevance: the surplus of information being its own commentary. However, Forster soon intrudes. (2) and (3) begin colourlessly, then tilt towards mild contempt through the insistence of their end-focus: a mantelshelf *bristling* with Cupids, one of the masterpieces of *Maud Goodman*. Like Galsworthy, Forster thinks the message is obvious enough. But (4) looks for extenuating circumstances, while (5) makes a more overt appeal for confirmation than Galsworthy would have thought necessary. Forster did not deplore 'social being', as Galsworthy did, or introduce an improved version, as Wells did; instead, he firmly regretted the necessity of drawing attention to it at all.

Hugh Walpole, whose 'condition of England' novels more or less drove the genre into the ground, also assumed that there was writing on every wall. *The Duchess of Wrexe* concerns the head of the Beaminster clan, a decrepit but still fearsome autocrat who inhabits a gloomy (and gloomily expressive) mansion in Portland Place. Young Rachel Beaminster's 'gaze' reveals, by way of a huge parenthesis, the representative contents of her sitting-room. The gaze is not Rachel's, of course, but Walpole's (1914, p. 17). The Duchess's secretary, Miss Rand, occupies an office which 'told you at once' everything about her. The table is so orderly that 'it made every other table the observer could remember seem untidy and littered' (p. 39). The 'observer' is there to lend a spurious authority to the ease with which Walpole interprets the writing on the wall. His talent, in fact, was for romance rather than realism: two of the more plausible characters in *The Duchess of Wrexe* – Arkwright, a brooding frontiersman, and the prodigal Francis Breton – are at their happiest without a roof over their heads. Like their author, perhaps, they seem to prefer the 'green mansions' popularized by W. H. Hudson's eco-romance of that name (1904).

Galsworthy, Forster and Walpole do indeed give us a house, and ask us to deduce from it the nature of its occupants. They make sure that we are equipped with the appropriate criterion of relevance. Woolf and Lawrence were right, I think, to see this as a limitation. Wells's preoccupation with irrelevance does make possible a larger and wilder inventiveness; but its purpose is to demonstrate the necessity of change, of a new, improved relevance. It rapidly became an interminable and obdurate self-absorption, as Lawrence was to point out in a trenchant review of *The World of William Clissold* (1955, pp. 133–8).

CONRAD

Joseph Conrad, a friend of Galsworthy and Wells and a wary onlooker at the scene of their triumph, began as a writer of exotic romances. His rooms reflect outwards rather than inwards; they are not the horizon of mental and emotional life, but a flimsy obtrusion on the wilderness. Almayer's 'folly' is a new house, less squalid than his old one, but no more imposing, which he will never complete (1976, p. 32). One look at the rooms occupied by Kayerts and Carlier, in 'An Outpost of Progress', tells us that they don't stand a chance.

More orderly white men construct more orderly habitats: the chief accountant, in *Heart of Darkness* (1902), who keeps up appearances amid 'the great demoralization of the land' (1973, p. 26); or Heyst, in *Victory* (1915), who furnishes his house with objects inherited from his father (1989, pp. 196, 205). Even so, these rooms are not the mirror-image of their occupants so much as a stage visible to a larger audience. Heyst and the chief accountant have bit-parts in the theatre of empire. Unfortunately for them, their performances may well prove as ineffectual as Carlier's old boots and half-empty boxes.

The minute Heyst and Lena leave their book- and portrait-lined living-room, Wang, their Chinese servant, 'materialises' inside it. 'The Chinaman stood still with roaming eyes, examining the walls as if for signs, for inscriptions; exploring the floor as if for pitfalls, for dropped coins' (p. 207). It is a marvellous, scary moment. The Sherlock Holmes who might have scanned the room for us, distinguishing relevant from irrelevant detail, only deepens the mystery. The list of things he could be looking for (signs, inscriptions, pitfalls, coins) bears no relation to the room's contents. For Conrad there are no diagnoses, no symptoms; only a performer and a less than enthusiastic audience.

In *The Rescue* (1920), a group of white people live in semi-captivity on the deck of a hulk moored across the river from a Malay settlement. A structure made out of wood and muslin protects them from mosquitoes. 'Rigidly enclosed by transparent walls, like captives of an enchanted cobweb, they moved about, sat, gesticulated, conversed publicly during the day; and at night when all the lanterns but one were extinguished, their slumbering shapes covered all over by white cotton sheets ... conveyed the gruesome suggestion of dead bodies reposing on stretchers' (1920, p. 250). As it so often does in Conrad, the view from outside destabilizes the colonists' presumption of self-control, of governance; it converts their reality into ghastly illusion. But who interprets this spectacle? Not, I think, the Malays.

Other writers who developed the view from outside tended to install an identifiable observer, a white man 'gone native': Kim reconnoitring Creighton's bungalow (Kipling 1978, pp. 44–6); Baden-Powell, on a scouting expedition in South Africa, recognizing a friendly establishment by the neat row of toothbrushes in the bathroom (1915, p. 70). Conrad's view from the outside is less reassuring. It is not that of our representative, a temporary outsider. At the same time, it is not that of the permanent outsider, the 'native' population. It simply inverts the view from inside.

Lord Jim (1900) divides into a tale of cowardice, objectively attested in a court of law, and a tale of redemption, subjectively attested by friendship, at Marlow's visit to Stein, in Chapter 20; just as Stephen Crane's *The Red Badge of Courage* (1895) divides at Chapter 12 into a tale of considered cowardice and a tale of fortuitous heroism; or as *Hamlet*, a play to which Stein alludes, divides at Act IV scene iv into a tale of inaction and a tale of action. Will Jim, like Hamlet, and Henry Fleming, be miraculously reconstituted? After dinner, Stein conducts Marlow to his bedroom, the light from their candles sweeping across polished, fragmentary surfaces, or flashing in and out of distant mirrors. Stein's house is as unreal, as hallucinatory, as the muslin tent. But Marlow uses the hallucination to create a new Jim (Conrad 1986a, p. 202). Stein finds him a job in Patusan: a new play, in a different theatre, which may please a different audience. As it passes from Stein's immaculately ordered study to the glimmer off fragmentary surfaces, the novel passes from one criterion of relevance to another, from realism to romance.

Conrad's most complex room is the grand *sala* of the Casa Gould in *Nostromo* (1904), which faces outward, as an emblem of prosperity and political stability, but also inward, as a reflection of domestic tensions. In Chapter 5 it witnesses an extraordinary gathering of the clans. Barrios has just departed with his army to confront the Monterist rebels, seen off at the harbour by the elite of Costaguana. Now the participants return to the Casa

Gould, to reassert ideals, or argue over policy. Familiar characters take up familiar positions; new ones are introduced. Conrad plots perspective and movement. Don José Avellanos, Mrs Gould, and eventually her husband, are the fixed points around which a nervous crowd assembles and reassembles. Decoud, the sceptic, the unfixed romantic opportunist, paces up and down. He takes Antonia Avellanos out on to the balcony, from which the street, another stage, is visible. They watch Nostromo ride by. Later, Father Corbelan, whom they had seen turn into the gateway of the Casa Gould, appears in the *sala*, silently observing. The Europeans drop off from the group around Charles Gould, leaving him strangely isolated. Later still, the last guest, 'looking in at the door of the empty *sala*', nods familiarly to the master of the house, 'standing motionless like a tall beacon amongst the deserted shoals of furniture' (1963, p. 177). This time there is no inversion of the view from inside, no dematerializing, for all the interplay of the literal and the metaphoric, of a solid existence. Instead, the business of tracking the characters takes the place of moral and political commentary – and this in a novel overburdened with moral and political commentary. It is the most audaciously choreographed scene in the fiction of the period – apart from the 'Wandering Rocks' episode in *Ulysses*, which it eerily anticipates.

IRRELEVANCE

In *Women in Love* Hermione Roddice examines the bedroom in the house Rupert Birkin has rented, 'as if absorbing the evidence of his presence, in all the inanimate things' (Lawrence 1987, p. 138). She is doing what dozens of Edwardian characters had done, and what Edwardian novelists had expected their readers to do. But her decipherments infuriate Birkin. They exemplify her desire to impose her will on him. Neither Birkin nor Lawrence believes that identity can be deduced from possessions, from environment.

Techniques of representation were changing, nowhere more radically than in the work of James Joyce. I shall devote Chapter 6 and parts of Chapters 14 and 19 to Joyce's finessing of the Principle of Relevance. But it is worth pointing out just how unlike Galsworthy's or Forster's his rooms are. In the 'Ithaca' episode of *Ulysses*, Bloom makes cocoa for Stephen and himself.

At some point in that process he hunts for the necessary ingredients and receptacles, and we are treated to an exhaustive inventory of the contents of his kitchen dresser (1960, pp. 788–9). It is safe to assume that no previous novel had delivered so much information about an act as commonplace as a man fetching a packet of cocoa from a cupboard. Some of it has a certain relevance. We might, for example, recall the occasion in 'Wandering Rocks' (pp. 291–2) when Blazes Boylan purchases the port and the pears whose remnants now occupy the middle shelf of Bloom's dresser. But the phial, the chipped eggcup, the olives, the onions, the cloves? Their point lies in an irrelevance far more radical than anything attempted by Wells.

The objects in the Blooms' various drawers would have much to tell a Sherlock Holmes, Kenner remarks (1980, p. 143). But there is no Holmes in the text, nobody to sift the evidence; and no casual observer to cue a symptomatic reading. The kitchen dresser tells us virtually nothing about Bloom, or about middle-class life in Dublin in 1904; nothing, at least, that we couldn't have found out for ourselves with a good deal less trouble. Wang, not Sherlock Holmes, is the model for the reader in *Ulysses*.

Virginia Woolf's essay 'Mr Bennett and Mrs Brown', an early acknowledgement that techniques of representation had changed irrevocably, was written in response to Bennett's review of *Jacob's Room* (1922). Bennett declared that the creation of character is the foundation of good fiction and that Woolf's characters 'do not vitally survive in the mind' (quoted in Hewitt 1988, p. 110). Jacob Flanders is not embalmed in habitat. His room does not express him any more adequately than his clothes, his habits or his appetites. There are several symptomatic rooms in *Night and Day* (1992b, pp. 9–11, 195–6), but *Jacob's Room*, an elegy for Woolf's brother, Thoby Stephen, who died of typhoid in Constantinople in 1906, was about the impossibility of biography, the uninformativeness of habitant.

Jacob's first room, in Trinity College, Cambridge, looks as though it will express him clearly enough.

> Then there were photographs from the Greeks, and a mezzotint from Sir Joshua – all very English. The works of Jane Austen, too, in deference, perhaps, to someone else's standards. Carlyle was a prize. There were books upon the Italian painters of the Renaissance, a *Manual of the Diseases*

of the Horse, and all the usual text-books. Listless is the air in an empty room, just swelling the curtain; the flowers in the jar shift. One fibre in the wicker arm-chair creaks, though no one sits there.

(1992a, p. 49)

Invitations, pipes, photographs, books: the room has a youthful homeliness comparable to Ernest Pontifex's, at Emmanuel (Butler 1923, pp. 198–9). But the change of tense destroys the elaborate Edwardian symptomatology. Jacob is not present in any way that matters in his possessions.

Jacob subsequently occupies other rooms, but they too are part of the problem rather than the solution, like his friends, or his lovers. After he has been killed in the First World War, Richard Bonamy and Mrs Flanders sift through his London lodgings. Nothing in this room expresses him – except a textual ghost which returns, in defiance of what Bonamy and Mrs Flanders might actually be thinking, from another room, another time. 'Listless is the air in an empty room, just swelling the curtain; the flowers in the jar shift. One fibre in the wicker arm-chair creaks, though no one sits there' (p. 247).

6

THE RELEVANCE OF
ULYSSES

If ever a book aspired to the status of a diamond rather than a
loaf of bread, it is surely *Ulysses*. 'I confess that it is an extremely
tiresome book,' Joyce told Harriet Weaver, a loyal and energetic
supporter, on 20 July 1919, 'but it is the only book which I am
able to write at present' (1957–66, I, p. 128). The only book he
felt able to write was a novel, but a novel which turned the
whole genre inside out. Its tiresomeness was its literary point;
and also, in a way, its marketability.

GETTING IT PUBLISHED

On 10 February 1915 J. B. Pinker wrote to Joyce, offering his
services. An agreement was signed in April. 'It did not work out
very well,' Ellmann concludes, 'for the agent was to have little
luck in marketing such peculiar merchandise' (Ellmann 1959, p.
395). Joyce wanted desperately to sell the merchandise, but it
was too peculiar; and about to get even more peculiar. Its
peculiarity would therefore have to be made its selling point.

A brief survey of the fate of Joyce's previous books will give
some idea of the trouble he was likely to have in disposing of his
most tiresome to date. *Dubliners* had finally been published, after
much prevarication and dispute, by Grant Richards, in 1914.
By the end of 1914 Richards had sold 499 copies, one short of
the number after which Joyce was to receive royalties. Pinker
managed to obtain a statement of sales for 1915: 26 copies in
the first six months. By 1916, sales were down to single figures.

A Portrait of the Artist as a Young Man completed its serialization
in the *Egoist* in September 1915. When Richards declined to
publish, Pinker offered it to Martin Secker, and to Duckworth –

with T. Werner Laurie and John Lane also in mind. Edward Garnett reported on the manuscript for Duckworth. He drew attention to passages which were likely to be regarded either as obscene or as 'tedious to the ordinary man among the reading public' (Ellmann 1959, p. 416). Still, the report did identify, albeit in negative terms, a potential readership: people with a taste for elegance and no objection to 'obscenity'.

With characteristic generosity, Harriet Weaver persuaded her editorial board to publish *A Portrait* in book form at the Egoist press. She sent Joyce an advance of £25. By 25 March 1916 a succession of seven printers, alarmed by the recent prosecution of *The Rainbow*, had refused to print the text as it stood. Ezra Pound suggested that large blank spaces should be left where obscene passages had been excised; he would paste in typed versions of these passages with his own hands. The public could be invited to buy the book 'with or without restorations', and the censorship evaded (Ellmann 1959, p. 417). Pound's scheme almost caricatures the contemporary assumption that the audience for fiction had split into orthodox and unorthodox elements. He did not have to put it into practice. *A Portrait* was published in America, on 29 December 1916, by B. W. Huebsch, with Harriet Weaver taking 750 copies for the English market; and in England on 12 February 1917.

Ulysses followed the same path: serialization in little magazines, until the censor caught up; then rejection by mainstream publishers. This time even Huebsch declined. In April 1921, Sylvia Beach, of Shakespeare and Company in Paris, came to the rescue. She proposed a de luxe edition of 1,000 copies, to be sold to subscribers of impeccable avant-garde pedigree. A decision had been taken to present the book as a diamond rather than a loaf of bread. Its selling point was to be its uniqueness. A four-page prospectus was mailed to several hundred potential subscribers. The most unexpected reply came from an Anglican bishop, the rudest from Bernard Shaw. When the de luxe edition was exhausted, in the summer of 1922, Harriet Weaver bought the plates and published an edition of 2,000 copies at the Egoist Press. Some of these actually found their way into the hands of readers. Between four and five hundred accumulated at post offices in America, and were confiscated and burnt. In January 1923 an edition of 500 copies was printed to replace them. Most of it was seized by English Customs authorities at Folkestone.

Ulysses finally became available in America in 1933, and in Britain in 1936.

Evidently, the book's exclusiveness did appeal to some readers. Joyce promoted it tirelessly (Ellmann 1959, pp. 545–6). He also began to circulate various kinds of readers' guides which both confirmed and (for the lucky few) eased its difficulty. These guides identified – or created – a readership by singling out those readers who were prepared to invest time and energy, as well as money, in the reading of fiction. Joyce also devised schemata, for admirers like Valéry Larbaud and Carlo Linati, which revealed the Odyssean parallels and the special techniques of each episode. Refusing his French translator access to the Linati schema, Joyce declared that his immortality depended on the 'enigmas and puzzles' he had sown in the text (Ellmann 1959, p. 535). Stuart Gilbert eventually published it in *James Joyce's Ulysses* (1930), at a time when readers' guides were easier to obtain than the book itself.

Ulysses is defined by its difficulty. I don't want to suggest that the conditions of its publication – the need to appeal to an elite readership – determined the way it was written. But I do think that those conditions encouraged Joyce to believe that he had in the end nothing to lose by complicating his style, since he would never achieve what the reading public at large understood by simplicity. He deliberately raised the stakes between one book and the next. The title of *A Portrait* categorizes it as a *Künstlerroman*, a familiar sub-genre. The title of *Ulysses* tells us, rather more alarmingly, that we will have to read Homer in order to read Joyce. Joyce advised his aunt to master Lamb's simplified *Adventures of Ulysses* before she attempted his novel (1957–66, I, p. 193).

That, of course, was by no means the end of it. Joyce's Homer was a Homer filtered through contemporary commentaries such as Victor Bérard's *Les Pheniciens et l'Odyssée* (1902–3). According to Bérard, the *Odyssey* was based on the Mediterranean voyages of Phoenician sailors. Its geography incorporates three distinct areas or theatres: the home island of Ithaca, off the western coast of Greece; a south-east axis down through the Peloponnese to the Levant; and a north-west axis up through the Mediterranean to the Straits of Gibraltar. At the beginning of the poem, Telemachus moves along the south-eastern axis, while Odysseus finds himself at the extreme limit of the north-western axis, in

Gibraltar. The action returns father and son to Ithaca from opposite directions. If we take the time and trouble to consult Bérard's 'bulky' work, as Stuart Gilbert did after a meeting with Joyce (Gilbert 1953, p. 11), we gain a new understanding of the novel. Traced on a map of the city (Hart and Knuth 1975), the movements of Bloom and Dedalus can be seen to mirror the wanderings of Odysseus and Telemachus (Seidel 1976). The very title of *Ulysses* is a threshold which makes manifest the author's intention to raise the novel-reading stakes substantially.

'My work,' Joyce told Adolf Hoffmeister in 1930, 'is a whole and cannot be divided by book titles ... from Dubliners on it goes in a straight line of development. It is almost indivisible, only the scale of expressiveness and writing technique rises somewhat steeply' (quoted in Coggrave 1991, p. 11). The thresholds which steepen that scale so dramatically are stylistic as well as titular. At each point on the curve, at each threshold, the cost of processing increases. So it is also within each work. The expressiveness of *Dubliners* rises from the 'scrupulous meanness' of 'The Sisters' to the lyricism of 'The Dead'. In *A Portrait*, the style develops as Stephen develops. The curve on which the episodes of *Ulysses* are plotted rises even more steeply. I now want to examine the beginning of that curve.

THE INITIAL STYLE

The words 'End of the First Part of *Ulysses*' appear on the last page of the Rosenbach fair copy of the ninth episode, 'Scylla and Charybdis', along with the date: New Year's Eve, 1918. If we add 'Wandering Rocks', as a kind of coda, we have, Hugh Kenner points out, 'a ten-episode block, homogeneous in its style and reasonably self-contained in its themes and actions' (1980, p. 61). It would be as though two stories of the kind found in *Dubliners*, one about a stoical cuckold-to-be, the other about a young artist turned drifter, had been woven together for purposes of ironic counterpoint.

Joyce himself referred to the style in which the first ten episodes are written as the 'initial style' (1957–66, I, p. 129). It combines dialogue, first-person present-tense interior monologue, and third-person past-tense narrative. Critics have treated it, productively, as a norm which the later episodes depart from and return to (e.g. Kelly 1988), and it does seem deliberately, almost parodically, normative. The elderly man who emerges from the sea as Buck Mulligan prepares to bathe (1960, p. 26) does so by means of the kind of informal, loosely structured sentence I have already discussed in relation to Lawrence. *Ulysses* is easy going at first. The elderly man disappears from the novel, but he leaves behind him a vivid impression. This is a world we can know intimately with relatively little effort.

And yet the informativeness seems more than a professional courtesy. It begins to niggle. What is the point of so much detail, so much that can be intimately known? What is its relevance? When Bloom mourns, loosely structured sentences spell out the self-consciousness of a non-Catholic at a Catholic ceremony.

> The mourners knelt^ here and there^ in praying desks.^ Mr Bloom stood behind^ near the font^ and, when all had knelt, dropped carefully his unfolded newspaper from his pocket^ and knelt his right knee upon it.^ He fitted his black hat gently on his left knee^ and, holding its brim, bent over piously.^
>
> (p. 130)

Kenner captures the edginess of this passage when he speaks of 'a *seriatim* accuracy of observation that hovers just this side of being malicious' (1980, p. 67). With the unimportant exception of two subordinate clauses, we decode each syntactic constituent as we come to it. Because we absorb the details of the scene seriatim, we are not taxed in any way. Indeed, it's all *too* easy. Some presence or figure – Kenner, following David Hayman, calls it the Arranger – has gone out of its way not only to describe a man exhaustively, but also to ensure that we assimilate as economically as possible every single detail of the description. The deference shown to the Principle of Relevance is so pronounced that we are tempted to imagine a motive (malice, say).

It is, in any case, too good to last. Gradually, the initial style tilts towards a periodic structure in which dependent constituents – those, like adverbials, which cannot be interpreted in isolation – are often anticipatory, and must be held in the memory until the major constituent of which they are a part has been interpreted (Leech and Short 1981, p. 226). Adverbials play an increasingly important, and mischievous, role. In 'Calypso', Bloom sets off to buy a kidney for his breakfast.

He approached Larry O'Rourke's. From the cellar grating floated up the flabby gush of porter. Through the open doorway the bar squirted out whiffs of ginger, teadust, biscuitmush.

(p. 69)

The adverbials of location ('From the cellar grating', 'Through the open doorway') have to be held in the memory until we discover exactly what will be done with them. Of course, it's only the tiniest of impositions, which may well have a reason. Perhaps the delay dramatizes Bloom's apprehensiveness, or the tang of early morning smells. But what exactly does the narrator wish us to notice? What is the focus of these sentences?

It might be that the adverbials, far from dramatizing Bloom's apprehensiveness, signify in their own right. As the initial constituent in their respective sentences, they provide a direct link between what has gone before and what is asserted in the main clause. They function as what some linguists would call the 'theme' of the sentence. They tell us what the sentence is going to be about. It is possible to argue that thematization varies according to genre: detective stories tend to thematize time adverbials, while travel brochures thematize adverbs of location (Brown and Yule 1983, pp. 131–3). The initial style consistently thematizes adverbials of location, especially in episodes like 'Wandering Rocks' which have Dublin, rather than individual characters, as their subject. Joyce did after all claim that if the city were to disappear, it could be reconstructed from his description of it (Budgen 1934, p. 69). One might argue that this deviation from loose sentence structure can be explained by a grammatical 'rule' (of thematization).

Such a rule could not, however, cope with the opening sentence of 'Lotos-Eaters':

By lorries along sir John Rogerson's Quay Mr Bloom walked soberly, past Windmill lane, Leask's the linseed crusher's, the postal telegraph office.

(p. 85)

Nobody, I think, has ever claimed that this sentence, or the episode it introduces, or the novel as a whole, is 'about' lorries. By thematizing these ostentatiously insignificant lorries, Joyce craftily varies the pattern. He surrounds the sedate verb phrase

100

'Mr Bloom walked' with such a thicket of adverbials that we can't really tell what he means us to notice. There is no grammatical rule to arrange the adverbials into an order of significance.

John Porter Houston, discussing the vital role played by adverbials in the initial style, concludes that they 'serve, more than anything else, to vary word order and sentence shape' (1989, p. 33). He admits that this variation cannot be explained by any grammatical rule. But his characterization of its function in rhetorical rather than grammatical terms – 'solemnity, a striking rhythmic effect, or remoteness from any concern over easy communication' (p. 22) – is too vague to be much of an improvement. He is quite right to speak of a pragmatic function ('concern over easy communication'), but doesn't develop the insight. All grammatical descriptions of the language of *Ulysses* (e.g. Gottfried 1980) suffer from a similar vagueness. They admit that grammar won't explain everything, but have no terms for what it won't explain.

We have reached the limits of the code model of communication, of grammatical and semiotic description. In 'Lotos-Eaters', Bloom halts before the Belfast and Oriental Tea Company in Westland Row, and reads the legends on the packets displayed. His reflections give rise to a reverie about the Orient.

> The far east. Lovely spot it must be: the garden of the world, big lazy leaves to float about on, cactuses, flowery meads, snaky lianas they call them.
>
> (pp. 86–7)

André Topia uses this incident as the basis for his description of Bloom's mind as a machine that ceaselessly decodes, alters and re-encodes cliché. 'Rather than a space of reverie we are dealing with a linguistic, a rhetorical, an encyclopaedic space' (1984, p. 109). The thoughts inspired in Bloom's mind by the idea of 'the far east' are all clichés, Topia argues, specimens of the Orientalist code operating in Dublin in 1904. But are they? Even Topia is obliged to admit that one would not automatically associate cactuses with the Far East, and we have no reason to suppose that people did so in Dublin in 1904. 'Flowery meads' is certainly a cliché, but meadowland surely belongs as much to an Occidental as to an Oriental topography. Lianas are tropical, rather than specifically Eastern, and here even Bloom, the cliché-machine, refers to his sources ('snaky lianas they call them'). The list, in short, is too idiosyncratic to be pure code, pure discourse, a linguistic 'space'. What has happened is that Bloom, at the window of the Belfast and Oriental Tea Company, has accessed the information filed in his memory at the conceptual address for 'the Orient'. The most stereotyped information ('the garden of the world') proves the most accessible. Thereafter the associations become more random. We assess their idiosyncrasy by accessing the information filed at the same address in *our* memories (and deciding, for example, that it doesn't include 'cactuses'). Bloom's reverie dramatizes the cognitive irregularities of memory, not the discursive regularities of a code. 'Wonder is it like that,' he reflects (p. 87).

If we are to understand the function of adverbials in the initial style, we must look not to their grammatical, rhetorical or semiotic coding, but to the inferences they support, and the principle which guides those inferences. Let us return to the opening sentence of 'Lotos-Eaters'.

> By lorries along sir John Rogerson's Quay Mr Bloom walked soberly, past Windmill lane, Leask's the linseed crusher's, the postal telegraph office.

Most readers will probably have little difficulty with this sentence, despite the proliferation of adverbials. The concluding words of the preceding episode – 'Poor Dignam!' (p. 85) – have reminded us that Bloom is due to attend a funeral. With that context in mind, we will, at a first reading, select the adverbial of manner ('soberly') as the focus of the sentence. Bloom's sobriety is relevant because it combines with what we already know (with what is stored in our short-term narrative memory) to produce a contextual effect: to reinforce our assumptions about his state of mind. The place adverbials may distract us momentarily, but are quickly subordinated by the dominant criterion of relevance.

It should be noted, however, that a second, complementary criterion operates on the initial style: relevance to the character described, what matters to him or her at a particular moment. What matters to Bloom, at this moment, is not so much his sobriety as the telegraph office. 'Could have given that address too,' he continues (p. 85). He is on his way to collect a letter addressed to him at the post office in Westland Row: a letter which might just as well have been addressed to him at the telegraph office on the Quay. Bloom's preoccupation supervenes on, or mixes with, the preoccupation signalled by the conclusion of the previous episode. The initial style often works by such a layering of relevance.

At subsequent readings of the sentence, yet other preoccupations may supervene. If we have looked at a map of Dublin in the interim, we may want to know what Bloom is doing on Sir John Rogerson's Quay. He's headed for the post office in Westland Row. But the Quay is by no means in a straight line between Eccles Street, his point of departure, and Westland Row. He has taken a considerable detour to the east. Why?

'Lotos-Eaters' begins on the Quay, further to the east than Bloom needs to be, because in the equivalent Homeric episode Odysseus sails south through the Aegean from the coast of Thrace, and then south-west through the Mediterranean until he lands at Djerba, on the African coast, the land of the lotos-eaters: according to Victor Bérard, that is (Seidel 1976, pp. 154–5, 177). Bloom's route takes him in a southwesterly direction from the Quay to Westland Row, and then to the baths in Leinster Street. With Odysseus's path through the Mediterranean in mind, rather than Bloom's sobriety, we may decide that the focus of the opening sentence of 'Lotos-Eaters' is in fact one of the adverbials of place: 'by sir John Rogerson's Quay'. That is the piece of information which now seems most relevant: which combines with a context created outside the book to produce a new understanding of Bloom.

We might seem to be in the presence of what critical theory would term 'intertextuality'. But Joyce does not posit any relation between his words and Homer's (or Bérard's). We should speak not of 'intertextuality', but (if the term was not so clumsy) of 'interpropositionality'. Joyce posits a relation between propositions which can be derived from his words, on one hand, and Homer's (or Bérard's) on the other. He complicates the linguistic structure of his sentence in order to ensure that it will *not* determine meaning. The complication allows us to suspend short-term narrative memory and retrieve other, less accessible contexts from encyclopaedic memory, from outside the text. In this respect it exemplifies the primary strategy of Modernism: one which readings based on a code model of communication will never grasp.

BEYOND THE INITIAL STYLE

The initial style is by no means utterly consistent. From the beginning of the book, there are intimations of other writing techniques, a different expressiveness. A narrative voice increasingly asserts its autonomy, its freedom to arrange and rearrange details without regard to the mundane business of story-telling. From 'Sirens' on, its performances seem as expressive as anything the characters do or say. In 'Sirens' Bloom is not even allowed to eat in peace. 'Leopold cut liverslices. As said before he ate with relish the inner organs, nutty gizzards, fried cods' roes ...' (p. 347). The magisterial 'As said before' refers us back to the opening of 'Calypso', where Bloom's culinary habits are first described (p. 65). It lets us know that everything that happens in the book happens at the pleasure of this anonymous obtrusive being (or function). 'Bloom ate liv as said before,' we are reminded a couple of pages later (p. 349).

In the later episodes, Groden observes, 'technique seems to dominate over content, parallels and correspondences override specific incidents, and the story seems buried under the surface' (1977, p. 17). This change of emphasis represents a rising curve of expressiveness rather than a break or transformation. While he was working on the last four episodes, which carried experiment to an extreme, Joyce also revised the earlier ones extensively. He thickened and complicated the initial style, and added a large number of Homeric and other correspondences. The most spectacular revision was the addition of subheads to 'Aeolus', breaking up an episode that would otherwise, in the manner of the initial style, flow smoothly. The subheads foreshadow the parodic styles of the later episodes, and the narrative voices which take over in the second half of the book. 'Aeolus' looks like a later episode, although it still more or less follows the precepts of the initial style.

Most recent attempts to explain the increasing dominance of technique over content have relied on a code model of communication. Jennifer Levine, for example, argues that the dominance of technique enforces a shift of attention 'from the signified to the signifier' (1990, pp. 156–7). Similar assumptions underlie many recent readings of *Ulysses* (MacCabe 1978; Attridge

and Ferrer 1984; Attridge 1988; McGee 1988; Benstock 1988).
Although often helpful, these descriptions are self-confirming.
The emphasis they discover in the later episodes is no more and
no less than the emphasis projected, to the exclusion of other
emphases, by the code model of communication. But if we shelve
that model, we will be in a position to ask whether the later
episodes do in fact enforce a shift of attention from signified to
signifier.

Their language, unlike that of *Finnegans Wake*, is easy enough
to decode. Problems arise when we have to decide what inferences
can be drawn from the output of decoding, and on what basis.
It is possible to 'read through' the successive styles, to make
inferences. At the same time, we cannot help being aware of the
disparity between the effort required to process these styles and
the rather meagre yield of information. The later episodes
systematically flout the Principle of Relevance, either by being
difficult to process, or by producing few cognitive effects.

In 'Wandering Rocks', the 'coda' to Kenner's ten-episode
Ulysses, a distinction emerges between what it is possible to infer
about one type of character and what it is possible to infer about
another. Some characters, the ones who belong in a traditional
novel, remain 'characters': figures about whose intentions there
is only ever one inference to be made. 'By the provost's wall
came jauntily Blazes Boylan, stepping in tan shoes and socks
with skyblue clocks to the refrain of *My girl's a Yorkshire girl*' (p.
327). In this section of 'Wandering Rocks', various people greet
the viceregal cavalcade, their exact location often thematized by
the sentences that describe their various gestures. There can be
no doubt, however, that the focus of the sentence that describes
Boylan is 'jauntily'. Boylan is all jauntiness, and forever jauntiness.
He is one of the very few characters in the book whose motive
and intention can be inferred from everything he says and does.
The provost's wall is a mere backdrop to his jauntiness. 'His
hands in his jacket pockets forgot to salute but he offered to the
three ladies the bold admiration of his eyes and the red flower
between his lips' (p. 327).

But what about Thomas Kernan, first presented by the same
kind of sentence as presented Bloom in 'Lotos-Eaters'? 'From
the sundial towards James's Gate walked Mr Kernan pleased
with the order he had booked for Pulbrook Robertson boldly
along James's street, past Shackleton's offices' (p. 307). His

boldness seems at this moment the most important thing about him; no Odyssean protocol is likely to attribute significance to his route. But by the time the Viceroy's cavalcade comes into view the boldness has subsided. 'At Bloody bridge Mr Thomas Kernan beyond the river greeted him vainly from afar' (p. 324). The three adverbials of location swamp the adverbial of manner. In Boylan's case, location is eclipsed by manner; here, manner ('vainly') becomes a feeble reflection, a mere consequence, of location ('from afar'). Each constituent is easy enough to decode, and the effort required to store 'At Bloody bridge' and 'beyond the river' temporarily will trouble few readers. But what should we infer? About Boylan, only one inference is possible: that he means to cruise the Viceroy's female companions. With Kernan, motive and intention slip from view. He means to greet the Viceroy; but his location at a distance, so roundly insisted upon, means that he cannot have expected to succeed. *Ulysses* has begun its long transmutation from novel into encyclopaedia. It has begun to provoke inferences which do not necessarily belong in a novel.

The progress of the cavalcade reveals just how hard it is, except in Boylan's case, to infer an intention from an act or a gesture. It also reveals how hard it is not to try to infer an intention. Even the Poddle River, hanging out 'in fealty' a 'tongue' of liquid sewage, finds itself included among the supplicants (p. 325). The Viceroy, programmed to infer fealty, is still at it in the episode's wonderfully sly concluding sentence.

> On Northumberland and Landsdowne roads His Excellency acknowledged punctually salutes from rare male walkers, the salute of two small schoolboys at the garden gate of the house said to have been admired by the late queen when visiting the Irish capital with her husband, the prince consort, in 1849, and the salute of Almidano Artifoni's sturdy trousers swallowed by a closing door.
>
> (p. 328)

This sentence seems to deliver relevant information as efficiently as one could wish, up to and including an adverbial of manner ('punctually') which we are happy to identify as a likely focus, since it confirms our assumption that the Viceroy takes his duties seriously. But with the business of reassurance safely out of the way, the sentence gains a second, and more mischievous, wind.

The identification of the house outside which the schoolboys stand might conceivably be said to have some slight bearing on the Viceroy's punctual response to salutes. But clearly the joke is on us, as we labour to make connections. A gap has opened between decoding and inference: between the ponderous but maddeningly feasible, maddeningly automatic decipherment of gossip about Queen Victoria, and the highly questionable relevance of the knowledge so laboriously produced.

In the later episodes of *Ulysses* we decode furiously, unremittingly, as though on a treadmill, but infer lamely: until 'Ithaca' and 'Penelope' redress the balance by providing, right at the death, a flood of information whose relevance cannot be doubted. I shall have more to say about these stylistic wanderings and homecomings in later chapters. Here, at the conclusion of 'Wandering Rocks', the conclusion of the initial style, the gap between decoding and inference, so characteristic of *Ulysses*, is confirmed by the Viceroy's acknowledgement of an act which was not even intended as a gesture: Artifoni's sturdy trousers swallowed by a closing door.

Part II

NATION AND SOCIETY

7

DEGENERATION

In Hubert Crackanthorpe's 'The Turn of the Wheel', Eardley Lingard, a successful businessman and politician who has just been elevated to the House of Lords, tries to decide which of the ills of the age he should address in his maiden speech. Most would feature in an account of any age. One, however, stands out: 'doctors, hurrying on the degeneration of the race' (1897, pp. 167–8). Degeneration – a falling-off from original purity, a reversion to less complex forms of structure – troubled many people during the second half of the nineteenth century. Unlike Lingard's other anxieties, it provides a key to the thinking of one age in particular. Also characteristic is his belief that the doctors have caused the disease they are meant to cure.

THEORIES

The theory of degeneration emerged in the natural and medical sciences. The age of 'evolution', 'progress' and 'reform' began to develop an urgent interest in regression, atavism and decline. Indeed, it was Darwin's theory of evolution by natural selection which, in Britain at any rate, provided a context. At first, the theory had seemed to suggest that evolution was inevitably progressive, slowly but surely transforming the simple into the complex, the primitive into the civilized. Increasingly, however, Darwin and his followers came to realize that 'evolution' was not synonymous with 'progress'. Environment operated in various ways to different effects, and the most adaptive inherited characteristics were not necessarily the 'highest' or most 'civilized' ones. Gradually, attention shifted to examples of regression. In *Degeneration. A Chapter in Darwinism* (1880), Darwin's disciple Edwin

111

Ray Lankester pointed out that parasites, which necessarily postdate their host organisms, are none the less '*simpler* and *lower* in structure' than those organisms (p. 30).

The implications for social theory seemed distressingly clear. Lankester himself talked of the decline of the 'white races' into parasitism (pp. 60–2). Paradigms of regression created by the natural and medical sciences began to play an important part in the analysis of social change (Pick 1989, p. 5). Production and consumption, the categories of political economy, define a cultural process; an identity constituted by producing or consuming is an identity *made*, either through the reciprocal alteration of man and world, or through the adoption of roles and images. Degeneration, on the other hand, defines an organic process; an identity constituted by it is an identity *given* – inherited – rather than made. It was seen not as the effect, but as the cause of crime, poverty, disease; a 'self-reproducing pathological process' (Pick 1989, pp. 21–2). The cultural 'decline' it caused was not susceptible to social or political determination.

It is this figuring of cultural change as a natural process outside human control which connects degeneration theory to an age-old anxiety about the end of the world. During the 1890s crisis-feelings intensified (Showalter 1991, ch. 1). Degeneration theory reinforced speculation about decadence in society and in the arts (Hennegan 1990). Max Nordau's *Degeneration*, a lurid and influential treatise published in translation in 1895, proclaimed the end of civilization in biblical cadence. But his conviction that the European races were degenerating derived from medical science rather than the Bible. Physicians, he said, had recognized in the behaviour of the European elites a 'confluence' of 'degeneracy' and 'hysteria'. All the new tendencies in the arts – decadence, naturalism, mysticism – could safely be regarded as 'manifestations' of this confluence (Nordau 1920).

The arrival of the new century did not altogether lay these anxieties to rest. H. G. Wells described its first years as a Balfourian age, an age which, like Balfour himself, Prime Minister from 1902 to 1905, called everything into question (James and Wells 1958, p. 145; Hunter 1982, ch. 1). However, the book in which Balfour called everything into question, *A Defence of Philosophic Doubt*, had been published as long ago as 1879. The book he wrote almost thirty years later, while Leader of the Opposition, defended not a 'philosophic doubt', but a biological near-certainty: a process of 'social degeneration' which had enveloped the nation in 'decadence' (Balfour 1908, p. 34).

Specific events such as the Boer War put the theory to the test. Recruiting campaigns revealed that 60 per cent of Englishmen were unfit for military service. This figure was bandied about to such effect that the government felt obliged to form an Inter-Departmental Committee on Physical Deterioration. The committee's report, delivered in August 1904, was meant to distinguish the real evidence of widespread poverty from fantasies about the decline of the race. However, the very existence of a report on 'Physical Deterioration' tended to fuel rather than allay anxieties. Sir John Gorst, MP for Cambridge University, referred to it as the 'recent report upon the degeneracy of our race' (Hynes 1968, pp. 23-4). The theory had become a habit of mind.

It also remained a habit of science. This was the era of eugenics (Searle 1976; Kevles 1985), the 'study', in Francis Galton's words, 'of agencies under social control that may improve or impair the racial qualities of future generations either physically or mentally' (quoted in Searle 1976, p. 1). Karl Pearson, who became Professor of Eugenics at University College London in 1911, insisted that 'a nation which has ceased to ensure that its better elements have a dominant fertility has destroyed itself far more effectually than its foes could ever hope to destroy it on the battlefield' (1905, pp. viii–ix). The eugenicists stirred the debate about racial decline by proposing a solution: the 'better elements' in society should be encouraged to breed, the 'very worst' should be sterilized. Their thinking found an echo in some unexpected places at the time (Trotter 1986), and in the subsequent history of European racism (Pick 1989, pp. 27-33).

It was, however, the habit of mind, rather than the scientific solutions, which had the greatest currency in intellectual life. The American historian Henry Adams pointed out in 1910 that Europeans had become obsessed with 'supposed social decrepitude', particularly in the cities. 'A great newspaper opens the discussion of a social reform by the axiom that "there are unmistakable signs of deterioration in the race". The County Council of London publishes a yearly volume of elaborate statistics, only to prove, according to the London *Times*, that "the great city of today", of which Berlin is the most significant type, "exhibits a constantly diminishing vitality"' (Adams 1958, p. 183). Evidence of diminishing vitality included not only the poor standard of health among army recruits, but also the falling birth rate, the decline of the rural population and the prevalence of alcoholism and nervous exhaustion. More or less any social 'problem' could be attributed to it. Lord Henry Hill, in *Suffragette Sally*, understands for the first time what his wife is up against when he hears people describe the suffrage campaign as an 'outcome of degeneracy' (Colmore 1911, pp. 114–15).

The assumption coloured all shades of political opinion, from the most reactionary to the most radical. Olive Schreiner was a socialist and a feminist, but her term for the redundancy which industrialism had enforced on women, 'sex-parasitism', connects her with Edwin Ray Lankester rather than Karl Marx (1978, p. 77). Parasitism and degeneration were the same thing (p. 78); the process they identified had been, and might again be, the cause of imperial decline (pp. 84–94, 101–2). The novel she worked at for much of her life, and finally published in 1926, *From Man to Man*, contains immense disquisitions on the fall of empires and the prospect of genetic engineering (1982, pp. 187–225). Fictional radicals like Barrington in *The Ragged Trousered Philanthropists* or Remington in *The New Machiavelli* are equally sure that the cause of the decline of nations is 'biological decay' (Tressell 1965, p. 473; Wells 1946, p. 306–10). The biologizing of social theory had become by the turn of the century an intense and widespread preoccupation, a subject-matter.

NATURALISM

The naturalist fiction which began to appear in the 1870s added a new pattern to the small stock of curves describing the shape lives take (or adapted an old one from classical and Shakespearean tragedy): the plot of decline, of physical and moral exhaustion (Fisher 1982, p. 271). Most Victorian novels divided existence into a long rise stretching to the age of sixty, measured in social and moral terms, and a short (physical) decline. Naturalist fiction envisaged instead a rapid physical rise to the moment of reproduction in the twenties, then a long redundancy accelerated by the emergence of some innate physical or moral flaw.

The most systematic and influential exponent of the decline-plot was Emile Zola, whose Rougon-Macquart novels (1871–93) analysed the effects of heredity and environment on the members of a single family, tracing the passage of a genetic 'flaw' down the legitimate line of the Rougons and the illegitimate line of the Macquarts. Henry James pointed out that the development of each section of the long chronicle was '*physiologically* determined by previous combinations' (1984b, p. 890). In each generation the inherited flaw topples an individual life into a downward spiral of disease, alcoholism, poverty or madness. This downward spiral was the way in which naturalist novels, in Europe and America, spoke about individual and social development.

In Britain, Zola may not have been the most respected of foreign novelists, but he was certainly the most notorious. There was, Gissing reported in 1896, 'no public for translated novels – except those of Zola' (1961, p. 219). James, in Paris in 1884, told W. D. Howells that he respected Zola, despite his pessimism and his 'handling of unclean things' (1974–84, III, p. 28). It was the handling of unclean things which dictated the British response to Zola. Henry Vizetelly began to issue translations in the same year; he was tried for publishing obscene books in 1889, convicted, and sent to prison for three months. By that time the other feature noted by James – pessimism – had made its mark on the English novel. George Moore's *A Mummer's Wife* (1885), for example, relates, in a detached manner, the long decline and sordid death of a provincial haberdasher, Kate Ede. Osmond Waymark, in Gissing's *The Unclassed* (1884), is praised for having written a novel which is 'hideous and revolting', but true to life.

Vizatelly's imprisonment seems to have taken the sting out of the moral objections to Zola. Thereafter, open hostility receded. In 1893 Zola was invited to London by the Institute of Journalists, and, much to Gissing's amusement, received by the Lord Mayor (1961, p. 177). Gissing noted that no prominent author had played any part in the welcome, and that a testimonial dinner arranged by the Authors' Club was 'in the hands of a lot of new and young men' (pp. 180–1). The young man most likely to further the cause of naturalism in England was Hubert Crackanthorpe, who, the year before, had conducted a long and respectful interview with Zola, which he published in his experimental magazine, the *Albemarle*. He certainly made full use of the decline-plot.

Eardley Lingard's wife, in 'The Turn of the Wheel', has a face absorbed by 'a lax and puffy lethargy' (Crackanthorpe 1897, p.

105); his mistress's edgy movements indicate the 'hysterical caging of spasmodic and inadequate emotion' (p. 159); Max Nordau would have enjoyed denouncing her boudoir. Lingard himself is formidably tenacious; but even he eventually runs out of energy.

In 'A Conflict of Egoisms', in *Wreckage* (1893), degeneration destroys a New Woman, the neglected wife of a novelist suffering from 'brain exhaustion'. Professionally mature but emotionally immature, she cannot cope with her husband's indifference, and retaliates by destroying the manuscript of his latest novel. He decides on suicide, but exhaustion gets him first; he drops dead as he is about to leap off a bridge. Crackanthorpe drowned himself in the Seine in 1896.

Naturalism's gift to British fiction was a subject-matter and a plot. Zola had 'done' peasant life in *La Terre*, slums in *L'Assommoir*, heavy industry in *Germinal*, and so on. His grim environments and plummeting protagonists became archetypes: a powerful stimulus to social criticism in fiction. In March 1887 Beatrice Potter shared a railway carriage with Sir George Trevelyan. 'I begged him to go into a smoking carriage ... for had I not in the pocket of my sealskin not only a volume of Zola, but my case of cigarettes! neither of which could I enjoy in his distinguished presence' (Webb 1986, I, p. 198). The novel was *Au Bonheur des dames*, in which Zola 'did' department stores. Sir George eventually settled down with *The Princess Casamassima*, James's most ambitious attempt at an unpoetic subject. Webb, for her part, remained enthusiastic about Zola: an enthusiasm shared by the exponents of two emerging genres, slum fiction and the New Woman novel.

FICTIONAL POLEMICS

Slum fiction, pioneered in the 1880s by Gissing and Besant and developed in the 1890s by Kipling, Morrison and Maugham, incorporated the decline-plot wholesale, but gave it a new spin. The most notable of these stories concern women whose lives follow a familiar pattern: courtship, and a glimpse of freedom, then marriage, marital violence, abandonment, and finally prostitution or death. What distinguishes them from French naturalism is that they place the blame on environment rather than heredity. The heroines are not degenerate. They are spirited women who have the vitality beaten out of them by an inhospitable environment. But the remorseless downward spiral of the plot still carries the message that there is no escape from deprivation. Morrison, however, did distinguish between a degenerate working class and one which is organically sound but damaged by its environment; he endorsed a plan to establish penal settlements in isolated parts of the country where working-class degenerates would be confined for life, and prevented from reproducing their 'type' (Morrison 1982, p. 32).

Heredity returned with a vengeance in the New Woman novels which began to appear in the 1880s. 'Frank Danby' (Julia Frankau) out-Zolaed Zola in *A Babe in Bohemia* (1889). Lucilla Lewesham, a young girl brought up by her decadent father and his shrieking mistress, escapes moral contamination but not hereditary epilepsy. The book was savagely denounced in the press, and banned by Mudie. Frankau had already caused a stir with her first novel, *Dr Phillips, a Maida Vale Idyll* (1887), whose 'hero' is a Jewish doctor with a large and profitable practice. 'He made money, bought a carriage for his wife, and Mrs Cameron for himself' (Danby 1889, p. 20). Fat, stupid, German Clothilde gets her emblem of respectability; he gets blonde, blue-eyed Mary Cameron. From then on, it's downhill all the way ('his character retrograded'). Degeneration theory served Frankau's sensationalism admirably. Meeting her in 1911, Arnold Bennett found her 'very chic' – and thoroughly ashamed of her novels (1932, II, p. 44).

'Doctors-spiritual must face the horrors of the dissecting-room,' Sarah Grand declared in the preface to *Ideala* (1889, p. viii). Her heroine decides that the future of the race is a question of morality and health. 'Perhaps I should ... say a question of health and morality, since the latter is so dependent on the former' (p. 289). Both heroine and author deploy the biomedical categories of late nineteenth-century social psychology. Ideala believes that the British Empire, like the Roman, has decayed internally, and that the solution is not reform, but a programme of physical and moral regeneration (pp. 287–91).

Grand's third novel, *The Heavenly Twins* (1894), was hugely successful, and established her as one of the leading writers of the day. It has been claimed as a precursor of Modernism (Bjorhovde 1987, ch. 4), and does experiment with tone and point of view. But the experiments are largely confined to one of its three loosely connected case studies, the story of the 'heavenly twins' Angelica and Diavolo. The other case studies can best be understood as versions of the naturalist degeneration-plot. Edith Beale marries Sir Mosley Menteith, a syphilitic degenerate, gives birth to a child famously likened to a 'speckled toad' (Grand 1894b, p. 301), and dies. The deformed child was a popular motif in naturalist fiction, incarnating degeneracy (Baguley 1990, p. 213). Evadne Frayling marries one of Menteith's fellow-officers. More worldly-wise than Edith, she recognizes his unsuitability at once, and declines to consummate the marriage. She remains unfulfilled, and cannot find a way to redeem her husband, whose habits are 'the outcome of his nature' (p. 337).

Book VI of *The Heavenly Twins* is narrated by Doctor Galbraith, a specialist in nervous disorders who examines and befriends Evadne. If Edith's story is a case study in degeneracy, Evadne's is a case study in that other 'modern' disease, 'hysteria' (p. 627). After her husband's death, Galbraith marries Evadne. But the outcome of his efforts to restore her to health remains uncertain. Paying a call in the neighbourhood, she encounters the 'speckled toad' once again, and suffers a relapse. Degeneracy and hysteria may yet have the last word.

As, indeed, they threaten to do in the conservative polemic of contemporary popular fiction. Professor Moriarty, in the Holmes stories, has 'hereditary tendencies of the most diabolical kind', a criminal 'strain' in his blood (Doyle 1981, pp. 470–1). According to Van Helsing, Count Dracula is a degenerate. 'Lombroso and Nordau would so classify him' (Stoker 1979, p. 406). Dracula's invasion of England dramatizes anxieties which were the stock in trade of theorists like Nordau and Césare Lombroso. He aims to pollute the entire race, beginning with his natural allies, the parasites, outcasts and madmen. In conservative polemic, however, unlike its radical equivalent, society's protectors usually prove strong enough to confine if not extinguish degeneracy.

THE AVOIDANCE OF NATURALISM

As soon as Cosima Chudleigh, in *A Writer of Books*, has established herself in London, she decides that she must witness an operation, as the 'French realists' did, in case any of her characters end up on the operating table (Paston 1898, p. 45). The novelist should be a 'scientific observer' (p. 58). Later, Mallory the critic persuades her to develop instead that 'personal flavour' which characterizes the English novel (pp. 170–1). Their discussion indicates that naturalism was still a force in the 1890s, but also that English writers were resisting it. For one thing, its champions had ceased to champion. During the 1890s Gissing concentrated on stories of intellectual life and middle-class rebellion. In 1891 Moore accused Zola of selling out (1914, p. 79). From *Confessions of a Young Man* (1888) through to *Evelyn Innes* (1898) and *Sister Teresa* (1901), Moore's major concern was the pathology of faith and creativity.

And yet there is *Esther Waters* (1894), a peculiar hybrid of the 'French' and 'English' traditions (Keating 1971b, pp. 134–6). Esther is, in the French manner, the victim of forces beyond her control; but she has been equipped, in the English manner, with moral resilience. Moore's mixed feelings encouraged him to anatomize working-class life by means of a decline-plot, and yet at the same time draw back from the apocalyptic determinism usually inscribed in such plots. *Esther Waters* is a novel made by the avoidance of naturalism.

William Latch's seduction and abandonment of Esther would not have been out of place in a novel by Mrs Gaskell or George Eliot. When she subsequently returns, pregnant and impoverished, to her equally impoverished family, and immediately quarrels with her drunken, brutal stepfather, it seems as though she will be drawn into the downward spiral of another kind of plot altogether. Mr Saunders, however, is, by a cunning displacement, merely her *step*father: the bloodlines through which contamination invariably flows in naturalist fiction have been cut. Esther is not doomed. Indeed, her experiences are sufficiently unpredictable for one critic to speak of the novel as 'picaresque' (Cave 1978, p. 73).

Like Bennett's Sophia Baines, Esther manages a business. She brings up her child. To be sure, motherhood does return her rather too easily to the English tradition. Esther fretting about her soldier son reminds one of Mrs Rouncewell, in *Bleak House*, fretting about Trooper George. Yet this interest in the making of identities is characteristic of the novel. For every degenerate, like Mr Saunders, there is someone who has identified, and been identified by, a talent or an occupation. Lanky, narrow-chested Arthur Barfield, the son of Esther's first employer, comes into his own whenever he mounts a horse (Moore 1936, p. 12). In naturalist novels, people don't come into a new individuality at

119

all. In English novels they do, but not, on the whole, by mounting a horse. Moore, like Bennett after him, avoided both 'French' determinism and the 'English' conviction that the only paths to self-discovery are introspection and marriage.

In Chapter 44 Esther, now a widow and once again destitute, returns to Woodview, the home of the Barfield family, which has itself been destroyed by gambling. The opening paragraph repeats word for word the opening paragraph of Chapter 1, which describes Esther's arrival at the local station. In Chapter 1 the first sentence of the second paragraph – 'An oblong box painted reddish brown and tied with a rough rope lay on the seat beside her' – is full of anticipation; the person it refers to has not yet been identified, and we read on eagerly, seeking clues. In Chapter 44 the sentence has been expanded. 'An oblong box painted reddish brown lay on the seat beside a woman of seven or eight and thirty, stout and strongly built, short arms and hard-worked hands, dressed in dingy black skirt and a threadbare jacket too thin for the dampness of a November day' (p. 346). Now there is nothing left to anticipate: the older Esther is the sum of the experiences which have shaped her appearance. The narrative loop confirms the decline-plot, returning her, roughened and diminished, to her starting point. But she is not defeated. Her decline cannot be attributed to the emergence of some moral or physical flaw. We are closer to the formal recapitulations of James and Joyce than to Zola's apocalypse.

Moore's avoidance of naturalism found an echo in the work of another Anglo-Irish writer, Sarah Grand. Unlike most New Woman novelists, Grand continued to evolve as a writer, remaining polemical, but modifying her earlier preoccupations. *The Beth Book* (1897) reworks the Evadne story from *The Heavenly Twins*. Like Evadne, Beth Caldwell, cramped by lack of education and experience, marries a man, Dr Dan Maclure, who turns out to be disreputable and corrupt. He has an affair with one of his patients, whom Beth regards as a 'parasite' (1980, p. 403). Both her husband and her most ardent admirer, a neurotic writer, are well embarked on decline: 'the one was earning atrophy for himself, the other fatty degeneration' (p. 480).

But Beth, like Esther Waters, refuses to decline with her menfolk. Nurtured by a community of intellectual women which includes the heroines of Grand's earlier novels, she discovers a talent for writing and public speaking. Grand cleverly alters the proportions of the decline-plot by devoting more than half the novel to Beth's childhood and youth. The talents and pleasures Beth develops are grounded in those early experiences. The book's conclusion, however, a mystical reunion with a man she has fallen in love with, somewhat qualifies the carefully accumulated stress on independence, female community and ordinariness.

Gissing, Moore and Grand all seem half-persuaded by Zola's determinism, by the plausibility of genetic explanations. But in the end they refuse apocalypse; partly, I think, because it seemed like a foreign invention. Galbraith reappears to counsel Beth, and to offer some gruff literary advice. Her husband is predictably fond of French novels. Galbraith, like Quentin Mallory, thinks that French novels have destroyed the French nation. Grand supports him, in a footnote, with an account of the cowardly behaviour of Frenchmen during a recent emergency (p. 367). The redefinition of Englishness which was in progress at the time, and which I shall explore in Chapter 10, helped to persuade English writers to steer clear of naturalism. Gissing relied heavily on it in his most popular novel, the semi-autobiographical *Private Papers of Henry Ryecroft* (1903). As for Moore, well, he learnt to despise the English during the Boer War, and took up Irishness instead.

IRONISTS

Gissing, Moore and Grand fell back on English moralism. Other writers tried to sidestep the downward spiral of the decline-plot without committing themselves to the counterbalance of moral absolutes. *The Picture of Dorian Gray* (1890) makes dazzling play with the idea of degeneracy. Constantly collapsing the metaphoric into the literal, the metaphysical into the organic, it none the less refuses to come clean, to own up, to disavow appearances. For Wilde himself, the metaphor became distressingly literal. Max Nordau had classified him as a decadent and an ego-maniac, claiming that his 'personal eccentricities' were the 'pathological aberration of a racial instinct' (1920, pp. 317–22). Wilde, at the end of his tether, complied with the metaphor. Submitting a plea for release from prison, he confessed to sexual madness, and endorsed Nordau's classification of him as a degenerate (Ellmann 1987, pp. 471–2).

Hardy came closer than Wilde, in his fiction if not his life, to acknowledging that sin is a disease. In *Tess of the D'Urbervilles* (1891), Angel Clare characterizes Tess as the product of a degenerate family (1978a, p. 302). He invokes against her the degeneration-plot which the novel has always harboured, but which it has so far resisted through its emphasis on her singularity. Hardy can scarcely be said to endorse Angel's point of view. But one might argue that Angel's degeneration-plot takes the novel over, carrying Tess through 'relapse' to murder and beyond.

One review of *Jude the Obscure*, headed 'Hardy the Degenerate', claimed that he had depicted a humanity 'largely compounded of hoggishness and hysteria' (quoted in Millgate 1982, p. 369). Jude does seem cloudily aware of degeneration theory. Depressed by interminable quarrels with Arabella, he decides that the best way to express his 'degraded position' would be to get drunk. 'Drinking was the regular, stereotyped resource of the despairing worthless' (1978b, p. 117). Jude will do what he thinks the hero of a naturalist novel would do. Appropriately enough, it is he who conveys the medical verdict on Father Time's massacre (pp. 410–11). Jude merely *quotes* degeneration theory. But he quotes it so convincingly that one cannot altogether avoid the suspicion that Hardy might have seen some truth in it. It would have suited his temperament. And *Jude the Obscure* does sometimes seem like a novel written by Angel Clare.

Wells took a more explicit interest in social and biological theory than Hardy or Wilde. *The Time Machine* (1895) explores the implications of the Second Law of Thermodynamics, formulated in the 1850s, which envisages the gradual heat-death of the universe. But its most gripping passages concern social rather than physical deterioration. When the time traveller reaches the year 802,701, he emerges into the middle of a crisis in the long-drawn-out feud between two degenerate species, the Eloi and the Morlocks (hysteria and hoggishness, again). Wells told Huxley that he had tried to represent 'degeneration following security' (quoted in Smith 1986, p. 48). *The Time Machine* is a vision of social apocalypse framed within a vision of global entropy, and the rhetoric of apocalypse overshadows the rhetoric of entropy. All that protects us from it is the studied normality of the audience which gathers to hear the time traveller's tale: an audience also on duty, in tales by Stevenson, James and Conrad, to hear of other abominations.

Later writers distanced themselves less equivocally. In *The Secret Agent* (1907), it is the loutish anarchist Ossipon who characterizes Stevie and Winnie as degenerates (1990, pp. 41, 222). On the latter occasion, Conrad speaks contemptuously of Ossipon invoking Lombroso 'as an Italian peasant recommends himself to his favourite saint'. In *Ulysses* it is Mr Deasy, the bullyingly Anglo-Irish headmaster, who bends Stephen Dedalus's ear with a diatribe on the degeneracy of the Jews: 'they are the signs of a nation's decay. Wherever they gather they eat up the nation's vital strength. ... Old England is dying' (Joyce 1960, p. 41). By that time degeneration theory no doubt seemed less compelling to some writers, though not to all. When the hero of *The Making of a Marchioness* deduces the villain's criminality from the shape of his skull, as Lombroso would have done, the heroine cannot agree; but he is proved right in the end (Burnett 1901, pp. 131–2).

DIVIDED NARRATIVES

One other response requires some discussion, because it had considerable formal and ideological consequences for the twentieth-century novel. It is a response present in the philosophy of the New Woman writers in the early 1890s, but not developed into a new narrative form until somewhat later. Grant Allen, whose *The Woman Who Did* (1895) was probably the most notorious of all the New Woman novels, preached a new hedonism, a revision of sexual relationships which would eliminate 'race-degradation' and promote 'race-preservation' (quoted in Keating 1989, p. 189). Women had either to separate themselves from men or mate with those men who were still, despite everything, racially sound. Thus Sarah Grand's Eugenia, who is herself racially sound, rejects Lord Brinkhampton, a 'neuropath' and degenerate (Grand 1894a, p. 169), and proposes to the aptly named Saxon Wake. Wake is a 'yeoman', but makes up racially for what he lacks socially. This will be the race-preserving, the eugenic – the Eugeniac – marriage. Such racially sound marriages should preferably be complemented, as Allen's language suggests and as the conclusion to *The Beth Book* makes clear, by a mystical union.

Mystical-eugenic unions were all very well, but they did presuppose an abundant supply of healthy, strong-willed young men and women. Narratives promoting race preservation had to balance the dream of a new hedonism against the reality, as it was perceived, of social decrepitude. Whereas the New Woman novelists tended to pair different types of degeneracy, the hoggish and the hysterical, Morlock and Eloi, their successors tended to pair a couple seeking regeneration with a couple or couples doomed to degeneracy. This new pairing emerges tentatively in Gissing, in the 1890s, then more strongly in Forster and Lawrence.

The Longest Journey (1907) incorporates two separate plots which just happen to coincide at a place called suburbia. In the first, sensitive Rickie Elliot's marriage to suburban Agnes Pembroke merely confirms the fatality of his physical disablement (hereditary lameness). Together, like a couple in a New Woman novel, they produce a horribly crippled daughter, who soon dies. Thereafter Rickie 'deteriorates' (Forster 1960, p. 197).

A second plot crosses this downward spiral. Rickie's race will die out, but his half-brother Stephen Wonham, the product of a more eugenic union with a staunch yeoman-farmer, may yet flourish. Distanced genetically from Rickie, as Esther Waters is from her stepfather, Stephen belongs to a different bloodline, a different plot. The genetic distance is also a moral and emotional distance. Agnes Pembroke, who has already drained the life out of Rickie, regards Stephen as a monster. 'He was illicit, abnormal, worse than a man diseased' (p. 145). Forster defends Stephen's abnormality against suburban convention, because he believes that it alone will preserve the race. There was some talk, at the time, of the appearance of a New Man who would complement the New Woman (Onions 1913, pp. 17, 76). Stephen Wonham, like Gissing's Everard Barfoot and Lionel Tarrant, might be regarded as a New Man.

In *Women in Love* (1920), the degeneration-plot and the regeneration-plot seem about to fuse, as Ursula is paired momentarily with Gudrun, Birkin with Crich. But in the end they diverge as emphatically as the bloodlines, the histories, of Rickie Elliot and Stephen Wonham. Degeneration theory circumscribes the 'barren tragedy' (Lawrence 1987, p. 476) of Gerald's life. It surfaces in Chapter 2, when the wedding party adjourns to Shortlands, and the talk turns to questions of race and nationality. Birkin has agreed with Gerald that 'race is the essential element in nationality' (p. 28), and is caught 'thinking about race or national death' (p. 30) when called upon to make a speech. Nobody else has mentioned race or national *death*. The thought disappears as Birkin rises to make his speech, but reappears in Chapter 5. Birkin and Gerald Crich meet on the platform of Nottingham station.

> 'What were you reading in the paper?' Birkin asked. Gerald looked at him quickly.
> 'Isn't it funny, what they *do* put in newspapers,' he said. 'Here are two leaders –' he held out his *Daily Telegraph*, 'full of the ordinary newspaper cant –' he scanned the columns down – 'and then there's this little – I dunno what you'd call it, essay, almost – appearing with the leaders, and saying there must arise a man who will give new values to things, give us new truths, a new attitude to life, or else we shall be a crumbling nothingness in a few years, a country in ruin –'
> 'I suppose it's a bit of newspaper cant, as well,' said Birkin.
>
> (p. 54)

The language of race degradation enters *Women in Love* as 'a bit of newspaper cant', a quotation.

> 'I believe the man means it,' [Birkin] said, 'as far as he means anything.'
> 'And do you think it's true? Do you think we really want a new gospel?' asked Gerald.
> Birkin shrugged his shoulders.
>
> (p. 54)

Birkin's analysis of national death, and his new gospel, are both a good deal more radical than anything envisaged by the leader-writer of the *Daily Telegraph*, or indeed any other newspaper. But he cannot very well dispute the contention that the country is in ruin, and that a new attitude to life is required, since this is what he himself believes. Birkin's shrug is also the text's.

Gerald Crich will act out, self-consciously but not parodically, this analysis of race and national death. He is no degenerate. He does not suffer from some inherited flaw. But he is constantly placed, both as an individual and as the member of a class, by quotations from the discourse of race and national death. His great achievement has been to make the mines profitable, breaking with his father's mid-Victorian philosophy of paternalism and muddling-through, and promoting a new creed of organization and efficiency. One of the issues which separates father from son is the proper attitude to the 'whining, parasitic' poor (p. 216). Thomas Crich feeds the supplicants; his wife and his son both want to turn them away. But the issue is framed in the son's terms rather than the father's, in the language of Lankester's Social Darwinism.

Gerald himself can be associated with early twentieth-century campaigns for 'national efficiency': physical health; scientific and technological training; military and naval preparedness; industrial modernization; a government of national unity (Searle 1971). Gudrun imagines that she might inspire him to become the Napoleon or the Bismarck of modern Britain. 'She would marry him, he would go into Parliament in the Conservative interest, he would clear up the great muddle of labour and industry' (p. 417). The application of business ethics and methods to public policy was one of the causes promoted by the 'national efficiency' movement. That would be Gerald's 'new gospel', if he could only bring himself to mean it.

That he can't is due to his failure in relationship. Gerald is not a degenerate destroyed by some inherited genetic flaw. He is a conditional degenerate – he often behaves *as if* he were drunk (pp. 70, 324, 443–4) – who is corrupted by the degenerate environments he encounters. Degeneracy exists in the two bohemias – Halliday's, Loerke's – which he inhabits briefly at the beginning and at the end of the novel. Halliday's circle is the kind that might easily have found itself denounced in Nordau's *Degeneration* (1895). Lawrence makes sure we get the point about Halliday: 'his face was uplifted, degenerate, perhaps slightly disintegrate, and yet with a moving beauty of its own' (p. 77). While Birkin observes bohemia coolly, then passes on, Gerald lingers, intrigued, appalled, fascinated, drawn inexorably into moral, sexual and physical conflict. He loses Minette to Halliday just as he will later lose Gudrun to Loerke.

Loerke, the 'mud-child', the 'very stuff of the underworld of life' (p. 427), is Lawrence's best shot at a degenerate. Extravagantly Jewish and homosexual, he fulfils to an almost parodic degree the requirements of stereotype. He is an evolutionary test-case, a parasite, a creature developed at once beyond and below humanity, into pure destructiveness. Gudrun succumbs to Loerke,

Gerald fights him and loses. Never himself a degenerate, Gerald, unlike Birkin, cannot create an alternative to degeneracy. His failure propels him, like Jude, into the final spiral of the degeneration plot. His desire for 'finality' (p. 461) drives him on to a conclusion, but his 'decay of strength' (p. 472) ensures that the conclusion will be death.

Gerald's story exemplifies the degeneration theory which glosses it so consistently. Rupert and Ursula's story, on the other hand, looks back to those tentative imaginings of mystical-eugenic union in Gissing and Grand, in George Egerton's 'The Regeneration of Two' (published in *Discords*, 1894), in Forster. Lawrence's parallel narratives are sometimes seen as part of a literary revolution, as distinctively Modernist. But they might also be regarded as the solution, at once formal and ideological, to a problem first articulated thirty years before.

8

DECLENSION

A passage in Arnold Bennett's journal for 15 June 1896 describes the aged male inmates of the Fulham Road workhouse. 'Strange that the faces of most of them afford no vindication of the manner of their downfall to pauperdom! I looked in vain for general traces either of physical excess or of moral weakness' (1932, I, p. 10). Armed with the mandate of naturalism, Bennett looks for evidence of degeneracy, but cannot find any. The faces shows signs of wear and tear, not monstrosity. Bennett's fiction was to avoid naturalism by confining itself to wear and tear, by not seeking any 'vindication' of biomedical theory. This chapter will describe his achievement, and relate it to the emergence of a new fictional territory, far removed from the Fulham Road, about which he had much to say: the suburb.

SUBURBS

By the end of the 1890s the brief phase of the slum novel was effectively over. The East End of London was still a point of automatic reference in many novels, but the portrayal of working-class life became increasingly light-hearted. Symptomatic of the new mood was the instant success of William de Morgan's genial old-fashioned romances (Keating 1989, p. 319). Dickens, not Zola, was the model. Addressing the Boz Club, William Pett Ridge claimed that Dickens had revealed the 'romance' and the 'cheerfulness' in the lives of 'hard-up people'. Some writers, he went on, described the poor as though they were 'gibbering apes'. But such 'naturalism' was outmoded. 'The reading public knows better; it knows that the Dickens view is the right view.' Ridge, like Edwin Pugh and W. W. Jacobs, was proud to be considered a disciple of Dickens (Ridge 1923, pp. 35–7). His best-known working-class novel, *Mord Em'ly* (1898), is a sentimental, facetious tale about a slum-girl whose vitality is nourished rather than impaired by London life.

At the same time, a new territory and a new class had become visible, as suburbia spread out from London and the major industrial centres and coastal resorts, boosted by railway expansion and the advent of the motor car. Suburbia was as tribal as the slums, as tempting to the cultural anthropologist; more so, perhaps, since the new tribe was composed of avid novel-readers. The result was a flourishing genre of fiction which, taking its tone from Jerome's *Three Men in a Boat* (1889) and the Grossmiths' *Diary of a Nobody* (1892), celebrated or gently mocked suburban lifestyles and values (Flint 1986; Keating 1989, pp. 319–26). The philanthropic Lady Harman, who wants inside information about suburbia, is advised to read Gissing, Pugh and Swinnerton (Wells 1986c, p. 347).

Ridge provided the 'Dickens view' of suburbia in *A Clever Wife* (1895), whose heroine, a feminist writer, agrees to marry the hero as long as she doesn't have to become 'domesticated and suburban, and interested in back gardens' (Ridge 1895, p. 131). On their honeymoon, she devotes more attention to the proofs of her first novel than to his expressions of bliss. Her second novel bombs, and her thoughts soon turn to domesticity, and even back gardens. There is a reconciliation scene on Clapham Common.

The Dickens view did not seek to conceal the essential monotony of suburbia. Pugh's *A Street in Suburbia* (1895) and Ridge's *Outside the Radius* (1899) describe an environment which regularly produces a certain type of person, and eliminates, by one means or another, any variants. Critics of suburbia seized on this monotony. Ruskin put the objection pithily when he alluded to 'those gloomy rows of formalised minuteness, alike without difference and without fellowship, as solitary as similar' (1903–12, VIII, p. 226). Suburbia permitted neither difference nor community. It denied the vision fostered by Romanticism and embedded in nineteenth-century social theory, of a society united by common human bonds but differentiated according to individual capacities and desires. In *Howards End* (1910), Mrs Munt, alighting at Hilton on her way to rescue Helen Schlegel from the Wilcoxes, wonders which 'country' the station will open into,

Suburbia or England, executive comfort or 'local life' and 'personal intercourse' (Forster 1941, p. 16). Forster's characters must choose between these alternatives. So must Shan Bullock's Robert Thorne. His father wants him to be a cowboy; he chooses the Tax Office, marriage, the suburbs. But he can't stand it. After a holiday spent on a Hampshire farm ('here at last were real men and women'), the Thornes emigrate (Bullock 1907, pp. 3, 279).

The uniformity of suburbia could be regarded as benevolent, according to the Dickens view, or petty and destructive, according to the Ruskin view. The real challenge was to see in it something other than uniformity.

INSIDE SUBURBIA

The best way to grasp how the challenge might be met is to compare a novel written according to the Ruskin view, Wells's *Ann Veronica* (1909), with one which begins according to the Dickens view, but modifies it in an enterprising way, Ridge's *From Nine to Six-Thirty* (1910). Both heroines, Ann Veronica and Barbara Harrison, leave their suburban homes and establish an independent life in London, eventually becoming engaged and reconciled to their families.

The uniformity of Wells's suburb, Morningside Park, is disrupted only by a family of arty, and much resented, outsiders, the Widgetts. Wells supposes that the imagination cannot develop in suburbia; it must be imported from outside. The Widgetts are Ann Veronica's escape route. Barbara Harrison, by contrast, doesn't need the example of glamorous outsiders. She rebels because she is sick of being bullied by her family.

A further difference of emphasis concerns the ways in which the two heroines, once established in rented rooms in London, embark on careers. Ann Veronica's disillusion is rapid. She dislikes the few occupations – shop assistant, secretary, nurse – which are open to her. Wells is not very interested in her perfunctory search for work; he installs her among a group of Fabian intellectuals, and then in a laboratory at Imperial College. Barbara Harrison, on the other hand, is a 'workaday woman'. She finds employment as a clerk in a travel agency, Warnett's World-Wide Wanderings, which expands and then goes bust; and as a clerk, and eventually manager, with a firm of process engravers. Her work experience shapes her identity.

In both novels the suffrage campaigns provide topical interest. For Wells, the suffrage movement is a 'phase' through which the exceptional individual, Ann Veronica, must pass on her way to self-determination. It is inconceivable in suburbia, and therefore a good thing; but it is also conceivable without the benevolent presence of H. G. Wells, and therefore a bad thing. The feminist Miss Miniver is mercilessly lampooned throughout the novel. Ann Veronica does take part in the suffragette raid on the House of Commons, but the episode reveals her immaturity as well as her courage.

Ridge handles feminism rather differently, allowing it a certain importance as a social and political movement. His feminist is a Miss Jane Collings, who used to live in the same suburban street as Barbara Harrison, but is now a suffragette, and a successful public speaker. Barbara remembers her as the archetype of suburbanism. But she has transformed herself, made her own way out of a suburbia which, if scarcely sympathetic, has not put up much of a resistance. Feminism fulfils her – a fulfilment which Barbara, unlike Ann Veronica, respects, even if she does not want it for herself.

The fourth and final difference concerns the men the heroines marry. Capes has an easy ride against Ann Veronica's other, culpably suburban wooers: the insipid Manning, the lecherous Ramage. He is a brilliantly innovative scientist turned communicator, with no respect for sexual conventions: a free spirit, an H. G. Wells. It is he who *gives* Ann Veronica her identity, as she realizes when he masterfully curtails a continental holiday:

'Can't we go down into Italy?'

'No,' he said; 'it won't run to that now. We must wave our hands at the blue hills far away there and go back to London and work.'

'But Italy –'

'Italy's for a good girl,' he said, and laid his hand for a moment on her shoulder. 'She must look forward to Italy.'

'I say,' she reflected, 'you *are* rather the master, you know.'

The idea struck him as novel.

(1980, p. 277)

Like hell it did. Wells couldn't conceive of men like Capes – like himself – as anything other than masters whose responsibility it was to liberate suburban maidens. The priggishness of the passage is compounded by Capes's attitude to work. When he talks of 'work', he means Work: saving the world. He does not mean that they are returning home to run a travel agency.

Barbara Harrison also has to put up with some rather slimy specimens. Like Ann Veronica, she wavers between contempt and reluctant dependence. But her feelings are complicated by her commitment to her career. She means to establish herself as a working woman first, and a wife second. The success of her career remains in doubt right up until the last moment; and while it remains in doubt there can be no salvation through marriage. She makes it clear that she will be a working wife. *Nine to Six-Thirty* is marred by sentimentality and facetiousness, particularly where babies are concerned, but it is a better novel than Wells's, because it gives suburbia a chance.

Another writer who gave suburbia a chance was Wells's friend and ally, Arnold Bennett: not perhaps in *A Man from the North* (1898), which is written according to the Ruskin view, but certainly in the later novels. In *Clayhanger* (1910), for example, the Clayhangers, having attained a certain status, move from the centre of Bursley to a new 'residential suburb', Bleakridge. The move has an individual significance for each member of the family, and no more than that. The house which the architect and developer Osmond Orgreave builds for Darius Clayhanger means one thing to him, another to Darius, and yet another to young Edwin. Edwin alone is 'capable of possessing it by enjoying it' (1954, p. 164); it becomes a part of his identity. None of them, though, would enjoy the house which Denry Machin builds for his mother, also in Bleakridge, in *The Card* (1911). *Hilda Lessways* (1911) unveils a London suburb, Hornsey, which is not at all like Bleakridge. There is nothing very startling, of course, about Bennett's discovery that suburbia exists in the eye of the beholder. But it did enable him to move beyond both the Dickens view and the Ruskin view.

WOOLF VERSUS BENNETT

Virginia Woolf's attack on Bennett as the (male) embodiment of conversative middlebrow taste still stands in the way of a proper appreciation of his achievement. 'Modern Fiction' (1919) and

'Mr Bennett and Mrs Brown' (1924) are among the most influential essays ever written about the modern novel (I shall quote from the versions of both essays which have had the widest circulation), while Bennett's criticism remains virtually unknown. When the quarrel began, however, in 1917, their roles were reversed. Bennett was fifty, and an immensely successful professional novelist; his name sold newspapers, people recognized him in the street. Woolf was younger, less famous, and less productive; she worked slowly and painfully, and was acutely sensitive to criticism. It was a conflict of temperaments, and of generations.

They quarrelled about characterization. Bennett thought that Woolf sacrificed depth of portrayal to cleverness. Woolf retorted that conceptions of identity were changing. New conceptions – new techniques – produced a new kind of 'character'. The older generation of novelists, she argued in 'Mr Bennett and Mrs Brown', had used 'tools' and 'conventions' which suited their purpose, did their business. 'But those tools are not our tools, and that business is not our business.'

She illustrated the difference between their business and her business by trying to imagine how the older generation would represent a scene she had witnessed on a train journey from Richmond to Waterloo: a desultory but faintly ominous conversation between two fellow-passengers, 'Mrs Brown' and 'Mr Smith'. Bennett, she decides, would invoke Mrs Brown's material and social circumstances. In doing so, he would miss her 'atmosphere', her essence.

In 'Modern Fiction' Woolf argued that identity is the 'pattern' which each sight or incident 'scores upon the consciousness'. Leopold Bloom is whatever is present to his mind (1919, p. 109). Identity can best by grasped by means of a poetic of awareness. The more aware a person is, the more representable he or she becomes; and, by implication, the more representable, the more aware. Modernism has often been construed as a poetic of awareness.

Woolf's description of Bennett's method is accurate. But she didn't ask why he had chosen to represent character through circumstance. Indeed, she doesn't seem to regard it as a choice. Bennett was incapable of seeing Mrs Brown at all, however hard he peered. The distinction between generations then becomes a distinction not between equally valid methods, but between blindness and insight. Bennett, however, was perfectly capable of seeing the world as Joyce and Woolf saw it. A journal entry for 19 February 1914 records an encounter with a middle-aged couple in a train. Disregarding material and social circumstance, Bennett captures the 'atmosphere' of the scene: the ripples of dissatisfaction – or is it tenderness? – that run beneath their exquisite restraint (1932, II, p. 79). But in his novels he chose to disregard atmosphere, and render circumstance. Why?

Woolf analyses a passage near the beginning of *Hilda Lessways*, where Hilda looks out of the window. Bennett does not disclose her state of mind. Rather, he describes what she might be seeing, or contemplating: the streets around her, their history, the house she lives in. Her reverie is interrupted by her mother's voice. 'But we cannot hear her mother's voice,' Woolf complains, 'or Hilda's voice; we can only hear Mr Bennett's voice telling us facts about rents and freeholds and copyholds and fines.' To make us believe in Hilda's reality, Bennett, 'being an Edwardian', describes the house she lives in, and the houses she can see from the window of the house she lives in. 'House property was the common ground from which the Edwardians found it easy to proceed to intimacy' (1924, pp. 121–2). This is witty, and just. The proof of its justness lies in the very similar opening of *The Old Wives' Tale* (1908), where Constance and Sophia Baines also stare out of a window, and Bennett does not describe them, but the geographic, economic and social position of the town they live in. It is Bennett's voice we hear, not theirs.

'Observation,' Bennett wrote in 1898, 'can only be conducted from the outside' (1932, I, p. 79). He believed that understanding depended on a recognition of difference, not similarity. The irreducible differences between people, particularly between men and women, were for him the incentive, not the bar, to characterization. So it was that in *Clayhanger* and *Hilda Lessways* he gave two versions of the same events, first from the man's point of view, then from the woman's; we cannot know Edwin Clayhanger until we have seen him through Hilda's eyes, and vice versa. Douglas Hewitt notes perceptively that Bennett, unlike most novelists of his time, wrote about people who were very different from himself. James, Hueffer, Wells, Forster, Lawrence, Richardson, Woolf: all wrote about experiences akin to their own. To be aware is to be representable; to be representable is to be aware. But the understanding we have of the Baines sisters or

Edwin Clayhanger is something we share with Bennett rather than the characters themselves (Hewitt 1988, p. 98). We know them as much by what they don't know as by what they do.

Hilda Lessways opens with Hilda a few weeks short of her twenty-first birthday. 'She was a woman, but she could not realize that she was a woman' (1991, p. 4). *Could* not. Hilda's ignorance is constitutive. She is a hollow place, a silence. The conversation which soon begins, between Bennett and the reader, is carried on around that silence. Out of it, out of unawareness, which is not a liability or oppression, but a potent force, develops the unique being who is Hilda Lessways. Bennett never stopped talking over the heads of his characters. It is that flow of comment, so irritating to Woolf, which preserves the constitutive difference of his characters: their right to remain unaware, to the bitter end, of themselves and of each other. To Modernism's poetic of awareness, Bennett opposed a poetic of unawareness.

DECLENSIONS

A poetic of unawareness required a new kind of plot, one that was not available to Bennett in either the 'French' or the 'English' traditions. Many, if not most, plots, and certainly those favoured by the great nineteenth-century English novelists, turn on moments of revelation, when the illusions nurtured by timidity, prejudice or habit fall away, and a naked self confronts a naked world. These are the moments when identity is begun, renewed or completed. French naturalism had added a different plot, in which the revelation is gradual, and of something already known, but temporarily concealed: a moral or physical flaw, an organic 'lesion'. Both kinds of plot favour awareness. Illusions are there to be stripped away. There can be no self-discovery, no personal development, whether into enlightenment or into degeneracy, until they have been stripped away.

A curious episode in *The Old Wives' Tale* suggests that Bennett was never really very happy with either kind of plot. Grouchy, fallible, cautiously opportunistic, waveringly tyrannical Samuel Povey is summoned from his bed one night by his more expansive cousin, Daniel, and transferred, effectively, to another novel. Daniel begins by confessing that his wife is an alcoholic, and so tears to pieces in a moment 'the veil of thirty years' weaving' (1964, p. 223). Hinting at even darker horrors, he leads Samuel through his shop and into the house behind, where his son, one leg broken by a fall, and his wife, whom he has murdered in a fit of rage, lie sprawled. The 'vile' Mrs Povey isn't merely drunken, and dead, but an emblem of degeneracy (p. 226).

The experience transforms Samuel. He regards Daniel as a martyr, a man goaded beyond endurance. 'Samuel, in his greying middle age, had inherited the eternal youth of the apostle' (p. 234). His new conviction makes him, for the first time in his life, a public figure. He launches a campaign to vindicate Daniel and secure his release. During the campaign, which fails, he contracts pneumonia, and dies. His death provokes the narrator into a startling display of mawkishness (p. 250).

Bennett finds himself caught between two traditions, French naturalism (Mrs Povey's degeneracy) and English moralism (Samuel's transformation), neither of which suits him at all. The whole episode seems like a lengthy quotation from a second-rate novel by someone else. One moment only sounds like Bennett. On the night of the murder, halfway through an anguished debate with Samuel, Daniel meticulously empties the surplus of the corn he had used to throw at Samuel's bedroom window out of his jacket pocket into its receptacle (p. 225). Bennett characterizes him, at this moment of crisis, through that part of his mind which doesn't yet realize what has happened. Crises are supposed to reveal, to set naked self against naked world. Bennett is more interested in the illusions that remain.

A new kind of plot was needed to demonstrate how such illusions – such nescience – might form, rather than deform, or form as well as deform, a personality. Bennett's protagonists advance their hollowness into a world which, as they age, becomes ever more crowded, ever more impenetrable. They feel the changes in pressure within them, but the shell of their nescience never cracks, as it would in a 'French' novel; nor is it ever filled up, with hard-earned wisdom, with love, as it would be in an 'English' novel. Leonora, watching her husband die, realizes that she has been created not by love, but by the 'constant uninterrupted familiarity' of married life. 'It was a trifle that they had not loved. They had lived. Ah! she knew him so profoundly that words could not describe her knowledge' (1903, p. 314). That knowledge, which has made Leonora what she is, is a knowledge produced not by revelation but by long familiarity, by mutually adjusted illusion. It is a necessary unawareness, and the most powerful thing about her.

The term Bennett found for lives not shaped by development or degeneration was 'declension'. A chapter in *Hilda Lessways* is entitled 'Miss Gailey in Declension' and describes the deterioration of Hilda's dancing-instructor. 'To Hilda Miss Gailey appeared no older; her brown hair had very little grey in it, and her skin was fairly smooth and well-preserved. But she seemed curiously smaller and less significant' (1911, p. 91). Declension involves a gradual loss of energy, will, presence, significance. But there is a gain to be had from the erosion of these qualities, which constantly demand that one live up to an ideal or self-image, or fashion oneself according to social convention. It is a gain of definiteness, of irreducible difference. I don't know whether Bennett had the grammatical sense of declension in mind. That sense is appropriate, because the declensions he portrays are not merely disablements, but variations in the form a person's life can take.

In the end, in Bennett's novels, loss and gain are hard to distinguish, as they are in many people's lives. Miss Gailey is a spinster, and his spinsters (Janet Orgreave, for example, in the Clayhanger tetralogy) remind us that an identity created by not willing, by not signifying, is at once, and inextricably, formation and deformation. In the early years of the century, the spinster novel became an identifiable sub-genre, a paradigm of declension. The narratives of Gissing's 'The Foolish Virgin' (reprinted in Fletcher 1987), F. M. Mayor's *The Third Miss Symons* (1913) and May Sinclair's *Life and Death of Harriet Frean* (1922) are as meagre, as eked out, as the lives they portray.

Few people, in Bennett's fiction, escape declension. At the end of *Whom God Hath Joined* (1906), Laurence Ridware, who has just survived a punishing divorce, wonders whether he should propose to a much younger woman, Annunciate Fearns. But he simply doesn't have the energy. Edwin Clayhanger is motivated during his youth by a fierce hatred of Methodism. But by the time he is asked, in *These Twain* (1916), to serve as District Treasurer of the Additional Chapels Fund, he doesn't even have enough animosity left for a contemptuous refusal (1916, p. 43). His ambition goes the same way: 'his life seemed to be a life of half-measures, a continual falling-short' (p. 221). Yet he is in his way fulfilled, even assertive.

Bennett regarded marriage as the test, and the fulfilment, of the identity which declension creates. Towards the end of *These Twain*, Hilda wants to move to the country, and persists in her arguments, even though she knows perfectly well that Edwin wants to stay in town. Edwin has to come to terms with the fact that his wife, in denying his clearly stated preference, is denying him.

> If Hilda had not been unjust in the assertion of her own individuality, there could be no merit in yielding to her. To yield to a just claim was not meritorious, though to withstand it would be wicked. He was objecting to injustice as a child objects to rain on a holiday. Injustice was a tremendous actuality! It had to be faced and accepted. (He himself was unjust. At any rate he intellectually conceived that he must be unjust, though honestly he could remember no instance of injustice on his part.) To reconcile oneself to injustice was the master achievement.
>
> (p. 506)

To reconcile oneself to injustice is to acknowledge the irreducible difference of other people, an acknowledgement enforced not by revelation, but by long familiarity. The passage brilliantly renders Edwin's habits of mind: the faint pomposity, the honesty which compels him *not* to confess to injustice and so claim the authenticity of sudden illumination. These habits are his difference from Hilda, and what she loves in him.

STUDIES ON HYSTERIA

In *The Old Wives' Tale* Constance Baines and Samuel Povey fall in love while absorbed in the manufacture of a new kind of ticket for the goods in the shop-window (1964, p. 103). They court each other unknowingly. Bennett promptly interpolates a treatise on the history of commerce in Bursley (pp. 103–5) which prevents us, like them, from registering the significance of the occasion. When Mrs Baines asks about the tune the town band has been playing outside in the Square, they can't help her (p. 106). Absorbed in their task, they haven't heard the band. Neither have we.

The scene demonstrates the lengths to which Bennett would go to keep his characters' ignorance of themselves, and to represent that self-absorbed self-ignorance. Sexual desire, which, traditionally, either reveals us to ourselves as we really are or destroys us, tested this technique to the limit, most notably in the account of Sophia Baines's elopement. Frank Harris expressed disappointment that there wasn't more of the 'superb wild animal' about Sophia; Bennett thought him dismally sentimental (Hewitt 1988, p. 95).

Bennett undid the wild animal in Sophia by so to speak writing his declension plot *over* the degeneration plot of Zola's *Nana*. Her Paris is Nana's Paris, Paris during the last celebration before the calamity of 1870. The mob yelling 'To Berlin! To Berlin!' while Nana dies horribly of smallpox is the mob Sophia encounters at the Place de la Concorde (p. 377). Zola described the theme of his novel as a pack of hounds after a bitch who is not even on heat. Sophia, the object of 'inconvenient desires', walks unscathed amid the 'frothing hounds' as though protected by a spell (p. 338). Sophia, unlike Nana, does not sell herself to the men who pursue her. It is the courtesan Madame Foucault, resplendent when first encountered, but increasingly abject and reduced finally to an 'obscene wreck' (p. 362), who plays Nana's part. Heredity does for Nana, the degenerate daughter of degenerate parents, but the Baines stock is sound (p. 357).

Even so, desire has left its mark on that inheritance. One day Sophia, now the prosperous owner of the Pension Frensham, wakes up semi-paralysed. Struggling to the foot of the bed, she examines herself in the wardrobe mirror, and sees that the lower part of her face has been twisted out of shape. The doctor offers a swift diagnosis. '*Paralysie glosso-labiolaryngée* was the phrase he used' (p. 450). By the early 1890s, facial, and specifically glosso-labial, paralysis had been recognized as one of the major symptoms of hysteria (Tuke 1892, I, p. 635; Tourette 1895, p. 35). Sophia realizes that the attack has been triggered by an encounter with a young man from Bursley, which destroys the barrier painstakingly erected between her two lives.

Mark Micale has described the second half of the nineteenth century as the *belle époque* of hysteria, and Paris and Vienna, the classically *fin-de-siècle* capitals, as its native environment (1990, p. 364). The master of ceremonies was Jean-Martin Charcot, who began to treat hysterics at the Saltpêtrière in 1870. By observation, examination and the use of hypnosis, he proved that their symptoms were genuine and genuinely disabling. Freud, who studied at the Saltpêtrière from October 1885 to February 1886, credited Charcot with establishing the legitimacy of hysteria as a disorder. Charcot demonstrated that it afflicted men as well as women, and was not simply related, as tradition had it, to the vagaries of the female reproductive system (the wandering womb). Even so, hysteria remained symbolically, if not medically, a female malady, and one associated with sexual disorders (Heath 1982, chs 3 and 4; Showalter 1987).

Psychoanalysis began with hysteria; according to some commentators, it could have begun nowhere else. 'Hysteria led Freud to what is universal in psychic construction and it led him there in a particular way − by the route of a prolonged and central preoccupation with the difference between the sexes' (Mitchell 1986, p. 386). The question of sexual difference was built into the very structure of the disease, into the hysteric's hesitation between sexual roles. But for Freud, as for Charcot, it was women who might provide the answer. It was women he and Breuer examined in the *Studies on Hysteria* (1895). The *Studies* inaugurated the 'talking cure', or 'listening treatment'.

In an obituary written shortly after Charcot's death in 1893, Freud summed up his mentor's understanding of the aetiology of hysteria: 'heredity was to be regarded as the sole cause' (1953–74, III, p. 21). French psychiatrists, like their English counterparts, were whole-hearted advocates of degeneration theory (Dowbiggin 1985; Clark 1981). Charcot's narratives of hysteria, with their genealogical trees full of interconnecting cases of alcoholism, epilepsy, criminality and suicide, resemble the storyline of Zola's Rougon-Macquart novels (Micale 1990, p. 383).

Freud argued, in a series of papers published in the 1890s, and in *Studies on Hysteria*, that Charcot and his followers had been 'dazzled' by the apparently all-encompassing concept of heredity. In this, he added, they were responding to a pervasive belief in the degeneracy of Western societies (1953–74, III, pp. 146–8). To reject heredity as a cause of mental illness was to reject determinism: a life story shaped by events not merely beyond the individual's control, but beyond his or her experience.

Freud began to study cases of 'acquired' rather than inherited hysteria, and to uncover a rather different storyline. He decided that hysteria did not begin in the life of an ancestor, with an organic 'lesion', but in the life of the patient, with a traumatic experience. During that experience the patient was confronted with a feeling which she could not bring herself to acknowledge, and which she repressed, thus dividing her consciousness. This feeling, which could neither be acknowledged nor ignored, was then converted, after a period of latency, into hysterical symptoms.

Hysteria, then, began and ended within individual experience. Where women were concerned, Freud said, the 'incompatible ideas' which produced trauma were likely to 'arise chiefly on the soil of sexual experience or sensation'. He gave two examples: a girl who blamed herself because, while nursing her sick father, she had thought about a young man; and a governess who had fallen in love with her employer (1953–74, III, p. 47). These two cases, written up in *Studies on Hysteria*, reveal the new storyline: the origin in trauma, the latency period, the physical symptoms.

We might compare the first to the case of Sophia. Left alone in the house to watch her paralysed father, Sophia spots Gerald and rushes down to speak to him. The encounter confirms her desire, her sexual awakening. When she goes back upstairs, she finds her father dead. Her body expresses the intensity of a guilt she can neither acknowledge nor ignore. 'As she stood on the mat outside the bedroom door she tried to draw her mother and Constance and Mr Povey by magnetic force out of the wakes into the house, and her muscles were contracted in this strange effort' (Bennett 1964, p. 94). Split between desire and remorse, she represses the latter, and elopes with Gerald. But it is surely the remorse which returns, converted into facial paralysis. Sophia's hysteria begins in trauma and ends in physical symptoms. If Zola's narratives resemble Charcot's, then Bennett's resemble Freud's.

Bennett was by no means the only writer to describe the dilemma of daughters left to care for a tyrannical, but physically or morally crippled, father. Sinclair, Joyce, Lawrence and Mansfield all used this dilemma as the basis for stories of declension. Jane Findlater's *The Green Graves of Balgowrie* (1896) varies it by installing a widowed mother as the tyrant. Vanessa and Virginia Stephen could be said to have experienced it in their lives, rather than represented it in their art.

9

FRONTIERS

In the previous two chapters I discussed the development of realist fiction in terms of characteristic territories (slum, suburb) and characteristic plots (degeneration, declension). I want to turn now to realism's great opponent, romance, which had been gaining commercial and aesthetic ground steadily ever since the success of Stevenson and Rider Haggard in the 1880s (Keating 1989, pp. 344–66). Romance created a new, and equally mythic, territory: the frontiers of empire. There destinies acquired a new (but very old) shape. If naturalist plots were informed by anxieties about social decrepitude, then romance plots were informed by anxieties about the state of a 'Derelict Empire' (Irwin 1912). Whereas declension novels avoided naturalism, or inoculated themselves against it by incorporating degenerative episodes, the new romances took it over and turned it around.

IMPERIALISM

By the end of the nineteenth century, empire had become the White Man's Burden, a dangerous project. 'At every turn,' the *Pall Mall Gazette* warned in 1885, 'we are confronted with the gunboats, the sea lairs, or the colonies of jealous and eager rivals. . . . The world is filling up around us' (quoted in Porter 1975, p. 117). The world was also filling up in economic and demographic terms. America and Germany were challenging the industrial and commercial supremacy of Britain, while the inexhaustible Russian and Chinese masses pressed in on her most valuable possession, India. 'Now,' Lord Salisbury declared in a speech in May 1898, which alarmed and offended foreign governments, 'with the whole earth occupied and the movements of expansion continuing, she will have to fight to the death against successive rivals' (quoted in Porter 1975, p. 126).

The new imperialism which emerged and gained strength during the 1890s was thus an act of reassertion rather than of assertion (Faber 1966, pp. 68–95; Porter 1982; Rose 1986, ch. 4). As a political movement, it had more downs than ups. The Liberal triumph of 1905 seemed fatal to any resurgence of imperial commitment. 'I began to have an ugly fear,' John Buchan was to say of the period, 'that the Empire might decay at the heart' (1940, p. 126). But it was precisely this anxiety, transmitted in warnings and denunciations, which proved the most potent expression of the new imperialism. Twenty years of degeneration theory had prepared the educated public for its diagnosis of a nation in decline. Its vision of imperial regeneration was over-ambitious in political terms, but compelling, and susceptible to endless reproduction in popular culture (Mackenzie 1984, 1986).

In recent years the study of the cultural effects of colonialism has tended, for understandable political and professional reasons, to concentrate on the colonized rather than the colonizers (Parry 1987; Gates 1989; Ashcroft et al. 1989). When the colonizers do appear, they tend to be analysed, in terms derived from Derrida and Foucault, as transmitters of a 'discourse' or component parts of a 'signifying system'. This approach can be illuminating (Bhabha 1989). But an analysis based on a code model of communication will invariably leave something out.

Being a white man in the colonies, Edward Said has argued, meant 'speaking in a certain way, behaving according to a code of regulations, and even feeling certain things and not others. It meant specific judgements, evaluations, gestures' (1978, pp. 226–7). Up to a point. Being a colonizer 'meant' the *use* of particular evaluations and gestures, at a particular time, in a particular place. There is no 'code of regulations', however imperial, powerful enough to override uniformly the different spin put on evaluations and gestures by different contexts. It is not enough, therefore, to reconstruct a way of speaking. We must also ask what people thought they were doing when they spoke. Power is a resource as well as a strategy.

I want to suggest that, for the colonizer, colonial experience did not so much confirm an old identity as create a new one. Kipling's Indian stories, for example, were meant to demonstrate that whiteness alone – an existing (European, metropolitan) identity – would never suffice on the frontiers of empire. Colonial life took strength and identity away before it gave anything back. 'Kipling was a provocation and a challenge,' the writer and explorer Edmund Candler recalled. 'I believe that the very hideousness of the picture in such tales as "At the End of the Passage", or "The City of Dreadful Night" was part of the lure of the East' (Candler 1924, pp. 26–7). Candler was incorrigibly romantic, but his emphasis on perpetual self-renewal did find a more sober echo in hundreds of adventure stories and, it may be, hundreds of lives. My subject here is the way that emphasis entered popular fiction, adding a new 'curve' to the repertoire of plots.

DYNAMOGENIC EFFECTS

Edwardian commentators knew a 'signifying system' when they saw one. Masterman recognized in the institutions grouped around a London suburb – prison, workhouse, fever hospital, lunatic asylum, cemetery – a habit of mind which had created an empire. 'For the spirit of that Empire – clean, efficient, austere, intolerably just – is the spirit which has banished to these forgotten barrack-prisons and behind high walls the helpless young and the helpless old, the maimed, the restless, and the dead' (1905, pp. 157–8). This is the empire as machine. But, unlike modern commentators obsessed with the 'rationality' of autonomous networks of power, Masterman could not altogether conceal his interest in motive. What did the austerity mean to those who enforced it?

One would expect the age which invented 'psychology' to have a lot to say about austerity and intolerable justice. William James wanted to develop a 'functional psychology' which would examine the 'amount of energy' people have for running their 'mental and moral operations'. He believed that most people live far within their limits, using only a fraction of their powers and abilities. Their horizons are contracted like the hysteric's field of vision: 'but with less excuse, for the poor hysteric is diseased, while in the rest of us it is only an inveterate *habit* – the habit of inferiority to our full self – that is bad' (W. James 1907, pp. 17–18). Behind James's functional psychology lay a conviction that the West was in decline.

The problem of subjectivity, and by implication of society as a whole, could thus be understood as a problem of renewal or regeneration. Identity *was* regeneration. Becoming yourself meant breaking through the inveterate habits which defined you as you were and becoming another person. James examined a whole range of stimuli, from anger and despair to the responsibilities of high office. He illustrated the regenerative powers of love with reference to Sydney Olivier's story 'The Empire Builder', about a young naval officer who bullies the Colonial Office into annexing the island home of his beloved (James 1907, p. 6). The banality of the example is striking. Colonial experience had become a storehouse of initiations, easily and casually plundered, fascinating even to those who had no thought of being initiated, or who were against empires, like James.

America already had a programme of individual and collective regeneration, which James didn't allude to. It had frontier myth. On 12 July 1893 Frederick Jackson Turner read his seminal paper on 'The significance of the frontier in American history' to the American Historical Association, which was meeting in Chicago during the World's Fair. 'American social development,' Turner claimed, 'has been continually beginning over again on the frontier. This perennial rebirth, this fluidity of American life, this expansion westward with its new opportunities, its continuous touch with the simplicity of primitive society, furnish the forces dominating American character' (Turner 1921, pp. 2–3). The frontier had served as a permanent rite of passage.

Turner was concerned primarily with social development, but he inserted an intriguing passage which spells out what the frontier had meant to the individual.

The wilderness masters the colonist. It finds him a European in dress, industries, tools, modes of travel, and thought. It takes him from the railroad car and puts him in the birch canoe. It strips off the garments of civilization and arrays him in the hunting shirt and the moccasin. It puts him in the log cabin of the Cherokee and Iroquois and runs an Indian palisade around him. Before long he has gone to planting Indian corn and plowing with a sharp stick; he shouts the war cry and takes the scalp in orthodox Indian fashion. In short, at the frontier the environment is at first too strong for the man. He must accept the conditions which it furnishes, or perish, and so he fits himself into the Indian clearings and follows the Indian trails. Little by little he transforms the wilderness, but the outcome is not the old Europe.... The fact is, that here is a new product that is American.

(p. 4)

Turner puts us in the place of the would-be colonizer, a person still defined by European technologies and habits of mind. He insists that they will have to be abandoned altogether. The colonizer becomes a colonizer by re-barbarizing himself, by shouting the war cry and taking the scalp in 'orthodox Indian fashion'. He must want to obliterate himself, to turn into his opposite. You have to become an 'Indian' in order to become an 'American'.

Turner's thesis had obvious applications to the British Empire, which Lord Curzon spelt out in his Romanes Lecture on 'Frontiers', delivered at Oxford in 1907. Curzon had travelled widely on the boundaries of the British Empire in Asia; as Viceroy of India, he had been responsible for 5,700 miles of sensitive border, and fully aware of their strategic significance. The lecture consists largely of a discussion of frontier policy in recent history, with much reference to buffer states, protectorates and spheres of influence. But its tone changes noticeably towards the end, when Curzon launches into some fervent remarks about the effect of 'Frontier expansion' upon 'national character', as illustrated in 'the history of the Anglo-Saxon race'. A school of American historians had, he says, traced 'the evolution of national character as determined by its western march across the continent'. Would the evolution of British national character be determined by marches across other continents towards other frontiers?

'I am one of those,' Curzon announced, 'who hold that in this larger atmosphere, on the outskirts of Empire, where the machine is relatively impotent and the individual is strong, is to be found an ennobling and invigorating stimulus for our youth, saving them alike from the corroding ease and the morbid excitements of Western civilization' (Curzon 1907, pp. 55–8). The victims of over-civilization, of social decrepitude, will be regenerated on the frontier. James, Turner and Curzon could be said to have sketched a social psychology which locks subjectivity into the politics of expansion.

WILD WEST, WILD EAST

On the night Turner delivered his paper on the significance of the frontier in Chicago, one young historian, Max Otto, chose to take in instead Buffalo Bill's Wild West Show, which was playing in a rented lot across the street from the main entrance to the World's Fair (Billington 1971, p. 172). He probably learnt as much about the American frontier from the popular myths generated by Buffalo Bill as he would have done from the academic myths generated by Professor Turner.

William F. Cody had always been an inveterate self-mythologizer. But he marketed himself most successfully in the Wild West Show first performed at Omaha, Nebraska, on 19 May 1883, and first taken to Britain in 1887. There was a special preview for the Prince of Wales on 9 May and a performance for the Queen on 11 May, the first public entertainment she had attended since the death of the Prince Consort twenty-five years before. She must have been amused, because a second command performance followed, on 20 June. Meanwhile the show, at Earl's Court, Kensington, had been attracting up to 40,000 people a day. During the European tours, the Wild West was augmented by representatives of what one might call the Wild East (German and English cavalrymen, Russian cossacks). It was now known as Buffalo Bill's Wild West and Congress of Rough Riders of the World, and displayed an international freemasonry of the regenerate (Blackstone 1986).

Cody's frontier thesis, like Turner's, had crossed the Atlantic successfully. Its spectacular mixture of parades, riding and shooting exhibitions, and dramatic episodes created a fantasy of barbarism. The programme for the 1899 season reveals the scope of the spectacle. Sandwiched between advertisements for such aids to regeneration as corsets, condensed milk, asthma cures, pepsin chewing gum and cough drops are sketches of the main performers and the 'types' they represent. An elegy for the cowboy describes him as 'a fit and manly type of the earlier civilization of the great West', now virtually extinct (Cody 1899, p. 24). During the European tour of 1889–91, we learn, Cody travelled to America to help resolve 'Indian difficulties' in Dakota. He brought some of the defeated chiefs back with him and displayed to them the wonders of European civilization. At Charlemagne's tomb in Aix-la-Chapelle, the assembled chiefs were told that 'after all his glory, his battles, triumphs, and conquests in which he defeated the dusky African prototypes of the present visitors to his tomb, peace brought him to pursue knowledge, to cultivate the arts and sciences' (p. 57).

The 'ethnological scope' of the Congress was completed by a display of 'Savage People from Our New Possessions' (Costa Ricans, Sandwich Islanders, Filipinos) who would provide 'living novelties and racial object lessons' (p. 63). In this respect it was comparable to other shows like Savage South Africa, which opened at the Empress Theatre, Earl's Court, on 8 May 1899, as part of a Greater Britain Exhibition, and included 'a horde of savages direct from their kraals, comprising 200 Matabeles, Basutos, Swazis, Hottentots, Malays, Cape and Transvaal Boers' (programme quoted in Shephard 1986, p. 97). According to the *Graphic*, the show was 'an agreeable blend of the Agricultural Hall, Buffalo Bill's Indians, and the march to Chitral, with a dash of the Somaliland natives who appeared a year ago at the Crystal Palace' (p. 99).

The Wild West Show rapidly assimilated the exploits of real empire-builders. When America declared war against Spain in 1898, Theodore Roosevelt, then Assistant Secretary to the Navy, seized the opportunity to put his doctrine of 'the strenuous life' into practice. Commissioned as Lieutenant-Colonel of the First US Volunteer Cavalry, he set about recruiting a band of heroes which would combine the two group he most admired, cowboys and sportsmen-aristocrats (Roosevelt 1926, XI, p. 14). The regiment, like Buffalo Bill's Wild West, included a number of Indians; indeed, it is said to have included a number of Indians *from* Buffalo Bill's Wild West. The First US Volunteer Cavalry quickly became known as the Rough Riders.

'Colonel Cody first introduced the name "Rough Riders" to the American public,' announced the 1899 programme. 'The manner in which Colonel Roosevelt subsequently introduced it to the Spaniards has made it historically immortal.' The show included a re-enactment of the regiment's assault on San Juan Hill by the very 'heroes and horses' who had participated in it. In the crucial scene, Roosevelt, casting 'theories, dictums and doubts' aside, leads his men up the hill, and into collective regeneration (Cody 1899, pp. 33–6). The dramatic episodes included in Savage South Africa were even more sacrificial: an attack on a white homestead, during which a woman hurls herself over a cliff, and the ambushing of the 'Shangani Patrol', who die with the national anthem on their lips (Shephard 1986, pp. 98–9). The frontier takes a lot away before it gives anything back.

HALF-HEARTEDNESS

The Wild West Show may have translated effortlessly to Europe, but the same could not be said of the fictional cowboy. The American frontier tale tended to focus on the Westerner. From Fenimore Cooper's Natty Bumppo to Owen Wister's Virginian, the hero was a man born and bred under primitive conditions, his essential self shaped by nature rather than culture, always already regenerate. It was the subsidiary characters – usually Easterners – who needed to obliterate and re-form themselves. The Westerner has analogues in British fiction. Rider Haggard's Quatermain stories transpose Cooper to Africa. Kipling's Kim is a young Virginian, Edgar Wallace's Sanders of the River an older, and distinctly unpleasant, version. But the British frontier tale tended to stress instead the experience of the 'Easterner': the man raised in comfort and privilege, crammed full of theories, dictums and doubts, who goes 'West' (i.e. 'East') to renew himself through conflict. One type of story deals in monumental constancy, the other in transformation. The second type suited the mood of a nation grown old in empire, and anxious about its ability to meet the challenge of more vigorous rivals.

John Buchan gave it a shape, and indeed a name, in *The Half-Hearted* (1900), whose hero – a supercilious, lethargic, 'over-cultured', 'enervated' young man – is persuaded to use his academic knowledge of the Indian frontier to help foil a Russian invasion. The Russians get him in the end. But he has saved India, and been regenerated in the process. He has mastered his disabling lethargy and understood the purpose of empire. This double awakening *is* his adventure (Buchan 1900).

India's Wild North-west became the site of many frontier tales like Maud Diver's bestselling *The Great Amulet* (1908), the surgingly romantic story of a mismatched couple whose love for each other, shallow at first, ripens and blossoms under pressure. Eldred

Lenox is a puritanical Scots artilleryman serving on the North-west Frontier. His wife, Quita, is a vivid, whimsical artist. They discover their incompatibility on the day of their wedding, and decide to separate, as they would have done in a New Woman novel. Eldred becomes addicted to work and opium, Quita to art, independence and flirtation. But this isn't a New Woman novel. Eldred is regenerated by an arduous expedition into the mountains north of Kashmir, Quita by motherhood ('a triumph of the essential woman over mere line and curve').

What the British frontier tale dramatizes, unlike its American counterpart, is the process of renewal: the creation of strength out of weakness. The Lenoxes are measured against Theo and Honor Desmond, 'Westerners' to the core, already regenerate, and celebrated, 150 pages apart, in identical terms (Diver 1908, pp. 57, 220). The Desmonds are monumentally constant: to themselves, to each other, to the empire. But the means by which Diver hopes to absorb the reader both in her narrative and in the project of empire is the far more problematic relationship between Eldred and Quita Lenox. Even after they are reunited, Eldred has still to overcome his opium habit, before it 'degener-ates into a craving' (p. 279). The only way he can succeed is to commit himself with renewed fervour and application to the cause of empire. Quita must commit herself to a man committed to empire. Her awakening, too, is both emotional and political: 'now, when she herself was called upon to obey the unwritten law of her husband's country and service, Lenox noted, with a throb of pride, that for all her artist's tendency to shrink from pain and suffering, she rose to the situation like a high-mettled horse to a fence' (p. 324). High praise indeed.

Half-heartedness regenerated became the hallmark of imperial fantasy. In Conan Doyle's *Tragedy of the Korosko* (1898), for example, a group of tourists travel up the Nile by steamer, venture ashore, and are promptly kidnapped by Dervishes. A half-hearted, middle-aged lawyer is just as promptly revitalized by the experience: 'he had begun to find himself – to understand that there really was a strong, reliable man behind all the tricks of custom which had built up an artificial nature.' The youth he had missed when young announces itself 'like some beautiful belated flower' (Doyle 1898, p. 270). (Another candidate for regeneration – he reads Walter Pater on the boat – is not so lucky, being dispatched by a Mad Mullah on page 140.)

As with the Rough Riders, art sometimes imitated the life which had already imitated art. Asked to pick a 'book of the year' for 1910, Arnold Bennett wrote instead about the grounds upon which such a selection might be made. No book would stand much of a chance, he reckoned, unless, like Forster's *Howards End*, it had been 'talked about' by the 'right people' (Bennett 1917, pp. 291–2). But was this the right criterion? What about 'the celebrated "Dop Doctor" ' which had 'sold very well indeed throughout the entire year', but not, as far as he knew, been talked about by the right people?

The Dop Doctor (1910) is an epic Boer War romance by Richard Dehan set before, during and after the siege of Mafeking (which appears as 'Gueldersdorp'). Owen Saxham, a brilliant young doctor, is falsely accused of performing an abortion, and has to give up his Harley Street practice. He hides himself away in Gueldersdorp, where he earns a reputation as a drunkard. If this was a naturalist novel, he would be well on his way to perdition. However, the town is besieged by the Boers, and the challenge revitalizes Saxham, who becomes right-hand man to the infinitely sagacious commanding officer (modelled none too loosely on Baden-Powell). Inspired by his new responsibilities, he begins the bitter struggle against alcoholism. After many complications, he wins the love of Lynette Mildare, an inmate of Gueldersdorp convent who was brutally raped when scarcely more than a child by a renegade Englishman. Her faith in Saxham at once secures and softens his redemption.

The most important of the many sub-plots concerns the parallel regeneration of the lower classes, in the shape of a cockney couple who redeem their urban fecklessness when under fire. The slum novel is thus the second genre to be inverted, its anti-heroes converted into heroes. Unflinchingly prurient, not to mention racist and sexist, *The Dop Doctor* is one of the most exuberant of Edwardian adventure stories. The regenerations are as crucial to its effect as the rapes and bombardments.

Imperial expansion, involving as it did repeated encounters with more 'primitive' cultures, made it hard to distinguish between the adventure story and historical romance, another bestselling genre. The message that all boys should be ready to answer the call of empire was the same, Keating points out, whether they were 'expected, to use the evocative titles of Henty's novels, to sail *Under Drake's Flag* (1883) or march *With Kitchener to*

Pretoria (1902)' (1989, p. 354). The apotheosis of historical romance was Anthony Hope's *The Prisoner of Zenda* (1894), whose hero is in such a bad way to start with that he can barely summon the energy to crack an egg (Hope 1966, p. 2). Three months in Ruritania bring him round nicely.

The point to grasp is not that the frontier tale endorsed imperial ideology, but that it did so by means of an awareness of genre which was both literary and political. The genres were so well defined that some writers, like Gissing's friend Morley Roberts, could switch between them at will. *Maurice Quain* (1897) is the story of a poverty-stricken classless intellectual, and includes a vivid portrayal of the degenerate humanity packed into the London slums (Roberts 1897, pp. 2–3). By contrast, Madge Gretton, in *A Son of Empire* (1899), is a New Woman transformed by the resurgence of imperialism into 'Romance itself, racial romance. "The world for England," was her motto' (Roberts 1899b, p. 3). Her New Womanly high spirits now take the form of a crush on military men. Roberts followed up the success of *A Son of Empire* with a Boer War romance, *Taken by Storm* (1901), whose sentimentality would have disgusted Gissing, if he ever read it. Dolf Wyllarde no doubt earned rather more from *Uriah the Hittite* (1904), a steamy romance, than she did from the spartan *Pathway of the Pioneer* (1906). But the somersaults between books matter less than the somersaults within books: Dehan's rewriting of the slum novel, Roberts's rewriting of the New Woman novel.

The adventure story takes the exhausted, purposeless men and women of naturalist fiction, whom we expect to degenerate or wither away, and transposes them to a new territory, the frontier, where a more vigorous identity can be created through emotional and political commitment. The curve of its plot dips sharply, bottoms out, then climbs steeply. The reversal of generic expectations fashions the bestseller, and the political message.

The only way to complicate the genre and the message was to keep both plots intact and run them in parallel. In *The Four Feathers* (1902), A. E. W. Mason juxtaposed a story of enablement with a story of disablement. Harry Feversham redeems an act of cowardice and marries his sweetheart, Ethne Eustace. His friend Durrance, a rival for Ethne, goes blind, and loses everything. The novel is as definite and incontestable about loss as it is about gain, refusing to allow enablement to supersede or conceal disablement. In its most moving scene, Durrance, now blind, retires to his study – which, as befits a man of action, is more of a gun-room – and runs his hands over the trophies which make the room 'a gigantic diary' (Mason 1986, pp. 152–3). The final scene is not of Feversham's triumph, but of Durrance leaning over the rail of a steamer anchored in Port Said, picturing to himself 'the flare of braziers upon the quays, the lighted portholes, and dark funnels ahead and behind in the procession of the anchored ships' (p. 263). *The Four Feathers* is the nearest popular equivalent to the divided narratives of Gissing, Forster and Lawrence.

10

ENGLISHNESS

Nothing infuriates Gissing's Henry Ryecroft more than the sight of foreign butter in a shop window. 'This is the kind of thing that makes one gloom over the prospects of England. The deterioration of English butter is one of the worst signs of the moral state of our people' (Gissing 1987, p. 152). The day has long gone, he complains, when an honest chap could expect to enjoy an 'honest chop' at an English inn (p. 78). At first glance, this glooming over butter and chops might seem like the Gilbert and Sullivan version of degeneration theory. But Ryecroft can be distinguished from the degenerationists by his aversion to apocalyptic thinking (pp. 40, 64), and from the regenerationists by his aversion to 'busy patriotism' (p. 174).

'Love of race, among the English,' wrote Sir Charles Dilke, 'rests upon a firmer base than either love of mankind or love of Britain, for it reposes upon a subsoil of things known: the ascertained virtues and powers of the English people' (1868, II, p. 403). Those virtues and powers became the focus of mainstream Edwardian patriotism.

England had possessed the attributes of a nation-state for longer than any comparable country: political, legal and administrative stability, and a widely intelligible vernacular. From the seventeenth century onwards, these attributes provided the basis for an account of the emergence and development of national identity. The account was, of course, a fiction; and England's expansion to Britain, then, by 1900, to Greater Britain, made it even harder to sustain. For the regional, social, political and religious divisions produced over the course of two centuries by rapid and effective industrialization were so deep that the British state, while it might secure widespread allegiance, could not be

154

said to embody nationhood. Monarch, Lords, Commons and the Church of England, while 'expressive of ancient cohesion', played no active part in the articulation of a new patriotism (Grainger 1986, p. 64). Given the indefiniteness of the political entity, cultural images of nationhood, cultural narratives, became increasingly important: a dictionary that would capture the 'genius' of the language; a workable definition of Standard English (Crowley 1989); the establishment of a canon of English literature (Baldick 1983; Doyle 1989; Collini 1991, pp. 354–68); the invention of 'rural England' (Howkins 1986).

The political synecdoche which, at the turn of the century, substituted England for Britain and Englishness for Britishness has recently been the subject of considerable debate (e.g. Colls and Dodd 1986; Bhabha 1990). This emphatic reassertion of an original and essential Englishness has been blamed for a whole range of evils, from the decline of the entrepreneurial spirit to the rise of literary criticism. I shall restrict myself here to two contrasting exponents: Kipling, who integrated his own 'discovery' of England into the regenerationist programme which was the subject of Chapter 10; and Ford Madox Hueffer, who, like Henry Ryecroft, wanted an England without programmes, an England *against* programmes.

KIPLING'S ENGLAND

Kipling described *Rewards and Fairies* (1910) as a 'balance' to, as well as a 'seal' upon, some aspects of his ' "Imperialistic" output' (1987g, p. 145). To us, it probably seems more like a withdrawal than a completion: proof that the late Victorian militant had finally given way to an Edwardian pastoralist (Batchelor 1982, pp. 8–17). But Kipling didn't go *that* quietly. He planted 'allegories and allusions' in *Rewards and Fairies*, coded affirmations of faith (1987g, p. 209). The Tory imperialist George Wyndham regarded the Puck stories as a 'masonic grip of secret fraternity' (1913, II, p. 201). Kipling's Edwardian writing grafts a new concern with the 'subsoil of things known' on to the old concern with empire: sometimes in ways so subtle that the subtlety becomes an end in itself.

In 1902, the year Kipling settled at Bateman's, in Sussex, his friend Rider Haggard undertook a study of 'rural England'. Haggard attributed the humiliations of the Boer War to the pitting of 'town-bred bodies and intelligences' against 'country-bred bodies and intelligences'. He thought that urban life was destroying the race, and that the only hope of recovery lay in 'the re-creation of a yeoman class, rooted in the soil and supported by the soil' (Haggard 1902, II, pp. 568, 575). The writer could best assist in that project not by making new territories conceivable, as Haggard and Kipling had done in the 1880s and 1890s, but by exposing the historical depth of old ones.

In *She* (1887) and *Kim* (1901), the frontier of empire is a space so vast, so abstract, that it permits encounters with timelessness. Where nothing can be certified, anything is possible. After *Kim*, Kipling confined himself to the here and now, the certifiable; even his ghosts have a local habitation and a name (' "They" ', 'The House Surgeon', 'The Wish House'). The creative pressure of the later writing is not at all expansive. It derives instead from an effort to ascertain the timeless – recurrent virtues and powers – within the limits of the narrowest of spaces: a Sussex valley, a spinster's or a scholar's mind.

The virtues and powers to be ascertained were moral (love, imaginative daring, the curative power of art), but also national, or racial. The immense scope of the latter can be glimpsed in the vision of a racially homogeneous Anglo-Saxon empire which united Kipling, Haggard, Roosevelt and Wister. In his auto-biography Kipling described how Roosevelt would come to his hotel in Washington and 'thank God in a loud voice that he had not one drop of British blood in him'. When the two men repaired to the Smithsonian, and Kipling accused the New England settlers of genocide, Roosevelt 'made the glass cases of Indian relics shake with his rebuttals' (Kipling 1987g, pp. 105–6). This was at a time, in 1895, when the two countries were momentarily on the brink of war. But the vision of race, of a recurrent Anglo-Saxondom, prevailed. 'There are two men left living in the world with whom I am in supreme sympathy,' Haggard noted in May 1918, 'Theodore Roosevelt and Rudyard Kipling' (Haggard and Kipling 1963, p. 99).

Roosevelt once told the diplomat Cecil Spring Rice that the proof of Britain's superiority to Russia was Kipling's superiority to Tolstoy; the author of 'Recessional' and the Mulvaney stories was obviously less decadent than the author of the *Kreutzer Sonata* (Roosevelt 1951, II, pp. 1052–3). When Owen Wister, a friend from Harvard days, began to publish stories about the frontier,

Roosevelt hailed him as an American Kipling (Wister 1930, p. 37). On 5 April 1895 he invited Wister and the artist Frederic Remington to dinner in Washington, to meet Kipling. As the three men travelled north the next day, they discussed a story Wister was writing about lawlessness in Arizona. Kipling, who was soon to publish *The Second Jungle Book*, with its vivid portrayal of the operations of the Law, no doubt had plenty to say on the subject (Remington and Wister 1972, pp. 117–18).

My point is that Kipling's England existed in the tension between a Sussex valley discovered one day in 1902, and an eternal recurrence of virtues and powers which knew no restriction of time or place. So we must look in the writing for the small-scale effects which clarify, and occasionally unsettle, a large-scale meaning.

DIALECT

In his Edwardian stories, Kipling aimed at renewals of idiom rather than plot structure. For the continuity of language had always been regarded as crucial to the continuity of 'national being': 1362, when English replaced Norman French in the law courts and at the opening of Parliament, marked a significant moment in the emergence of nationhood; 1835, when English became the language of education in India, marked a reinforcement of empire. By the end of the century, however, some observers had begun to wonder whether the language itself was degenerating, along with everything else. In their eyes, the discourse of the new mass-circulation dailies represented a loss of Anglo-Saxon vigour and purity. One commentator considered this 'white peril' a greater menace than the 'yellow peril' of the Asiatic hordes (Trevelyan 1901, p. 501; Lee 1976).

In his massive epic, *The Dawn in Britain* (1906), Charles Doughty declared that every patriot should keep 'reverently clean and bright' the language which 'lies at the root of his mental life', 'putting away all impotent and disloyal vility of speech, which is no uncertain token of a people's decadence' (1906, VI, p. 243). William Barnes, Gerard Manley Hopkins and Ezra Pound were among the writers who took an interest in Anglo-Saxon.

Barnes thought that English derived its vitality from its Teutonic origins, and that the introduction of Latin or French words had only served to weaken it. The purest English was now spoken by those furthest from the international centres, especially the Wessex 'landfolk'. He meant, he said, to uphold 'our own strong old Anglo-Saxon speech' (1878, p. iii). Wessex dialect was not a 'corruption of the written English', but 'a separate offspring from the Anglo-Saxon tongue', 'purer, and in some cases richer, than the dialect which is chosen as the national speech': a statement quoted with approval by the most prominent linguist of the day, Max Muller, in his *Lectures on the Science of Language* (1861, p. 49). According to Muller's theory of dialectal 'regeneration', literary language, the language of the cities, decays as it develops away from experience, and must be reinvigorated by input from the regional frontiers, where the forms of speech still touch the forms of experience.

The use of dialect in fiction no longer seemed an irritating eccentricity. Hardy insisted that Hermann Lea's guidebook should identify the Wessex of the novels not with Dorset, but with 'the Wessex of history': the original Anglo-Saxon kingdom. The speech recorded in them, Lea said, was 'the outcome of the Anglo-Saxon language' rather than a mere dialect (Lea 1977, pp. xvii, xx). This renewal of language was seen as a source of ideological and aesthetic unity (Cox 1970, pp. 343, 349–51, 393–4, 411–19).

Dialect authenticates the speech of Kipling's characters, as it does that of Hardy's; more significantly, it identifies a narrative voice. In *Puck of Pook's Hill* (1906) and *Rewards and Fairies* (1910), this voice establishes imaginative continuity between the world inhabited by the children and the dream-world conjured by Puck, and ideological continuity between the English present and the English past. Dialect words tend to occur at moments of transition, when the reader is being prepared for a change of scene, a move either into fantasy or back out again. In aesthetic terms, their unfamiliarity anticipates or recalls the dream-world. In ideological terms, they seem at once more vigorous and more ancient than the language of cities.

'Simple Simon', in *Rewards and Fairies*, establishes a continuity between the landfolk of present and past: between the carter Cattiwow and the shipbuilder Simon Cheyneys, a friend of Francis Drake. Both know how to handle men and materials. Dan and Una intercept the carter and his team of horses on the way to extract a log from the mud at Rabbit Shaw. 'Cattiwow never let them ride the big beam that makes the body of the timber-tug, but they hung on behind while their teeth thuttered' (1987e, p. 228). 'Thuttered' has the vividness of a word formed to imitate what it represents – and it derives from Old English. 'At the top of Rabbit Shaw half-a-dozen men and a team of horses stood round a forty-foot oak log in a muddy hollow. The ground about was poached and stoached with sliding hoof-marks, and a wave of dirt was driven up in front of the butt' (p. 228). 'Poach' and 'stoach' were both dialect words, one in general use, the other restricted to Kent, Surrey, Sussex and Hampshire. Here, they set the scene for the appearance of Puck and Simon Cheyneys. They trap the eternally recurrent in the here and now. Hopkins said that Barnes's use of dialect narrowed his 'field' but heightened his 'effects' (1935, p. 87). We might say the same of Kipling's Sussex stories.

QUOTATIONS FROM AN UNKNOWN LANGUAGE

One product of empire was enigma. In *Allan Quatermain*, Haggard's adventurers visit a buried city, where they unearth a couple of stone doorways, which are unfortunately too heavy to loot. For them, the significance of the ruins lies not in their picturesque disposition, as it might have done for earlier travellers, but in their mystery. The fragments of carved stone are enigmatic signs which stimulate thoughts about the rise and fall of empires (Haggard 1951, p. 432).

Africa's most impressive ruins lay at Zimbabwe, in South Mashonaland. 'It is the loneliness of the landscape in which they stand,' wrote James Bryce, 'and still more the complete darkness which surrounds their origin, their object, and their history, that gives them their unique interest' (1899, p. 82). Dispel the mystery, and the interest – the provocation to thoughts of empire – dies. A little archaeology enhanced the frontier; too much archaeology would close it for ever (Stein 1909, p. 22).

England, of course, was well supplied with monuments and ruins. The National Trust was set up in 1895 to safeguard those 'records written in brick and stone, in the presence of which, more movingly than anywhere else, a people recalls the dim centuries of its past' (Anon. 1911, p. 165). Forget about Zimbabwe. There was plenty of enigma just up the road (Austin 1902, pp. 23, 163, 168–9; Newbolt 1906; Wyndham 1913, II, pp. 477, 490). Indeed, the road itself often provided the enigma (Kipling 1987e, pp. 106, 123; Belloc 1904).

Just up the road usually meant the southern counties. Hardy, Haggard and W. H. Hudson were all to be found pondering on the mysterious past encoded by Stonehenge (Hardy 1967, p. 200; Haggard 1902, I, p. 8; Hudson 1908, p. 67). In *The Longest Journey*, the sight of the Cadbury Rings stimulates patriotic, though not imperial, sentiment (Forster 1960, pp. 131–2). Several years (and a world war) later, a visit to Silbury Hill and Stonehenge was still enough to revitalize the weak and indolent hero of H. G. Wells's *The Secret Places of the Heart* (1922, p. 127). For Hudson, the Wiltshire Downs proved as regenerative a frontier as the plains of Patagonia. This time it was not natural or native enigma which sharpened his faculties, but 'chance hieroglyphs' scored on the hills, 'the signs and memorials of a past life' (1910, p. 115). The habit of mind which had mythologized the South American frontier proved more than adequate to the south of England.

'There stood an abbey,' wrote Hudson's friend Edward Thomas, in similar mood, 'now speaking only through a curve added to the undulations of the land.... A dolmen rises out of the wheat in one field, like a quotation from an unknown language in the fair page of a book.' The traces lead him to a disused road: 'worn to the depth of some feet below the surrounding fields by the feet of adventurers, lovers, exiles, plain endurers of life, its end is to become a groove full of hazels and birds, the innermost kernel of the land, because nobody owns it and nobody uses it' (Thomas 1982, p. 114). This innermost kernel is a purely symbolic centre, without content or function. 'Puck's Song' commands us to observe these chance hieroglyphs, these quotations from an unknown language: traces of mound and ditch, of the boundaries of a city. 'And so was England born!' (1987d, pp. 41–2).

Enigma spoke of decline, of redundancy. Musing on the encroachment of 'scientific industrialism', Henry Ryecroft complains that the older, truer England of the southern counties now 'signifies little save to the antiquary, the poet, the painter' (Gissing 1987, p. 157). The respecters of redundancy were themselves becoming redundant. Even Kipling, with his vision of Anglo-Saxon hegemony, knew that an understanding of how England was born could be made accessible only to children, only in the occluded space of a Sussex valley, and even then only by magic.

In Kipling's 'An Habitation Enforced', George Chapin, an American businessman recovering from a heart attack, buys an abandoned manor house in Sussex. His wife, Sophie, discovers that her ancestors lived in this part of the country. 'Her folk come out of the ground here,' one of the locals remarks, 'neither Chalk nor Forest, but Wildishers' (1971, I, p. 142). According to W. D. Parish's *Dictionary of the Sussex Dialect* (1875), the Weald of Sussex 'is always spoken of as The Wild by the people who live in the Downs, who by the same rule call the inhabitants of the Wealden district "the wild people"'. The Chapins – unlike one of their neighbours, a vulgar Brazilian parvenu – are at home in the south of England. Their return to origins establishes the continuity and regenerative power of the Anglo-Saxon race, and is sealed by the birth of a son.

Being American, the Chapins can see the funny side of the vigorous landfolk. Their status as outsiders exposes the fragility, the obsessiveness, of their investment in the Heart of England. Like a James heroine encountering the codes of European society, Sophie learns to adjust to a pathologically secretive world. She 'gets back' at the English by generating a secret of her own (her ancestry). But an identity founded on retaliatory secretiveness is not a very secure one. For all the talk of land and landfolk, the Chapins inhabit a hieroglyph rather than an aboriginal *patria*. Commercial and political England bypasses their remote estate, their 'hidden kingdom', as it had Edward Thomas's innermost kernel. This kingdom is the grown-up equivalent of the secret world where Puck appears to Dan and Una.

It is this awareness of redundancy which sharpens the threat implicit in the title of the story – from Thomas Tusser's sixteenth-century manual of husbandry (Tusser 1878, p. 27) – and in its ending. The Chapins' return to origins is a return to symbolism, a withdrawal from the influential and effective life they have led. It will confine them to their habitation, their redundancy, for ever. In the final scene, George wants to build a bridge out of larch, but is treated to a homily on the enduring qualities of oak, on the ascertained virtues and powers of the English people. He gives in. ' "Make it oak then. We can't get out of it" ' (p. 152). So subtle are the means of ascertaining those virtues and powers that they have become an end in themselves: an enriching but ultimately fruitless pastime.

Giving in because he can't get out is also the fate of Lawrence's most undilutedly English protagonist, 'perfect in his race', the hero of 'England, My England' (first published 1915, revised 1922). The effect of the revisions Lawrence made to the story is to align the hero more closely with the occluded, redundant England of Gissing, Hudson, Thomas and Kipling. In the first version, he is called Evelyn, in the second Egbert (Egbert was the West Saxon king under whom 'the whole English race in Britain was for the first time knit together under a single ruler ... England was made in fact if not as yet in name' (Green 1916, p. 44). The first version tells us little about the cottage he occupies with his wife, Winifred; the second locates it in Hampshire, and identifies it with 'the old England of hamlets and yeomen' (Lawrence 1960, p. 8). 'The spear of modern invention had not passed through it, and it lay there secret, primitive, savage as when the Saxons first came. And Egbert and she were caught there, caught out of the world' (p. 11).

Lawrence also gave his hero Viking eyes and the agility of an English archer (pp. 7–8). Indeed, the density of the references suggest that he was not simply alluding to, but parodying, contemporary versions of Englishness. An inveterate amateur, Egbert cannot commit himself to anything. His daughter is crippled as a result of his carelessness, and his wife drifts away from him. A congested, repetitive story, 'England, My England' is notable chiefly for the rather overbearing assurance of the narrator, who is keen to let us know at every opportunity that he has seen through the miserable Egbert. Its first and second versions bracket the writing and publication of *Women in Love*, and we might think of it as Lawrence's warning to himself not to put too much faith in Rupert Birkin: a man who shows some signs, on occasion, of wanting to withdraw into a fantasy of Englishness, to renovate mill-houses and restore furniture ('My beloved country – it had something to express when it made that chair' – (Lawrence 1987, p. 355).

HUEFFER'S ENGLISHNESS

In March 1924, Ernest Hemingway, recently installed as assistant editor of the *Transatlantic Review*, favoured Ezra Pound with his opinion of the editor, Ford Madox Ford. Ford, he admitted, could 'explain stuff' – but 'in private life he is so goddam involved in being the dregs of an English country gentleman that you get no good out of him' (Hemingway 1981, p. 113). Pound thought that Ford's impersonations contradicted his salutary emphasis on precision of language (Pound 1983, p. 59). To these young Americans intent on 'making it new', Ford's Englishness was at best a mannerism, at worst a betrayal of aesthetic principles.

Ford's Englishness had begun when he was German Hueffer, not English Ford. It was only in 1915 that he dropped his middle name, Hermann, and only in 1919 that he changed Hueffer to Ford. His Anglicization was a strenuous and not entirely consistent process. In the 1890s Hueffer adopted Toryism, medievalism and 'the simple life'. D. H. Lawrence remembered him posing as an agricultural expert; another version of the story has Hueffer insisting that cabbage was a profitable crop because the stalks provided canes for the British army (Nehls 1958, I, p. 410; Garnett 1954, p. 37).

But Hueffer tried to get out of English society, as well as in; and his foreignness was no less bogus than his Englishness. At one point, he thought he had succeeded in becoming a German citizen. In the preface to Violet Hunt's *The Desirable Alien* (1913) he referred to Germany as 'my beloved country' (Mizener 1972, p. 240). He could play the desirable alien, too. Douglas Goldring was so taken in by the latter performance that he made fun of Hueffer's devotion to cricket and the old school tie, while admiring uncritically his fraudulent references to an extensive continental education (Goldring 1943, p. 9). Hueffer never stopped performing. But the performance varied. To that extent we can credit it with a measure of control. I shall argue that, in the writing if not the life, it served as what he himself would have termed a 'critical attitude'.

Hueffer regarded the Boer War as the end of the kind of Englishness he himself embodied, 'a chasm separating the old world from the new' (Mizener 1972, p. 52). In *The Inheritors* (1901), he championed the old, with its respect for tradition and individuality, against the heartless collectivism of the new: Arthur Balfour's Toryism against Joseph Chamberlain's Social Imperialism. Invaders from the Fourth Dimension take over the world, transforming it into 'an immense machine' (Hueffer 1901, p. 206). As Robert Green has pointed out, the hero's impeccable Englishness represents a despairing protest against the inhumanity of the new political doctrines (Green 1981, pp. 18–19).

And yet, Green adds, there is 'a strange disjunction' between the apocalyptic tone, and the rather dull slide into dystopia which the novel actually describes; Hueffer's pessimism 'appears not to have engaged his full creative energies'. This disjunction seems to me less a failure of creative energies than a political and literary consequence of the way in which Hueffer defined his Englishness. That Englishness did, of course, express his opposition to the new politics. But it was also a criticism of apocalyptic thinking of any kind, a criticism which he extended and refined over the next fifteen years, both in his novels and in the three books he wrote about England and Englishness: *The Soul of London* (1905), *The Heart of the Country* (1906) and *The Spirit of the People* (1907).

In *The Soul of London*, Hueffer examined the 'images' which social theory offered as axioms. In one image, London is about to be overwhelmed by 'Neurasthenia' and 'Decay'; in another, it will, 'humanity being redeemable', become 'a gigantic, bright, sanitary and sane congeries of little white houses that can be folded up and carried off in the night' (Hueffer 1905, p. 168). Roughly speaking, the first fiction is die-hard Tory, the second Fabian or social imperialist. Hueffer's objection to both was that they employed damagingly abstract models of social change. He was equally sceptical about attempts to identify the Heart of England, and always put 'the country' in inverted commas: it was a fantasy, an abstract model, an invention of people who lived in cities, not a source of essential English virtues.

In *The Spirit of the People*, the wittiest and most incisive of the three books, he developed his own view of English virtues. The English, he said, would never modernize themselves, because they had always prospered by averting rather than fomenting crises. Their most significant achievement had been 'the evolution of a rule of thumb system by which men may live together in large masses' (1907, p. 126). They were the least apocalyptic people on earth: 'this ferocious lack of imagination has made, in the English race, for an almost imaginative lack of ferocity' (p. 28). The English temperament prescribed patience and long-suffering, a self-suppression at once admirable and terrible. Hueffer illustrated this temperament with two anecdotes. One, the germ of *The Good Soldier* (1915), concerns an English country gentleman who falls in love with his young ward, but heroically suppresses his feelings. The other concerns a father awaiting the return of his son, who has been horribly crippled in the Boer War (1907, pp. 148–51).

Such was the temperament that Hueffer imagined himself to possess, and that he attributed to his most complex protagonist, the immensely patient and longsuffering Christopher Tietjens, in *Parade's End* (1924–8). (By that time the temperament had been subjected to a much cruder assault in Michael Arlen's *The Green Hat*, a bestseller which combined the elegiac tone of *The Good Soldier* with plenty of explicit sex – Arlen 1924, pp. 80–1, 309, 320). Hueffer's desire to understand the alchemy which combines lack of imagination and lack of ferocity into Englishness also explains the pairing of a stupid Englishman with a lazy Englishman in *A Call* (1910), *Mr Fleight* (1913) and *The Good Soldier* (1915): Dudley Leicester and Robert Grimshaw, Mr Fleight and Mr Blood, Ashburnham and Dowell (who is, of course, not an Englishman, but a Europeanized American).

Hueffer's leisurely narratives, fictional or non-fictional, are a protest against apocalypse. A world described in such fashion is not likely to come to a sudden and bloody end. Dowell, the narrator of *The Good Soldier*, admits that he has told his story in 'a very rambling way'. His world *has* come to a sudden end, with the disclosure of his wife's adultery. But he responds by slowing down rather than speeding up: 'when one discusses an affair – a long, sad affair – one goes back, one goes forward' (Hueffer 1972, p. 167). Going back and forwards in memory across the rupture in his life – the event which has separated old self from new, innocence from experience – is Dowell's way of restoring continuity, and thus identity. Hueffer once said that the kind of 'good leisurely novel' written by the Victorians had come close to being a 'philosophic rendering' of the English mind (Hunt and Hunt 1912, p. ix). His own novels are as leisurely as their compact form will allow; the leisureliness makes a point.

At the beginning of *Mr Fleight*, Mr Blood, the lazy Englishman, sits at the window of his club on Derby Day, calculating the proportion of mechanical to horse-drawn vehicles on the Embankment. At the end of the novel he sits at the same window on Christmas Day, doing the same thing. In between, he has masterminded the successful election campaign and engagement of the stupid Englishman, Mr Fleight. His promotion of Mr

Fleight does not redeem him, or revitalize him – or Mr Fleight; they are, respectively, as lazy and as stupid at the end of the novel as they were at the beginning.

Mr Blood is a monster, an anachronism whose violence (he is rumoured to have strangled his groom) throws into doubt his claims to represent the virtues of the landed gentry. His aversion to modern politics is expressed in apocalyptic terms (Hueffer 1913, p. 194). Mr Fleight is an equally unlikely representative of Englishness. The son of a Jewish soap-manufacturer, he survives in the course of the campaign a formidable amount of racial violence and abuse, some of it from Mr Blood himself. And yet, like his mentor and occasional tormentor, he is fundamentally decent. Hueffer's achievement was to incorporate a monster and an alien into his representation of Englishness, without compromising it or them.

At the end of the novel, a plan to modernize milk production provokes from Mr Blood a surly but by no means predictable testament:

> 'Well, that's all right,' Mr Macpherson said amiably; 'that's the spirit of the time.'
>
> 'So it is,' Mr Blood answered. 'I've got nothing against it, except I don't like being here on Christmas Day instead of Derby Day. It's a personal deterioration in myself. I don't like it. I foresee that I, too, shall die a British peer.'
>
> 'I don't see how you get at that,' Mr Macpherson said. But Mr Blood only nodded his head with an expression of the deepest gloom.
>
> (p. 306)

That ironic measuring of 'personal deterioration' establishes a critical attitude impervious both to sentimentality and to paranoia. Hueffer subsequently adopted the persona of Mr Blood in some of his polemical writings, much to Pound's disgust. His allegiance, he made clear, was to the old world, not the new. Yet he had always stated that allegiance in such a way as to distinguish it from any infatuation with crisis. Pound and Hemingway must be counted among those who couldn't see how he got at that.

11

SPIES

Towards the end of John Buchan's *The Thirty-Nine Steps* (1915), Richard Hannay, who has been chased up and down the length of the land by ruthless German agents and obdurate British detectives, arrives in leafy Berkshire, 'a land of lush water-meadows and slow reedy streams' (Buchan 1947, p. 94), to meet an important contact. This landscape, in the Heart of England, is a part, at least, of what he is fighting for. But it is no 'innermost kernel', no occluded centre. For his contact is Sir Walter Bullivant, Permanent Secretary at the Foreign Office. Buchan's Heart of England, unlike Kipling's, or Thomas's, or Lawrence's, is also the heart of the political system.

It is no 'idle' Englishness which is at stake in the spy story, no mending of chairs or speculation about dialect words, but a heavy-duty patriotism more preoccupied with empire than with leafy Berkshire. The genre established itself as a market leader in Britain at the turn of the century, gradually displacing the imperial adventure story, as the focus of anxiety shifted from frontier wars to Great Power rivalry. It offers a perfect opportunity to examine the interconnections of ideological and narrative renewal.

REAL INTELLIGENCE / CARICATURE INTELLIGENCE

In Chapter 4 of *Greenmantle* (1916), Richard Hannay encounters his implacable adversary, the ruthless Colonel Stumm. 'Here was the German of caricature, the real German, the fellow we were up against. He was as hideous as a hippopotamus, but effective' (Buchan 1956a, p. 50). In popular fiction, the real invariably *is* the caricature. Popular fiction is peopled by caricatures; but those caricatures can be mistaken for real because the anxieties they crystallize are real anxieties. Colonel Stumm, with his pyramidal head and suspiciously effeminate habits, is a caricature – but one which Buchan's readers had, in 1916, good cause to fear.

The years between 1900 and 1914 saw the establishment, not at all coincidentally, of the British spy novel and the British secret service. Before 1907 espionage was largely passive, based on amateur agents and casual informants. In that year the appointment of Lieutenant-Colonel James Edmonds as head of M05, the secret services section of the directorate of military operations, marked a change of emphasis. By the end of 1910 a more active and professional system was in place: a secret services bureau with a Foreign Section and a Home Section (subsequently known as MI6 and MI5). The new professionalism, however, depended very much on old assumptions, as Nicholas Hiley has shown (1983, 1985; see also French 1978, Andrew 1985).

The bureau assumed, erroneously, that Germany was preparing to invade Britain, assisted by an army of spies and saboteurs. Any information that appeared to confirm this assumption was regarded as true. In 1912 the uncovering of a modest network of German agents only convinced the director of the Home Section that he had hitherto under- rather than overestimated their presence: those agents as yet undiscovered must of course be 'the cleverest and most adroit' – the ones entrusted with sabotage after the outbreak of war (Hiley 1985, p. 855). The British secret service, like the British spy novel, invested in fantasy.

Indeed, they invested in the same fantasy. When Edmonds took over at M05, the files contained a few papers relating to the Boer War, and some relating to France and Russia, but nothing about the new opponent, Germany. He badly needed evidence to confirm his suspicions about Germany, which were not shared by the Secretary of State for War, Richard Haldane. Fortunately, literature came to his aid. In 1909 the sensational novelist William Le Queux published *Spies for the Kaiser. Plotting the Downfall of England*, in which two lawyers expose 'the vast army of German spies spread over our smiling land of England'. His aim was to kindle in his readers a conviction that German agents were hard at work everywhere, reconnoitring beaches and preparing acts of sabotage. When the novel was serialized in the *Weekly News*, the paper appointed a spy editor, and ran the headlines 'FOREIGN SPIES IN BRITAIN. / £10 Given For Information. / Have You Seen a Spy?' Le Queux received a large number of letters which denounced perfectly innocent people for swearing in German or sporting a wig. He passed them on to Edmonds, who used them to persuade the Committee of Imperial Defence to set up a new secret services bureau. As late as July 1908, Haldane had remained sceptical about the extent of German espionage. Edmonds's new 'evidence', nearly all of it fantasy rather than fact, seems to have changed his mind (Hiley 1985, pp. 843–4). In Edwardian Britain, real intelligence *was* caricature intelligence.

If literature coloured politics, politics also coloured literature. Edwardian spy novels were, as David Stafford has pointed out, unashamedly didactic: a political response to the erosion of Britain's status and prestige in a period marked by relative economic decline, armaments races and crisis diplomacy. Distinguished by his Englishness from unreliable foreigners, and by his gentlemanliness from working-class agitators and delinquents, the secret agent became a 'symbol of stability' in a changing world (Stafford 1981).

However, there was, as I have shown in previous chapters, a widespread suspicion that the English gentleman was no longer all that he might be, an anxiety that the rot which had already destroyed the working-classes might also be reaching the upper and middle classes. The suspicion produced, in imperialist circles, an emphasis not on stability in a world of flux, but on the necessary flux which, however painful, would create a more stable world. Popular fiction echoed this propaganda by creating heroes who must endure flux in order to achieve a properly founded stability. The adventures of the secret agent do not simply confirm what he already is: they regenerate him, physically, morally and, most important of all, politically. I shall argue that spy novels are at their most effective, both in literary and in ideological terms, when they explore the instability of their protagonists.

Historians of the genre (Merry 1977; Atkins 1984; Denning 1987; Cawelti and Rosenberg 1987) have been reluctant to discuss it in relation to other contemporary genres. We must start, I believe, with its immediate predecessor, the terrorist novel of the 1890s.

TERRORISTS

Bestselling literature often sells because it addresses the anxieties aroused by real events. The sensation novels of the 1860s fed off scandals involving bigamy and the forcible incarceration of the sane in lunatic asylums. The 1880s provided real events in the shape of terrorism. The British public felt most immediately threatened by the Fenian bombing campaign of 1884–5; but it would also have been aware of the assassination of Tsar Alexander II on 13 March 1880, and of the attempt to blow up Kaiser Wilhelm I on 28 September 1883. Terrorism was international in scope; it reminded people that Britain did not in fact enjoy a splendid isolation, but belonged to a large and threatening world. On 24 November 1883, when 'infernal machines' intended for the German embassy were found in a London lodging-house, *The Times* remarked that Europe was bound together by a network of railways and telegraph lines, and that a blow struck at any part would be felt throughout the whole.

The appeal of the new scandal lay in its production of enigma: 'the sense,' as Hyacinth Robinson puts it in James's *The Princess Casamassima* (1886), 'vividly kindled and never quenched, that the forces secretly arrayed against the present social order were pervasive and universal' (1907–9, VI, p. 275). Dynamiters were even more secretive than bigamists. They made a point, a ceremony – paradoxically, a display – of secrecy. Initiation into the secret societies of terror was attended by the most bloodcurdling oaths and pledges. Once inside the mystery, you could never get out, as Robinson discovers. The dynamiter did not conceal a secret, like the bigamist; he or she *became* a secret. To stop being that secret was to stop being; traitors met a sudden and inevitable death.

Writers and publishers were quick to exploit the commercial possibilities of secrets kept for ever. The publishers of Edgar Wallace's *Four Just Men* (1905) offered substantial prizes to the readers who could explain most convincingly how the terrorists had murdered a British cabinet minister – something the novel itself had not disclosed. Enigma could be exploited for ideological as well as commercial ends. In Robert Cromie's *The Crack of Doom* (1895), Herbert Brande, a crazed anarcho-scientist, invents a kind of atom bomb. He means to detonate two bombs simultaneously, in Labrador and the South Seas. The hero sabotages one expedition; the other 'has not returned, nor has it ever been definitely traced'. The danger was not yet over.

Terrorism politicized mystery and mystified politics. People who married bigamously, or committed their best friends to asylums, usually had a pefectly intelligible, if criminal, motive. Dynamiters did not. Their grievances and aspirations related to archaic (foreign) regimes. Driven by obscure personal insults and injuries, they killed, as often as not, for revenge. Terror was political, but also foreign and private.

Sensation novelists went to great lengths to preserve these qualities. They did not write about Fenians, whose political motive was not at all hard to understand (though see Kernahan 1897). They wrote about obscurely injured foreigners, and notably about foreign women, whose politics were always likely to remain inscrutable. The heroine of Joseph Hatton's *By Order of the Czar* (1890), Anna Klosstock, starts life in a Jewish village in Russia. She is raped by the governor of the district, General Petronovitch, and then brutally flogged. She becomes a nihilist, marries a rich sympathizer, and inherits his wealth. Moving now in the highest society, she seduces and murders Petronovitch. When Philip Forsyth, a young English painter who has fallen in love with her, joins the secret society, she finally reveals her past and demonstrates her right to vengeance. Asked to provide a motive, she answers with her body.

> As she spoke she tore open her dress, exhibiting a lovely white arm and part of a beautiful bust, turning at the same time with swift rapidity to exhibit her right shoulder and her neck, no further than is considered correct by ladies of fashion at balls and in the opera stalls, but sufficient to thrill iron men who had themselves been witnesses of the worst of Russian tortures. Red and blue, deep ridges and welts crossed and recrossed each other, with intervals of angry patches of red, and weird daubs of grey that blurred and blotted out all remains and tokens of the beautiful form with which nature had endowed one of its loveliest creatures.
>
> (Hatton 1890, p. 357)

Anna's disfigured, denaturalized body is her politics; an anti-politics, rather, for she would repay this violation of nature by violating (political) culture. Her gesture fails because it is uninterpretable. It disappears into the vast enigma out of which it arose. Returning to Russia, Anna and her colleagues are arrested and sent into exile.

Hatton meant his novel to have a political impact. But his most potent symbol, Anna's back, is a hieroglyph rather than a manifesto; the injury condensed in its ruin will never enter fully into political process. Hatton doesn't really know what to do with it. His hero, Philip Forsyth, faints at the sight. Instead of accompanying Anna into exile, he returns to London and a miserably diminished existence, though his painting of a group of exiles, including Anna, does win the Royal Academy's Gold Medal. Hatton, in short, can incorporate Anna's face into his narrative, by way of the painting, but not her back, her enigmatic injury.

The heroine of L. T. Meade's *The Siren* (1898) has also been converted to nihilism by a brutal public flogging; her mission is to secure her English father's fortune, then assassinate him and the Tsar with bouquets of poisoned roses. She is immensely desirable, and wreaks havoc among the respectable English, both men and women, but tormented by the memory of the flogging, the politics (or anti-politics) inscribed on her body. She learns to love her English father, and longs to exchange Russian magnetism for English respectability. But the memory, the secret inscription, keeps her loyal to the cause; there can be no compromise between a daughter's love for her father and a terrorist's eroticized dedication to the Russian people. She commits suicide.

Both novels aspire to political commentary, but their fascination with women's bodies deflects them into sado-masochism. Other writers were not so easily deflected. In *Angel of the Revolution* (1893), George Griffith enlisted his hero, Richard Arnold, an engineer whose design for an airship has been rejected by the British government, into the Brotherhood, an international secret society. The Brotherhood is led by Natas, a Russian Jew who has suffered terribly at the hands of the Tsarist police. Its council chamber contains vivid paintings of scenes of exile and torture. Colston, the Englishman who recruits Arnold, has himself been flogged for coming to the aid of a defenceless woman: ' "That is the sign-manual of Russian tyranny – the mark of the knout!" '

(Griffith 1893, p. 14). Arnold builds airships for the Brotherhood, which uses them to foment and regulate a world war between Britain, Germany and Austria, on one hand, and France, Russia and Italy, on the other. Although in theory neutral, the Brotherhood brings America into the war on the side of Britain and Germany, and thus ensures their triumph. Arnold marries Natas's daughter (her back seems to have escaped damage).

Without airships, Britain and Germany would have been defeated; without the Brotherhood, there would have been no airships. Griffith uses terrorism's violation of the British way of doing things to suggest that the British way is outmoded, and that Britain will not survive into the twentieth century (the novel is set in 1904) unless it adopts an imperial outlook and a new and much harsher political creed (p. 307): the last battle the Anglo-Saxon Federation wins is against Muslim hordes pouring out of the East. Arnold's political awakening is as crucial a part of his adventure, and of our enjoyment of his adventure, as the expeditions and battles. Hatton and Meade had broached the subject of politics, but didn't really know what to do with it. Griffith incorporated it fully into his narrative.

SPIES

The agenda pursued by Griffith – the awakening of a complacent ruling class – had been set by George Chesney's *The Battle of Dorking* (1871), the first invasion-story (Clarke 1966). The identity of the invader varied according to political circumstances. The visit of the Russian fleet to Toulon in 1893 inspired the threatening Franco-Russian alliances of *Angel of the Revolution* and William Le Queux's *The Great War in England in 1897* (1894), which went through sixteen editions after it had been endorsed by Lord Roberts, Britain's most famous military strategist. Roberts and Le Queux also collaborated on *The Invasion of 1910* (1906). This time it's the Germans, now perceived as the greater threat (Kennedy 1980), who impale English babies on their bayonets. The story was serialized in the *Daily Mail*, and the invaders were ingeniously routed through towns where the paper sold particularly well.

The problem with Chesney's formula was that it was altogether *too* cautionary. The British always lost. What the agenda demanded was a political regeneration which would *avert* military defeat. Fortunately, however, invasion had its acknowledged preliminaries. The theorists agreed that its success would depend on secret preparations (Gooch 1981, ch. 1). There would be no invasion, in short, without spies.

In the early years of the century spy fever superseded terrorist fever (French 1978). 'How little the public knows,' Le Queux complained, 'of the stealthy treacherous ways of modern diplomacy' (1901, p. 7). Fifteen years later, he was to claim that before the war German agents had 'ranked among the leaders of social and commercial life, and among the sweepings and outcasts of great communities' – some of them had even been 'on golfing terms with the rulers of Great Britain' (1916, pp. 106, 189).

In Headon Hill's *The Spies of the Wight* (1899), Philip Monckton, a journalist holidaying on the Isle of Wight, encounters an artillery officer, Arthur Doring, and a mysterious stranger, the bloated and wheelchair-bound Mr Campion. A missing cufflink reveals Doring's implication in a conspiracy to steal the plans of some new forts guarding Portsmouth. He has been enmeshed by Campion's daughter, whose androgynous beauty recalls that of the terrorist sirens. Campion himself is only pretending to be a fat cripple, and soon sprints nimbly away from his wheelchair; he is in fact the Baron von Holtzman, German master-spy. But there is, from the ideological point of view, a flaw in Hill's narrative. Monckton wants above all to secure a scoop for his paper. When he unmasks the spies, his editor congratulates him on a 'neat bit of up-to-date journalism' (Hill 1899, p. 279) – rather than a neat bit of up-to-date patriotism. Monckton's adventures, unlike Richard Arnold's, do not include a political awakening.

If the spy novel was to fulfil its ideological agenda, and thus supersede the terrorist novel and the invasion-story, it had to produce a different kind of hero, one changed in every way by his experiences. It found that hero in the amateur agent or accidental spy, the sleepy young Englishman whose complacency is shattered when he stumbles across some fiendish plot. In Erskine Childers's *The Riddle of the Sands* (1903), Carruthers, the bored and complacent narrator, joins his friend Davies for a spot of yachting and duck-shooting in the Baltic, and benefits immediately from the experience. Childers describes his gathering enjoyment in intricate detail because, although there is not yet

174

a storm or a Hun in sight, the real adventure – the regeneration of Carruthers – has begun. More importantly, Davies is a staunch patriot who believes that Germany is preparing for war, and that British complacency may well ensure defeat (1978, pp. 118–19). Government will continue to ignore the danger unless roused into action by 'civilian agitators' like himself (p. 119).

When they discover the identity of the treacherous Dollmann, Carruthers, the civil servant, wants to return to England and inform the Admiralty or Scotland Yard. Davies, the civilian agitator, believes that the authorities will do nothing, and persuades him that they must settle the matter themselves. Just as the 'peevish dandy' has been transformed into an outdoorsman, so the civil servant now joins the agitators. The narrative turns as much on the second as on the first of these transformations (an experience denied to the scoop-happy Philip Monckton).

The elision of politics and adventure distinguished the spy novel from the terrorist novel; the emphasis on enigma rather than battles distinguished it from the invasion-story. 'This ... is a narrative, not a criticism,' Le Queux insisted in *Secrets of the Foreign Office* (1903, p. 72), after launching a savage attack on British apathy and conceit. But in the spy thriller, the criticism *was* the narrative.

OPPENHEIM

The most prolific and successful, if by no means the most accomplished, exponents of the spy novel were William Le Queux and E. Phillips Oppenheim. They set the tone and reaped the rewards. Since David Stafford has already said much of what needs to be said about Le Queux (Stafford 1982), I shall concentrate here on Oppenheim.

The Mysterious Mr Sabin (1898) created his formula of intrigue in high and luxurious places. Sometimes described as the first spy novel, it in fact relies heavily on the potency of terrorism. Lord Deringham, a retired admiral, writes feverishly, day and night, in his study. He is generally considered crazy but harmless, until various criminal masterminds start to show an interest in his work, which turns out to include a detailed survey of Britain's coastal defences. Mr Sabin, a sinister cosmopolitan who walks with the aid of a jewelled stick, succeeds in stealing Deringham's papers. He will hand them over to the Germans in exchange for help with his plan to restore the French monarchy. He is stopped not by the British, who prove completely ineffectual, but by a secret society, to which he once belonged and which still exercises over him an authority greater even than that of the Kaiser. 'A war between Germany and England,' one character declares, 'is only a matter of time – of a few short years, perhaps even months' (Oppenheim 1898, p. 64). The German threat was just one element in an all-purpose brew of paranoia.

International secret societies continued to fascinate Oppenheim. But the alignments in his novels began to shift as his perception of the German threat sharpened, and with it his sense of the need for a political awakening. In 'An Accidental Spy', the opening chapter of *A Maker of History* (1905), Guy Stanton – 'just a good-looking, clean-minded, high-spirited young fellow, full of beans, and needing the bit every now and then' (p. 40) – stumbles across a secret meeting between the Kaiser and the Tsar in a forest on the German border. A page of secret treaty, which floats out of a window and lands close to his hiding place, reveals that they are coordinating an attack on Britain. Stanton, who can't speak the lingo, and is in any case too full of beans to be interested in politics, becomes the focus of deadly intrigue. The French get hold of him before the Germans, but won't admit it to anyone. Sir George Duncombe, a friend of a friend, who has fallen in love with a photograph of his sister, herself a captive by this time, eventually tracks him down. The fatal page persuades the French government to ally itself with Britain rather than Russia, and the new alliance proves strong enough to avert war.

The Anglo-French alliance of 1904 had enabled Oppenheim to produce a narrative based not on the intervention of a secret society, but on political awakening. What connects the protagonists now is not membership of an order or clan, but their status as amateurs. They are *all* 'accidental spies'. Stanton, the callow tourist, receives a political education. Sir George Duncombe, galvanized by the photograph, passes into 'the shadows of the complex life' (p. 251). Duncombe's assistant, a journalist, learns how to reconcile patriotism with the desire for a scoop. One of the French kidnappers, a 'drug-sodden degenerate' (p. 272), goes over to the enemy; but another, who has always posed as a 'decadent', turns out all right. The ruling classes on both sides of the Channel have awoken to their responsibilities. The French leader concludes that 'We amateurs have justified our existence' (p. 313).

In *The Secret* (1907), a British amateur justifies his own existence without any help from the French. J. Hardross Courage, man of leisure and accomplished cricketer, is implicated in yet another scheme to restore the French monarchy, this time backed innocently by some American millionaires whose wives want to become titled ladies, and less innocently by the Germans, who plan to invade Britain after the forts protecting London have been put out of action by a fifth column masquerading as the German Waiters' Union. Courage, who had previously found life 'a tame thing', becomes a new man. But the authorities refuse to believe him. So the 'civilian agitator' forms an alliance with the scaremongering press, the main platform during the pre-war years for those who felt that the politicians would continue to ignore their warnings (Morris 1984). He takes his story to the editor of the *Daily Oracle*, who decides to print it, even though his office is under siege by heavily armed German waiters.

Oppenheim stuck by his accidental spies (e.g. 1915). In his most elaborate thriller, *The Great Impersonation* (1920), Major-General Baron Leopold von Ragastein encounters in Africa an Englishman, Everard Dominey, whom domestic tragedy has reduced him to a drunken wreck. Noticing a distinct physical resemblance, Von Ragastein decides to kill Dominey and take his place in English society, in order to gather information about the mentality of the ruling classes. Dominey, however, is not so drunk that he fails to notice what's going on. Getting his retaliation in first, he disposes of his would-be attacker, and from then on impersonates Von Ragastein impersonating himself. This causes immense confusion to his English wife, Rosamund, with whom he won't sleep because he's pretending to be Von Ragastein, and to Von Ragastein's voluptuous Hungarian mistress, with whom he won't sleep because he's not Von Ragastein. However, the Germans think he's their man and, on the outbreak of war, entrust him with their invasion plans. He passes these on to the authorities, who have by this time learnt to respect amateurs.

The Great Impersonation embeds a spy novel in a domestic drama which might easily have been written by M. E. Braddon. Ten years before his encounter with Von Ragastein, Dominey had been attacked by Roger Unthank, a rival for Rosamund's hand, and had apparently killed him. Unthank, however, lives on, in a loathsome pestilential thicket at the bottom of their garden, emerging every night to terrorize Rosamund by hallooing outside her window. But the Everard Dominey who returns from Africa is a different man; he has assimilated the discipline and resolution of his Prussian opponent. He catches Unthank and razes the thicket to the ground, thus purging his marriage and his ancestral estate. It would seem that you have to become a Prussian in order to become an Englishman. In the spy novel, as in the adventure story, the hero's renewal, and ideally the reader's, is accomplished by a generic renewal. The expectations aroused by naturalist fiction or domestic melodrama are aroused again – and then confounded.

FRONTIERSMEN

The spy novel is a frontier tale transposed to the new arena of Great Power rivalry. Chapter 11 of *The Riddle of the Sands*, in which Davies and Carruthers begin their exploration of the Frisian coast, is entitled 'The Pathfinders'. Davies is a North Seas pathfinder, a nautical Natty Bumppo equipped with the intuition which is 'the last quality of the perfect guide or scout' (Childers 1978, p. 143). If Davies is Natty Bumppo, a cowboy, then Carruthers is a greenhorn 'Easterner', like the narrator of Owen Wister's *The Virginian* (1902).

On Christmas Eve 1904, Roger Pocock, a Davies-like 'civilian agitator', wrote to ten newspapers announcing the formation of a Legion of Frontiersmen. Pocock had led an adventurous life in the colonies and held firm views about degeneration (Pocock 1896). He believed that renewal could only come from outside the system, through the creation of a Kiplingesque 'Lost Legion' (Kipling 1940, p. 195). 'Many men were awake,' Pocock recalled in his autobiography, 'manning the outposts and the frontiers, whose training in war, in wild countries and at sea had made them vigilant' (1931, p. 23). His description of the recruitment of legionnaires recalls Roosevelt's description of the recruitment of Rough Riders for the war in Cuba (p. 32; Roosevelt 1926, XI, pp. 8–20). Like Roosevelt, he wanted to combine the strenuous life with imperialism.

But there was a quite specific focus to Pocock's patriotism: the

German threat. He added to the 'visible Legion' of frontiersmen a hidden corps of counter-intelligence experts, which included Erskine Childers and William Le Queux, and which specialized in unearthing invasion plans. Of the two invasion plans Pocock mentions, one derived from *The Riddle of the Sands*, while the other was written up as *The Invasion of 1910* (1931, pp. 150, 61–3). The Legion receives honourable mention in the latter. Other writers known to have been members were Rider Haggard, Edgar Wallace and Conan Doyle. The only political home they could find was among patriots who had renounced party politics.

Pocock was ousted from the Legion in 1909, but his departure did not lead to any change of emphasis. The Legion's official gazette, the *Frontiersman*, relaunched in 1910, continued to stress the German menace. The front cover provided a glimpse of the strenuous life in the shape of an advertisement for the Imperial School of Colonial Instruction at Shepperton-on-Thames, complete with pictures of lasso practice. Support was given to the Boy Scout movement, which by 1910 had successfully elided scouting and spying. The front cover of *Scouting for Boys* (1908) shows a scout observing from behind some rocks as an invasion party lands. In *My Adventures as a Spy* (1915), Baden-Powell celebrated spying as an extension of scouting by other means, and as the best possible form of regeneration. 'For anyone who is tired of life, the thrilling life of the spy should be the very finest recuperator!' (p. 45).

Richard Hannay certainly finds spying a fine recuperator. The opening chapter of *The Thirty-Nine Steps* finds him back in London, having made his 'pile' in South Africa, and thoroughly sick of its amusements and its complacency. His complaints recall the 'restlessness' and 'distaste' Buchan himself had felt on returning to England from South Africa, where he had held the responsible post of private secretary to Lord Milner, in 1903 (1940, pp. 126–8). Then Franklin P. Scudder blunders into his life. After Scudder's death, Hannay's first thought is to find the nearest frontier, where his 'veldcraft' might be of some use. Once out in the wild, he experiences, like Carruthers, a delicious physical awakening.

Buchan also gives his hero a literary awakening. Carruthers has a dip, Hannay has a hike across the heather, followed by 'The Adventure of the Literary Innkeeper'. The literary innkeeper wants to write like Kipling and Conrad, and it doesn't take him long to place Hannay's yarn. ' "By God!" he whispered, drawing

179

his breath in sharply. "It is all pure Rider Haggard and Conan Doyle."' The fact that the yarn is 'pure' romance – that it defies the conventions of domestic realism, and the comfortable view of the world they sustain – makes it all the more credible to the innkeeper. 'He was very young, but he was the man for my money' (1947, pp. 24, 39). The reader for Buchan's money will be the one who realizes that, in a complacent world, literary romance is political truth.

Hannay's second generic awakening is as much political as literary. It occurs during 'The Adventure of the Radical Candidate', when he deciphers Scudder's notebook. Scudder had originally told Hannay that an international anarchist conspiracy, backed by Jewish financiers, is fomenting revolution. In his paranoid fantasy 'the Jew' is 'the man who is ruling the world just now', and the Jew 'has his knife in the Empire of the Tzar, because his aunt was outraged and his father flogged in some one-horse location on the Volga' (p. 12). Hannay, we might think, has found himself in a terrorist novel. The notebook, however, tells a different tale, about a German plot to provoke war with Britain (p. 45). This is a spy novel. The knowledge Hannay has gained enables him to refute the Radical candidate's claim that the 'German menace' is a Tory invention, and provoke a further awakening. Once awoken, Sir Harry, the Radical candidate, directs him to Sir Walter Bullivant, Permanent Secretary at the Foreign Office. The accidental spy now has access to the heart of the political system.

But Buchan never forgets that Hannay is a frontiersman, and that frontiersmen are outsiders. The final scene of *The Thirty-Nine Steps*, where he finds the German spies embedded, like Headon Hill's, in a suburban villa, is not only a brilliant denouement, but also a poignant reminder of his status as an outsider, his hatred of bourgeois convention. The conventions momentarily destroy his self-belief. No wonder Roosevelt liked the book. If Carruthers is the most memorable of the 'Easterners' who go 'West' to regenerate themselves through counter-espionage, Hannay is the most memorable of the 'Westerners' who go 'East', but stay true to the frontier. He is nomadic, protean, occasionally violent, a symbol of the instability needed to revitalize a complacent, suburbanized society.

12

AWAKENINGS

Chapters 10 and 11 have dealt, respectively, with the subtle regenerations envisaged by Kipling and Hueffer and the unsubtle regenerations envisaged by Childers and Oppenheim. This distinction between highbrow and lowbrow fiction is harder to maintain when we turn to an increasingly popular genre: the romance of sexual 'awakening'.

A crucial term in definitions of highbrow (Modernist) fiction is parody: the *locus classicus* being the 'Nausicaa' section of *Ulysses*, which parodies sentimental Victorian fiction. Parody has suited the critical mood of the last twenty years because it proclaims 'intertextuality'. It illustrates the thesis that all writing is rewriting, and exemplifies the 'self-reflexivity' which has been said to characterize twentieth-century culture (Hutcheon 1985, p. 2).

Most commentators have insisted that Modernist parody does not create a hierarchy of discourses so much as an equivalence, an ambivalence (Barthes 1975, p. 9; Heath 1986, pp. 141–2; Hutcheon 1985, p. 6). Even so, it is the parodic text, in these accounts, which does the *work* of transformation, critique or inversion. The parodied text, whether highbrow or lowbrow, remains so much raw material. Thomas Kent, for example, speaks admiringly of works that 'deform' and 'recombine' the predictable elements of popular, 'automatized' texts (1986, p. 103). I want to examine here the ways in which *both* kinds of writing rework the conventions they inherit.

BESTSELLERS: ROMANCING WOMANHOOD

Bestsellers were the books which sold best: a minimum of 50,000 copies (Keating 1989, pp. 439–45). But the level of sales was not the only qualification. Controversial books (*The Woman Who Did*), genre books (*The Adventures of Sherlock Holmes*) and good books (*Tess of the D'Urbervilles*) all sold very well indeed without being considered, in the strict sense, bestsellers. Bestsellers were likely to be regarded as bad books. Yet they somehow transcended questions of propriety, genre and literariness. They radiated self-assurance. They promised not only to entertain, or to shock, but also to inspire, redeem, heal.

Spirituality sold books, as Marie Corelli and Guy Thorne found out. So did almost any well-hyped declaration of faith in absolute values. Even sexuality could be converted into an absolute value if it was presented as regenerative. The massive success of Elinor Glyn's *Three Weeks* (1907) was a sign that Corelli's days were numbered; in 1911 the literary agent J. B. Pinker told Violet Martin that middle-class readers were getting 'beyond' her (Somerville and Ross 1989, p. 292). Thereafter, absolute sex sold more books than absolute divinity, though few things could beat a skilful combination of the two.

When his 'episode' begins, Paul Verdayne, the hero of *Three Weeks*, is an average upper-class Englishman. He courts his dog rather more fervently than his girlfriend, a parson's daughter with large red hands. He is a reluctant traveller. Paris bores him, Versailles is 'beastly rot' (Glyn 1907, p. 11). One day he is sitting in his Swiss hotel, reading the sports pages, when a woman walks by. He is besotted. Fortunately she has brought with her a tiger-skin rug, on which a famous initiation soon takes place. The woman turns out to be the queen of a remote East European state. Eventually she is murdered by her jealous husband, but not before she has given birth to Paul's son, who will rule in her place.

The politics which converts this awakening into an absolute value is quite explicit. 'You must not just drift, my Paul, like so many of your countrymen do,' coaxes the queen. 'You must help to stem the tide of your nation's decadence, and be a strong man' (p. 199). The tiger-skin rug awakens him politically as well as sexually. When he returns to England he becomes a leader, a figure of authority: 'the three weeks of his lady's influence had changed the inner man beyond all recognition' (p. 254). Since his son will rule in Eastern Europe, he can even be said to have extended the British Empire.

Paul Verdayne's is a heavy-duty regeneration, comparable to

those experienced in the frontier tale or the spy thriller. The paradigm's power can be seen in the ease with which it incorporates and justifies illicit sexuality. So politicized were the new genres that the fragile coincidence of event and meaning which constitutes an adventure could be made to happen anywhere, in any fashion: on the thirty-ninth step or a tiger-skin rug. For a man, in these genres, committed by stereotype to the life of action, the only failure is not to have an event, an 'episode', at all. For a woman, however, committed by stereotype to passivity, things were not so simple.

If the average British male had to be delivered from eventlessness and the lack of identity it entailed, the average British female had to be delivered from the bland, uniform identity too often imposed by marriage or spinsterhood. The objective of the Edwardian romance of womanhood was to *uncouple* event and meaning, temporarily. In that hiatus, that free fall, regeneration could take place. A proposal is made, an engagement announced, a wedding celebrated, then the heroine calls a halt; the deferral creates a time between innocence and experience, a time for adventure. Where the 'average' woman submerges herself in marriage or celibacy, the romantic heroine hesitates; her hesitation permits, or creates, desire, the full recognition of sexual difference. When consummation does take place, it will be for her sake as well as for the hero's. This awakening is every bit as powerful, as necessary to the health of the nation, as his; but more dangerous, harder to contain within the bounds of social and literary propriety. It is dangerous because it is labile, founded on the separation rather than the coincidence of event and meaning, and on the recognition of difference rather than identity.

The heroine of Florence Barclay's *The Rosary* (1909), Jane Champion, is part Jane Eyre, part champion golfer. She rejects beautiful, artistic Garth Dalmain, with his lilac shirts and red socks, because he seems unmanly, a 'mere boy'. But the rejection makes her wonder whether she herself is not too manly. Rather than disavowing it defers, and in deferring recreates, her femininity. Dalmain goes blind. Nursing him, in disguise, Jane nurses her femininity until, a woman at last, she can declare her love. However, the free fall, the delirium of concealment, is severely curtailed by Dalmain's steadily increasing remasculinization. 'The sense of manhood and mastery; the right of control, the joy of possession, arose within him. Even in his blindness, he was the stronger' (Barclay 1922, p. 288).

Deference does not come after desire, as the price willingly paid for pleasure. It is already there. It is what makes for a woman's pleasure. These heroines want to defer consummation, to fall free; they also want an end to deferral, they want deference. In Ethel M. Dell's *The Way of an Eagle* (1912), Nick Ratcliffe, a young subaltern, rescues Muriel Roscoe, then little more than a child, from an uprising on the North-west Frontier. She becomes engaged to him, through a sense of obligation, but then withdraws. He releases her, confident that he can win her back. Nick is small and repulsive, but iron-willed. It is his ruthlessness which appals, then fascinates and finally conquers Muriel. Somehow he has 'kindled' within her the 'undying flame'. 'Against her will, in spite of her utmost resistance, he had done this thing' (Dell 1912, p. 298). Muriel has become a woman, and discovered sexual difference, through masochism alone; indeed, she has discovered it *as* masochism. That squaring of assertion with submission, deferral with deference, was the ideological work accomplished by the Edwardian romance of womanhood.

THE SHEIK

As the female reading public expanded, stories about the liberation of modern young women became virtually synonymous with bestsellerdom. By the 1920s, one historian observes, the bestseller had come to be regarded as 'a feminine artefact, produced by women for women' (Melman 1988, p. 45). These stories have recently become a focus of enquiry for feminist critics challenged by the connection they suppose between pleasure and submissiveness (Modleski 1982; Radway 1984; Radford 1986; Kaplan 1986). Does the female reader of *The Way of an Eagle* (or *Gone with the Wind*, or *The Thorn Birds*) put herself in the place of the heroine to the extent of enjoying her ultimate submission to a man? And should feminism seek to cure her of this dangerous identification through stern prophylactic measures?

Cora Kaplan has argued that psychoanalysis can help us to understand how romance works because it understands fantasy as the foundation of social and psychic identity, as a scenario in which the subject plays different roles at different times, and in which various identifications are possible. Something similar may happen in the reading of mass-market romances. Instead of identifying consistently with a 'feminine' heroine pursued and captured by a 'masculine' hero, the reader may identify with different characters, or with different aspects of the same characters. For example, the hero of Colleen McCullough's *The Thorn Birds* (1977) is a Catholic priest whose beauty and virginity give him a 'feminine side'. 'As a beautiful and pure object of desire he stands in the text in place of the woman, often obscuring [the heroine]' (Kaplan 1986, p. 141). He remains in that 'place' right up until the final seduction scene, when he becomes unequivocally a man.

The desert romances – stories of sexual violence set, more often than not, in the French Sahara – provide an interesting test-case for Kaplan's hypothesis. The most successful of them all was E. M. Hull's *The Sheik* (1919), which had gone through 108 impressions in Britain alone by 1923. (The audience for the film version, made with Rudolph Valentino in 1921, was estimated in millions.) Diana Mayo, an Englishwoman travelling in the desert, is abducted and raped by Sheik Ahmed Ben Hassan. A few weeks later, she is deeply in love and would rather kill herself than leave him. Robert Hichens's *The Garden of Allah* (1904), also set in the French Sahara, is a (less violent) forerunner. Domini Enfilden, a young and fervently Catholic Englishwoman travelling in Algeria, meets and marries a mysterious Russian, Boris Androvsky. Disappointingly, Boris turns out to be a renegade monk. Appalled by his betrayal of God, Domini packs him off back to his monastery, and brings up their child on her own. *The Garden of Allah* and *The Sheik* represent the two main tendencies of desert romance, towards mysticism and towards sexual violence.

At first sight, neither novel offers much scope for multiple identification. Both relish polarity. Topographically, they are divided between city and desert, civilization and barbarism. The barbaric men who inhabit the desert are all man, mighty, muscular and iron-willed. It is at their hands alone that the half-women who set out from the decadent cities will become all woman.

Still, the polarity of Domini Enfilden and Boris Androvsky is softened by her Amazonian mannishness and his fumbling hesitancy. Androvsky, as befits a monk, is clumsy and virginal. Domini teaches him the ways of the world, initiates him. At first it seems that marriage will put an end to this role-swapping and re-establish Androvsky as master. But then he confesses that he has betrayed God, and the confession reduces him to a second childhood. Domini takes charge again. In a final assertive stroke, she conceals from him the fact that he is a father; she herself will be the only creator, the only authority. She retires to an Edenic walled garden on the edge of the desert. The polarities of male and female, city and desert, collapse. There *is* a third way. The reader can identify with man, woman or androgyne.

In *The Sheik*, however, polarity rules. At the beginning of the novel Diana is boyish, haughty and indifferent to men. 'God made me a woman,' she complains. 'Why, only He knows' (Hull 1919, p. 15). Ahmed Ben Hassan, however, has no doubts about himself, or Diana. His 'fierce burning eyes' sweep her until she feels that the 'boyish clothes' which cover her 'slender limbs' have been 'stripped from her, leaving the beautiful white body bare under his passionate stare' (p. 58). Diana is not so much stripped as polarized by this passionate stare. Gone with the boyish clothes is her youthful androgyny. Soon she will be raped into a recognition of the difference between men and women. The morning after, she tries to resume her androgyny by putting on the boyish clothes: 'in them she would feel herself again – Diana the boy, not the shivering piece of womanhood that had been born with tears and agony last night' (p. 65). It doesn't work, of course, because feeling herself now means feeling a woman. Once a woman, she never dominates, never controls. It is impossible to identify with her in anything except her sexual submissiveness.

The Sheik closes off every 'subject position' except one to the female reader. It is a sorry tale of polarity converted into hierarchy by sado-masochism. And yet there is a kind of fluidity, a change of mood, a liberation even. The worst thing that could ever happen to the heroine turns out to be the best thing that could ever happen. It is through this reversal that fantasy takes hold. The heroine can do nothing; but the narrative can do what it wants with her, and for her. It all depends not so much on the reader's identification with Diana Mayo as on her understanding of genre.

No sooner has Diana acknowledged that she loves Ahmed Ben Hassan than the whole captivity narrative is replayed, this time as a conventional romance, with all the main figures occupying their 'correct' positions. Ahmed's bitter enemy and rival, Ibraheim Omair, captures Diana, and is just on the point of raping her in his turn when Ahmed arrives. Her role in the narrative remains the same, but Ibraheim Omair has taken Ahmed's place as villainous rapist, while Ahmed appears as the gallant rescuer. The novel has cited itself transformatively, reworked its own basic element, the captivity narrative; it has declared its power to institute at will the free fall of relativity, of a perpetually renewed desire.

However, this narrative abandon is itself regulated by a further constraint. Diana's sexual role may remain the same the second time 'round, but she does awaken to a new understanding of cultural difference. She realizes that she should treat Ibraheim and his followers with the contempt due to an inferior race – a habit learnt in India the previous year (p. 204). India, from the British point of view a more politicized territory than the French Sahara, has taught her the habits of rule. Now, for the first time, she begins to exercise them in Africa, thus producing a new alignment. Ahmed she now regards as her equal. Ibraheim, meanwhile, has taken Ahmed's place not only as rapist, but as Arab. He is 'the Arab of her imaginings' (p. 210): gross, ugly, ignorant, utterly depraved. Even his tent smells in a way Ahmed's doesn't (p. 204). The boundary between civilization and barbarism has been redrawn: it now runs, not between the white woman and the two sheiks, but between Diana and Ahmed on one hand, and the villainous Ibraheim on the other.

The second captivity narrative has reclassified Ahmed. In rescuing Diana, he behaves like a white man. Indeed he is, it transpires, a white man: the foundling son of an English father and a Spanish mother, brought up in the desert by an Arab sheik. Cultural difference unites him to Diana, rather than separating him from her. The final revelation is that the motives for his brutal treatment of her were cultural rather than sexual. He was avenging himself upon the English for what his drunken, degenerate father had done to his saintly mother. Diana's love will redeem him. The plot which frames and connects the two captivity narratives is a regeneration-plot. Sado-masochism has been reclaimed for empire, though not without some tricky moments – the odd free fall – along the way.

ROMANCE IN THE NOVEL OF IDEAS

It is the tricky moments in the romance of sexual initiation, the moments when desire seems to be acknowledged and celebrated in its own right, which are closest to serious fiction of an innovative or polemical kind. To be sure, the ambiguities of awakening were more apparent to Katherine Mansfield, in 'Bliss', or to Forster and Lawrence, than they ever were to Glyn, Dell or Hull. Even so, it isn't always easy to tell the realists and the romancers apart.

The supposedly regenerative effects of a sojourn in Italy seem to be much the same whether they are being promoted by Forster, in *A Room with a View* (1908), or Hichens, in *The Call of the Blood* (1906). In both novels, Italy awakens a fascination with violence and sensuality; in both, lower-class Italians are introduced to exemplify a life lived according to instinct. Of course, there are differences. Forster dramatizes what Hichens laboriously spells out. But both exploit romantic stereotype. Aware of this, Forster incorporated a popular novelist, Miss Lavish, whose version of Lucy Honeychurch's awakening is duly derided by the other characters. But the description attributed to Miss Lavish (1978, p. 179) isn't all that much more trashy than the one he himself offers as narrator (p. 89).

Lawrence also worried about the resemblances between his own radical revaluation of sexuality and the purple passages of the romancers. A crucial scene between the two lovers in 'The Captain's Doll' (1923) is interrupted by the sight of a young woman with a huge woolly dog who poses like a heroine on a novel cover, and is surrounded by admirers pretending to be 'elegant Austrians out of popular romances' (Lawrence 1982b, p. 125). Lawrence kept his distance from popular romance by at once invoking and denigrating it. Ursula Brangwen and Anton Skrebensky, staying at a hotel in Piccadilly, express their proud independence from 'mortal conditions' by acting like aristocrats. 'Thus a tissue of romance was around them .... The days went by – they were to have three weeks together – in perfect success.' Ursula, however, wants to leave Skrebensky (Lawrence 1989, p. 420–3). The allusion to *Three Weeks* establishes for us the 'tissue of romance' which she must break through if she is ever to become her own woman.

Lawrence has been seen as an innovator who, like Dostoevsky and Joyce, extended the polyphonic and carnivalesque capacities of the novel. *Women in Love* switches rapidly between points of view without delivering a final judgement. It incorporates a whole range of idioms which allow us to measure the progress of those who use them towards regeneration. Ursula's feelings after her reconciliation with Birkin in 'Excurse' are expressed in the language of popular romance; the expression demonstrating that she still perceives the relationship in unregenerate – sentimental – terms (Lodge 1990b).

Later on in 'Excurse', Ursula kneels before Birkin, exploring the 'floods of ineffable darkness' that well from somewhere 'further in mystery than the phallic source' (Lawrence 1987, p. 314). Lodge suggests that Lawrence is again employing 'stylized discourse', this time of biblical or occult origin (1990b, p. 101). The spell of mysticism has superseded the spell of romance. Ursula is still unregenerate. In fact the whole chapter, which comes as close as any to articulating Lawrence's creed, thrives on comic juxtapositions. It is, in stylistic as well as thematic terms, an 'excurse', an interruption or wandering. Take the conclusion of the roadside quarrel.

'Shall we go,' she said.

'Yes,' he answered. And they mounted the car once more, and left behind them this memorable battlefield.

(p. 311)

Lawrence had originally written 'went to the car' rather than 'mounted the car'. The revision ensures that the episode ends on a mock-heroic note – a note faintly reminiscent of the instant translations of vernacular into epic language which comprise the 'Cyclops' section of *Ulysses*. Indeed, Lawrence revises here in the same way that Joyce revised the early sections of *Ulysses*, elaborating and embellishing, thickening the verbal texture. There are grounds, then, for describing at least parts of *Women in Love* in the terms one would use to describe Dostoevsky or Joyce.

Parts only. The Gudrun–Gerald Crich story is not in the least carnivalesque, and the 'language' it incorporates, of degeneration theory, proves all too prophetic of its outcome. There plot endorses idiom, rather than revealing its limitations (see Chapter

7, above). Conceptions of parody or carnival will not help us to understand how Lawrence saw Gudrun's sexuality. For that, we must turn back once more to popular romance.

FANTASY

Gudrun Brangwen and Diana Mayo both discover their identity as women through relationships with physically and socially powerful men. In both cases the construction of sexual difference is mediated by sado-masochism, and by a scene in which the women watch a horse being brutalized.

In 'A Child Is Being Beaten' (1919), Freud collated and analysed the fantasies of four young women (1953–74, XVII, pp. 179–204). These fantasies all involve scenes in which children are beaten. In the first phase, the author of the fantasy watches her father beating a child who is clearly a rival for his love. Her motives are neither sexual nor sadistic, Freud suggests, but rather the raw material out of which both feelings will be shaped. In the second phase the fantasist imagines herself being beaten by her father. The fantasy is now an expression of her guilt, to which her love for her father has succumbed. Guilt transforms incipient sadism into masochism. The beating is both a punishment for imagining the forbidden genital relation, and a regressive substitute for it. Desire and prohibition have been created together. In the third phase the fantasist is once again a spectator; she watches a teacher or some other authority-figure beating a number of children, usually boys. The form of the fantasy is now sadistic, its content masochistic and libidinal, since the boys are substitutes for the author herself.

Both Gudrun and Diana undergo experiences which correspond roughly to the three phases of this fantasy. We know nothing of Gudrun's previous lovers, so the relationship with Gerald represents an initiation into sexual difference. In Chapter 9, 'Coal-Dust', Gudrun and Ursula watch while he drives his terrified Arab mare at a colliery train which rumbles through the crossing. Gerald's brutality appals Ursula, but fascinates Gudrun. 'Gudrun was as if numbed in her mind by the sense of indomitable soft weight of the man, bearing down into the living body of the horse' (Lawrence 1987, p. 113). Later, when Gerald seduces her, she becomes the mare, receiving him 'in an ecstasy of subjection, in throes of acute, violent sensation' (p. 344). This ecstatic subjection polarizes Gudrun, creates her as woman.

Her third episode occurs in Chapter 30, as the novel moves towards its conclusion, and demonstrates the fundamental incompatibility between the degeneration-plot and the regeneration-plot. The quartet, ensconced in the Alps, resolve, or fail to resolve, their differences, with Loerke acting as catalyst. Gerald and Birkin dismiss him as a degenerate. Ursula and Gudrun talk to him about his work, specifically about a statuette of a naked girl sitting on a horse (p. 429). The horse, a stallion, represents male control and its rider female submissiveness. But Gudrun's response, of 'supplication', 'dark homage', affected indifference, is the same. Ursula insists that Loerke has represented himself in the stallion; he admits, casually, that he had assaulted the young girl who modelled for him (p. 433). This time, by a further perversion, it is the horse (or the man it represents) which does the beating. Gudrun is again a spectator; we do not know whether she will submit to Loerke as she had once submitted to Gerald. The episode revolts Ursula, who decides that she and Birkin must leave immediately (p. 434).

Diana Mayo is raped by the Sheik on page 61; by page 132 she knows that she loves him. During that interval, there are three significant moments. She watches the Sheik taming a colt with extreme brutality (Hull 1919, p. 103). Later that day, when he takes her in his arms, she can see only the tortured animal, blood and foam dripping from its mouth, between herself and his broad chest (p. 114). She is the horse. Four weeks later she attempts to escape. Ahmed Ben Hassan chases her down, and shoots her horse, one of his favourites, from beneath her. As he carries her back to camp she discovers that she loves him (p. 132). The Sheik had said that he valued his horses more highly than her. Now he has sacrificed one of them in order to get her back.

All three texts describe a womanhood attained through sado-masochism. Freud treats the fantasy as a symptom of mental illness, of hysteria or obsessional neurosis; and the mental illness as a symptom of discrepancies in the evolution of the species. The impulses repressed in hysteria or obsessional neurosis derive from 'man's archaic heritage' (1953–74, XVII, p. 204).

In *Women in Love* Gerald's construction of sexual difference on the figure of the Pussum, with her 'inchoate look of a violated slave, whose fulfilment lies in her further and further violation'

(p. 80), completes his fascinated but terrified response to a 'primitive' sculpture of a Negro woman in labour. 'He saw the Pussum in it. As in a dream, he knew her.' Gerald, being a civilized man, wants to maintain 'certain illusions' against this weight of sensation, 'certain ideas like clothing' (p. 79). But it is his acknowledgement of the 'primitive' in himself which has taken him back to the Pussum, and will take him on to Gudrun, on into sexual difference.

Unlike Freud, Lawrence also invokes degeneration theory. Gudrun's three-phase initiation is at once into sexual difference and into degeneracy. Chapter 9, first entitled 'Colliery', then 'Coal-Dust', describes her incorporation into the underworld of the mines. As Gudrun and Ursula walk away from the crossing, two labourers openly evaluate Gudrun as a sexual object (p. 114). She finds the 'voluptuousness' of the mining district both 'potent' and 'half-repulsive' (p. 115). The men's voices arouse in her 'a strange, nostalgic ache of desire, something almost demoniacal, never to be fulfilled'. Drawn inexorably into this world, she parades her sexuality in the streets like 'any other common girl of the district' (p. 117).

Ursula, one might note, has already encountered the fatal voluptuousness of another mining district, in Chapter 12 of *The Rainbow*, 'Shame'. The 'homogeneous amorphous sterility' of the place, its 'Zolaesque tragedy', appals her, but fascinates her companion and ex-lover, Winifred Inger. Winifred is attracted to, and eventually marries, Tom Brangwen, the colliery manager, whose 'slight sense of putrescence' reveals his inert subjection to mechanism (1989, pp. 322–5). Winifred disappears into the downward spiral of Zolaesque tragedy. Ursula escapes.

In *Women in Love* Lawrence characterizes this regression to primitive voluptuousness as a collective degeneration, a 'fatal half-heartedness', a 'sort of rottenness in the will' (p. 118). Gudrun revels in the 'abandonments of Roman licence': the corruption and excess, so ominously reminiscent of contemporary Britain, which had destroyed Rome from within (p. 287). In the end, it is Loerke, the honorary primitive, who will complete her corruption. Or may do. For Gudrun, like Freud's patients, has been reduced by the fantasy she lives out to spectatorship.

In *Women in Love* fantasy is powerfully over-determined, by 'man's archaic heritage', by a nation's decline. The first factor is represented as the catalyst, the second as the cause, of the sado-masochistic episode. If Gerald had not studied the sculpture, the 'sheer African thing' (p. 79), he might not have been able to recognize the Pussum's sheer femininity. His subsequent recognition of Gudrun, and her recognition of him, on the other hand, are *produced* by their degeneracy: their fatal desire for a 'finality' that a corrupt society offers but cannot deliver.

'The mass of the populace "find themselves",' Lawrence remarked, in popular novels. 'But nowadays it's a funny sort of self they find. A sheik with a whip up his sleeve, and a heroine with weals on her back, but adored in the end, adored, the whip out of sight, but the weals still faintly visible' (1955, p. 116). He himself, however, had produced a hero and heroine whose fatal attraction is every bit as funny as the one Ahmed Ben Hassan conducts with his whip. *The Sheik* is preposterous, and in many ways deplorable. But there is something attractive about Hull's refusal to characterize the sado-masochistic episode between Ahmed and Diana as unequivocally monstrous, as a consequence of the painful death of liberal England. Unlike Lawrence, like a number of other popular writers, she was able to free herself, for a moment, from the determinism of the degeneration-plot.

Part III

THE PSYCHOPATHOLOGY OF MODERNISM

13

SEX NOVELS

In the first two Parts of this book I attempted to provide contexts – one economic, the other social and political – for the development of the English novel during the period. I now want to isolate, and explore in greater depth, two preoccupations which seem to me characteristic of turn-of-the-century fiction: desire and disgust.

Of course, Edwardian writers were not the first to notice desire and disgust. Romance is inconceivable without the former, satire without the latter. But the economic and social changes sketched in Parts I and II did foster a renewed, a more overt, attention. In many novels, from *A City Girl* to *The Old Wives' Tale*, the heroine's desire for clothes, her investment in fashion, is a prelude to sexual awakening. The new commerce invited women to resemble prostitutes in their 'commodified self-display' (Bowlby 1985).

Desire, however, could be conceived only in relation to other feelings. The economist Stanley Jevons paired utility, the 'production of pleasure', with disutility, the 'production of pain'. He appropriated the term 'discommodity' to signify 'any substance or action which is the opposite of *commodity*, that is to say, *anything which we desire to get rid of*, like ashes or sewage' (1888, pp. 57–8). Ashes, sewage: these are objects not of desire, but of revulsion; a feeling increasingly apparent, towards the end of the century, not just in consumer behaviour but in social theory. The concept of degeneration, dwelling on a rottenness at once cultural and biological, multiplied images of monstrosity: Mr Hyde, Moriarty, the Morlocks, Count Dracula, Quint and Miss Jessel, the picture of Dorian Gray, Kurtz's abominations. Naturalism not only gave prominence to filth, disease and putridity (Baguley 1990, p. 211), but orchestrated them into a new narrative teleology.

In each case the fiction of the period renewed, or diversified, an already existing preoccupation. I shall argue here that one source of its innovativeness, and of its excellence, lay in this diversification.

SEX NOVELS

In 1910 Edward Garnett, by that time an influential literary adviser and talent-spotter (Jefferson 1982), wrote a preface to Maud Churton Braby's *Downward. A 'Slice of Life'* which provided a defence and a short history of the 'Sex Novel'. Such novels were valuable, he thought, because, like the greatest works of art, they challenged orthodoxy. The first wave – the New Woman novels of the 1890s – had caused outrage because it seemed to threaten the institution of marriage; though in fact the average heroine wanted nothing better than to marry the 'strong man of her dreams'. The second wave – launched, one might say, around 1905, at the same time as the militant suffrage campaigns – should be seen as part of the women's movement. Braby herself had already published a book called *Modern Marriage and How to Bear It* in which she discussed the 'problem novels' of the 1890s, and recommended Gribble's *Pillar of Cloud* and Wyllarde's *Pathway of the Pioneer* (Braby 1910a, pp. 6, 38).

The sex novel should not be identified too closely with the women's movement. It overlapped on the one hand with popular genres like desert romance, and on the other with *Bildungsromane* by Masefield, Lawrence, Cannan, Mackenzie, Maugham, Joyce and others. Even so, women's sexuality, and their right to express it as they chose, was a prominent theme, and the cause of a great deal of controversy.

In Gissing's novels of the 1890s the woman is no longer expected to provide money, social status, beauty or adoration; instead she must prove, through an 'elaborate test of her unconventionality', her 'worthiness' for marriage to a particular, equally unconventional man (Keating 1989, p. 203). In *The Odd Women*, Everard Barfoot declares his contempt for 'the typical woman'; he thinks he may have met his match in the undeniably atypical Rhoda Nunn. Rhoda has chosen oddness. But even she cannot altogether impose her singularity on the men she meets, or on her author. Virginia Madden's first sight of her, after a gap of several years, is unceremoniously hijacked by the narrator. Is she beautiful, or not? 'At first view the countenance seemed masculine, its expression somewhat aggressive – eyes shrewdly observant and lips consciously impregnable. But the connoisseur delayed his verdict' (Gissing 1980, p. 20). The connoisseur delays *his* verdict, sensing 'subtle feminine forces that might be released by circumstance' (p. 21) – by male circumstance. Barfoot appreciates oddness. But Rhoda is too odd for him, and he reverts to evenness, marrying a nice respectable girl.

The most ambitious and influential attempt to represent atypicality was Hardy's *Tess of the D'Urbervilles*. Tess provokes a typifying sexual response in every man who sets eyes on her, including the narrator. Her attributes, one reviewer noted, 'are paraded over and over again with a persistence like that of a horse-dealer egging on some wavering customer to a deal, or a slave-dealer appraising his wares to some full-blooded pasha' (quoted in Boumelha 1982, p. 124). The pasha-like Alec D'Urberville packages her as a *femme fatale*; Angel Clare, ever the wavering customer, as a rustic innocent.

At the beginning of Phase the Second the narrative circles around her, as though trying to find a new and less invidious angle. Surveying women at work in a field, the narrator's eye 'returns involuntarily', as Alec's and Angel's had done on previous occasions, to one in particular. It seems that Tess will once again become the object of erotic appraisal. This time, however, the narrative pauses long enough to register the difference made to her body by something other than male circumstance. Her arms have been scratched and torn by the stubble, and this scarification identifies her (Hardy 1978a, pp. 137–8). It is, after her pregnancy, a new and different embodiment. Only when it has been registered are we allowed to glimpse her face. Hardy's interest in work, and the identity it confers, has allowed Tess some respite from the rapists and voyeurs who surround her.

In the end, Angel Clare's idealizing priggishness will take even that from her. But she does experience one remarkable moment of 'exaltation' as she is falling in love with him. Hearing the sound of his harp, she approaches through the uncultivated garden, gathering cuckoo-spittle on her skirts and cracking snails underfoot (p. 179). The description is close to farce. Yet it also conveys movingly, through its obstinate accuracy, its refusal of the connoisseur's gaze, her determination to be herself. Angel Clare, of course, will have none of that.

Yet the problem remained that minutely differentiating descriptions of women, and of women's bodies, often did no more than reactivate the connoisseur's gaze. Something of this kind happens in *The Old Wives' Tale*, once Bennett gets Sophia to Paris. Her pleasure is said to lie in the spectacle of luxury. Yet Bennett's syntax displays this spectacle to us first, and only then, belatedly, to her.

> Sophia, thrust suddenly into a strange civilization perfectly frank in its sensuality and its sensuousness, under the guidance of a young man to whom her half-formed intelligence was a most diverting toy – Sophia felt mysteriously uncomfortable, disturbed by sinister, flitting phantoms of ideas which she only dimly apprehended.
>
> (1964, p. 305)

Sophia's moral and grammatical subjectivity is suspended while Bennett investigates the world around her; it resumes only in division, by this time as much object (Gerald's diverting toy) as subject, and reduced from pleasure to dim apprehension. Here Bennett's 'poetic of unawareness' seems to disable rather than enable. In Edwardian fiction, the tendency to differentiate and individualize frequently loses out to the connoisseur's gaze. But not always.

EDWARDIAN BODIES

H. de Vere Stacpoole's *The Blue Lagoon* (1908) must be one of the few stories about sexual awakening in which gratification precedes desire. The young lovers, Dicky and Emmeline, shipwrecked as children on a remote island in the South Seas, dispense altogether with preliminaries. Their lovemaking is spontaneous, and all over before either of them realizes it's begun. Only after the event do they become interested in each other's bodies. 'Her breasts, her shoulders, her knees, her little feet, every bit of her he would examine and play with and kiss' (Stacpoole 1908, p. 184). Made visible by Dicky's desire, Emmeline's body becomes its emblem. Similarly, Hewlett's young 'forest lovers' marry to save each other's skins, and *then* fall in love; the hiatus allows for a protracted investigation of teenage desire (Hewlett 1909).

Stacpoole's departure from the literary conventions by which the body was usually represented signals Dicky and Emmeline's departure from moral conventions. It's a diffident signal, of course. They only make love because they don't know any better; they are parents before they have stopped being children. Even the description of foreplay is calculatedly detumescent in its progress from breasts to shoulders, knees and dainty feet. But other Edwardian novelists wrote less equivocally about sexual awakening; they too represented desire by representing the body in new ways.

It would be wrong to suppose that Victorian novelists drew a veil across the body. We need only think of Maggie Tulliver's irresistibly dimpled elbow, in *The Mill on the Floss* (1860), to realize that they didn't (Eliot 1979, p. 561). However, there isn't all that much enticing flesh in Victorian fiction. It was only towards the end of the century, as description in general became more minute, that writers started to supply a fuller range of erotic detail. The irresistibly dimpled elbows of Winifred Varley, in Lawrence's 'The Witch à la Mode', are merely the prelude to yet more arousing, and carefully specified, surfaces and textures (Lawrence 1971, pp. 102–8).

One of the reasons why H. G. Wells's *Ann Veronica* (1909) caused so much offence was that it showed a woman making advances to a man. Ann Veronica awakens sexually while working in the laboratory with her instructor, Capes. She notices a 'fine golden down' on his cheeks: 'at the sight something leapt within her. Something changed for her' (Wells 1980, p. 147). Not so much a feature as a space between features, the golden down becomes the evidence and emblem of Ann Veronica's desire. Her apprehension of it eroticizes Capes, and enables her to take pleasure in her own body (pp. 148–9).

The sight of golden down seems also to have aroused some eminent male Edwardians, real and fictional. Wells himself reported that Dorothy Richardson, his lover from 1905 to 1907, was 'most interestingly hairy on her body, with fine golden hairs' (Wells 1984b, p. 64). Gerald Scales, in *The Old Wives' Tale*, takes a similar if less comprehensive interest in the hairiness of Sophia Baines, with whom he has just eloped. Embracing her, he notices the beauty of her face, 'viewed so close that he could see the almost imperceptible down on those fruit-like cheeks', and suddenly desires her (Bennett 1964, p. 289). Scanning Clara

Dawes, in *Sons and Lovers*, Paul Morel sees 'a fine down, almost invisible, upon the skin of her face and arms ... and when once he had perceived it, he saw it always' (Lawrence 1948, p. 322). 'And it sent hot flashes through his blood,' Lawrence added in the manuscript. The nape of Mary Cartaret's neck, 'shining with golden down', has the same effect on *her* suitor (Sinclair 1982, p. 241). Golden down was still causing havoc, it would appear, in the 1920s (Arlen 1924, p. 249).

Such attention was scandalous because it ignored the assumption, widespread in Victorian fiction, that a face consists of features rather than surfaces, and that those features express character (Fahnestock 1981). These men's glances freed the body from the necessity to symbolize. But they may have freed it only in order to subject it to a different necessity. Wells remarked that Dorothy Richardson had wanted a 'complex intellectual relationship', but that for him it had been no more than a 'sensuous affair, for Dorothy was a glowing blonde' (1984b, p. 64). Even so, the body was beginning to be described in new ways, ways that revalued, or refigured, desire.

Victorian scars, like Victorian noses and foreheads, expressed moral identity. They were created rather than inherited features, but still *expressive*. When Count Dracula is cornered, the red scar on his forehead shows 'like a palpitating wound'; it voices his 'hellish rage' (Stoker 1979, p. 365). In *David Copperfield*, Rosa Dartle's scar, cutting down through both lips, embodies a violent passion she is otherwise able to suppress; when she turns pale with anger it becomes apparent 'like a mark in invisible ink brought to the fire' (Dickens 1966, p. 353).

If Victorian scars express moral identity, Edwardian scars provoke desire. What finally arouses the heroine of *The Awakening* (1899) is the scar, at once fascinating and repulsive, on a man's wrist (Chopin 1978, p. 127). In 'The Prussian Officer', the scar on a young orderly's thumb drives his superior to distraction (Lawrence 1983, p. 4). These scars are not symbols, but traces of an event (a duel, an accident). They demonstrate that the body has been culturally inscribed, (dis)figured. Somehow that inscription, which has a history but no meaning, stirs desire.

Such marked bodies appear not only in the work of innovators like Chopin and Lawrence, but also in more formulaic fiction. The heroine of *The Hard Way* (1908) marries a young artillery officer, who promptly goes mad and is locked up. She eventually establishes herself in society and meets a darkly interesting grandee with a darkly interesting scar; this one runs from forehead to earlobe. 'It fascinated her, made her long suddenly to run her fingers down the line of silver hairs, caressing it. The thought recalled her to herself with a jerk, as it were: she could caress no man, being wife to a lunatic' ('A Peer' 1908, p. 100).

In Edwardian fiction scars are even more fascinating than golden down. Both eluded the physiognomic code of the Victorian novel: one by not being a feature, the other by not being a natural feature. Both gave bodies a new presence in writing.

SOCIAL PURITY

Stories about sexual awakening are shaped, more directly than other stories, by social conventions: what people agree to speak about, what they agree to be shocked by. The bodies which appear in Edwardian fiction appear by grace of the censor.

In the thirty years before the First World War public morals were subjected increasingly to state regulation (Bristow 1977; Mort 1987; Keating 1989, pp. 241–84). It was usually not the government which took the initiative, but one of the proliferating social purity groups. Launched by the militant evangelicalism of the 1880s, these groups represented a new force in British politics, quite distinct from the professional experts who had attempted to regulate public morals in the years from 1830 to 1860. Probably the most influential, and certainly the most censorious, was the National Vigilance Association (NVA), which grew out of campaigns to promote the Criminal Law Amendment Act of 1885.

A series of articles about child prostitution in the *Pall Mall Gazette*, with titles like 'Strapping Girls Down' and 'I Order Five Virgins', had speeded the legislative process considerably. Their author, W. T. Stead, was subsequently jailed for abducting his main witness, and his six months of martyrdom did the cause no harm. Indeed, the cause flourished with the passing of the Criminal Law Amendment Act and the inauguration of the NVA at a rally in Hyde Park. The rally drew large crowds headed by wagonloads of virgins dressed in white and sporting the slogan 'The Innocents, Will They Be Slaughtered?'

William Coote, a compositor on the *Standard* and minor official of the Working Men's League, helped to organize the rally and was appointed secretary of the NVA. The success of the campaign for the 1885 Act taught him that the criminal law could be used to reform public morals. 'You can, and do, keep men sober,' he asserted, 'simply by an Act of Parliament; you can, and do, chain the devil of impurity in a large number of men and women by the fear of the law' (Coote 1902, p. 69). One devil he certainly meant to chain was the taste for popular entertainments. The NVA led a campaign to clean up the Empire Music Hall in Leicester Square, a notorious resort of prostitutes. Screens were erected to partition off the promenade, and promptly torn down again by a gang of toffs led by Winston Churchill, who made his first political speech from the pile of debris (Jones 1983, p. 233).

Erotic fiction provided another target. In 1888 the NVA had encouraged the prosecution of Zola's English publisher, Vizetelly. In 1911 they persuaded W. H. Smith to ban an issue of the *English Review* because it contained a faintly lubricious story. Libraries also felt the force of their disapproval. In 1910 Canon Lambert, of the local NVA, told the Hull Public Libraries Committee that he 'would as soon send a daughter of his to a house infected with diptheria or typhoid' as put *Ann Veronica* into her hands; the novel was withdrawn. Other authors suffered the same fate. Nietzsche was banned in Belfast, Fielding in Doncaster (Thompson 1975, p. 3). In December 1909 the Circulating Libraries Association announced that it would henceforth censor itself. Austin Harrison, editor of the *English Review*, protested about the withdrawal of Neil Lyons's *Cottage Pie*, in February 1911, and Gilbert Cannan's *Round the Corner*, in February 1913.

Cottage Pie concerns village life in Sussex and Buckinghamshire; at one point the narrator feeds strawberries, Alec D'Urberville fashion, to the local beauty. *Round the Corner* includes a couple of bathing scenes, in one of which a young man emerges from the undergrowth to find a young woman swinging naked from a tree. The young woman has already been dismissed from her post as governess for bathing naked in the presence of her charge. And that's about it.

There was no government censorship of fiction. Prosecutions had to be brought, pressure exerted, by individuals or groups. What could and could not be represented on the written page was a matter of dispute between factions. Take the case of W. B. Maxwell's *The Devil's Garden*, banned by the circulating libraries in 1913. William Dale, postmaster in a Hampshire village, discovers that his wife has been seduced by the local MP, Barradine. He manages to kill Barradine, without arousing suspicion, and eventually becomes a prosperous farmer and captain of the local fire brigade. He dreams of seducing Norah, a young servant; but before he can do so, an orphanage endowed by Barradine burns down, taking most of the fire brigade with it.

On 9 September 1913 Maxwell wrote to *The Times* to protest. He admitted that *The Devil's Garden* was 'outspoken', but felt confident that 'no-one, man, woman, or child, will be the worse for reading it'. Two days later, Clement Shorter, editor of the *Sphere* and literary man about town, took up the issue. He was not in favour of state censorship, but did object to one of Dale's fantasies about Norah, in which they both dance naked in a stream. Maxwell replied that the passage had been read out of context; Dale is half mad, and anyway never yields to temptation.

The idea of context seems to me crucial. *The Devil's Garden* admits the existence of rape fantasies. Its offence is that it doesn't succeed in framing or regulating this idea by the explanation that such fantasies occur only to mad or bad people. The novelty of the idea, in fiction, is such that it eclipses any explanatory context (of the kind Maxwell was able to provide in his letter). The problem was precisely that the passage might be read out of context and, just conceivably, acted upon.

It did Lawrence no good to explain in *The Rainbow* that Ursula Brangwen's passion for Winifred Inger was only a phase in her life, and a decadent one at that. He had described two naked women embracing, and the sheer novelty of the scene eclipsed the framing narrative. Clement Shorter, among others, was again on hand to condemn it. The book was banned. But another novel published by Methuen in 1915 does not seem to have caused any offence at all, even though it implicitly endorsed lesbianism. Christopher St John's *Hungerheart* is about a woman who loves and lives with other women. However, it doesn't contain any lesbian bodies or lesbian bathing scenes. St John leaves it to her readers to interpret her rejection of the roles prescribed for women and her condemnation of marriage. There is no lesbian text, only a lesbian context, in the minds of some of her readers. The book was not banned.

SOCIAL HYGIENE

In his preface to *Downward*, Edward Garnett drew on degeneration theory to explain the polemical intention of the modern
sex novel. ' "We are no longer breeding from our best but from
our worst equipped stocks," our sociologists tell us' (Braby 1913).
The sex novel, like the New Woman novel, had a diagnostic
function. Again, however, the diagnosticians were sometimes
regarded as the source of infection. Both they and their accusers
subscribed to the same social theory.

During the years before the First World War a new emphasis
emerged: on hygiene rather than purity, on training rather than
denial. The books about sex education which had been appearing
since the 1880s were prompted, like the purity campaigns, by a
sense of social decline, and directed primarily at young people
between the ages of sixteen and twenty-three. 'There is,' the
hygienists warned, 'too long a period between the awakening of
strong sexual desire in adolescence and the possibility of regular
gratification' (Thomson and Geddes 1914, pp. 151–2).

In 1912 one expert argued that knowledge could not and
should not be withheld. The choice lay 'between healthy open
teaching or evil and distorted instruction' (Andrews 1912, p. 92).
Margaret Bondfield, the first woman to serve as a cabinet
minister, described in her autobiography how one organization,
the Women's Co-operative Guild, had set out to provide healthy
open teaching. At the lectures it organized, many women 'heard
the names and functions of their bodily organs for the first time';
these women wanted above all to know 'the "words"' (Bondfield
1949, p. 128). The Guild drew its membership from the respectable working class (Lawrence's mother was secretary of the
Eastwood branch; in *Sons and Lovers*, Paul attends a meeting
addressed by 'Margaret Bonford'). Sex education, for audiences
of any age or class, meant providing the words.

But they had to be the right words, provided by the right
people. The Guild insisted that its lecturers should pass an
examination. E. B. Kirk published two books, one for boys, one
for girls, which offer alternative descriptions of intercourse,
one a literal account of what happens, the other a virtually
incomprehensible effusion about notes joining together to make

a perfect chord. These descriptions appeared on perforated pages, so that parents could tear out the version they did not want their children to read (1905a, 1905b). Increasingly, however, such knowledge was controlled by experts rather than parents, by teachers and doctors. 'It is always correct to employ the right words, which are used in physiology and by doctors and educated people, and to discourage the use of the vulgar expressions and gutter-slang' (Gallichan 1920, p. 26).

What had to be controlled was the recognition of sexuality. 'If a new word occurs in a book,' Frederick Gould told his young readers, 'you wish to know its meaning. If a new activity occurs in your body, you wish to know its meaning' (1909, p. 32). The meaning universally attributed to this new activity was procreation. The books provided two contexts for the erotic text: God's will, the divine plan for human progress; and racial evolution, the genetic plan for human progress. The sexual 'word' did not mean pleasure; it meant the future of the race.

But other (less well controlled) interpretations were available: from idle talk with servants and friends, which carnivalized sacred themes and spoke only of gratification; and from erotic novels, which had much the same effect. 'Too often,' warned Mona Baird, 'this class of reading so excites the sexual instincts as to lead desire to outweigh prudence, and every other sensible consideration' (1916, p. 19). Every young man and woman would know the kind of novel she meant. Respectable libraries banned them; where they did appear on the shelves, they were likely to show signs of unusual wear and tear.

When facts about the 'sad things of life' pass through the brain of a Dickens or a George Eliot, another commentator observed, they become 'purified and educative'; when they pass through the brain of a Zola, they become 'pernicious and infective as with deadly moral plague' (March 1915, p. 180). The solution was to 'pre-occupy' the adolescent mind with healthy books, with literary classics (Bullen 1886, p. 12). The National Home-Reading Union was founded in 1889 to do just that (Radford 1910). It issued primers and reading lists, and established reading circles in schools and libraries. Despite gaining recognition from boards of education, it fought a losing battle. Its 1909 report described the flood of 'worthless and demoralising publications' aimed at young people as a 'grave national peril' (NHRU 1909, p. 6).

The sex novel, which flourished in the 1890s and then from

1905 to 1914, seemed dangerous to the purity groups because it was explicit, and to the hygienists because it was misleadingly explicit. Its advocates subscribed to the same theory of social decline, the same piety about 'racial health', as its opponents. Their disagreement centred on the extent to which sexuality ought to be acknowledged, and on the extent to which a freely acknowledged sexuality might promote racial health.

Even the pornographers subscribed to the theory. By 1900 most publishers of erotica had gone out of business or skipped to Paris; by 1910 the supply had dried up completely (Kearney 1982, p. 151). What Edwardian pornography there was resembled the spy novel in its depiction of a hidden world beyond the rule of law: a world created and sustained by social decay (Hiley 1990). In *The Modern Eveline* (1904), Inspector Walker of the Special Branch explains that his undercover investigations have revealed a society 'rotten to the core'; he is, however, trouserless at the time (Hiley 1990, p. 67).

The secret society of hedonists whose activities are chronicled in *Pleasure Bound 'Afloat'* (1908), *Pleasure Bound 'Ashore'* (1909) and *Maudie* (1909) is united by the considerations which unite the secret societies of the terrorist novel: an affinity of suffering (in this case, perversion), combined with access to modern technology (a powerful yacht, a communications system, up-to-date type-writer girls). The room where Anna Klosstock strips, in *By Order of the Czar*, or the council chamber equipped with torture scenes where the Brotherhood meets in *Angel of the Revolution*, have their equivalent in Maudie's photographic studio, the walls of which display pornographic versions of biblical stories (Anon. 1909a, pp. 33–7). Terrorist, spy, pervert: all feed parasitically on social decay. All respond to a comparable anxiety about the decline of the race.

OLDER WOMEN

Lawrence once advised a friend looking for translation work to try 'Wm Heinemann or Methuen – or if it's anything racy, John Long' (1979–89, I, p. 306). During the Edwardian period Long published two writers, Hubert Wales and Victoria Cross (both pseudonyms), whose greatest success came with novels about older women who seduce young men: an event invariably represented as an education in 'racial health'.

Wales's favourite subject was the separation of physical from spiritual love. The husband and wife in *Mr and Mrs Villiers* (1906) have not slept together for six years. Any allusion to sex makes her feel as though a snake is creeping down her back. He leaves home, moves in next door to his mistress, and is soon interrupting a celebration dinner to press 'burning lips' on 'every little space which her evening bodice left open to his ravages' (1906, p. 62). His mistress's ravages prove just as searching. He goes into a decline and eventually, spitting blood, a coma; at which point he is returned, with thanks, to his wife. Since he's now a semi-invalid, their marital problems may be over.

Cynthia in the Wilderness (1907) tells a similar story. Cynthia's husband, Harvey, reveres her spirit and is consistently unfaithful to her body. She meets a man who appreciates both. They become lovers. However, the increasingly brutish Harvey catches them in the act and beats her lover over the head with a golf club. The lover survives. Meanwhile one of Cynthia's friends has self-sacrificingly poisoned Harvey and taken the rap. Cynthia returns from the wilderness to marry her lover.

Racier still was *The Yoke* (1907). Angelica Jenour, still a virgin at forty, realizes that her twenty-year-old ward, Maurice, is awakening sexually, and fears that he will resort to prostitutes. One of Maurice's friends contracts venereal disease and commits suicide. Angelica decides that she will save Maurice from a similar fate, and herself from the 'yoke' of repression, by becoming his lover. After educating him in love, and in 'racial health', she passes him on to his future wife.

Angelica does all that the reformers could have asked of her. She prepares Maurice for hygienic reproduction. Yet she clearly transgresses the limit set to sexual knowledge. She offers more than knowledge: she instructs not with motherly words, but with her body, with her own sexuality. *The Yoke* was suppressed after a vigorous campaign by the NVA, which denounced it as 'immoral garbage'.

Adolescence also appealed to Victoria Cross. In *The Greater Law* (1914), Roland West impregnates young Hilda Thorne and then, to avoid scandal, marries her to Clive Talbot, whom he has discovered in the local lunatic asylum. Talbot has the capacities of a man, but the consciousness of a child. Hilda falls in love with him, but doesn't know how to set about awakening him: 'if, as it were, his body should awake before his mind, from

209

that wonderful sleep that now enfolded both, he might become, instead of the splendid human being she hoped, merely an erotic maniac' (1914, p. 264). She decides to broaden his mind by making him read the kind of books in which love is represented as both a physical and a spiritual passion: the works of Milton, Bulwer Lytton and Victoria Cross. The sex novel incorporates itself as sex tract, becoming the limit of knowledge.

The novel which most profitably troubled that limit was Elinor Glyn's *Three Weeks* (1907). Paul Verdayne's 'episode' is curiously bodiless, its eroticism transferred from body and event to setting. (The tiger-skin rug on which the queen famously stretches might perhaps be seen as a displaced body surface, golden down.) Paul rains kisses on his queen which make up in vigour for what they lack in subtlety:

> The lady gasped. She looked up at him in bewildered surprise, as a child might do who sets a light to a whole box of matches in play. What a naughty, naughty toy to burn so quickly for such a little strike!
>
> But Paul's young, strong arms held her close, she could not struggle or move. Then she laughed a laugh of pure glad joy.
>
> 'Beautiful, savage Paul,' she whispered. 'Do you love me? Tell me that.'
>
> 'Love you!' he said. 'Good God! Love you! Madly, and you know it, darling Queen.'
>
> 'Then,' said the lady in a voice in which all the caresses of the world seemed melted, 'then, sweet Paul, I shall teach you many things, and among them I shall teach you how – to – LIVE.'

> *   *   *   *   *

> And outside the black storm made the darkness fall early. And inside the half-burnt logs tumbled together causing a cloud of golden sparks, and then the flames leapt up again and crackled in the grate.
>
> (1907, pp. 44–5)

In fact, despite the suggestive asterisks, nothing has happened.

This is a metaphorical consummation, a consummation in metaphor. The real thing, when it happens, seems like an afterthought. In *The Blue Lagoon* gratification precedes desire; in *Three Weeks*, desire precedes gratification, and precedes it, and precedes it. Until, suddenly, out of the confusion of skins and scents, there's a child. The Queen dies, but the child, in the pink of racial health, inherits her throne. This is teleological sex with a vengeance.

The Yoke was banned; *Three Weeks* wasn't. Both challenge a limit they ultimately respect. Wales, Cross and Glyn all owed their popularity to their ability to convert sexual expression into an absolute moral (and even political) value. The miniature transgressions that occur in Edwardian fiction whenever anyone glimpses a scar or a patch of golden down were not developed or amplified by the narratives which, in every sense, contain them. Transgression remained irreversibly local. Thus, young men like Angel Clare (Hardy 1978a, p. 172), Philip Carey (Maugham 1990a, pp. 154–76, 183–4, 232–3), Cecil Reeve (Leverson 1950, pp. 103–4), and, hypothetically, Stephen Dedalus (Joyce 1960, pp. 814–15) can be seen to have uneducative affairs with older women, without being formed by them.

SPLITS

Anxieties about adolescence were also exploited in novels where the hero's mistress fails to take the place of his mother, leaving him hopelessly divided between physical love for one and spiritual love for the other. 'The son decides to leave his soul in his mother's hands, and, like his elder brother, go for passion. He gets passion. Then the split begins to tell again. But, almost unconsciously, the mother realises what is the matter, and begins to die. The son casts off his mistress, attends to his mother dying.' This is Lawrence's account, in a letter to Edward Garnett, of Paul Morel's affair with Clara Dawes (1979–89, I, p. 477). It would also describe, with minor alterations, the plot of a sex novel published ten years before *Sons and Lovers*, Robert Hichens's *Felix*.

Felix Wilding falls in love with his mother's friend Mrs Ismey; or, to be precise, with her beautiful arms. When she prepares to take off her long white gloves he practically has to be helped from the room. But he is in for a shock.

Slowly she pulled the long glove lower till her wrist was bare. Felix's eyes began to shine. He bent a little forward. Then, abruptly, he turned away and looked at the other people in the room. He felt quite sick, almost as if he had seen a crime committed.

(Hichens 1902, p. 207)

Mrs Ismey's hands are filthy, and the reason for this turns out to be her addiction to morphia. Morphia became a recreational drug in bohemian circles in England during the 1890s (Berridge 1988). Bernard Shaw once scolded the actress Janet Achurch for reverting to her deceitful, 'heavy eyelidded, morphia injecting self'; he advised her to eat stewed fruit and Hovis (Holroyd 1988–92, I, pp. 371–2). Other cures on offer included Turkish baths, hot-water enemas and turtle soup (Parssinen 1983, p. 97). Mrs Ismey is beyond stewed fruit and turtle soup. Felix has to choose between her and his mother, who is about to undergo major surgery. He returns to his first love, his mother, Mrs Ismey to her husband.

Sons and Lovers, like *Felix*, like many sex novels, is about the split between abuse and sanctification of the body. Lawrence had already written a sex novel, *The Trespasser*. In 1911 he withdrew it from Heinemann, who were willing to publish, because he regarded it as 'pornographic'. 'Is the book so erotic?' he asked Edward Garnett anxiously: 'I don't want to be talked about in an *Ann Veronica* fashion.' He didn't want to be known as the author of a sex novel. Yet he did eventually publish *The Trespasser* in 1912, knowing it to be a sex novel; and he did declare that the self-division anatomized by *Sons and Lovers* was 'the tragedy of thousands of young men in England' (1979–89, I, pp. 229, 275, 339, 477).

This 'tragedy' afforded Lawrence a familiar theme and an opportunity. It enabled him to describe passion isolated from soul and to re-figure the body. The novel explores activities which enmesh the body without absorbing it, which give it form and purpose, but not meaning. Work, for example, eroticizes Clara Dawes. When Clara operates her spinning jenny, her body comes into its own. 'He saw the arch of her neck from the shoulder, as she bent her head; he saw the coil of dun hair; he watched her moving, gleaming arms' (1948, p. 318). Such rhythms intensify her presence. It is then that Paul notices the spaces between features, the golden down. Robert Hichens would not have taken the opportunity. Nor would Elinor Glyn, or Hubert Wales, or Victoria Cross. But without them it might not have been given to Lawrence.

Lawrence and Garnett knew perfectly well what a sex novel was, and didn't want *Sons and Lovers* to seem like one. Garnett edited the manuscript heavily. He cut several passages concerned with the split William Morel feels between soul and passion, and thus inclined the novel away from the tragedy of thousands of young men, and towards the tragedy of a single young man, the author himself. He also cut passages that describe Clara's maternal feelings for Paul, and Paul's uncertain sexuality (the occasion, for example, when he puts on Clara's stockings). Whatever the intention, the effect of these cuts was to diminish Lawrence's portrayal of a relationship with an older, fully embodied woman.

The representation of sexuality in turn-of-the-century fiction was constrained by a number of factors: censorship, the residual perspective incorporated in the (male) connoisseur's gaze, the emphasis on 'race-preservation'. But we should also acknowledge, here and there, a tendency to differentiate and individualize.

14

DISGUST

In the early years of the century, as in the later, sex sold books. It made for the writing of good bad books, but not good books. Bennett and Conrad avoided sex, Wells eugenicized it, Lawrence in the end took it too seriously, Hueffer was too happy feeling miserable about it, Sinclair lost interest, Forster censored himself, Kipling stuck to people whose youth or misfortune ruled them out, Richardson refined it out of existence. Only Maugham, Joyce (Brown 1985) and, in a very different way, James had anything memorable to say on the subject.

Disgust, on the other hand, is a feeling which animates, and is memorably represented in, a wide range of early twentieth-century writing. It preoccupied the best and most innovative writers of the period: James, Conrad, Kipling, Lawrence, Joyce, Wyndham Lewis. It was also an important factor, I shall argue, in the success of an enduringly popular genre: detective fiction. But I want first to establish its presence more generally.

BAD MOMENTS

One of the emotions whose expression was analysed by Charles Darwin in a famous book on the subject was disgust:

> The term 'disgust', in its simplest sense, means something offensive to the taste. It is curious how readily this feeling is excited by anything unusual in the appearance, odour, or nature of our food. In Tierra del Fuego a native touched with his finger some cold preserved meat which I was eating at our bivouac, and plainly showed utter disgust at its softness; whilst I felt utter disgust at my food being touched

by a naked savage, though his hands did not appear dirty.
A smear of soup on a man's beard looks disgusting, though
there is of course nothing disgusting in the soup itself.
                                        (Darwin 1904, p. 268)

Disgust is a gut feeling, a dis-taste. Caused, primarily, by the
ingestion of something which tastes bad, it provokes expulsion:
vomiting, spitting. A bad smell can have the same effect. Disgust
is spontaneous, absolute, all-or-nothing. It is also, to some extent,
culturally determined. The 'native' finds preserved meat revolting
to *touch*: soft when it should be baked hard. Darwin, in his turn,
is revolted by a purely cultural transgression: the fact that his
food has been touched by a 'naked savage', even though the
savage in question has evidently washed his hands first. There
are boundaries which define us, distinctions which enable us to
make sense of the world: soft/hard, raw/cooked, primitive/
civilized, and so on. If the boundaries are crossed, or the
distinctions blurred, we feel threatened, and act immediately to
re-establish them. What revolts us is not matter, but matter out
of place: soup on a man's beard.

The matter out of place in late nineteenth-century fiction often
marks the closeness of a social and psychic abyss, an outside, an
absolute difference. The ancient carriage that conveys Tess and
Angel Clare to church on their wedding day is driven by a
postilion with 'a permanent running wound on the outside of his
right leg' (Hardy 1978a, p. 278). Neither of them notices the
wound, but we do, surely, because open sores throw doubt on
the body's ability to heal itself, to stay intact, to seal us off from
the world; while the fluid they secrete is 'unnatural', neither
blood nor water, the product of some microbiological battlefield
or laboratory. Equally repellent is Billy Grainy's sore shin, in
The Real Charlotte (1894), which 'had often coerced the most
uncharitable to hasty and nauseated alms-giving' (Somerville and
Ross 1990, p. 69). These encounters bring us to the edge of
something we cannot confront rationally, but only reject, expel.

The distinctions disgustedly insisted on in turn-of-the-century
fiction are often class distinctions. 'The bourgeois subject con-
tinuously defined and redefined itself through the exclusion of
what it marked out as "low" – dirty, repulsive, noisy, con-
taminating.... The low was internalized under the sign of
negation and disgust' (Stallybrass and White 1986, p. 191). In

The Nether World the physical disgust Sidney Kirkwood feels at the 'fume of frying' emanating from a fish and chip shop is also a social disgust: although he has known the locality since childhood, he is not yet 'subdued' to it (Gissing 1974, p. 31). Working-class smells, and a considerable virtuosity in their description, are features of middle-class autobiography from Gosse (1974, pp. 74–5) to Orwell (1962, pp. 112–13).

Such feelings were a response to something which threatened not merely to subdue, but to abolish, identity. In *Marcella*, the reforming MP Aldous Raeburn visits a slum behind Drury Lane whose odours bear 'the inmost essence of things sickening and decaying'; the children playing amid the garbage seem remote from any 'tolerable human type' (Ward 1984, p. 418). There he encounters Marcella Boyce comforting a battered wife; what appals him is not the 'conventionalized' signs of ruin which surround them, but the woman, the 'breathing death' interposed between himself and Marcella (p. 422). Disgust has no truck with convention, with signs; it does not interpret or signify, but rejects.

For some among the next generation of writers, it was the system itself, not its edges and interstices, which provoked revulsion. Dispatched to renovate a cafe, Tressell's workmen find the kitchen and scullery in an 'unspeakable condition'. The worst abomination of all is a trough between window and table filled with matter out of place: fragments of fat and decomposed meat, broken cutlery, human hair (1965, pp. 406–7). Not surprisingly, anti-vivisection novels (Maugham 1991a, pp. 201–7) and anti-war novels (Herbert 1929, p. 105) were equally unsparing with abominable detail.

Other writers harnessed revulsion to projects of self-transformation. Beth, for example, turns against her husband when she discovers that he has been conducting hideous experiments in the study of their house (Grand 1980, p. 437). Thereafter he himself becomes an object of disgust: 'when he touched her, her delicate skin crisped with a shudder. She used to wonder how he could eat with hand so polluted, and once, at dessert, when he handed her a piece of orange in his fingers, she was obliged to leave it on her plate, she could not swallow it' (p. 445). This revulsion separates her more effectively from her earlier, cowed self than any amount of gloomy introspection.

After the death of his wife, Captain Hepburn feels utterly changed. He doesn't know why. 'But then one never can know the whys and wherefores of one's passional changes' (Lawrence 1982, p. 90). Again, the abruptness and depth of the change are measured by a revulsion from his friends and acquaintances: 'the moment they approached him to spread their feelings over him or to entangle him in their activities a helpless disgust came up in him, and until he could get away, he felt sick, even physically' (p. 91). Grand and Lawrence wanted to describe the formation of identity at a level 'below' conscious thought: a process which had eluded the moral, social, psychological and literary vocabularies of the time. Disgust gave them a point of entry into the subconscious. Passional changes, violent fluctuations of feeling which form and deform identity in an instant, were the great, unprecedented subject of Lawrence's fiction. Disgust, in short, could be conservative or radical in its effects. It could preserve class distinctions, or change someone's life.

BLOOMERS

Lawrence's exploration of violent fluctuations of feeling may have been unprecedented, but it was not unparalleled. In 1918, Joyce told Frank Budgen that *Ulysses* was to be, among other things, 'the epic of the human body'. 'In my book the body lives in and moves through space and is the home of a full human personality. The words I write are adapted to express first one of its functions then another' (Budgen 1934, p. 21). Lawrence would surely not have disputed the aim, even though he was to prove critical of its expression.

The episode Joyce had in mind was 'Lestrygonians', where, he claimed, the stomach dominates: Bloom, looking for lunch, puts his head into the Burton, is revolted by the sight of men 'swilling' and moves on to Davy Byrne's and a cheese sandwich. Bloom's physical revulsion – 'Smells of men. His gorge rose. Spaton sawdust, sweetish warmish cigarette smoke, reek of plug, spilt beer, men's beery piss, the stale of ferment' (1960, p. 215) – is connected subtly, either as cause or as catalyst, to his mounting anxiety about Molly and Blazes Boylan, whom he narrowly avoids at the end of the episode. Leaving Davy Byrne's, he witnesses an appetite far more desperate, more impervious, than his own. 'At Duke lane a ravenous terrier choked up a sick knuckly cud on the cobble stones and lapped it with new zest. Surfeit. Returned with thanks having fully digested the contents' (pp. 228–9). Odysseus-like, he coasts 'warily' on, ruminating about ruminants, the phrase he has found for the terrier's regurgitation more appropriate to the loan of a book than a knuckly cud. This, he has already complained, before he reached the Burton, is the worst hour of the day. 'Feel as if I had been eaten and spewed' (p. 208). But the worst hour of the day is also the worst hour of his life, as cuckoldry approaches: a crisis comparable to Beth's, or Hepburn's.

To cope with disgust, and self-disgust, himself eaten and spewed, Bloom wanders. From 'Sirens' onwards, the styles, the techniques, wander in sympathy. In that episode the precision of the initial style gives way to 'a more arbitrary use of language' (Kelly 1988, p. 25). For a moment, during the overture to the episode, a selection of 'onomatopoeic junk' arranged in a 'thematic catalogue' (Kenner 1980, p. 88), narrative ceases altogether. It has been set adrift (Attridge 1988, pp. 136–57, 160–72). Throughout the episode we struggle to find a criterion of relevance which might bind it into sense.

> A hackney car, number three hundred and twentyfour, driver Barton James of number one Harmony avenue, Donnybrook, on which sat a fare, a young gentleman, stylishly dressed in an indigoblue serge suit made by George Robert Mesias, tailor and cutter, of number five Eden quay, and wearing a straw hat very dressy, bought of John Plasto of number one Great Brunswick street, hatter. Eh? This is the jingle that joggled and jingled.
>
> (Joyce 1960, pp. 360–1)

On a second reading, equipped by then with the knowledge that Boylan and Bloom share both tailor and hatter, we may feel the ironic effect of some of these details. On a first reading they are likely to seem excessive, a puzzling, possibly even sickening, surfeit.

The passage draws attention to the gap between decoding (what the words might mean) and inference (what they might be intended to mean on this occasion) which characterizes the later episodes of the book, by asking what the data add up to ('Eh?'), and providing an answer, as though to a child, which merely reinforces in a small way what we already knew: Boylan's clothes, like everything about him, embody his jauntiness ('This is the jingle...'). Such moments, in the episodes from 'Sirens' to 'Circe', are likely to do little more than strengthen existing assumptions, existing knowledge. It is in 'Sirens', after all, that the Arranger announces himself by repeating what he has already told us: 'Bloom ate liv as said before' (p. 349). The criterion of relevance is as readily infringed by telling us something we already know as by telling us something for which we cannot provide a context. In 'Sirens' we are well and truly on the 'treadmill of recapitulation' (Kelly 1988, p. 16). The text has begun to spew what it has eaten, to lap its own vomit.

By 'Cyclops', the initial style no longer exists. A garrulous Thersites delivers bar-room opinion, his monologue interrupted by thirty-two comically elevated set-pieces. These set-pieces violently flout the Principle of Relevance: they cost a lot to process, but yield very little by way of contextual effect. There is no knowing what to make of the Citizen, Bloom's future antagonist. What is it important to know about him? That he has frank eyes and hairy legs? Or a deep chest and a large nose? Again, we suffer from a surfeit of information.

Still, our appetite for relevance is not easily extinguished. Every now and then we may be able to seize upon a statement which, when combined with what we already know, will enhance our cognitive environment. At one point, J.J. O'Molloy enters, to be described instantly as 'a comely hero of white face yet withal somewhat ruddy' (p. 414). Stylistically, the epithet is adrift, excessive; yet it does combine with what we already know about Bloom, who had earlier noticed O'Molloy's 'hectic flush' (p. 158), to enable us to acknowledge his shrewdness and compassion.

On the whole, though, our experience of the wandering styles is likely to be one of surfeit, of an appetite fed by statements which can with some difficulty be decoded, but which yield virtually nothing in the way of contextual effect. The orthodox view, now, is that we should suspend our appetite for relevance, and simply take pleasure in the hyperbole, the excess, the 'play' of language. My argument is that the appetite for relevance is not easily suspended, as Joyce very well knew, and that our response to stylistic excess is likely to involve not only pleasure but fatigue, boredom, frustration and, yes, disgust. Furthermore, the whole tendency of his extensive revision of the earlier episodes was to increase the surfeit: to thicken their texture until they failed to resemble altogether the Imagist prose-poem that Pound had hoped he was writing (Groden 1977).

'Circe', with its ritual debasements, its annihilation of identity, its flourishing of secret anxieties and desires, is the climax of Bloom's wanderings; yet it is, in many ways, anticlimactic. Kenner entitles his chapter on it 'Death and Resurrection'; the Bloom who emerges from Nighttown is a new Bloom, courageous and composed (Kenner 1980, p. 120), regenerated. But for the reader, I think, there is no rite of passage. We are still on the treadmill of recapitulation. Generically, the episode may gesture towards Shakespeare, Goethe, Flaubert; but it also recycles more banal precedents. When Bloom enters Nighttown, he enters a slum novel complete with whores, dribbling idiots and rubbish tips (p. 562). When he submits to Madame Bella, he enters the sado-masochistic fantasy world of late Victorian pornography (Gilbert 1982, pp. 196–7). Stephen Dedalus's mother, rising stark through the floor in leper grey, rises stark out of a ghost story (p. 680). The whole episode, as Kenner points out, is a play to outrival Synge and Yeats in offensiveness (1980, pp. 118–19).

More significantly, 'Circe' is a gigantic recapitulation of incidents, thoughts and phrases from the previous fourteen episodes, a 'jumbled reprise of what the reader has left behind' (Mahaffey 1988, p. 107). We are still, at this stage of the book, eating what we have been forced to vomit, what the recapitulations have brought up. 'Circe' is an offence to that appetite for relevance which Joyce had nurtured so carefully through the initial style, and then systematically frustrated through stylistic excess. There may be pleasures in 'Circe'. But it is also revoltingly dull.

THEORY AND DETECTIVE FICTION

I shall return to the relation between disgust and stylistic excess in Chapter 18, when I discuss Wyndham Lewis's writing. But I want to turn now to a popular genre which has usually been thought to exclude the depiction of passional changes, partly because it is English, and partly because it concentrates on the hermeneutic powers of the detective.

Originally an urban genre, in Conan Doyle's early stories, English detective fiction was transformed by the reinvention of Englishness. Doyle himself liked to contrast old world with new. In 'The Adventure of the Dancing Men', Hilton Cubitt, squire of Riding Thorpe Manor, a 'man of the old English soil' (Doyle 1981, p. 513), is murdered by his wife's former lover, a swaggering

American gangster. *The Valley of Fear*, a longer story, has two parts: one describing a violent death in an ancient English manor house, the other the origins of the crime in industrialized, brutalized America. Imported crimes served to clarify and strengthen the Englishness they had momentarily disrupted (Bentley 1913). By the 1920s detective fiction had taken over rural, country-house England; it became a part of the heritage industry. W. H. Auden, an addict, said he would only read stories set in 'rural England' (Auden 1948, p. 146). To more recent commentators this emphasis, which invariably conceals the social origins of crime, has seemed a damaging inhibition.

Equally damaging has been a perceived complicity with nineteenth-century realism – and all that that entails. 'The project of the Sherlock Holmes stories,' Belsey argues in an influential essay, 'is to dispel magic and mystery, to make everything explicit, accountable, subject to scientific analysis' (Belsey 1980, p. 111; the chapter is reprinted in Ashley 1989, Bennett 1990). The detective's interpretations sustain and extend the 'positivism' which supposedly enabled the bourgeoisie to make sense of the world. This argument has the force and the limitations of the critical theory which engendered it.

During the 1970s semiotics converted itself into a critique of ideology by incorporating a theory of subjectivity derived from the work of Jacques Lacan. Lacan was understood to argue that the unconscious, and therefore subjectivity, is structured like a language; that 'the process of signification is the process of the subject itself' (Coward and Ellis 1977, p. 94). The human subject, like the grammatical subject, is defined by its 'position' in discourse. This rhetoric of position was meant to close off subjectivity to avowals of essence or completeness, and open it to 'scientific analysis': to Althusser's theory of ideology or, later in the decade, Foucault's theory of the relation between knowledge and power. It anchored poststructuralism's semiotic delirium in a psychology and a politics.

What *could* be avowed, as well as analysed, in the 1970s, was desire. '*Desidero* (I desire) is according to Lacan the Freudian *Cogito*, since what is essential in the primary process (the play of combination and substitution in the signifier which determines the institution of the subject) traces the route of desire' (Coward and Ellis 1977, p. 120). Desire, produced by difference, by a lack, was the one politically correct human energy which conformed to the Saussurean model of signification, and to the model of subjectivity derived from it. This conformity sponsored Kristeva's work on desire in language, and Barthes's *The Pleasure of the Text* (1973), which had become, by the end of the decade, the acceptable face of *nouvelle critique*. It also led cultural historians like Stallybrass and White, when they analysed the politics of fascination and disgust, to put the stress on fascination (Stallybrass and White 1986).

Belsey reiterates the stress when she points out that, although the overt aim of the Sherlock Holmes stories may be 'total explicitness', they also include women whose sexuality has a 'dark and magical' quality 'beyond the reach of scientific knowledge' (1980, p. 114). 'The Dancing Men', for example, is about Holmes's ability to break a cipher. But the victim's widow already knows both the code and her own feelings about the murderer, a former lover; and divulges neither. 'As a result, the text with its project of dispelling mystery is haunted by the mysterious state of mind of a woman who is unable to speak' (Belsey 1980, p. 115). Desire undermines the power claimed by Holmes's scientific method, on behalf of justice, and by Doyle's story, on behalf of realism.

These women are marginal figures only. English detective fiction's overriding positivism, combined with its overriding Englishness, has been enough to condemn it in the eyes of many professional commentators. I am not convinced, however, that complacency alone would have been enough to secure so many readers over such a long period. There are other disturbances in detective fiction than desire; disturbances which have contributed significantly to its broader appeal.

CORPSES

Death is the salient feature of English detective fiction, not sexuality. Death activates the hermeneutic powers of the detective, and the healing powers of Englishness. There is always a moment, before those powers are fully operational, when death holds the stage. The corpse in the first Sherlock Holmes story, *A Study in Scarlet* (1887), is studiedly inaugural, a show-stopper. 'I have seen death in many forms,' Watson records, 'but never has it appeared to me in a more fearsome aspect than in that dark, grimy apartment, which looked out upon one of the main arteries of suburban London' (Doyle 1981, p. 29). *The Return of Sherlock Holmes* (1905), from which Belsey draws her examples, contains its full quota of crushed skulls and slit throats, not to mention a man pinned to the wall by a harpoon.

Marxist and deconstructive readings construe these corpses as pure signs, a challenge to the detective's hermeneutic powers. 'He is not moved by pity for the victim, by moral or material horror at the crime, but by its *cultural quality*: by its *uniqueness* and its *mystery*' (Moretti 1988, p. 135). His refusal to be horrified ensures the triumph of (bourgeois) mind over matter. Or does it?

It seems to me that the physical disgust aroused by a corpse, the moral disgust aroused by murder, are not so easily suppressed; indeed they are rhetorically powerful, and therefore ever-present in detective fiction. These are feelings which have received a certain amount of attention from philosophers (Sartre 1957, pp. 604–15; Pole 1983), anthropologists (Douglas 1966), psycho-analysts (Kristeva 1982) and cultural historians (Stallybrass and White 1986). The terms they use can help us to understand the psychological and rhetorical power of disgust.

Kristeva tries to imagine a life sustained not by desire but by exclusion, by the memory of some primordial separation which is the future subject's first effort to distinguish itself from the 'maternal entity'. This violent, clumsy breaking away does not achieve the separation of subject from object which will eventually make possible both desire and meaning, but rather an 'abjection', an expulsion which is also self-expulsion. If the object draws us into a desire for meaning, the 'abject', the (waste) product of expulsion, draws us towards death. It evokes horror and disgust.

The abject is 'the in-between, the ambiguous, the composite' (Kristeva 1982, p. 4); whatever has been expelled but not obliterated, for to obliterate it would be to obliterate ourselves. It is a disturbance of boundaries, systems and identifications which becomes evident in the physical gestures and the cer-emonies we devise to conceal it, thus provoking further expul-sions.

A wound with blood and pus, or the sickly, acrid smell of sweat, of decay, does not *signify* death. In the presence of signified death – a flat encephalograph, for instance – I would understand, react, or accept. No, as in true theatre,

223

without makeup or masks, refuse and corpses *show me* what
I permanently thrust aside in order to live.

(p. 3)

In fiction, of course, there is no 'true theatre', no unmediated
representation. However, fictional corpses may evoke a comparable response. Confronted by the abject, we do not desire or
interpret, Kristeva says, but 'faint away'. We are paralysed, Pole
argues, by the effort to extrude what is actually or prospectively
a part of ourselves. 'At which point we find the only positive
action closely connected with disgust; that of retching or vomiting'
(1983, p. 225). Similarly, the phantom disgust aroused by a
fictional corpse may persist alongside the phantom pleasure we
take in the resolution of an enigma.

'The corpse must shock,' Auden said, 'not only because it is a
corpse but also because, even for a corpse, it is shockingly out
of place, as when a dog makes a mess on a drawing-room carpet'
(1948, p. 151). In detective fiction the corpse is always out of
place, incongruous, like shit on a carpet or soup in a man's
beard. Murder makes a mess in a clean (English) place. Stories
about murder are stories as much about dealing with mess as
about deciphering clues.

Neither Freud nor Proust allowed their interest in signification
and desire to obscure the fact that murder makes a mess of
both – indeed, the fact that murder can be used to symbolize
the messes both make. In *Moses and Monotheism* Freud remarked
that the distortion of a text (in this case, scripture) 'resembles a
murder: the difficulty is not in perpetrating the deed, but in
getting rid of its traces' (1953–74, XXIII, p. 43). The analogy
with murder suits his view that the text – scripture, dream,
symptom – is never simply an encoded message, but the site of
a (potentially bloody) conflict between impulses. The traces left
by murder or by distortion continue to bear witness to the
violence that produced them. To that extent, they are objects
not of interpretation but of horror, disgust, fascination. They
continue to provoke these feelings even after the interpreter has
drained them of significance. The same is true, I would suggest,
of detective fiction.

In one of the creepiest episodes in *A la recherche*, at the beginning
of *Sodome et Gomorrhe*, the narrator listens to the sounds made
when the Baron de Charlus seduces Jupien: 'these sounds were

so violent that, if they had not always been taken up an octave higher by a parallel plaint, I might have thought that one person was slitting another's throat within a few feet of me, and that subsequently the murderer and his resuscitated victim were taking a bath to wash away the traces of the crime.' He concludes that pleasure is the one thing in life as 'vociferous' as pain, especially when it induces 'an immediate concern about cleanliness' (Proust 1983, II, p. 631). Transgression is provoked, measured and perhaps betrayed by the mess it makes.

It is to dirt, to refuse, to matter out of place, that the detective looks first: the dirt which is the corpse, and the dirt which surrounds the corpse. Footprints, fingerprints, hairs, threads, bloodstains. Holmes seems able to discern an entire body-print in the traces left at the scene of a crime. He is the proud author of monographs on the identification of footsteps and 'the influence of a trade upon the form of the hand', and an essay entitled 'The Book of Life'. 'By a man's fingernails, by his coat-sleeve, by his boots, by his trouser-knees, by the callosities of his forefinger and thumb, by his expression, by his shirt-cuffs – by each of these things a man's calling is plainly revealed' (Doyle 1981, p. 23). Of course, Holmes's business is to convert material traces into signs, into clues. But the matter to which his activities have drawn attention remains, for us, as we await his interpretation, unconverted, unresolved.

In detective fiction, the stuff to be deciphered is also the stuff of horror and disgust. Recognizing this, Dennis Wheatley and J. G. Links went so far as to produce, in the late 1930s, a series of dossier-books which contained not only facsimile documentation but material 'evidence': a scrap of bloodstained fabric, a cigarette-butt, an arsenic tablet ('Note to readers. The poison has been extracted from this tablet') (Wheatley and Links 1936, 1937, 1938, 1939). By converting such traces into clues, the detective dissolves them. But the traces must be registered in order to be converted. It is that process which makes detective fiction something other than a dispute between the power of signs and the power of desire.

'I COULDN'T TOUCH A BIT OF BREAKFAST'

Dorothy L. Sayers's *Whose Body?* (1923) immediately offers what its title has promised: matter out of place, in a bath in a suburban flat. Since no one can identify the body, its materiality remains unavoidable: calloused hands, blistered feet, dirty toe nails, all contradicted by a faint violet perfume, manicured finger nails and a pair of gold pince-nez. Lord Peter Wimsey proceeds to convert these traces into clues. But the owner of the flat, an architect, hasn't quite got the knack. The sight of the body – the mess on his carpet, so to speak – makes him feel sick. 'I couldn't touch a bit of breakfast,' he says, 'nor lunch neither' (Sayers 1989, p. 14).

The narrative, in other words, provides a position from which death seems merely disgusting or horrifying, rather than a stimulus to interpretation. Many detective stories, novels and films include a similar scene in which someone sees the corpse and just feels terribly ill. What they are confronting, and we may confront through them, is the abject.

G. K. Chesterton built such positions into some of his best stories. In 'The Secret Garden' a succession of beheadings makes Commandant O'Brien, an exotic Irish soldier, feel 'decidedly sick'. Father Brown, of course, is unmoved (Chesterton 1981, pp. 33–4). But his hermeneutic virtuosity does not altogether overshadow the Irishman's feeling that the murders have horribly confused life and death, reality and dream (p. 37). Murder has forced O'Brien to confront the abject: the in-between, the indeterminate, the composite, the monstrous.

In 'The Invisible Man', a young Scotsman, John Turnbull Angus, accompanies Father Brown to the home of Isidore Smythe, an inventor who has made millions out of designing robots. A robot stands guard over the spot where murder has been committed. Angus wonders whether the machines have killed their master and eaten him; 'and he sickened for an instant at the idea of rent, human remains absorbed and crushed into all that acephalous clockwork.' (Chesterton 1981, pp. 74–5). The narrative acknowledges his nightmare: the blurring of distinctions between man and machine, inside and outside, subject and object. Unlike the women in the Sherlock Holmes stories, Angus expresses his horror. The story does not need to be deconstructed.

The detective never sickens: his insulation safeguards him against nightmares. But it would be a mistake to assume that he is entirely immune. Holmes is never simply the voice of positivism, as Belsey suggests (1980, p. 112). True, he is a scientist, and he does object rather cold-bloodedly to Watson's tendency to 'slur over work of the utmost finesse' in order to dwell upon 'sensational details' (Doyle 1981, p. 636). But he is himself notably slurred over, a double nature (p. 185). Although neat and methodical, a guardian of distinctions and taxonomies, he is also extremely untidy. He keeps his cigars in the coal scuttle, his tobacco in a slipper, and his unanswered correspondence pinned to the mantelpiece by a jack-knife (p. 386). This comic confusion asserts his kinship with the abject world he will become immersed in, the mess he will have to clear up.

Later writers tended to tone this duality down into eccentric mannerisms: Wimsey's whimsicality, Hanaud's (Mason 1910) or Poirot's foreignness. But other detectives also assert their kinship with an abject world. Freeman's Dr Thorndyke, the most convincingly scientific of them all, does not regard scientific evidence as infallible (Freeman 1911). Ernest Bramah's Max Carrados is blind, and therefore unable to participate in the totalitarian project which detective fiction has been said to underwrite: 'the dream of rendering society totally visible to the gaze of power' (Bennett 1990, p. 216). Carrados has to rely on the senses of hearing, touch, smell and taste: senses which immerse him, frighteningly at times, in the world his deductions are meant to regulate (Bramah 1914). Nor should we imagine that the women detectives of the period had a straightforward relation to 'the gaze of power' (Orczy 1910; Craig and Cadogan 1986).

Father Brown is every bit as untidy as Holmes. 'The Absence of Mr Glass' pits him against an eminent criminologist, Dr Orion Hood, whose apartments, like his mind, are a miracle of tidiness. Enter their opposite, 'a shapeless little figure, which seemed to find its own hat and umbrella as unmanageable as a mass of luggage' (Chesterton 1981, p. 172). 'The Queer Feet' finds him in London's most exclusive hotel, hearing a dying man's confession. His presence that evening seems to the owner as offensive as 'a speck of dirt on something just cleaned' (p. 41). Father Brown's affinity is not with the 'gaze of power', but with the abject, with the mess on the carpet. In 'The Salad of Colonel Kray' he dives into a dustbin in order to examine its contents. 'Dust and other discolouring matter shook upwards as he did so; but Father Brown never observed his own appearance, whatever else he observed' (p. 285).

'STAMPED WITH SLIME'

English detective fiction is often accused of treating small matters in a small-minded way. I have tried to show, however, that it can encompass some fairly major phobias and disruptions. Criminals, Father Brown remarks, always end up 'stamped with slime' (Chesterton 1981, p. 163). They are identified, stamped; but only by an act which has created waste, indeterminacy, matter out of place. The qualms evoked by detective fiction stamp us, too, pending the detective's clarification, with slime.

Elizabeth Bowen, who began to publish after the First World War, at a time when detective fiction enjoyed enormous popularity, recognized its capacity to horrify as well as intrigue (Kemp 1990). In 'The Cat Jumps', Harold and Jocelyn Wright move into a house whose previous owner, Harold Bentley, had killed and dismembered his wife. The Wrights are a modern, ultra-rational couple, with 'thoroughly disinfected minds' and 'no inhibitions' (Bowen 1983, p. 362). They have the house stripped and scrubbed. Even so, a strange smell persists, 'a smell of unsavoury habitation, of rich cigarette-smoke stale in the folds of unaired curtains, of scent spilled on unbrushed carpets, an alcoholic smell'. Dismayed by this unsettling odour, they set out to 'expel' the Bentleys, by whatever means possible (p. 363).

The Bentleys, however, return to haunt the Wrights, and the guests invited down for their first weekend party. Disgust turns into horror. At dinner, the flow of ultra-rational conversation peters out.

> In fact, on the intelligent sharp-featured faces all round the table something – perhaps simply a clearness – seemed to be lacking, as though these were wax faces for one fatal instant exposed to a furnace. Voices came out from some dark interiority; in each conversational interchange a mutual vote of no confidence was implicit. You would have said that each personality had been attacked by some kind of decomposition.

> (p. 366)

The bad smells, the ghostly presences, have destroyed the clarity of outline which certifies identity. Bowen, too, 'decomposes' the clear outlines of generic convention, mixing horror with comedy and social observation in a way that Chesterton alone, among crime writers, was capable of. But her subject was their subject: matter out of place. And no small matter. I will now pursue the matter of bad smells and ghostly presences in the work of a very different kind of writer: Henry James.

15

HENRY JAMES'S ODD WOMEN

Between 1896 and 1899, Henry James published a series of remarkable novels and stories which are told primarily from the point of view of a girl or a young woman: *The Other House*, *What Maisie Knew*, *The Turn of the Screw*, *The Spoils of Poynton*, 'In the Cage' and *The Awkward Age*. According to Leon Edel, the series belongs to a period of experimentation in James's career, between the humiliating collapse of his theatrical venture in 1895, and the triumphant inauguration of his 'major phase' in 1900, when he began work on *The Ambassadors* (Edel 1969, pp. 246–50). During this period, Edel suggests, James was preparing the ground for the achievement of the late novels, extending and refining his narrative technique, attempting the unusual.

Edel's account is too confidently teleological. James was certainly experimenting, but his experiments didn't always take him in the direction of *The Ambassadors*. The woman-centred stories are among his least mandarin. He put himself out, as he rarely did before or after, to write from the point of view of protagonists who did not resemble him. The heroine of 'In the Cage', for example, is his most convincing lower-middle-class character. These protagonists are not innocents abroad, like Daisy Miller and Isobel Archer. They are innocents at home, menaced by what is most familiar, by family itself. The woman-centred stories represent an interlude in James's career.

They are preceded by one story about a male protagonist in obsessive pursuit of knowledge, 'The Figure in the Carpet' (1895), and followed by another, *The Sacred Fount* (1901). In these stories the desire for meaning becomes itself the only meaning of desire, its articulation the only possible activity. What is different about the woman-centred stories is that they suspend this obsession

230

with interpretation and, by the same stroke, allow for something other than desire.

SCREWED UP

The place to start is *The Turn of the Screw* (1898), a text which has provoked almost as much theoretical debate as Poe's 'Purloined Letter' or Conrad's *Heart of Darkness*. It is a ghost story, of course, a story meant to provoke horror: a feeling which combines revulsion with dread. I shall argue here that James wrote a horror story in order to articulate feelings of revulsion which were of natural rather than supernatural origin. But I must first of all confront a debate which, ignoring horror altogether, has centred on interpretation and desire.

In 'The ambiguity of Henry James' (1934), Edmund Wilson gave the governess a motive for deception, arguing that she is a 'neurotic case of sex repression', and that she hallucinates the ghosts (Wilson 1962, p. 102), The ghost story is really a madness story. In 1963 Oscar Cargill drew parallels between the governess and Miss Lucy R., who features in Breuer and Freud's *Studies on Hysteria* (essay reprinted in James 1966a, pp. 156–9). Both are Englishwomen of depressive tendencies who have charge of two small children and fall in love with their employers. Alice James had been diagnosed as a hysteric. William James was certainly familiar with *Studies on Hysteria*. Henry had of necessity to be interested in the subject, the argument goes, and it is possible that he knew about Breuer and Freud, though Cargill clearly overstates the case for direct influence.

In the first phase of the debate, critics tried to decide what the story means. In the second phase, inaugurated by Shoshona Felman's 'Turning the screw of interpretation' (1977, in Felman 1982b), they decided that its meaning is its undecidability. The story became an allegory of the will, or the desire, to interpret. The general context for Felman's essay is that combination of linguistics and psychoanalysis which produced, during the 1970s, a new way of talking about subjectivity (see above, pp. 221–2).

Like her predecessors, Felman concentrates on the governess. But for her the governess is not a 'character' so much as a 'position' which the reader drops into. 'Since it is the governess who, within the text, plays the role of the suspicious reader, occupies the *place* of the interpreter, to *suspect* that place and that position is, thereby, *to take it*' (1977, p. 90). Just as the governess compels the children to reveal their meaning and their pleasure, Felman argues, so an interpreter like Edmund Wilson compels the text to reveal its meaning and its pleasure. Opening the text, each of us becomes the governess. Felman's reading of James, like Belsey's reading of Conan Doyle, allows no room for anything except signification and desire.

ACROSS DANGEROUS PLACES

It is striking that James himself, when he was planning the story, paid little attention to the governess. His original notebook entry (12 January 1895) concentrates on the corrupt servants and the corrupted children. 'The servants *die* (the story vague about the way of it) and their apparitions, figures, return to haunt the house *and* children, to whom they seem to beckon, whom they invite and solicit, from across dangerous places, the deep ditch of a sunk fence, etc. – so that the children may destroy themselves, lose themselves, by responding, by getting into their power' (1987, p. 109). The emphasis is on evil, and deliberately vague, except when James specifies that the inviting and soliciting should happen 'from across dangerous places'. In the text, Quint and Miss Jessel appear beyond a window, or on the other side of a lake, or significantly above or below the observer. A gap opens in the assumptions of distance and relation which measure domestic surroundings, in the tissue of domesticity. Crossing the gap means death. 'It is a question of the children "coming over to where they are"' (1987, p. 109).

The Turn of the Screw is about a crossing which extinguishes the desire (the meaning) it has solicited. Only at the very end of the notebook entry, apparently as an afterthought, does James mention the figure who will become the governess. He told Wells that he had ruled out 'subjective complications' on the governess's part and allowed her only 'the most obvious and indispensable little note of neatness, firmness and courage – without which she wouldn't have had her data' (1974–84, IV, p. 86). Her data are, of course, all we have to go on. But we need not assume that she does no more in the story than (mis)interpret them. She acts in other ways. It is those other actions which open up for us, not her own subjectivity, but the dangerous place across which evil solicits. They reveal horror, not desire; death, not meaning.

The text in which Freud spoke most powerfully, if elliptically, about those things was not *Studies on Hysteria* but *Beyond the Pleasure Principle* (1920). 'In the theory of psycho-analysis,' he begins, 'we have no hesitation in assuming that the course taken by mental events is automatically regulated by the pleasure principle' (1953–74, XVIII, p. 7). James also begins by granting the pleasure principle, in the shape of the governess's employer, an uncontested mastery. 'One could easily fix his type,' Douglas remarks; 'it nevèr, happily, dies out' (1907–9, XII, p. 153). Happy and immortal, the Master embodies pleasure.

Thereafter both arguments hesitate, systematically, as they disclose examples of the regulation of mental events by a principle other than pleasure. Having seduced the governess into working for him (p. 155), the Master insists that she should 'take the whole thing over and let him alone' (p. 156). She is there, in her place, to safeguard his gratification. But the gesture which frees him for pleasure – handing over the headmaster's report on Miles, unopened – is also a first, and ominous, hesitation. The report hints at forces beyond the pleasure principle.

One way to look past the governess, and the smothering desires she has been invested with, is to situate the story as a whole in a series (potentially a history) of representations of 'evil'. I shall read the next book in the series, *Beyond the Pleasure Principle*, with the help of Jacques Derrida, who reads it with Rousseau's help; and, since I have already expressed considerable scepticism about the critical project of which Derrida is a part, I should explain his presence in the argument at this juncture. What interests me is Derrida's sense of (his own place in) a series of efforts to represent the demise of representation: to bring out (or back, or forward) what lies 'beyond' the pleasure principle, 'beyond' the desire for meaning. Rousseau, Freud, Derrida: for each, what lies beyond is repetition. Establishing as much, they repeat each other. And yet there is always a difference to be established, too. The irreducibility of what lies 'beyond' has always to be reasserted, to be wrenched away from the constructions placed upon it: the pleasure, the meaning, it has accrued since the last assertion.

Derrida's writing could be seen as a reiterated, differentiated wrenching away. 'To speculate – on "Freud" ' (1980) is concerned with what binds the question of life and death to 'the question of positionality in general, of positional (oppositional or juxtapositional) logic, of the theme or the thesis' (1987, p. 259). Derrida understands Freud's move beyond the life-instincts as a move beyond position, beyond thesis; and rejects those readings, including Lacan's, which have drawn theses out of Freud's text (p. 377). He wants, instead, to make legible its 'non-positional structure' (p. 261). I want to look past the figure of the governess to the question of life and death formulated by a story which remains, when all is said and done, a *ghost* story.

PLAYING THE DEVIL

What is the gap, the dangerous place, across which evil solicits? Like James, Freud and Derrida approach it from the direction of the pleasure principle. The dangerous place emerges in the fading of the pleasure principle.

Freud's second chapter provides examples of compulsive repetition, including, famously, the game in which a one-year-old boy compensates himself for his mother's absence by endlessly restaging the disappearance and return of objects within his reach. These examples show that unpleasurable experiences can be worked over in the mind, mastered, converted into pleasure.

A different kind of evidence emerges from the psychoanalytic treatment of neurotics. Patients resist analysis by compulsively repeating, in the transference, their failures and humiliations. Such resistance is not pleasurable. It suggests, on the contrary, that 'some "daemonic" force' is at work (Freud 1953–74, XVIII, p. 21), some force more powerful than the pleasure principle. Beyond the pleasure principle is the devil's work, or death. Freud went on to distinguish between the sexual instincts, which seek to prolong life, and the 'ego-instincts', which seek to 'prolong' death – to restore, through compulsive diabolical repetitions, the inanimate state out of which life arose.

Derrida glosses the devil's appearance in Freud's argument with a footnote from Rousseau's *Letter to D'Alembert* which concerns a play featuring the devil. When he appeared on stage, Rousseau records, the devil 'appeared double, as if the original had been jealous that they had had the audacity to imitate him'. The audience took to its heels. Rousseau can only imagine one other sight as terrible: the writing on the wall at Balthazar's feast. He grasps the demonic – what Derrida terms *différance*, 'an alterity more irreducible than the alterity attributed to opposition' – as a threat to representation: an uninterpretable writing, a 'double apparition' which confuses person and mask, original and simulacrum. The demonic, Derrida suggests, is this effect of 'duplicity without an original' (1987, pp. 279–82).

In *The Turn of the Screw*, two revenants, two devils, the ghosts of Quint and Miss Jessel, come back in order to ensure their hold on the two children, and come back double. When Quint first appears to the governess, he appears as his master's double. She (mis)recognizes him in 'two distinct gasps of emotion' (James 1907–9, XII, p. 176). Her first shock is that the Master should have returned home and be standing on the tower. The second is 'a violent perception of the mistake of my first'. The second perception only has a meaning in relation to the first; it has no origin, no reference to the world. Indeed, the world no longer exists. 'It was as if, while I took in, what I did take in, all the rest of the scene had been stricken with death' (p. 176). She and the figure later identified as Quint continue to confront each other 'across our distance' (p. 177). The duplicity in which (or as which) the devil returns has already begun to infect her way of thinking.

The next time he comes back he gazes in at her through a window. Her response is to double him: to place herself where he stood, to look into the room. 'As if, at this moment, to show me exactly what his range had been, Mrs Grose, as I had done for himself just before, came in from the hall. With this I had the full image of a repetition of what had already occurred' (p. 185). The devil's range, the gap across which he solicits, can be gauged only by reproducing it. Mrs Grose, in her turn, blanches, retreats, comes round to the outside. The devil compels repetition, a duplicity without original. He is, Derrida remarks, 'the *revenance* which repeats its entrance, coming back [*revenant*] from one knows not where ('early infantile influences,' says Freud), inherited from one knows not whom, but already persecutory, by means of the simple form of its return, indefatigably repetitive, independent of every apparent desire, *automatic*'. This automaton 'produces effects of ventriloquism without origin, without emission, and without addressee' (1987, p. 341) When Peter Quint and Miss Jessel speak, they speak – and this is perhaps the most frightening thing about them – through Miles and Flora.

Freud defined the 'uncanny' as 'whatever reminds us of this inner compulsion to repeat' – a compulsion which solicits death

(1953–74, XVII, p. 238). In James's story, each turn of the screw provides further reminders, takes a further step 'beyond', a step towards the decisive confrontations, with Miss Jessel in Chapter 20 and Quint in Chapter 24. During both confrontations, the diabolic revenants find their range by keeping their distance. The uncanny emerges, horrifyingly, *in* that distance, as the children, interposed between devil and guardian, are forced to repeat (double, supplement) one or the other. Flora turns on the governess an expression which converts the little girl into an old woman, 'hideously hard' (1907–9, XII, p. 281). The expression may appear new on Flora's face, but it is in fact an old one, since it is Miss Jessel's: Flora's violent rejection of the governess comes back in her from somewhere else; it is a ventriloquism without origin. The second confrontation, between the governess and Quint, catches Miles at precisely the same range: *in* the dangerous crossing, *in* repetition (p. 309).

It is the turn, not the screw, which is demonic, uncanny, horrifying. In James's story, the children, by their compulsive repetitions, their doubling of the already double, are the next turn. What of the story itself? Does it claim a place, as the next turn of the screw, in a series of representations of evil?

The purpose of Rousseau's footnote had been to complain about the feebleness of contemporary representations of the devil. James certainly took up the challenge. No sooner has his story encountered the full effects of the devil's work, with Flora's turn against the governess, than it finds itself visited by a revenant, a literary ghost.

When Mrs Grose leads Flora away, the governess collapses. 'Of what first happened when I was left alone I had no subsequent memory. I only knew that at the end of, I suppose, a quarter of an hour, an odorous dampness and roughness, chilling and piercing my trouble, had made me understand that I must have thrown myself, on my face, to the ground and given way to a wildness of grief' (p. 282). The encounter with evil has emptied out consciousness, even the 'little note of neatness, firmness and courage' (of hysteria, if you prefer). 'I got up and looked a moment, through the twilight, at the grey pool and its blank haunted edge, and then I took, back to the house, my dreary and difficult course' (p. 283).

What comes back here is not just her residue of consciousness, but the High Romantic representation of that horror which is

the other side of a powerfully renovating imagination: the landscape of 'La Belle Dame sans Merci', the 'visionary dreariness'
which, in Book II of *The Prelude*, invests 'moorland waste' and
'naked pool' (Wordsworth 1979, p. 433). Such visions unseat the
mind, but also prove its power; they disable and enable. The
governess's vision of dreariness is her last, diminished, chance at
identity.

But for her, and for James, there is yet one more step to take,
a step beyond the 'lyric poets' and their enabling disablements.
The final encounter with Quint removes even this impoverished
residue. Trapped in the spacing of repetition, not knowing who
to repeat, Miles dies. His death abruptly halts the sequence of
horrifying events; a sequence which will come back in ghostly
form when the governess hands her manuscript to Douglas,
shortly before her death; and then again when Douglas hands it
to the narrator, shortly before *his* death.

The governess's desire to interpret is less remarkable than her
solitary patrol on the edge of a dangerous place: her terror, her
disgust, her fainting away, her disappearance. She has no position,
by the end, no place from which she could desire or interpret.
When Mark Seltzer, in the course of an analysis heavily influenced
by Foucault, describes her as occupying 'the power roles of the
"medico-tutelary complex"', he surely attributes to her too great
a degree of identity (Seltzer 1984, p. 157). James was less
interested in her than in the space between her little note of
neatness, firmness and courage and the devil's solicitations.

VULGARITY

To say that James wrote a ghost story, rather than a madness
story, is not to say that he believed in ghosts. It is to say that
the response ghosts traditionally provoked, horror, is one that
interested him. I now want to explore the reasons for that
interest, and in doing so to connect horror to disgust.

Allon White points out that in his later writing James explored
the idea of vulgarity in its four main 'areas of application'; as
language, vernacular, 'vulgate'; as an index of class; and as
sexual, or aesthetic, lapse. In each area, White observes, 'the
active, evaluative restraint is the fear of vulgarity' (1981, p. 134).
That restraint endlessly acts upon a scandal which both confounds
and confirms it. We consider the vulgar 'common' because it is

what we have in common; we consider it 'base' because it is the basis of individual and collective identity. Vulgarity is James's version of the abject. It represents (and is represented by) loss, waste, permeability.

This was, in one aspect, a question of aesthetics. The doctrine of organic form James evolved was his antidote to vulgarity in literature. He believed that a work of literature can be counted a success only if it fulfils the 'law of entire expression' (1984b, p. 1159) – only if there is a perfect fit between form and meaning. But the law of entire expression, like most laws, is apparent more in the breach than in the observance.

A metaphor James frequently used to define it was that of leakage: the fit between form and meaning must be so perfect that nothing intrinsic leaks out and nothing extrinsic leaks in (1974–84, IV, p. 619; 1984b, pp. 138, 1053). The metaphor insists, if only with the aim of prevention, on permeability, on porosity. Confronted by the exquisite facade of D'Annunzio's novels, for example, James wonders what might be escaping from it.

> We feel ourselves somehow in presence of a singular incessant *leak* in the effect of distinction so artfully and copiously produced, and we apply our test up and down in the manner of the inquiring person who, with a tin implement and a small flame, searches our premises for an escape of gas. The bad smell has, as it were, to be accounted for.
>
> (1984b, p. 935)

The bad smell that James gags on here, the 'leak of distinction', is sexual. For all its stylishness, D'Annunzio's *Il Fuoco* (1900) merely proves that 'there is an inevitable leak of ease and peace when a mistress happens to be considerably older than her lover' (p. 930): a theme we have already encountered in the fiction of the period (see Chapter 13). The discrepancy between low theme and high style constitutes the aesthetic 'leak' which troubles the reader.

In the woman-centred tales James courted and transformed vulgarity. *The Turn of the Screw*, for example, leaks from the very beginning, when Douglas reveals that as a young man he had fallen in love with a woman ten years older than him (1907–9, XII, pp. 149–50). Relationships, potential or actual, between young men and older women also feature in *What Maisie Knew*

(1897) and *The Awkward Age* (1899). The bad smell which suffuses the prologue to the first novel, and the whole of the last two, is sexual talk: chatter, innuendo, speculation, rumour. James fosters such talk, then seals it off.

He described *The Turn of the Screw* as a 'pot-boiler' redeemed from 'vulgarity' by its 'difficulty' (1974–84, IV, p. 86). His position in the literary marketplace was not so secure that he could afford to despise pot-boilers. He knew that the novel had been 'vulgarized', like all other kinds of literature, indeed more so; and he acted upon this pragmatic assessment. The experimental writings of the 1890s put the law of entire expression under considerable strain by incorporating not only vulgar meanings but also vulgar forms.

By the mid-1890s sexual talk meant a particular genre, the so-called 'dialogue novel'. In the preface to *The Awkward Age*, James suggested, skittishly perhaps, that he had modelled the book on the dialogue novels of the French writers Gyp and Henri Lavedan. But British writers like F. Anstey and Violet Hunt had also enjoyed success with the formula. Furthermore, novels about sexual intrigue in high society – E. F. Benson's *Dodo* (1893), or Ellen Fowler's *Concerning Isabel Carnaby* (1897) – were often written largely in dialogue. James's interest no doubt reflected his determination to learn from his experiences as a dramatist, and to compose according to a 'scenic method'. *The Other House* (1896) was a direct adaptation of a play scenario; as late as 1910, he was to remember it as a valuable 'precedent' and 'support' in this respect (1987, p. 261). But dialogue in novels was often, he felt, a flagrant breach of the law of entire expression, a source of leakage. Whenever it was introduced for its own sake, or simply as a means of conveying information about plot, it opened a gap between form and meaning. The dialogue novel was a porous form which expressed porous meanings.

Sam Carter, the hero of Anthony Hope's *The Dolly Dialogues* (1894), is a permanent bachelor who enjoys flirting – like Vanderbank, the hero of *The Awkward Age* – with married women. He does so graciously, on the whole. But one of his married friends, Mrs Hilary Musgrave, shows some concern lest his flirtatious chatter will corrupt Phyllis, an adolescent girl she has in her charge; particularly when he describes how, as a young man of twenty, he fell in love with his sisters' governess (pp. 117–21). Hope colludes with this leakage to the extent that the dialogue in his novel is unashamedly there for its own sake. It does not express character so much as create an atmosphere of intrigue.

For James, dialogue should express character. The successive conversations Nanda holds with Vanderbank, Mitchy and Mr Longdon establish exactly what she has learnt, and declined to learn, from her experiences. Nanda, unlike Phyllis, has a point of view. James does not display his heroine's innocence for the entertainment of his experienced readers, as Elinor Glyn was to do in *The Visits of Elizabeth* (1900). But, having granted Nanda a consciousness, indeed a moral influence, James won't allow it any scope. Glyn allows her heroine an easy passage from innocence to experience by marrying her off, after the approved eighteenth-century manner, to a reformed rake, Lord Valmond. James withdraws his from the fray before there is any fray to speak of, and places her under the protection of an 'American uncle', Mr Longdon. Neither resolution seems entirely satisfactory.

What Maisie Knew is a different proposition. Here James attempted the tightest of forms, representing everything that happens from Maisie's point of view. And Maisie, although younger than Nanda, plays a far more active, and evaluative, part in the connections which form and reform around her. She brings her stepfather and stepmother together, thus contributing to the creation of a fresh tie from which, 'as if through a small demonic foresight', she derives great benefit. She has the devil within her, as well as around her. She becomes 'a centre and pretext for a fresh system of misbehaviour, a system moreover of a nature to spread and ramify' (1984b, p. 1158).

Tight form restrains loose meaning, but only by allowing it, on occasion, a bizarre licence. In a remarkable scene towards the end of the novel, Sir Claude wants to show Maisie a letter which her father has written to his second wife, informing her that their marriage is over. Mrs Wix staunchly intervenes to prevent him. But the vulgarity of the whole complicated exchange has already, in a sense, leaked out. Sir Claude wants to know why she thinks that his lover's new freedom, announced in the letter, will free him as well, and she responds by an 'extraordinary' demonstration. She gives Sir Claude 'a great giggling insinuating naughty slap' (1907–9, XI, p. 256). Maisie and Sir Claude are dumbfounded. The pressures that have built up inside James's tight control over their tight self-control can only be contained, perhaps, by a strategic leak: a giggle and slap.

Not all of James's assimilations of vulgarity were so felicitous. *The Other House* is a melodramatic story about commercial and sexual rivalry which ends with the murder of a four-year-old girl. The place to read it is in the *Illustrated London News*, where it ran between 4 July and 26 September 1896. In the 4 July issue the opening section of the story is preceded by visual and verbal reports concerning the Prince of Wales, the Matabele revolt, the restoration of Norwich cathedral, and the birth of a kangaroo, among other things. The conversation between Rose Armiger and Mrs Beever which concludes this episode is interrupted by an illustration of recent trouble in Crete. The opposite page presents a scene from the Matabele revolt ('On the track of the rebels: murderous work'). The issue also contains advertisements for Cockle's anti-bilious pills, Scrub's cloudy household ammonia, and other domestic items. Rarely can James have found himself in such mixed company.

The novels he published during the 1890s were as porous as any he ever wrote. That he should so often take the risk of being vulgar in order to write about vulgarity indicates the depth of his preoccupation. *What Maisie Knew* and *The Turn of the Screw* are masterpieces of measured but none the less powerful revulsion at social and sexual vulgarity. We learn that Quint's social status had been, according to Mrs Grose, 'dreadfully below' that of Miss Jessel (1907–9, XII, p. 207). Their relationship, in other words, was vulgar before it became terrifying, material for a novel by D'Annunzio before it became material for a ghost story. When the ghostly lovers return across an even more sensitive boundary, between life and death, they cause the world to 'reek', James says, with 'the air of Evil' (1984b, p. 1187). Faced by such porosity, by classes mingling promiscuously, by death permeating life, what can the governess do but faint away? She is terrified not so much of the ghosts, Woolf argued, as of 'the sudden extension of her own field of perception, which in this case widens to reveal to her the presence all about her of an unmentionable evil' (1986–8, II, p. 219).

That widening also characterizes two childhood memories which haunted Woolf herself. One would not have been out of place in naturalist fiction. It concerns an 'idiot boy' who 'sprang up with his hand outstretched mewing, slit-eyed, red-rimmed;

and without saying a word, with a sense of the horror in me, I poured into his hand a bag of Russian toffee'. The other would not have been out of place in James's story. 'There was the moment of the puddle in the path; when for no reason I could discover, everything suddenly became unreal; I was suspended; I could not step across the puddle; I tried to touch something' (1985, p. 78). A monster, a gap which cannot be crossed: both experiences convert disgust into horror, both paralyse. There may well be madness in them, as there was for Woolf. But it is not the madness which counts, in the end, so much as the widening itself, the fatal step 'beyond' the pleasure principle.

INTERPOSED: GOVERNESS, COMPANION, CLERK

Maisie Farange and Nanda Brookenham are vulnerable because they are both *intermediate*: Nanda at the awkward age between childhood and maturity, Maisie in an awkward role as object of contention between warring parents. The heroine of *The Turn of the Screw* is vulnerable because she is a governess, someone interposed between guardian and wards, between employer and servants. All three have the responsibility of stopping up the holes through which vulgarity pours; all three find themselves in an awkward position (or inter-position) which, however heroically they perform, denies them an identity of their own. 'I give it its foundation,' Sartre says of the disgusting or horrifying object, 'but it does not furnish any foundation for me' (1957, p. 608). Maisie alone has enough of the devil within to confound the devils without.

Fleda Vetch, in *The Spoils of Poynton* (1897), is equally interposed: as companion, as 'messenger and mediator' (1907–9, X, p. 147) between Mrs Gereth and her increasingly estranged son, Owen, then as rival to Owen's fiancée, Mona Brigstock. The vulgarity that will compound her awkwardness is introduced in comic terms, in the shape of the Brigstocks' home, Waterbath. Viscosity, Sartre observes, is 'the agony of water' (1957, p. 607); at Waterbath the 'worst horror' is the 'acres of varnish, something advertised and smelly, with which everything was smeared' (James 1907–9, X, p. 7). The smelly, advertised stickiness that suits them so admirably, and looks as though it may suit Owen, amuses Fleda and revolts Mrs Gereth.

Mrs Gereth responds by abandoning her own house, Poynton, to the barbarians, and taking the best of its 'spoils' with her. This act spoils the spoils for ever, by removing them from their context. Fleda, visiting Mrs Gereth in her new home, sees not a reconstituted harmony, but 'far-away empty sockets, a scandal of nakedness between high bleak walls' (p. 72). The removal is a catastrophic separation which Fleda, the awkward intermediary, feels within herself. James's language registers the aftermath of some primordial violence. 'Fleda tried to think of some of the things at Poynton still unappropriated, but her memory was a blank about them, and in the effort to focus the old combinations she saw again nothing but gaps and scars, a vacancy that gathered at moments into something worse' (pp. 78–9).

Mrs Gereth, meanwhile, tries to 'knock' her 'into position' (p. 31): a position, that is, where she will embody and act out her mistress's feelings, seal her off both from the Brigstock vulgarity and from the implications of her own response. It is the latter which most threatens Fleda. Mrs Gereth, in an outburst worthy of Mrs Wix, though less benevolent, salivates over Fleda's desire for Owen. ' "*I* know what you are.... You're not quite a saint in heaven yet. Lord, what a creature you'd have thought me in my good time!" ' The outburst strikes Fleda as 'a blind profanity' (p. 205); it exposes in Mrs Gereth a vulgarity as merciless as anything the Brigstocks are capable of, and makes Fleda's position, awkward already, impossible.

The dismemberment of Poynton, the vision of gaps and scars, contaminates the friendship between Fleda and Owen. As he tries desperately to express his love for her, Owen strays further and further into a 'grey suburb' of life, a 'vulgar and ill-lighted region' of which he has had no previous experience (pp. 86–7). This 'suburb', incarnated by her father's sordid rooms in West Kensington, where Mrs Brigstock surprises them, is a fatally indeterminate zone, neither one thing nor the other. Desire leaks away into its grey recesses.

The heroine of 'In the Cage' is a counter clerk in the telegraph department of a Mayfair shop, awkwardly positioned between two types of vulgarity: the lower-middle-class world inhabited by her drunken mother, her boring fiancé, Mr Mudge, and her pushy friend, Mrs Jordan; and the world of the telegram-sending classes, whose attachments and liaisons would not be out of place in the novels she borrows, 'very greasy, in fine print and all about fine folks, at a ha'penny a day' (1907–9, XI, p. 371). The counter where she works is pervaded, in winter, by the 'poison of perpetual gas', and at all times by the 'presence of hams, cheese, dried fish, soap, varnish, paraffin, and other solids and fluids that she came to know perfectly by their smells without consenting to know them by their names' (pp. 367–8). The worlds of unnamed solids and fluids and the world of signification, of telegrams and anger, meet at the 'lattice' which forms her cage. Smells (of food, of the abyss) leak out; significance (wealth, status, intrigue) leaks in. Her position, like Fleda's, or the governess's, is one of 'servitude and promiscuity' (p. 396). The only identity these odd, awkward women derive from their exposure to vulgarity is a refusal both of desire and of revulsion. In this respect, they are unique in the fiction of the period.

16

IRONY AND REVULSION IN KIPLING AND CONRAD

'Mrs Bathurst', published in *Traffics and Discoveries* (1904), is one of Kipling's most enigmatic and most admired tales. Set in South Africa, on a railway siding at False Bay, it tells how four men while away an afternoon discussing the obsessive love of a warrant officer named Vickery for Mrs Bathurst, a widowed hotelier. Vickery eventually disappeared up-country. One of the men, Hooper, describes how, travelling in the same region, he was taken to a place where two tramps had been found dead after a thunderstorm, one upright, one squatting, both turned to charcoal. 'They fell to bits when we tried to shift 'em. The man who was standin' up had the false teeth. I saw 'em shinin' against the black. Fell to bits he did too, like his mate squatting down an' watchin' him, both of 'em all wet in the rain' (Kipling 1971, I, p. 91). All that is left of Vickery, if it *is* him, is the part that wasn't him, the false teeth. The incongruity of this detail halts the scene a half-step short of horror. It is, in its stress on the texture of the corpses, disgusting rather than horrifying.

Barbara Everett has discussed the 'primitivism' of the story, the way it reaches 'something buried, infantile, vulnerable in the reader'. This primitivism is 'equalled and balanced by everything in the telling which is cold and detached, so formally ironic as to make Kipling sometimes the easiest of great writers to find repellent' (1991, p. 13). The balance of detachment and primitivism leads her to suggest that we should not read the story as a narrative, puzzling over the identity of the tramps, but as the unfurling of a metaphor: the *coup de foudre*, love's lightning-stroke which at once illuminates and destroys, turning the lovers into charcoal. In its favouring of metaphor over metonymy, in its resolute indeterminacy, it is thoroughly Modernist (Lodge 1989).

And yet the story remains a narrative, to the bitter end. Hooper has kept a memento, possibly Vickery's false teeth, which he declines to produce, for the reason that 'he was a friend of you two gentlemen, you see' (p. 91). His gesture brings back, from earlier in the narrative, from up-country, the disgust aroused by the crumbling corpses. Disgust, or the memory of disgust, threatens to unbind the social cohesiveness which the story insists on: four men yarning, the air filled with the chatter of a nearby picnic party. And cohesiveness, mutual understanding, is the prerequisite of irony.

The story maintains an uneasy truce between two opposing imperatives: a revulsion which, if expressed, would sweep irony away; and an irony which carries on as though nothing could ever unsettle it. In this respect, it is characteristic of its time.

TORTURE

One scene in particular, which recurs throughout his *oeuvre*, tested Kipling's detachment to the limit: that of torture. He wrote about torture from the torturer's point of view, and the pleasure he took, and encouraged his readers to take, in these scenes throws their equally palpable detachment into question.

In a penetrating essay on torture, Elaine Scarry argues that it involves three processes. First, pain is inflicted. 'Second, the pain, continually amplified within the person's body, is also amplified in the sense that it is objectified, made visible to those outside the person's body. Third, the objectified pain is denied as pain and read as power' (1985, p. 28). The pain inflicted undoes meaning. It replaces consciousness with sentience. Either the universe contracts to the immediate vicinity of the body, or the body swells to fill the entire universe (p. 35). The torturers externalize this sentience through their actions: 'in the conversion of a refrigerator into a bludgeon, the refrigerator disappears; its disappearance objectifies the disappearance of the world (sky, country, bench) experienced by a person in great pain' (p. 41). As the prisoner's world contracts, so the torturer's expands, so he feels less and knows (himself) more. 'It is not merely that his power requires blindness; it is, instead, quite simply that his blindness, his willed amorality, *is* his power, or a large part of it'

(p. 57). One person's pain has become a regime's fiction of power: this, not the extracting of information, is the real purpose of torture.

Kipling's first novel, *The Light that Failed* (1890), contains a scene in which the war artist Dick Heldar, just back from the Sudan, bullies the head of the syndicate which employs him into returning his sketches, while his friend Torpenhow looks on. Heldar realizes that his victim has a weak heart. He walks round and round him, pawing him 'as a cat paws a soft hearth-rug' and tracing with his forefinger 'the leaden pouches underneath the eyes' (1988, p. 36). This physical remarking of symptoms, an objectification of imminent pain more effective than mere assault and battery, destroys the man's faith in himself. The sentences describing it are the only memorable ones in an otherwise unmemorable piece of writing.

The insignia into which the man's pain has been converted are those not of a regime's power but of male companionship. Torpenhow thoroughly approves of his friend's actions, and is amused by the ironic comments that accompany them. Scarry observes that torture 'has as its centre the single, overwhelming discrepancy between an increasingly palpable body and an increasingly substanceless world, a discrepancy that makes all the lesser discrepancies we normally identify as "ironic" seem as remote and full of dissolution as the world to which they belong' (1985, p. 30). But to the torturer, irony, the enjoyment of discrepancies, is still available. Indeed, its availability is an important sign of his omnipotence. Torture makes Heldar *more* of an ironist.

In Kipling's stories the victim of torture is from the start beyond irony, beyond companionship. The aim is to reduce him *yet further*. Heldar's first act is to expose his victim. 'He put one hand on the man's forearm and ran the other down the plump body beneath the coat.' The 'thing', he complains to Torpenhow, is 'soft all over – like a woman' (Kipling 1988, p. 35). The plump body disgusts him because it is contourless, featureless, indeterminate: neither male nor female. In this scene, torture does not overcome resistance, and thus create a fiction of power. It dramatizes the unresolved coexistence, within Heldar, and within the writing, of two imperatives, two constitutive processes: revulsion and detachment. It is their coexistence which conjures a crazy enjoyment out of the contemplation of suffering.

MARKING THE BEAST

One of Kipling's most troubling torture scenes occurs in an early story, 'The Mark of the Beast', which he himself described as 'rather nasty', and which some reviewers considered excessive (Page 1984, p. 106). It appeared in *Life's Handicap* (1891), which was subtitled 'Stories of Mine Own People' and dedicated to E. Kay Robinson, his chief on the *Civil and Military Gazette* at Lahore. His own people were the members of the Anglo-Indian community, the people he had written for and about in the collection which made his name, *Plain Tales from the Hills* (1890).

It was Kipling's habit, and not his alone, to convert difference into absolute distinction, between genders, races, nations. Some of the best stories in these early collections describe relationships between white men and black women. They insist that white society is not as honourable and law-abiding, and black society not as frank and brutal, as they have been made out to be. But they also insist that in the end there cannot and ought not to be any union between the races. 'A man should, whatever happens, keep to his own caste, race and breed. Let the White go to the White and the Black to the Black. Then whatever trouble falls is in the ordinary course of things – neither sudden, alien, nor unexpected' (1987a, p. 162).

In 'The Mark of the Beast' Kipling's own people – planters, soldiers, administrators – gather from 'the uttermost ends of the Empire' (1987b, p. 195) to celebrate the New Year. One of them, a planter called Fleete, gets riotously drunk, and on his way home stubs out his cigar on the forehead of a temple idol. A leper – a Silver Man – appears from a recess behind the image of the god, and touches Fleete on the chest. Within twenty-four hours, Fleete begins to develop a disease diagnosed as hydrophobia, but closer to lycanthropy. He howls, craves raw meat and frightens the horses. He has crossed the boundary between cultures, and is being made to pay for it. However, the narrator and his friend Strickland, a policeman who 'knows as much of natives of India as is good for any man' (p. 195), capture the leper, and torture him until he agrees to lift the curse.

'The Mark of the Beast' is a fairly commonplace Gothic tale

about a man who is transformed into a beast because he has been behaving like one. What lifts it above the commonplace, for better or worse, is the imagination Kipling invested in the torture of the leper. Scarry argues that the torturer converts pain into a fiction of power through a display of agency. Torture victims frequently describe how they were forced to examine the weapons soon to be used against them (Scarry 1985, p. 27). So Kipling forces us, if not the leper, to examine the instruments that Strickland has fashioned: gun barrels heated in the fire, a walking stick broken in two, one yard of fishing line, 'gut lapped with wire, such as is used for *mahseer*-fishing' (Kipling 1987b, p. 254). The obsessive, finicky detail launches what is in effect a story within the story.

The scene itself, like much of Kipling's best writing, is at once compellingly lucid and touched by uncertainty.

> Strickland wrapped a towel round his hand and took the gun-barrels out of the fire. I put the half of the broken walking stick through the loop of fishing-line and buckled the leper comfortably to Strickland's bedstead. I understood then how men and women and little children can endure to see a witch burnt alive; for the beast was moaning on the floor, and though the Silver Man had no face, you could see horrible feelings passing through the slab that took its place, exactly as waves of heat play across red-hot iron – gun-barrels for instance.
>
> (p. 205)

The adverb 'comfortably' seems to have strayed in from some other scene, some other text. Neither the victim nor his torturers are in a position to feel comfortable. But perhaps the incongruity is the point. The torturers are acting to restore a white man's comfort. Their acknowledgement of comfort, and of the irony of its presence at such a scene, is part of their power.

The next sentence sets out to justify what they are doing, hesitates, acknowledges the pain they have caused, is deflected into literariness (simile), and returns finally to a clinching display of agency. As the prisoner's world contracts to a pinpoint of 'horrible feelings', so the torturer-narrator's world expands – comfortably – through the employment of a figure of speech. While the syntax falters, hinting at uncertainty, the figure of speech – the expansive irony of an effect (waves of pain) which resembles its cause (waves of heat) – secures the fiction of omnipotence. The leper will submit.

The torturers want to damage someone who is already damaged beyond repair, who has no feet, no hands, no face. The leper, like Dick Heldar's victim, is utterly indeterminate, utterly abject. Instead of speaking, he mews 'like a she-otter'. Hearing this sound, the narrator feels sick, 'actually and physically sick' (p. 252). The story within a story glimpses not only power but disgust. When they capture the leper, Strickland knocks his legs from under him, while the narrator stamps on his neck. 'He mewed hideously, and even through my riding-boots I could feel that his flesh was not the flesh of a clean man' (p. 206). This disgust enforces a ritual expulsion. When the leper leaves he is made to take 'the gloves and the towels with which we had touched him, and the whip that had been hooked round his body' (p. 206). The torturers feel that they have disgraced themselves as Englishmen for ever.

The First World War encouraged Kipling to make further distinctions between his 'own people' and a new set of 'barbarians'. In 'Sea Constables' (1915), the terminally ill skipper of a blockade-runner is refused medical assistance. *A Diversity of Creatures* (1917) contains within its diversity not only verse and prose celebrations of Englishness, but the notorious, and celebrated, 'Mary Postgate'. Mary Postgate discovers a German airman who has (bizarrely) fallen out of his aeroplane after bombing a nearby village and killing a child. Her behaviour, in ignoring his pleas for help, surely qualifies as torture. He, too, is already defeated, broken by his fall. Indeed, he is barely human, his head as pale as a baby's, 'and so closely cropped that she could see the disgusting pinky skin beneath' (1987f, p. 352). He has been reduced from a person to an assemblage of body parts. 'The mouth even tried to smile.... A tear trickled from one eye, and the head rolled from shoulder to shoulder' (p. 353). The only connection Mary Postgate can see is between the object resembling an airman and the dead child. 'This thing hunched under the oak-tree had done that thing' (p. 354).

During the torture scene Kipling concentrates on a kind of displaced agency. While she waits for the German to die, Mary incinerates the belongings of her employer's nephew, Wynn, a young airman killed in a training accident. 'Now Wynn was dead, and everything connected with him was lumping and rustling and tinkling under her busy poker into red black dust and grey leaves of ash. The thing beneath the oak would die too.' As the victim contracts to a 'thing', the torturer expands into an almost lyrical display of agency. Kipling pays extraordinary attention to her every act: 'she wielded the poker with lunges that jarred the grating at the bottom, and careful scrapes round the brickwork above' (p. 354). She invents herself, through these scrapings and jarrings which obliterate the thing beneath the oak tree.

Torture gives Mary Postgate a job. She has never believed in 'advanced views' of 'woman's work in the world'. But she realizes that letting the airman die is work she can do, work that a man, wanting to behave like a 'sportsman', could not have done (pp. 354–5). She stops worrying about the husband and the children she lacks. '*But* it was a fact. A woman who had missed these things could still be useful – more useful than a man in certain respects. She thumped like a pavior through the settling ashes at the secret thrill of it' (p. 355). She is suddenly, unashamedly masculine: a stoker, a pavior. The italicization rearranges the information structure of the first sentence, blurring its focus: is the fact important, or its unexpectedness? Mary's new identity has emerged confusingly, against the grain.

The description of her 'increasing rapture' – the glow which reaches 'to the marrow of her bones' (p. 354) – aligns the story, disturbingly, with narratives of sexual awakening like Katherine Mansfield's 'Bliss' or 'A Cup of Tea'. She savours the airman's death. One person's overwhelming sentience (pain) has been converted, not into the insignia of power, but into another person's overwhelming sentience (pleasure). The result is that, at the conclusion of the story, desire and irony (the irony of her desire) entirely subsume disgust. ' "*That's* all right," said she contentedly, and went up to the house, where she scandalised the whole routine by taking a luxurious hot bath before tea, and came down looking, as Miss Fowler said when she saw her lying all relaxed on the other sofa, "quite handsome" ' (p. 355). Her own, newly determinate body supervenes on the airman's shattered, revolting indeterminacy.

The torture scenes establish a framework of rough justice which makes it clear, to the protagonists at least, what has to be done, and done quickly. Yet in all three cases torture proves nothing, because it has no resistance to overcome. It merely exposes the already broken, the already abject: something which the torturer may reduce even further, but can never measure himself or herself against in any coherent way. Detachment and primitivism combine to create the imaginative power of these scenes: but not a stable identity, or a community of the just. If Strickland feels dishonoured by his night's work, what about Mary Postgate, once the handsomeness fades?

It is precisely such a torturing of the already abject which appals Stevenson's Archie Weir in *Weir of Hermiston*, when he witnesses his father, the Lord Justice-Clerk, pronouncing sentence of death on a 'whey-coloured, misbegotten caitiff' called Duncan Jopp, a being 'sunk beneath the zones of sympathy'. The judge brings a 'monstrous, relishing gaiety' to his task. 'It is one thing to spear a tiger, another to crush a toad; there are aesthetics even of the slaughter-house; and the loathsomeness of Duncan Jopp enveloped and infected the image of his judge' (1979b, p. 77). Stevenson put his feelings about his own father into that 'image'. Archie Weir's revulsion marks a limit: the point at which son separates from, and turns equivocally against, father. Kipling remains in imagination with the torturing father, not the victim, not the appalled onlooker; or, rather, with the act itself, for his trinity of torturers includes a father (Strickland), a son (Heldar) and, if not a holy ghost, then a holy mother (Mary Postgate).

CONRAD'S ODD MEN

Conrad has seemed the Modernist writer with the nearest thing to a moral and political philosophy. Jacques Berthoud, for example, has argued eloquently that Conrad's major creative phase rests on 'a continuous and consistent effort of thought', and that his writing should be valued for its 'intelligibility and control' as well as its 'power and profundity' (1978, p. 186). Berthoud is able to show that, even at their most schematic, the novels dramatize moral and political dilemmas effectively.

But a question remains as to the limits of this proven moral and political intelligence. There are Kiplingesque 'things' in the novels which seem beyond its range. In *Nostromo* (1904), Berthoud suggests, Charles Gould and Martin Decoud are contrasted as the man of action and the man of thought; both, however, recognize the futility of politics in Costaguana. 'This view,' he adds, 'is vividly confirmed by the endless cortege of political delinquents that Conrad parades with his customary sardonic zest' (1978, p. 186): Pedrito Montero, the demagogue Gamacho, the parliamentarian Lopez. Indeed. But is that *all* the parade confirms?

After welcoming Pedrito Montero to Sulaco, the 'enormous Gamacho', Commandante of the National Guard, retires to rest. Montero's cavalry rout his troops while he lies drunkenly at home, his bare feet 'upturned in the shadows repulsively, in the manner of a corpse' (Conrad 1963, pp. 325–6). Gamacho is a mere opportunist. His conduct tells us nothing about the future of Costaguana. So why is the description of his conduct so spiteful? Why should the adverb 'repulsively' be held back just long enough to become the undisputed focus of the sentence describing his feet? It is the gross physicality of the enormous Gamacho, not his fleeting appearance as an orator, which seems to hold Conrad's attention. He is quite simply disgusting, like Señor Hirsch, whom Nostromo and Decoud discover aboard their lighter (p. 227). Hirsch is a corpse, a mass, a void across which the more determinate and transitive characters gaze at each other. Gamacho and Hirsch are disgusting because they are indistinct, neither dead nor alive. Figuring them out, Conrad's sardonic zest must redouble itself in order to impose the distinctions they lack.

There are an awful lot of fat greasy men in Conrad. They constitute a sub-group within the group of European renegades who populate the tales of the Far East. These renegades – Almayer in *Almayer's Folly* (1895), Willems in *An Outcast of the Islands* (1896), Schomberg in *Victory* (1915) – are distasteful mainly because they blur the boundary between races. Unable or unwilling to conduct themselves according to the white man's codes, they yet have no interest in brown men other than to exploit them. They occupy the margin, the void, between cultures. Sloth and obesity incarnate their cultural indistinctness.

Cornelius, in *Lord Jim*, Stein's agent and Jewel's stepfather, is 'marked' by the 'abjectness' which seems to Marlow 'the stamp of the man': 'I am sure his love would have been the most abject of sentiments – but can one imagine a loathsome insect in love?' (1986a, p. 254). Cornelius, Marlow adds, belongs neither in the background nor in the foreground of the story: 'he is simply seen skulking on its outskirts, enigmatical and unclean'. His presence collapses another necessary distinction: between foreground and background, between characters we know extensively from within and characters who command no more than a vignette. He is a minor character; yet his abjectness represents in some way the obstacle Jim must overcome. Jim is the butterfly to Cornelius's beetle (Tanner 1963, pp. 40–1).

The equally monstrous Captain of the *Patna* receives even harsher treatment. He is shown, for the space of several paragraphs, trying to cram his vast bulk into a gharry (Conrad 1986a, p. 39). The narrative responds to this spectacle by cordoning it off with a flurry of comic comparisons. But in his enthusiasm Conrad overdoes the 'sardonic zest'. The description balloons like the Captain himself. There is an energy here, an anxiety, which is more than ironic, more than philosophical.

Abjectness is Conrad's subject. It is what his protagonists – Jim, Marlow, Kurtz, Nostromo, Decoud, Gould – must confront. It is what the novels themselves must confront, in their ironic detachment, their effort of thought. On his way to Patusan, Marlow visits a wretched little place on the coast run by 'a third-class deputy-assistant resident, a big, fat, greasy, blinking fellow of mixed descent, with turned-out, shiny lips' (1986a, p. 248). The poor man can scarcely find the energy to pass on some news about Jim, and yet he both fascinates and repels Conrad. Racially mixed, physically intransitive, he embodies abjectness. The frenzy of these descriptions makes me wonder whether narratives so intent on nosing out the abject should be valued primarily, as Berthoud suggests, for their 'intelligibility and control'.

SECRET AGENTS

There were fat men everywhere, in popular fiction. Capitalists (Tressell 1965, p. 106), lechers (Abbott 1908, pp. 40–6), agitators (Irwin 1912, p. 40), German spies (Buchan 1956a, p. 50), war profiteers (Ruck 1918, p. 341), necromancers (Maugham 1991a, p. 178), and, of course, comic bounders (Wodehouse 1961, pp. 34, 41, 242). Chesterton once remarked that Dickens's Mrs Gamp is 'a sumptuous study, laid on in those rich, oily, almost greasy colours that go to make the English comic characters, that make the very diction of Falstaff fat, and quaking with jolly degradation' (1987, p. 98). Conrad's fat men certainly quake, though there is nothing jolly about their degradation. He knew that he was dipping his ironist's bucket into a much-used stream.

There are fat men in *The Secret Agent* (1907), which is usually thought to diverge significantly from the conventional thriller (Berthoud 1978, p. 148; Kermode 1983, p. 47); and *Under Western Eyes* (1911), which has been acclaimed as a Modernist classic that systematically flaunts its own artifice (Kermode 1983, ch. 6).

The fat men in *The Secret Agent* (Verloc, Michaelis, Sir Ethelred) don't belong to any particular racial or cultural group, and are not noticeably more disgusting than the thin men. This equitable distribution of nausea supports Berthoud's argument that the novel's chief concern is with the prevailing conservatism of English life (1978, pp. 132–7). With two exceptions, all the characters – statesmen, policemen, anarchists, spies, wives – struggle to maintain the status quo. The two exceptions are the Russian *agent provocateur* Vladimir and the terrorist known as 'the Professor'. These two, Berthoud points out, are at odds not only with English political moderation, but also with the very idea of 'social life' (p. 134).

The Professor, the one politically motivated individual whose views are not flatly contradicted by his behaviour, ought to be the standard against which the hypocrisy of terrorists and policemen alike can be measured. He ought to be unique, a reproof to literary as well as social convention. And yet there were equivalents in popular fiction. Dr Andrew Fernandez, for example, in Hume Nisbet's *The Great Secret* (1895), whose gang hijacks a cruise liner, has all the Professor's charismatic inhumanity, with some to spare. Conrad, I think, never forgave the Professor for *not* being unique.

He did everything he could to prevent any vulgarizing charisma from attaching to the Professor. 'His clothes, of a nondescript brown mixture, were threadbare and marked with stains, dusty in the folds, with ragged button-holes' (1990, pp. 5–6). Utterly nondescript, selfless, he is meant to expose the affectations and hypocrisies of those who surround him. Yet this nondescriptness is dwelt on with such fierce insistence that he becomes if anything *over*descript, a compound of bizarrely luxuriant reductions (p. 52, lines 26–35). Again, Conrad overdoes what he termed the 'ironic treatment' of his subject. His reduction has the paradoxical effect of enlarging its intended victim. We cannot be surprised that the Professor, for all his miserable banality, is still a force at the end of the novel. His charisma, like Fernandez's, survives intact.

Recognizing, perhaps, the inadvertently aggrandizing effect of

255

so much scorn, Conrad tried another tactic: summariness. The best way to cut the terrorists down to size is to tag them with ironic epithets (Michaelis as the 'ticket-of-leave apostle', and so on). Their weakness is their conventionality; this the ironist has exposed by the brusqueness of his characterizations. But such stereotyping is itself, on the level of representation, a kind of conventionality: the common currency of popular journalism and popular fiction. To characterize Señor Hirsch by his Jewish features, or Ossipon ('the robust Ossipon') by the 'negro type' of his face, is to reproduce convention. So Conrad cannot let his epithets alone. The supposedly summarizable Ossipon acquires a monumental sentence which gobbles so many ironies that it finally becomes a paragraph in its own right (pp. 40–1).

The sentence is so drawlingly dismissive of Ossipon and those who have put their faith in him that it effectively turns its contempt on itself. It is, after all, representations like this which have given people like Ossipon the currency they enjoy. There is a wobble in Conrad's 'ironic treatment', apparently so stable, so inflexible, so unlikely to be taken in. The scorn that exceeds irony in all these descriptions is directed not at the delinquents themselves but at the way they have been described, over and over, in popular journalism and fiction: a way which Conrad has had no choice but to emulate. The treatment oozes disgust: disgust, in part, at its own failure to be fully, uniquely ironic.

Under Western Eyes poses the same problem, only more explicitly. Some of the conspirators, like Tekla and Sophia Antonovna, are treated carefully. Others, however, like Madame de S———, Peter Ivanovitch and Nikita, are as savagely reduced – and thereby, perhaps, expanded – as anyone in *The Secret Agent*. In the preface to the 1920 edition, Conrad established three categories of representation: Tekla and Sophia Antonovna, who have been treated sympathetically; Peter Ivanovitch and Madame de S———, who have been exhibited as monsters; and the executioner Nikita (another abnormally fat man, we might note), who is merely banal, having been 'exhibited to the public eye for years in so-called "disclosures" in newspaper articles, in secret histories, in sensational novels' (1957, p. 8). These three categories had provoked in him, respectively, no animus, an entirely justified animus, and an animus directed not at a particular type of terrorist but at the way that type has been represented. It is when Conrad switches from the second to the third category

256

that we hear the unmistakable accent of hatred. At that point, disgust becomes a matter of form rather than content, because it is directed at vulgar techniques of representation which the ironist had thought to expel from his writing, but in the end must rely on. The problem is not the fat men, but their inevitability, their familiarity.

DIALOGUE AS TORTURE

If we attribute the 'intelligibility and control' for which Berthoud rightly values Conrad to his 'ironic treatment' of complex issues, then we must attribute the note of exasperation which threatens both intelligibility and control to a kind of 'primitivism': a revulsion at the world, and at his own inability to treat it with a sufficiently annihilating irony. This note is to be heard routinely in the overdone descriptions I have cited, but also in the crises: Kurtz's exterminatory postscript, Decoud's suicide, the polymorphous loathing which makes Jim complicit in some way with Gentleman Brown, Heyst with Mr Jones. The primitivism counts for as much in our response to Conrad as it does in our response to Kipling.

But Conrad exceeded Kipling by writing, on one occasion, from the point of view of the victim rather than the torturer. *Nostromo* has its quota of torturers, of course; notably Guzman Bento, who unifies the newly independent state of Costaguana by force. His victims include the diplomat and patriot Don José Avellanos, who seems only to exist 'in order to prove how much hunger, pain, degradation, and cruel torture a human body can stand without parting with the last spark of life' (1963, p. 123). Amazingly enough, Don José has not parted with any information, either, which cannot be said of another victim, the English doctor Monygham, who blames himself for his own weakness (pp. 308–12). Their suffering has helped to create the 'fiction of power' which sustains Guzman's brutal regime.

Another torturer, Colonel Sotillo, desperate to discover the missing cargo of silver, thinks he can extract the information from one of his prisoners, Señor Hirsch. Hirsch is beaten, and subjected to the 'estrapade': his arms are tied behind his back and then lifted, so that his shoulders dislocate. However, he knows nothing. Realizing that there is no way out, he spits in Sotillo's face. Sotillo panics, and shoots him dead.

The torture scene is at once brutal and self-consciously formal (Fogel 1985, p. 29). It has a rhythm characteristic of Conrad's writing, in which demands for information alternate liturgically with silences until they finally provoke an obliterating explosion. For Conrad, dialogue is a forced relation, 'not meeting, not philosophy, not conversation, not dialectic, but only persons making persons speak in a continuous, unresolved, and finally unresolvable field of force' (p. 226). Stevie, Winnie, Verloc, Razumov, Whalley, Nostromo and Heyst are all 'cornered people' who, in the end, 'detonate' (p. 27).

The climax of the scene, as Sotillo makes one last effort to extract the information he requires, epitomizes this unresolvable field of force:

A slight quiver passed up the taut rope from the racked limbs, but the body of Señor Hirsch, enterprising business-man from Esmeralda, hung under the heavy beam per-pendicular and silent, facing the colonel awfully. The inflow of the night air, cooled by the snows of the Sierra, spread gradually a delicious freshness through the close heat of the room.

'Speak – thief – scoundrel – *picaro* – or—'

Sotillo had seized the riding-whip, and stood with his arm lifted up. For a word, for one little word, he felt he would have knelt, cringed, grovelled on the floor before the drowsy, conscious stare of those fixed eyeballs starting out of the grimy, dishevelled head that drooped very still with its mouth closed askew. The colonel ground his teeth with rage and struck.

(pp. 369–70)

Fogel notes the 'peculiar and punctilious sadism' (1985, p. 28) of the weather report; a freshness as bizarre as the comfort attained in 'The Mark of the Beast'. Here, though, nobody pays any attention to the incongruity. A different game is afoot. The epithet hung around Hirsch's neck – 'enterprising businessman from Esmeralda' – makes it hard to know where Conrad himself stands. Will the banal anti-Semitism of earlier descriptions be vindicated or disproved? In the event, it simply detonates. The object of so much revulsion – Gould's, Sotillo's, ours – expresses his own revulsion, and in a way so revolting that the torturer, 'as if aspersed by a jet of deadly venom' (p. 370), kills him instantly. This jet of sputum, an act of expulsion, not triumph or forgiveness, is the only redemption Conrad ever imagined for any of his fat men. Irony, for once, has come and gone, as unnoticed as the inflow of night air. Disgust remains.

17

WAITING: JAMES'S LAST NOVELS

Kipling, Conrad and James incorporated into their writing something of the turbulent fascination with impurity which had previously characterized satire and tragedy, but not, to any comparable extent, the novel. It is this, as much as their celebrated irony, which makes them modern and, a different matter, interesting. They wrote about lives shaped, as Kristeva might put it, not by desire, but by exclusion; and they did so in ways that were at times almost impure, almost vulgar.

Kipling and Conrad continued in this vein until the end of their careers. Kipling was no easier on German airmen than he had been on lepers. Conrad evolved a metaphysic of disgust, identifying his protagonists by their revulsion from an abjectness for which they must all, in complicated ways, take responsibility: the heart of darkness, the abyss of cowardice, the silence of the Golfo Placido, the 'death-ridden earth' of Samburan. Kipling remained the inventor or cannibalizer of popular genres; Conrad their envious, exasperated parodist. James, however, changed direction. The last three novels he completed – *The Wings of the Dove* (1902), *The Ambassadors* (1903), *The Golden Bowl* (1904) – are about lives shaped by desire, not exclusion; and they make no concessions at all to the vulgar reader.

AVOIDING MATERIAL CLUES

The idea for *The Wings of the Dove*, of a man who gives a sick woman a 'taste of happiness' by marrying her, came to him in 1894, and from the very beginning its potential vulgarity alarmed him:

It has bothered me in thinking of the little picture – this idea of the physical possession, the brief physical, passional rapture which at first appeared essential to it; bothered me on account of the ugliness, the incongruity, the nastiness, *en somme*, of the man's 'having' a sick girl: also on account of something rather pitifully obvious and vulgar in the presentation of such a remedy for her despair – and such a remedy only.

(1987, p. 103)

So much so, apparently, that in the final version Merton Densher saves Milly Theale without actually 'having' her. James's determination to avoid obviousness and vulgarity illuminates both the risks he subsequently took, on occasion, in *What Maisie Knew* and *The Spoils of Poynton* and the meticulous restraint of the last three novels.

The novel which preceded the last three, *The Sacred Fount* (1901), has usually been considered his most vulgar; he may have thought so himself, since he omitted it from the New York Edition. However, it certainly isn't obvious in its treatment of a vulgar subject: the detection of adultery. At one point, the narrator discusses the propriety of his project with a companion who insists that it will remain 'honourable' as long as the researchers confine themselves to 'psychologic signs' and don't play 'the detective at the keyhole'. The narrator agrees that the really shameful liability would be possession of a 'material clue' (James 1923, pp. 52–3). The material clue revolts them, and James, since it would turn his tale into a vulgar detective story. By avoiding it, by sticking to 'psychologic signs', as he was to do consistently in his late novels, James avoided at once a moral and a generic indecency.

The notoriously indirect style of the late novels was James's protection against vulgarity. It created moral and literary value by 'making the reader's purchase of significance difficult and costly' (White 1981, p. 147). If enjoyment of a work of art constitutes 'our highest experience of "luxury",' James wrote in the preface to *The Wings of the Dove*, then 'the luxury is not greatest ... where the work asks for as little attention as possible'. Enjoyment is greatest when the reader is obliged to bring to bear the maximum 'attention of perusal' (1907–9, XIX, pp. xx-xxi). James's defence of difficulty is compatible with the account I

261

have given in Chapter 4 of the emergence of Modernism; my aim here is to extend that account by examining the 'attention of perusal' demanded by the last novels.

Acknowledgement of that defence, combined with the awe in which difficulty has been held by the critical theories of the last twenty years, has led to his virtual recanonization: as Modernist, this time, not as literary moralist. The 'theoretical dimensions' of his writing (Rowe 1984) have been ransacked (Bradbury 1979, 1984; Kappeler 1980; Carroll 1982; Caws 1985; Bloom 1987; Tallack 1987; McWhirter 1989). His narrative strategies are said to have shifted the emphasis of the novel from 'constructing life-like worlds' to 'exploring the dynamics of world construction', and thus contributed to a 'wide-spread awareness in the literature of our century that we live in a world of signs that ... lead only to other signs' (Armstrong 1987, p. 1). While I agree that there is something new going on, in the last novels in particular, I wouldn't put it in quite those terms.

EVENTS

Events create material clues, which are, as often as not, vulgar. So why not dispense with them? Or at least recess them in some way. In the last novels, meaningful events often take the form of recognitions rather than actions (Cave 1988). Strether discovers that Chad and Madame de Vionnet are lovers. Milly Theale makes the same discovery about Merton Densher and Kate Croy, Maggie Verver about the Prince and Charlotte Stant; in each case, the revelation shows what they are made of. Even here, though, there is a tendency towards recessiveness. Strether's discovery, like Isabel Archer's, in *The Portrait of a Lady*, is presented directly, with full dramatic, even melodramatic, force. Milly Theale's and Maggie Verver's are presented indirectly; we don't see them tested, we don't see their visionary response take shape (Horne 1990, pp. 214–18). James, in short, is as far as he possibly could be from the unshaded staging of disablement and re-enablement so characteristic of contemporary popular fiction.

Equally crucial, as events, are the conversations during which the characters reveal themselves to each other. In *The Wings of the Dove* James speaks of the 'intensity of relation' and the 'face-to-face necessity' into which Densher and Kate Croy have been thrown, whenever they meet, by their crisis (1907–9, XX, p.

326). It is through a series of face-to-face necessities, encounters with the Prince, with her father, with Charlotte Stant, that Maggie Verver saves her marriage. These occasions destroy old understandings and create new ones; they are the medium through which identity is expressed. For the reader, they bring 'much relief' (Yeazell 1976, p. 83). They clarify rather as duels and awakenings do in another kind of fiction.

And yet the clarity can be deceptive. Consider the scene in which Kate Croy and Merton Densher commit themselves to a conspiracy against Milly Theale:

> 'Don't think, however, I'll do *all* the work for you. If you want things named you must name them.'
>
> He had quite, within the minute, been turning names over; and there was only one, which at last stared at him there dreadful, that properly fitted. 'Since she's to die I'm to marry her?'
>
> It struck him even at the moment as fine in her that she met it with no wincing nor mincing. She might for the grace of silence, for favour to their conditions, have only answered with her eyes. But her lips bravely moved. 'To marry her.'
>
> (1907–9, XX, p. 225)

The two lovers declare themselves; their language *performs* that declaration. Kate doesn't merely assent to Densher's propositions. She repeats them word for word, imitating, as in a ceremony, the very shape of his syntax. Such repetitions signify agreement not only with a proposition in general, as a simple affirmative might, but with every part of it. Kate is fully present in every word of the pledge which has sealed their mutual commitment; her reiteration wills Densher to be fully present in a proposition he has put, it might seem, hypothetically. Such reiterations, which also occur at crucial moments in *The Golden Bowl* (Normann 1982, pp. 84–107), serve as a model for meaningful event in late James.

And yet these climactic disclosures take place only at the far end of the vista provided by James's exploration of consciousness. Kate Croy's invitation to name things is followed, in our unfolding awareness of the event, not by Densher's response, but by a narrative hiatus. 'He had quite, within the minute, been turning names over; and there was only one, which at last stared at him there dreadful, that properly fitted.' Clearly, this hesitation provides a context for the name he eventually produces. But the context provided is by no means easily accessible. We hesitate over his hesitation. James could have written 'He had been turning names over; and there was only one which fitted', and still indicated Densher's reluctance. As it is, we have to deal with interleavings, like the pointedly withheld 'dreadful', which complicate the focus of the sentence. Why dread, rather than shame or embarrassment? What is he afraid of? The characteristic obliquity of James's syntax (Chatman 1972; Leech and Short 1981, pp. 97–110) forces us to access relatively remote contexts in an effort to understand Densher's meaning.

In late James even the most emphatic affirmation is doubly recessed: by the narrative interventions which frame, and space out, dialogue; and by the difficulty the reader has in processing those interventions. Far from being everything, as the post-structuralist might suppose, the words themselves are nothing; nothing at all without the contexts, some relatively inaccessible, which might allow us to infer what the speaker means by them. Kate Croy, we realize after a certain familiarity, overstates; Densher understates. In a world where speech is event, inference becomes a crucial and an arduous task. Densher finds it more or less beyond him. There is too much in Kate's words, and not enough in his. The conclusion of their pact reveals the degree by which they have both missed explaining themselves:

> 'Oh, oh, oh!' Densher softly murmured.
> 'Yes, yes, yes.' But she broke off. 'Come to Lady Mills.'
>
> (p. 225)

The parallelism of this exchange draws the distinction between them: Kate emphatically affirming, Densher at a loss, his words expressive, but without reference – indeed not, strictly speaking, words at all.

Later, Mrs Stringham visits him in his rooms with the hope that he will reveal what he knows, and feels, about Milly. ' "That I shall really tell you?" With which, as she hesitated, and it affected him, he brought out, in a groan, a doubting "Oh, oh!" It turned him from her to the place itself, which was a part of what was in him' (pp. 272–3). The place is a part of what is in him because it is there that his relationship with Kate Croy has been consummated. Again, the hesitation reveals the impossibility of telling everything, or anything. It produces a non-statement. Indeed, a helpless 'oh' remains his note throughout the conversation with Mrs Stringham.

Densher's 'oh' raises the question of the extent to which the novel as a whole should be regarded as a kind of encyclopaedia. Do we associate it, for example, with Lord Mark's 'oh'? Lord Mark is a kind of 'malignant blank', an incarnation of the menace latent in his name that a sign may signify nothing beyond itself (Poole 1991, p. 116). When introduced, he gives an 'oh!' which Densher recognizes as that of 'the clever, the accomplished man': 'it was the very specialty of the speaker, and a deal of expensive training and experience had gone to producing it' (1907–9, p. 232). It sounds a note, not of helplessness, but of self-evident, albeit empty, authority. He uses it as a weapon when probing Milly about her feelings for Densher, and then as a territorial marker when Densher himself is announced. ' "Oh!" said Lord Mark – in a manner that, making it resound through the great, cool hall, might have carried it even to Densher's ear as a judgement of his identity heard and noted once before' (p. 167). Connected across sixty-odd pages of text, the two exclamations constitute a basis for inference: about Lord Mark's intentions, and Densher's. It is possible, though by no means probable, that a reader might interpret Densher's note of helplessness in the light of Lord Mark's note of judgement, to which James has explicitly drawn attention; the novel serving us in this instance as encyclopaedic memory. James's writing, like Joyce's, obliges us to base our inferences about what a character might mean by his or her eventful words on an attention to such relatively inaccessible contexts.

KEPT WAITING

What happens both in the recognition scenes and in the momentous conversations is that identities are declared once and for all. For Lambert Strether, there is no way back from the discovery that Chad Newsome and Madame de Vionnet are lovers; for Merton Densher and Kate Croy, there is no way back from conspiracy. And yet event and meaning seldom coincide, in late James; identities are seldom declared once and for all.

A more characteristic scene, in many ways, is one in which somebody is kept waiting; and when one person delays and

265

another is delayed, there can be no 'intensity of relation', no 'face-to-face necessity'. James was fascinated by delay as well as by coincidence. It is a subject present in his early writing, but given greater prominence in the later. Mrs Bellegarde keeps Newman waiting in the revised version of *The American* (1907–9, II, pp. 180–1), but not in the original.

In Book I of *The Wings of the Dove*, Kate Croy waits for her father, in his apartment in Chirk Street; in Book II, Merton Densher waits for Maud Lowder, at Lancaster Gate. We approach them by way of the fantasies they evolve while waiting. 'She waited, Kate Croy, for her father to come in,' the novel opens, 'but he kept her unconscionably, and there were moments at which she showed herself, in the glass over the mantel, a face positively pale with the irritation that had brought her to the point of going away without sight of him' (1907–9, XIX, p. 3). Her irritation has already taken in Lionel Croy's thoroughly abject belongings, including a slippery, sticky armchair, and the 'vulgar little street' outside.

It's all very reminiscent of Mr Vetch's 'little place' in West Kensington, in *The Spoils of Poynton*, whose sordidness overshadows Owen Gereth's love for Fleda. When Mrs Brigstock surprises them there together, the first thing she notices is a half-chewed biscuit on the carpet: 'Owen at any rate picked it up, and Fleda felt as if he were removing the traces of some scene that the newspapers would have characterised as lively' (1907–9, X, p. 169) – a material clue, no less. But Kate Croy and a mirror is a more powerful combination than Fleda Vetch and Owen Gereth. What she sees in the mirror is not the stickiness of her surroundings but her own beauty; in this scene a narcissism produced by sight overwhelms a disgust produced by smell and touch. Kate is the most relentlessly handsome of James's heroines: 'she was somehow always in the line of the eye – she counted singularly for its pleasure' (XIX, p. 5). While her father delays, desire emerges; desire, after all, *is* delay, and disappears once the wait is over. It overshadows the vulgarity of the room, generating a fantasy of masculine power. 'There was a minute during which, though her eyes were fixed, she quite visibly lost herself in the thought of the way she might still pull things round had she only been a man' (p. 6).

Densher has less use for mirrors; but delay stiffens his resolve, as well as his indifference to vulgarity. The vulgarity in this case is the message of wealth and power conveyed by Aunt Maud's 'conclusively British' furniture. 'He had never dreamed of anything so fringed and scalloped, so buttoned and corded, drawn everywhere so tight, and curled everywhere so thick' (pp. 78–9). His fantasy of power, of revenge, is to write an article about these 'heavy horrors'. When Aunt Maud finally appears, she conveys the same message as her furniture, with just the faintest suggestion of desire, amid all the heaviness, in the admission that she cannot altogether hate him.

From the start, James had emphasized that Densher and Kate Croy desire each other passionately, and that they have been forced to delay by poverty alone. 'If the young couple have at any rate, and for whatever reason, to *wait* (say for her, or for *his* father's death) I get what is essential. *Ecco.* They are waiting' (1987, p. 104). These were to be lives shaped by desire rather than exclusion. In one aspect *The Wings of the Dove* is a novel about a long secret engagement, as the brief account of assignations in Kensington Gardens makes plain (1907–9, XIX, pp. 47–50). In another aspect, Milly Theale's, it isn't, of course. What does *she* want?

Milly is most memorably kept waiting by her doctor, Sir Luke Strett:

> She should be intimate with the great bronze clock and mantel-ornaments, conspicuously presented in gratitude and long ago; she should be as one of the circle of eminent contemporaries, photographed, engraved, signatured, and in particular framed and glazed, who made up the rest of the human comfort; and while she thought of all the clean truths, unfringed, unfingered, that the listening stillness, strained into pauses and waits, would again and again, for years, have kept distinct, she also wondered what *she* would eventually decide upon to present in gratitude.
>
> (p. 237)

The leisureliness of the sentence allows not only for the accumulation of solidifying detail, but for remarkable analysis, of the stillness 'strained into pauses and waits'. And yet it arrives unmistakably at a focus on Milly ('what *she* would . . .'); it reveals her at a stroke. Her talent is to feel at home in a strange place; she sees not only the vulgar presents, but the truths – 'unfringed, unfingered' – they have been exchanged for. The truths don't invalidate the presents, though they do encourage a certain discrimination. 'She would give something better at least than the brawny Victorian bronzes' (p. 237). This is what she wants: to give a fiction (a present is a fiction, a symbol) in exchange for a truth (a diagnosis). In the end, she will bequeath her fortune (a symbol as well as a material fact) to Merton Densher in return for the bitter truth that he doesn't love her.

Milly Theale waits, because everyone must learn to wait in a book about desire. Even the rather abrupt Lord Mark waits well (1907–9, XX, pp. 143–4). But James's narrative obliquity allows her to wait, on this occasion, without having been made to wait; the truth-producing interview with Sir Luke is already under way before we hear about the great bronze clock. There is no question of Sir Luke manipulating her as Lionel Croy manipulates his daughter and Aunt Maud manipulates Densher. For her, event and meaning, the face-to-face necessity and the desire produced by deferral, do after all coincide.

OLD FELLOWS

The Ambassadors announces by its title that it will be a book of interviews, of encounters more or less ceremonial, of performative utterances. It ought to resemble a dialogue culminating in two emphatic affirmations, as Chad agrees to return to Woollett, Massachusetts, and Mrs Newsome agrees to marry Lambert Strether. But Strether is kept waiting from the start. His friend Waymarsh does not meet him at Liverpool, as planned, and the ensuing 'duration of delay' (1907–9, XXI, p. 5) allows him to pick up, without the looming presence of his American friend, the 'note of Europe', and Maria Gostrey, in whose company he absorbs the note.

Kate Croy and Merton Densher recognize and desire in each other a 'precious unlikeness' (XIX, p. 50). Dining with Maria Gostrey before a visit to the theatre, Strether notices her difference from Mrs Newsome: the low-cut dress, the red velvet band around her neck, a 'starting point for fresh backward, fresh forward, fresh lateral flights' (XXI, p. 51). These flights are all into difference: into what might have been, what might yet be. The scene has a fine comic rhythm which keeps them airborne by setting Maria's bold intrusive wit against Strether's slow courtesy.

Their pact is, in one aspect, to ignore vulgarity, to stop short of revulsion. They agree to include rather than exclude: to keep their differences, and all the other differences Strether will encounter in Europe, alive.

> He felt as if the play itself penetrated him with the naked elbow of his neighbour, a great stripped handsome red-haired lady who conversed with a gentleman on her other side in stray dissyllables which had for his ear, in the oddest way in the world, so much sound that he wondered they had n't more sense; and he recognized by the same law, beyond the footlights, what he was pleased to take for the very flush of English life.
>
> (p. 53)

The great 'stripped' handsome lady is unmistakably vulgar; and the vulgarity, the display of nakedness, seems to influence, in a strange way, Strether's perception of the 'flush' of English life. In the play, a bad, and possibly older, woman makes a good-looking young man in perpetual evening dress do the most dreadful things: leakage, indeed. Strether finds himself drifting into a 'kindness' for the young man, and by analogy for the object of his own embassy. 'Would Chad also be in perpetual evening dress?' (p. 54). Of course, as it turns out, Chad's relation with the older Madame de Vionnet does leak terribly; and Strether, although deeply shocked, will have a certain kindness for that, too. The night at the theatre introduces him to complicity.

In Paris, Strether is once again kept waiting. Chad has left town in order to create a further duration of delay which will allow his mother's ambassador another fresh start. His apartment, which Strether has already visited, speaks for him. Chad is a meaning before he is an event. When he does appear, it is as an intruder, whom Strether does not at first recognize, in Maria Gostrey's box at the theatre: an event without, for a split second, an identifiable meaning. From now on, Chad will never quite coincide with himself. Strether can neither emulate this perpetual difference nor call its bluff (discern, as Mrs Newsome would have done, an essential sameness beneath the perpetually renewed exterior).

His predicament is contained in the anecdote which started James: W. D. Howells telling Jonathan Sturges to live all he could while still young.

I seem to see something, of a tiny kind, springing out of it, that would take its place in the little group I should like to do of *Les Vieux* – The Old. (What should I call it in English – *Old Fellows*? No, that's trivial and common.) At any rate, it gives me the little idea of the figure of an elderly man who hasn't 'lived', hasn't at all, in the sense of sensations, passions, impulses, pleasures.

(1987, p. 141)

The idea skirts the trivial and common, the '*banal* side' of a Parisian awakening (1907–9, XXI, p. 141), but not in order to invite revulsion. What was to stir the protagonist, instead, was the 'sense that he may have a little super-sensual hour in the vicarious freedom of another' (p. 142).

Strether's super-sensuality frees him, but only for a more elaborate, more pleasurable captivity. He has found his measure of absolute difference in Madame de Vionnet, whom he values for her 'rare unlikeness to the women he had known' (p. 157). It is not a woman he desires, perhaps, so much as an unlikeness from the women he has known. But he won't drive home his advantage with her, his attractiveness, because he has resolved not to derive any benefit to himself from his embassy.

Such renunciation is noble; or, from another point of view, selfish. Densher, having waited youthfully for so long, seems to age dramatically with Milly's death, because he realizes that he has missed his opportunity; thereafter he prefers the permanently inaccessible Milly to the accessible and already sampled Kate Croy. Strether, having been kept waiting for so long, and liberated in the process, decides to keep everyone else waiting. His perverse genius is to defer consummation indefinitely. The consequence of the complicity inaugurated by his arrival in England is to 'make him want things that he should n't know what to do with'; indeed, to 'make him want more wants' (XXI, p. 40).

With Densher and Strether, noble renunciation and selfishness are hard to tell apart. But James did create one indisputably selfish old fellow: John Marcher, in 'The Beast in the Jungle' (1902). Marcher believes that his life will be distinguished by some extraordinary crisis, some 'unprecedented stroke'. May Bartram, to whom he once revealed this conviction, becomes, on their reacquaintance, its guardian. But his wait multiplies

270

meanings, and the meanings defer endlessly the event that might resolve them. May Bartram, by now desperately ill, gives him, through her hesitation before speaking, a last chance to recognize that *she* is his event (James 1962–4, XI, p. 386). However, his recognition does not come until much later, as he stands beside her grave. He will always be too late. 'It was the truth, vivid and monstrous, that all the while he had waited the wait was itself the portion' (p. 401).

But is Marcher merely selfish, as he himself concludes, in his refusal to acknowledge, until it is too late, May Bartram's love? Eve Kosofsky Sedgwick has complicated our understanding of the story by suggesting that his 'secret' is not May Bartram, but 'homosexual panic': a refusal to acknowledge the possibility that he might desire a man (Sedgwick 1989). According to this account, what he accepts at the graveside is the heterosexual compulsion – the obligation to desire a woman – which will close off his homosexual possibilities, and make him truly the man of his time to whom nothing was ever to happen. Sedgwick argues that May Bartram wants above all to help Marcher through his crisis: to cure his 'vexed and gaping self-ignorance', and nurture whatever kind of sexuality emerges from the struggle (1989, p. 262). The advantage of her argument is that it makes his self-suppression the result, not of a puzzling obtuseness, but of an unresolvable conflict between a socially instituted heterosexual compulsion (the Law) and homosexual possibilities.

Section 4 of the story includes May Bartram's hesitation, the moment at which she realizes that, 'far from helping dissolve Marcher's closet, she has instead and irremediably been permitting him to reinforce it' (Sedgwick 1989, p. 262). She reveals to him that his secret lies not in the future, but in the past (the secret is the closet). It is indeed a critical moment; although Sedgwick, in attending perceptively to May Bartram's story, somewhat underestimates the appearance May has for Marcher during the crisis.

Visiting May in April, Marcher finds her for the first time in the year without a fire; the room has 'a smooth and ultimate look, an air of knowing, in its immaculate order and its cold, meaningless cheer, that it would never see a fire again' (1962–4, XI, p. 380). May herself has the waxy pallor of an artificial lily, the inscrutability of a sphinx whose person 'might have been powdered with silver'. The pallor is reminiscent of Kipling's

271

leper, the Silver Man. May Bartram, too, has her associations
with death, with the abject. Like Quint and Miss Jessel appearing
to the governess, she communicates with Marcher 'as across
some gulf, or from some island of rest that she had already
reached, and it made him feel strangely abandoned' (p. 380).
Her 'cold charm' dominates the encounter.

Telling him that it is never too late, May moves closer to him,
for a moment, 'as if still full of the unspoken'.

> Her movement might have been for some finer emphasis
> of what she was at once hesitating and deciding to say. He
> had been standing by the chimney-piece, fireless and sparely
> adorned, a small, perfect old French clock and two morsels
> of rosy Dresden constituting all its furniture; and her hand
> grasped the shelf while she kept him waiting, grasped it a
> little as for support and encouragement. She only kept him
> waiting, however; that is he only waited.
>
> (p. 386)

The description of the chimney-piece creates for us her hesitation,
a space in which something might have been said, but wasn't.
Her action is, or might have been, a supplement to speech. But
since the speech never comes, the supplement supplements
nothing. The syntax – 'She only kept him waiting, however; that
is he only waited' – mimics, demonically, this doubling without
origin. The wait itself is the meaning, and the end of meaning,
the impossibility of self-recognition. What May has to tell him
glitters, 'almost as with the white lustre of silver, in her expression'.
She presents it as 'inordinately soft'.

Marcher's secret may be, as Sedgwick suggests, his homosexual
panic. To him this secret is, although he won't admit it, leprous,
abject, disgusting. What James dramatizes so well, through May
Bartram's appearance, is Marcher's paralysis. The truth sickens
him. Like the governess, he faints away, at the end of the
story, in view of this beckoning from across a dangerous place.
Marcher's is a life founded on rejection, not desire. It might
make us think again about those other old or rapidly ageing
fellows, Lambert Strether and Merton Densher, whose lives are
apparently founded on desire, but who also, in their fashion,
reject.

VERVE

In *The Golden Bowl* James allowed Maggie Verver to consummate Milly Theale's dream of loving and being loved, and so to escape from the 'prison-house of desire' (McWhirter 1989, p. 147). Strether's freedom, his super-sensuality, had depended on ignorance. Maggie's depends on knowledge, of the Prince's relationship with Charlotte Stant. Strether, like Densher, like Marcher, wants more wants. Maggie has an aim in mind: to win back her husband. She is determined to get something out of the affair for herself.

The balance of power begins to tilt in the opening scene of Book II, where Maggie is kept waiting, for the Prince's return from Matcham; or, rather, and this is her difference from Strether and Densher, keeps herself waiting. The Prince is, as anticipated, very late, and she suffers accordingly all the torments, the exacerbated attentiveness, of those who are kept waiting. She has, however, *chosen* to be kept waiting, and her duration of delay is filled not with lateral flights, but with 'an infinite sense of intention' (1907–9, XXIV, p. 9). She knows that she has given her husband the first surprise of his married life. It is she who has taken the initiative, made a difference: 'he had come back, had followed her from the other house, *visibly* uncertain' (p. 15). She has made him understand that she loves him and wants him.

Maggie has taken control of her life; but not in such a way as to remove control altogether from her husband, her partner. The man who has already kept her waiting once does so again, this time on his own initiative. He retires to dress for dinner, a process which takes an hour to complete. Once again, the delay generates meaning: an awareness of subjection, of 'the fullest surrender' (p. 22), which balances the mastery achieved during her previous wait. Once again, the Prince, on his return, confirms that meaning. In *The Golden Bowl*, unlike *The Wings of the Dove* and *The Ambassadors*, event and meaning do coincide, and James is therefore able to describe the Prince's entrance; the narrative no longer hesitates over, or despairingly attenuates, or recesses, the moment of encounter, of union.

One small proof of Maggie's moral stature, which emerges

during her final triumph over Charlotte Stant, is her ability to laugh at herself; not a talent given to many of James's protagonists. Her dominance is such that she is able to confront Charlotte, in the garden at Fawns, without appearing to confront her. 'She herself could but tentatively hover, place in view the book she carried, look as little dangerous, look as abjectly mild, as possible; remind herself really of people she had read about in stories of the wild west, people who threw up their hands on certain occasions for a sign they were n't carrying revolvers' (pp. 310–11). Abjectness, skilfully concealed but none the less impossible to shake off, has been a quality associated with Charlotte from the outset. Assuming it for a moment, Maggie acknowledges her own fallibility; she might. so easily have lost. That acknowledgement is her main strength. She is the only one of the quartet who can conceive of herself as ordinary. At this crucial, resolving moment, James deploys sub-literary stereotype; few of his contemporaries would have taken that risk, would have acknowledged their own fallibility.

So much for Maggie's verve. What about James's? Does the novel's obliqueness, the 'extreme convolution' of its syntax, merely distract, or, worse, intimidate (Hewitt 1988, pp. 22–3)? I would like to approach this question by way of Virginia Woolf's review (I shall quote from the text she had in front of her, the 1904 edition). Woolf criticized James's style in terms which are sufficiently close to those I have used in discussing Mansfield, Lawrence and Joyce for some conclusion to be reached. 'Mr James,' she observed, 'tortures himself and wearies his readers in his strenuous effort to get everything said that there is to say' (1986–8, I, p. 23). Her first example of an 'overburdened' sentence is the one which describes Adam Verver's recognition that his daughter is troubled by his familiarity with the gold-digging Mrs Rance. 'It was *really* remarkable: this perception expanded, on the spot, as a flower, one of the strangest, might, at a breath, have suddenly opened' (James 1966b, p. 130). James insists, almost punitively, that the perception is remarkable; but the syntax of the subordinate clause then distends so remarkably itself that we rather lose sight of any other remarkableness. What *is* the point of the flower? Its strangeness, or the suddenness of its flowering? And would either quality be remarkable in the response of a father caught in a mildly compromising situation by his daughter? James seems to be admiring a verve of his own rather than Verver's. Woolf may well be right to protest. James more or less admits as much a couple of pages earlier, when he observes that he may be drawing his circle 'too wide' around this particular incident (p. 128).

Woolf's second example is a sentence which describes a crucial moment in the brief encounter between the Prince and Charlotte Stant at Portland Place (she wants him to let her buy Maggie a wedding present). 'She had stood a stair or two below him; where, while she looked up at him beneath the high, domed light of the hall, she rubbed with her palm the polished mahogany of the balustrade, which was mounted on fine ironwork, eighteenth-century English' (p. 90). Woolf's objection is to the mahogany and the ironwork. 'These are trivial instances of detail which, perpetually insisted on, fatigues without adding to the picture' (1986–8, I, p. 23). The detail is irrelevant; it does not combine with what we already know about the Prince and Charlotte to tell us something we don't yet know; in Relevance Theory terms, it increases the cost of processing the sentence, without producing a significant contextual effect (adding to the picture).

But is the detail irrelevant? It certainly blurs the focus of the sentence, forcing us to look beyond short-term narrative memory for a context. The mahogany and the ironwork distract us from what is going on, at a crucial moment, in the minds of the characters. But do they not fix the moment itself, in time and space? James has already described the encounter as an 'exceptional minute', a 'mere snatch' (p. 89). Charlotte's palm rubbing the balustrade establishes its critical nature. For Charlotte and the Prince, every encounter is a mere snatch, an opportunity that will evaporate unless it is grasped firmly, aggressively. Charlotte loses because she is committed, by temperament and circumstance, in a way that Maggie is not, to the exceptional minute. James overburdens his sentence because the occasion it describes is hopelessly overburdened.

There may also be another relatively inaccessible context for the Portland Place balustrade, in Charlotte's potentially destructive cosmopolitanism, her curious 'neutrality' (p. 64). The chapter opens with the couple strolling in Hyde Park, on a day of a 'rich, low-browed, weather-washed English type' (p. 88). But what has Englishness, of weather or ironwork, to do with Charlotte? She is the permanent 'desirable alien', in Violet Hunt's phrase. James's distended syntax forces us to suspend short-term narrative memory, to cast around for significance. But if we work hard enough we can find reasons for the detail that annoyed Woolf; it does 'add to the picture', it does produce contextual effects which could not have been produced in any other way. An awareness of James's tendency to draw too wide a circle around events, on occasion, need not, and should not, prevent us from recognizing that it is the width of the circle which makes him, on other occasions, a great writer.

18

WYNDHAM LEWIS

Modernism began as a formal and literary-historical category. It has since become political (Jameson 1988b, I, ch. 2; II, chs 6, 7; Eagleton 1989) and gendered (Scott 1990). Here I shall resume the discussion of its psychopathology initiated in Chapter 14. 'The contemplation of the horrid or sordid or disgusting, by the artist,' T. S. Eliot wrote, 'is the necessary and negative aspect of the impulse toward the pursuit of beauty.' Eliot thought Dante one of the few writers to encompass 'the complete scale from negative to positive'. Most gravitate towards the lower end of the scale. 'The negative is the more importunate' (1932, p. 169). In Modernism, the negative was always importunate.

Eliot himself succumbed often enough. When, towards the end of 1925, Conrad Aiken complimented him on a recent book of poems, he received through the post an article about vaginal discharges torn from the *Midwives' Gazette*. Eliot had underlined several words and phrases: 'blood', 'mucus', 'shreds of mucus', 'purulent offensive discharge' (Ackroyd 1984, pp. 150–1). Women were, notoriously, the main, though by no means the only, source of disgust in his early poems. In *The Waste Land*, the 'hearty female stench' excised from the manuscript re-emerges in the various portraits of ladies. This revulsion is central to the poem's Modernism, as Maud Ellmann has shown (1990). In his later writing Eliot moved at once beyond Modernism and beyond revulsion, up towards the positive end of the scale.

Wyndham Lewis has usually been regarded as the most Modernist of Modernists (Kenner 1972, pp. 232–6, 240; Jameson 1979; Dasenbrock 1985). I shall characterize him here as a writer importuned by the negative; an innovator, certainly, but one limited in his departures by the scope of his subject-matter. To

277

do this, I shall trace his development from the very early prose sketches of 1908 through to *Tarr* (1918).

WILD BODIES

Lewis's earliest surviving prose pieces are descriptions of peasant life in Brittany. A journal he kept in 1908 describes a 'pardon', or *fête*, at Clohars. The people who interest him are not the participants but the spectators, the older men who attend because they find in resisting participation 'the acrid savour of their own personality' (Lewis 1982, p. 193). Lewis the writer announces himself, I think, in the word 'acrid' (bitterly pungent, irritating, corrosive: *OED*). He does not care about what unites the revellers. Holding aloof from the *fête*, 'the enemy of such orgaic participation of life' (p. 195), he enjoys the bitter pungency of an apartness which seems to revolt everyone else. Acridity mattered because it was a subject-matter he could claim as his own.

Later in the same journal Lewis describes the acrid life – heat, sweat, oiliness, tar – of a harbour after a violent squall; but rather spoils the effect by adding that the acridity has been 'render'd more intense' by the grey light and the purple gleam of the wet houses (p. 198). What he 'notices', in short, is a painting by Whistler, a poem by Arthur Symons, a prose sketch by Hubert Crackanthorpe. Finding the subject-matter was one thing, relieving it of previous representations quite another.

'Crossing the Frontier' (1909–10) imagines acridity as the absolute difference created by boundaries. Entering Spain from France, Lewis talks to a Spaniard whose occasional impassive 'yes' contrasts vividly with the volubility of the French. 'But his vitality is even greater, and behind this silent mask, and this solitary word, entire speeches of cataclysmic violence are clamouring and surging for utterance' (1982, p. 205). Lewis discovers himself as an Englishman and a writer by confronting his acrid opposite (and potential ally), just as the young Rudyard Kipling had done thirty years before, by entering and describing Patiala Palace, or Peshawar, the City of Evil Countenances, where the Afghans scowl at the Englishman and 'spit fluently on the ground after he has passed' (Kipling 1986, pp. 27–31, 81–5).

Another strategy was to claim a philosophical or sociological basis for the enquiry, as Lewis did in 'Our Wild Body', an essay first published in the *New Age* on 5 May 1910. Here he attributed the healthy egotism of the Spaniard and the Basque to the primitive respect in which they held the body; something the Englishman had long since forgotten, despite his baths, his Indian clubs and exercise charts. 'The bath is, figuratively, to drown it in, the instruments on the wall to indebt it to science and tame it' (p. 251). The distinction is wittily drawn, but commonplace. George du Maurier's *Trilby* (1894), for example, pays a great deal of attention to the baths and Indian clubs of its pseudo-bohemian English artists. Lewis's vitalism, a temporary phase, provided a reason for admiring the wild body, but sentimentalized it in the process.

By this time, however, Lewis had done enough to convince Ford Madox Hueffer, who published some of the Breton material in the *English Review*: 'The "Pole" ' (May 1909), 'Some Innkeepers and Bestre' (June 1909), 'Les Saltimbanques' (August 1909). These sketches, travel-writing transmuted uneasily into fiction, avoid aestheticism and sentimentality. They find a language for attitudes and gestures which had not yet been represented convincingly in fiction. 'Mine was now a drowsy sun-baked ferment,' Lewis recalled in his autobiography, 'watching with delight the great comic effigies which erupted beneath my rather saturnine but astonished gaze: Brotcotnaz, Bestre, and the rest' (1984, p. 125).

'Some Innkeepers and Bestre' begins as an essay on French innkeepers and their cultivation of attributes: oiliness, breeziness, pomposity, rotundity and even, in one case, a wooden leg (1982, pp. 221–2). 'These emotions, like the body, develop if constantly used ... to prodigious proportions; until, to pursue the physical simile, the original frame and structure is no longer discernible beneath a bulging mass of the strangest excrescences' (p. 227). The bulging mass of excrescences overflows and thus obliterates the original 'frame and structure'. Lewis's comic effigies are a motivated version of Conrad's fat men, shapeless physical and moral monstrosities which challenge our ability to enforce limits and make distinctions. Their shapelessness is acrid, aggressively distasteful.

Bestre, for example, a Breton innkeeper of Spanish descent, specializes in 'dumb-passive' provocation (p. 229). He defeats one opponent simply by looking at her: 'looking with such a nauseating intensity of what seemed meaning, but in truth was nothing more than, by a tremendous effort of concentration, the transference to features and glance of all the unclean contents of his mind, that had he suddenly laid bare his entrails she could not have felt more revolted' (p. 230). In the later, revised version of this story, Bestre revolts the painter's wife by exposing himself (1927a, pp. 131–2). The earlier version – the concentrated gaze which stops just short of meaning – seems to me the better, if necessarily more enigmatic, one. Self-exposure may be nauseating, but it is rather obviously nauseating: a commonplace violation, an encoding into sexual violence of behaviour that is neither sexual nor violent, but acrid, abject. That Lewis should subsequently resort to translation demonstrates how uncategorizable the behaviour was, as originally conceived, and how hard to represent.

At this stage in his career Lewis relied on a different translation, into social theory. Bestre is 'degenerate'. 'As to the *raison d'être* of these campaigns ... of his pugnacity, I think this is merely his degeneracy – the irritable caricature of a warlike original' (1927a, pp. 232–3). Degeneracy seems a rather weak, not to say boring, explanation for Bestre's capacity to nauseate, lumping him in, as it does, with all the other misfits and monsters projected by late Victorian anxieties. The point about acridity, after all, is that it evades, indeed defies, the categories of social theory.

SOLDIERS OF HUMOUR

Lewis's boldest attempt to resolve the problem of representation was *Enemy of the Stars* (1914, revised 1932), not so much an unstageable play as the description of a play being performed, in the future, for a phantom audience. The stage directions (1979, p. 98) are comparable to those for Oscar Kokoschka's *Murder the Woman's Hope*, an expressionist play which caused a great stir when it was first performed in 1907 (Sokel 1963, p. 17). So is some of the action. But no performance, however expressionist, could do justice to Lewis's text. 'Very well acted by you and me,' leers the 'advertisement' printed in *Blast*. 'We go abroad for the first scene of our drama' (Lewis 1979, pp. 95–6). 'Abroad' is the space beyond genres where the unrepresentable may yet put in a fugitive appearance.

In so far as there is any action, it concerns two male protagonists, Hanp and Arghol, who work in a wheelwright's yard owned by the latter's bullying uncle. Their mutual antagonism spills over into violence. Hanp murders Arghol and then commits suicide. Hanp is a descendant of Bestre, Arghol of the detached observer of Bestre's campaigns. The relation between peasant and intellectual, between abjectness and irony, has now been incorporated fully into the text. Arghol succumbs to Hanp, then rejects him. 'This pip of icy spray struck him on the mouth. He tasted it with new pleasure, before spitting it out: acrid.' Lewis's dramaturgy has finally caught up with the implications of that key-word. The fate of the abject is to be 'spat back among men' (1979, p. 101).

'Always à deux' (p. 115), Arghol and Hanp are separate yet utterly dependent, bonded by mutual antagonism. Unlike the other male couples of the period, Bloom and Dedalus, or Birkin and Crich, they possess neither psychic unity nor a socially symbolic role. They constitute, as Jameson perceptively notes, a 'pseudo-couple' (1979, ch. 2). The term is Samuel Beckett's, and characterizes the strange pairings in his work: Vladimir and Estragon, Hamm and Clov, Mercier and Camier. The pseudo-couple emerges as a distinct relationship with its own ceremonies, as a narrative device, in nineteenth-century fiction, in Flaubert and Dostoevsky. The most striking examples in British and Irish fiction before Beckett are Sisson and Lilly in Lawrence's *Aaron's Rod* (1922), Callcott and Somers in Lawrence's *Kangaroo* (1923), and Pullman and Satterthwaite in Lewis's *The Childermass* (1928).

Jameson regards the pseudo-couple as a 'structural device' for preserving a narrative tradition which would otherwise have gone on repeating itself for ever, or succumbed to delirious instability (1979, pp. 59–60). Lewis fits into this scheme somewhere between Flaubert and Beckett. The scheme, however, may be the problem. It is, in its dovetailing of realism into Modernism, and Modernism into postmodernism, *very* schematic. And it presupposes a formal imperative – to preserve narrative 'as such' – which can be connected to the practice of individual writers only with some difficulty. It empties writing of content. 'Lewis's relational universe has no place for a thesis about human nature,' Jameson argues (p. 47). But it does, in fact, propose a thesis, a carnivalized version of Romantic theories of the origin and growth of the self. 'Men,' Arghol affirms, 'have a loathsome deformity called Self: affliction got through indiscriminate rubbing against their fellows: social excrescence'. This affliction cannot be cured because it is oneself. 'I have smashed it against me, but it still writhes, turbulent mess' (Lewis 1979, p. 107).

Mutual disgust, and parallel self-disgust, provoke the pseudo-couple to physical violence. Hanp and Arghol lash out at a turbulent mess which could just as easily be themselves as each other.

> The attacker rushed in drunk with blows. They rolled, swift jagged rut, into one corner of shed: large insect scuttling roughly to hiding.
> Stopped astonished.
> Fisticuffs again: then rolled kicking air and each other, springs broken, torn from engine.
>
> (p. 111)

Colons establish the rhythm of this passage, and of several others in the play. They mark a pause, a hiatus; and at the same time throw our attention forward, across the gap. At once separating and connecting, impeding and propelling, they reproduce the collapse of all distinctions within the pseudo-couple. 'Flushes on silk epiderm and fierce card-play of fists between: emptying of "hand" on soft flesh-table' (p. 111). The joke about card-play might be the grimly ironic reflection of a Kiplingesque narrator settling down to enjoy a little torture. Except that it is now impossible to distinguish the ironist from the leper. Everything happens 'between', or 'between:', along an infinitely porous dividing line.

Lewis's thesis about the origin and development of identity veers towards the metaphysical or the ontological, but its main point of reference is physical. It turns self-knowledge into a knowledge of the abject, into nausea. 'Just now,' Hanp reflects after the bout of fisticuffs, 'the blows had leapt in his muscles towards Arghol, but were sickened and did not seem hard.' But abject blows are enough to see off an abject opponent. 'Thick sickly puddle of humanity, lying there by the door' (p. 116). Arghol's epic snores, a 'peachy, clotted tide, gurgling back in slimy shallows', the sound of a 'malodorous, bloody sink, emptying its water', provoke Hanp beyond endurance. Aching with 'disgust and fury', peering through 'patches of tumified flesh', he stabs his partner to death (p. 117).

The thesis is that identity is created by excluding rather than desiring – by negotiating with the abject, which never negotiates, only attracts and repels. Kipling and Conrad thought that, given an adequate display of resoluteness, and of civilizing irony, the negotiation might be concluded: just. The next generation of writers – Joyce, Lawrence, Lewis – was not inclined to be so sanguine. *The Enemy of the Stars*, though never as systematically uninformative as 'Circe', is equally hard to take. Outside the history of the novel, it none the less contains that to which some novels have tended.

LAUGHTER

In 1917, in 'A Soldier of Humour', Lewis invented a protagonist-narrator for the Breton stories which were to be collected in *The Wild Body* (1928). Pine (later renamed Ker-Orr) sports an excrescence of self every bit as alarming as those which encumber his various antagonists. 'My body is large, white and savage. But all the fierceness has become transformed into laughter. It still looks like [a] Visi-Gothic fighting machine, but is really a laughing. machine' (1982, p. 323). His antagonist is a Frenchman he meets during a holiday in Spain, M. de Valmar, whose peculiarity is to behave as though he is an American. Together they make a perfect pseudo-couple.

The story is not, in most respects, innovative, or Vorticist. For example, Pine's impressions of the scene outside a hotel in a small Spanish town (p. 334) recall Dickens's description of the approach to Todgers's boarding-house, in *Martin Chuzzlewit* (1968, p. 185). Lewis borrows the comic fatalism, but doesn't want, or more likely can't manage, Dickens's mazy syntax.

Lewis had clearly been reading *American Notes* (1842) as well. His description of the idle curiosity inflicted on foreign-looking travellers in trains (1982, p. 335) owes something to Dickens (1972, p. 161). Pine's exploitation of the American delight in military titles (1982, p. 339) may derive from Martin Chuzzlewit's discovery that, in his boarding-house, 'there were no fewer than four majors present, two colonels, one general, and a captain, so that he could not help thinking how strongly officered the American militia must be' (1968, p. 335). Both writers regard self-consciousness as an excrescence produced by physical discomfort, or anxiety about social status. For Dickens it is a temporary, and avoidable, indignity; for Lewis it is the human condition.

These continuities of comic technique indicate that Lewis was,

in orthodox fashion, still learning. But his distinctive preoccupation emerges during an account of Pine's first meal at a
new boarding-house:

> My presence caused no stir whatever. Just as a stone
> dropped in a small pond which has long been untouched
> and has a good thick coat of mildew, slips dully to the
> bottom, cutting a clean little hole on the surface slime, so
> I took my place at the bottom of the table. But as the pond
> will send up its personal odour at this intrusion, so these
> people revealed something of themselves in the first few
> minutes, in an illusive and immobile way. They must all
> have lived in that pension together for an inconceivable
> length of time.
>
> (1982, pp. 339–40)

Dickens was certainly interested in sedimentation, mildew,
excrescence, armature: but only as an obstacle to that mobility,
that free circulation of energies and feelings, on which the well-
being of individual and society depended. Lewis likes them for
themselves. He sees the disgust they arouse, and the laughter, as
great motive forces. Personality is a unique odour chemically
produced beneath the crust of habitual behaviour. In order to
count at all, it must amuse or repel.

A great deal of odour is released in Lewis's first published
novel, *Tarr* (1918; revised 1928), which concerns two painters
living in Paris, Tarr and Kreisler, who share a lover, briefly, but
very little else. Tarr is English and sardonic, and more or less
keeps his crust intact. Kreisler is German and romantic, and
blows his spectacularly, killing a man in a duel, and then hanging
himself. Tarr is a relative of Arghol and Pine, Kreisler of Hanp
and M. de Valmar. Both are wild bodies framed by a novel
which, written during wartime, signalled Lewis's temporary withdrawal from abstraction: that is, from the concept of the wild
body articulated in the early stories. 'The geometries which had
interested me so exclusively before, I now felt were bleak and
empty. They wanted *filling*' (1984, p. 139). The geometries derived
from painting, from Dickens, and from Dostoevsky, whose novels
Lewis read not as 'sinister homilies' but as 'monstrous character
patterns, often of miraculous insight' (1984, p. 158). The relation
between the geometries and the filling, between abstraction and
detail, reproduces that unending, fruitless negotiation with the

abject which was his subject-matter, and which occupies the lives of his characters.

In his autobiography Lewis commented that *Tarr* should really have been called 'Otto Kreisler', because Kreisler is the main character. But the part of the book he then went on to discuss is the first part, 'Overture', in which Tarr meditates on, and in the process thoroughly exacerbates, his own wild body (1984, p. 165). The conflict is between the severity of his artistic creed, which Lewis seems to endorse, and his indulgence in sensuality and sentiment. Like Arghol, he smashes his indulgence, which is also his humanity, against him; but it still writhes, a 'turbulent mess'.

Tarr warms up for a meeting with his girlfriend, Bertha, by launching, in the presence of his friend Hobson, a diatribe against women made even more violent by Lewis's eccentric use of equal signs as dashes. 'They are everywhere! = Confusing, blurring, libelling, with their half-baked, gushing, tawdry presences! It is like a slop of children and the bawling machinery of the inside of life' (1973, p. 115). The misogyny is commonplace: women confuse and blur the distinctions upon which men rely; they produce slop; they turn insides out. This is the creed of a life based on expulsion. It is enough to see off Hobson's 'vulgar Bohemianism'.

> 'You are concentrated, systematic slop. = There is nothing in the Universe to be said for you. = Any efficient State would confiscate your property, burn your wardrobe, that old hat and the rest, as "*infecté*" and insanitary, and prohibit you from propagating.'
>
> (p. 17)

Hobson's 'flabby potion' is no match for puritanism dressed up as eugenics. 'You are meaner spirited than the most abject tramp,' Tarr tells him, before knocking the old hat into the road (p. 19).

Bertha, however, is another matter. Approaching her house, Tarr sees her regarding him with an indifference every bit as practised as his own. 'This familiar life, with its ironical eye, mocked at him, too' (p. 37). The familiar life, with its systematic slop, is all excrescence, waste product. And yet it scrutinizes him as fiercely as he scrutinizes it. Tarr has to acknowledge, in a new photograph which Bertha has placed on her writing-table, his

285

own abjectness. 'A set sulky stagnation, every violence overgrown with this strange stuff – that twist of the head that was him, and that could only be got rid of by breaking' (p. 40). The twist, the excrescence, the odour produced by stagnation: these, not the ironical eye operating in their midst, make the man. Bertha and Tarr mirror each other. 'Bertha's numb silence and abandon was a stupid tableau vivant of his own mood. In this impasse of arrested life he stood sick and useless' (p. 47). By the end of the chapter, the room, Bertha's chief expression and weapon, has overwhelmed Tarr's Visi-Gothic fighting machine (pp. 61–3). His discovery that sloppiness is not the waste product of irony, of the geometric mind, but its inherent obverse, is the best thing in the book, and indeed in Lewis's writing before *The Childermass* (1928). In Modernist fiction, the ironical eye is replaced by filling, slop, interiority, passional changes, the whole stupid tableau vivant; and by outbreaks of fury as, every now and then, someone tries to scrape off a piece of excrescence.

INFERIOR RELIGIONS

During his conversation with Hobson, Tarr articulates an aesthetic of disgust. '"I gaze on squalor and idiocy, and the more I see it, the more I like it . . . I laugh hoarsely through its thickness, choking and spitting; coughing, sneezing, blowing"' (1973, pp. 9–10). The artist should not survey slop, but ingest and expel it. Rembrandt painted 'decrepit old jews', Shakespeare dealt in 'human tubs of grease' like Falstaff (p. 10). Tarr's facile anti-Semitism reveals the dark side of an aesthetic which will become inflexibly authoritarian if the artist forgets that what he spits out is actually or prospectively a part of himself. In the novel, Tarr is not allowed to forget. Lewis, who endorsed Tarr's views, did on occasion forget.

Flaubert, Tarr says, had 'an appetite like an elephant' for squalor and idiocy. 'But he grumbled and sighed over his food. = I take it in my arms and bury my face in it!' (p. 9). The difference between the language teacher's attitude to the abject Russian *émigrés* in Geneva, in Conrad's *Under Western Eyes*, and Tarr's attitude to the abject Russian and German *émigrés* in Paris, is that Tarr belongs among them: he has taken them in his arms and buried his face in them. Despite his cultivation of an ironical eye, he neither understands nor desires detachment. His aesthetic takes us beyond James, Conrad and Kipling.

Lewis's most complex and brilliant statement of his aesthetic was 'Inferior Religions', published in the *Little Review* in 1917, and revised for *The Wild Body* (1928). He begins anthropologically, with an account of the small Breton communities whose 'inferior religions' had inspired his earliest writings, and derives from his observations a theory of comedy. A comic type, he argues, is the 'laziness of a successful personality', part of ourselves become a 'fetish' (1982, p. 316). The emphasis is now, as it had not been in the Breton journal, on familiar life rather than oddness, and on complicity rather than detachment. The comic object cannot be laughed away because it is often a part of ourselves. Laughter does not distinguish us from the absurd, the comically uniform; it is an outburst against inseparability. 'Laughter is the climax in the tragedy of seeing, hearing and smelling self-consciously' (p. 317).

Lewis's satire derives from a thesis about human nature. 'The chemistry of personality (subterranean in a sort of cemetery whose decompositions are our lives) puffs in frigid balls, soapy Snowmen, arctic Carnival-Masks, which we can photograph and fix' (p. 317). Satire fixes the carnival masks. It immobilizes, without diminishing, the acrid savour of personality. If the 'cadaveric travail' beneath is vigorous and bitter, 'the mask and figurehead will be of a more original and intense grotesqueness'. The opposing armies in Flanders stuck up dummy men on poles for their enemies to pot at, in a spirit of 'fierce friendliness'. 'It is only a dummy of this sort that is engaged in the sphere of laughter. But the real men are in the trenches underneath all the time, and are there on a more "decisive" affair' (p. 318).

'Inferior Religions' has an enigmatic and perfectly phrased conclusion which turns from the exigencies of trench warfare to Lewis's primary vocation, painting.

> Beauty is an icy douche of ease and happiness at something suggesting perfect conditions for an organism. A stormy landscape, and a pigment consisting of a lake of hard, yet florid waves; delight in each brilliant scoop or ragged burst, was John Constable's beauty. Leonardo's consisted in a red rain on the shadowed side of heads, and heads of massive

female aesthetes ... Cezanne liked cumbrous, democratic
slabs of life, slightly leaning, transfixed in vegetable intensity.

(p. 319)

The extraordinary lucidity of these descriptions bears no direct
relation to the theory of comedy. They suggest, by implication
only, by association, that the satirist's dummies aspire to beauty
as well as instruction. Laughter is the iciest of beauty's icy
douches. This connection cannot be stated directly. But it is in
the end what characterizes Lewis's treatment, between 1914 and
1918, of a subject-matter he had first discovered in 1908: acrid
human nature. At some cost, perhaps, since thereafter the acridity
of his own at times less than human nature became increasingly
apparent.

THE HISTORY OF GRATIFICATIONS

In 'Psycho-Analysis and the History of Art', a lecture delivered
in 1953, Ernst Gombrich observed that the increasing complexity
of 'modes of representation' has always gone hand in hand with
an ever more fervent appeal to 'regressive' pleasures (1963, p.
36). Thus, political caricature emerged relatively late in the
history of art because its aggressiveness was only acceptable when
articulated by a complex, ironic technique. The sophistication of
caricature, requiring a trained response, paradoxically justified
the regressive pleasure taken in violence (pp. 36–7).

Gombrich argues that the development of nineteenth- and
twentieth-century European art can best be understood in these
terms. He cites Bouguereau's *The Birth of Venus* (1879) as an
example of official art whose erotic appeal revolts us now because
it is too flagrant, too obvious. In the final decades of the
nineteenth century this resentment stimulated a search for difficulty, for more demanding gratifications. 'The fault of fault-
lessness,' Gombrich observes, with Browning's view of Andrea
del Sarto in mind, 'is a discovery of the nineteenth century' (pp.
37–8).

Painters like Renoir and Cézanne withheld passive pleasures
and demanded activity from the viewer. 'Impressionism succeeded in excluding literary association and in confining the give
and take to the reading of the scrambled colour-patches.' In
return for this effort of shared activity, it yielded a 'premium' of

regressive pleasure. 'For the first time in several centuries the public were allowed to see real splashes of loud, bright, luminous colours which had been banned as too crude and primitive by academic convention.' Van Gogh, Gauguin and Picasso subsequently developed an openly regressive, 'primitivist' art (p. 41).

No doubt Gombrich's emphases would be challenged by art historians today. Modernism has been superseded by post-modernism, which does not attempt the same balance between difficulty and regression. But they are emphases which would certainly have been recognized at the time: for example by Philip Carey and his fellow students in *Of Human Bondage* (1915), who find a 'cheerful disgustingness' in Bouguereau's name (Maugham 1990a, p. 212). Carey, motivated by an 'abhorrence of the chocolate box' (p. 255), teaches himself to reject Watts and Burne-Jones in favour of Monet, Manet, Degas and Ingres (pp. 225, 233). Clutton, a more adventurous colleague, discovers Gauguin (p. 278).

I have argued that the development of literary 'modes of representation' can be understood as a raising of the interpretative (inferential) stakes which paradoxically justifies a more direct treatment of emotions like desire and disgust. There are plenty of Bouguereau equivalents in popular fiction (the sickly eroticism of Hewlett's *The Forest Lovers*, for example). The ironies of James, Conrad and Kipling constitute a reaction against too much sickliness, and sometimes produce – in Kipling's torture scenes, in the lapses of Mrs Wix and Mrs Gereth – a direct treatment of the most regressive pleasures. The next generation of writers developed an even greater complexity, and an even franker description of desire and disgust. I shall conclude my account of that development by returning to James Joyce.

19

STEPHEN HERO AND
BLOOM THE OBSCURE

I have suggested two motives for Modernism: the desire to exploit a more diversified market for fiction by establishing stylistic thresholds which test the reader's powers of inference, and thus offer an increased effect in return for an increased effort; and the fascination of the unusually wide range of new subject-matters thrown up by the pace of economic, social and political change. If there is one novel which exemplifies the convergence – the interlocking – of these motives, it is Joyce's *A Portrait of the Artist as a Young Man* (1916).

According to Stephen Dedalus, beauty precludes emotions such as desire and loathing which are kinetic rather than static, and directed towards a physical rather than a spiritual end (Joyce 1976b, p. 206). Yet his exposition, which takes the form of a dialogue with Lynch as they walk through the Dublin streets, is itself both kinetic and physical. One of his speeches is obliterated by a 'harsh roar of jangled and rattling metal', when a dray laden with old iron turns the corner (p. 209). A vivid awareness of desire and disgust – the insistence, more marked than in any other contemporary novel, of subject-*matter* – punctuates Stephen's aspirations to theory. He may turn his back, in theory, on subject-matter. But Joyce does not.

The famous proposition that the artist, like God, 'remains within or behind or beyond or above his handiwork, invisible, refined out of existence, indifferent, paring his fingernails' (p. 215) exalts impersonality and stasis. Lynch's less famous rejoinder – ' "Trying to refine them also out of existence," said Lynch' – reinstalls personality, kinesis and matter. The artist's indifference is an activity, a paring away of his or her own self, a refinement which creates a far from invisible waste product. In Joyce's

novels, waste product is everywhere, although it will be Leopold
Bloom rather than Stephen Dedalus who takes the time to review
his 'well pared' fingernails (1960, p. 115).

A PORTRAIT

A Portrait is a *Künstlerroman*, a study of development, of 'flight',
but one freighted with desire and disgust. Stephen's biological
immersion is every bit as striking as his determination to 'fly by'
the nets of nationality, language and religion (1976b, p. 203).
The 'cold slime' of the ditch into which he is pushed at Clongowes
becomes a memory as fundamental as his discovery of the magic
of words (pp. 10, 14). Even after he has left the school, the
indignities he suffered there come back in the guise of different
nauseas. On one occasion, he cannot enjoy his mutton hash
because 'the mention of Clongowes had coated his palate with
the scum of disgust' (p. 71). From the very beginning, his
subjectivity is an 'economy of flows': secretions, issues, ejacu-
lations, invasive odours (Ellmann 1982, pp. 87–97). His sins don't
blaze out; they trickle squalidly from a soul 'festering and oozing
like a sore' (Joyce 1976b, p. 144). Stephen's is a subjectivity
founded on desire *and* exclusion; but disgust is his true virtuosity,
the more varied register. He is such a connoisseur of bad smells
that he has some trouble finding one that will serve the purpose
of mortification (p. 151). He leaks more often and more colour-
fully than James's intermediaries. The breakwater of 'order and
elegance' he constructs against the 'sordid tide' within him and
without proves utterly ineffectual. 'From without as from within
the water had flowed over his barriers' (p. 98).

Richard Ellmann suggests that Joyce found for himself a
principle of order and elegance in the metaphors of immersion
and flight (1959, p. 307). If beetle and butterfly symbolize the
contrary directions in which Lord Jim is pulled, then the amniotic
tides and the flight of imagination circumscribe Stephen Dedalus.
For Jim, immersion and flight are alternatives; he is transferred
from one to the other, from realism to romance, by the agency
of Marlow and Stein. For Stephen, there is only a spiral of
interlocking forces. Language, which might have imposed order
and elegance, merely intensifies his susceptibility to nausea.
Invited to inspect the lecture theatre where his father had once
sat, Stephen comes across the word 'foetus' cut several times into

the wooden desks. The word unleashes a vision whose horror is grossly disproportionate to the mild irritation his father's reminiscences have so far produced. 'His recent monstrous reveries came thronging into his memory. They too had sprung up before him, suddenly and furiously, out of mere words.' The monstrous reveries 'abase' his intellect (Joyce 1976b, pp. 89–90). The experience demonstrates the under-determination of meaning by linguistic structure; bad news for the aspiring theorist and writer, though news which Joyce himself was to spread more effectively than any of his contemporaries.

Stephen, however, responds by evolving a literary style capable of abstract order, if not total authority. He derives less pleasure from the reflection of the sensible world in language than from 'the contemplation of an inner world of individual emotions mirrored perfectly in a lucid supple periodic prose' (pp. 166–71). When, a few minutes later, he dedicates himself to the creation of beauty, he dedicates himself – in a periodic prose which mirrors the emotion, and which we can sense him admiring – to a style, a theory, rather than a subject-matter. Joyce just as evidently does not follow suit, since he punctuates the reverie with the sound of young men bathing: 'O, cripes, I'm drownded' (pp. 169–70).

Stephen's devotion is immediately rewarded with a vision, in another famous passage:

> A young girl stood before him in midstream, alone and still, gazing out to sea. She seemed like one whom magic had changed into the likeness of a strange and beautiful sea-bird. Her long slender bare legs were delicate as a crane's and pure save where an emerald trail of seaweed had fashioned itself as a sign upon the flesh. Her thighs, fuller and softhued as ivory, were bared almost to the hips where the white fringes of her drawers were like featherings of soft white down. Her slateblue skirts were kilted boldly about her waist and dovetailed behind her. Her bosom was as a bird's soft and slight, slight and soft as the breast of some darkplumaged dove. But her long fair hair was girlish: and girlish, and touched with the wonder of mortal beauty, her face.
>
> (p. 171)

Chiasmus (the inversion of word order in parallel clauses) marks a stylistic threshold. It encourages us to scan carefully a passage which it has identified as copybook: 'not exactly an experience we are to share with Stephen, but something like a piece he might have written out afterwards, practising his new vocation' (Kenner 1980, p. 8). The threshold is in fact doubly marked. For Stephen, like James's governess, has his encounter with High Romantic sublimity. The construction 'seemed like one whom' is most strikingly evident in Wordsworth's encounters with admonitory figures who restore his faith in humanity, and serves a comparable purpose in poems by Hardy, Edward Thomas, Eliot and Auden (Trotter 1984, pp. 15–20). Here it indicates the lengths to which Stephen will go to summon up sublimity.

The encounter with the girl occurs at the end of Chapter 4. Chapter 5 dumps us straight back into the abject, in the shape of Stephen's breakfast. 'The yellow dripping had been scooped out like a boghole and the pool under it brought back to his memory the dark turfcoloured water of the bath in Clongowes' (1976b, p. 174). All five chapters of *A Portrait* conclude with a moment of self-transcendence; four times, the next chapter opens with a harsh reversion to squalor and to a plain style.

The sentences which describe Stephen at breakfast are notably informal. There is no anticipatory structure, either between sentences or between major constituents within sentences. We decode as we go along, holding in our syntactic memory only the immediately preceding grammatical context, a task made even simpler by the cohesiveness of the passage. We have no trouble assigning a reference to the grammatical subject of each sentence.

The same cannot be said of Stephen's vision of the bird-girl. Chiasmus exemplifies the greater demands made by a periodic sentence structure, withholding the main constituent and requiring that subordinate or dependent constituents be held in the mind until its belated appearance. Furthermore, the construction 'seemed like one whom' impairs the cohesiveness of the passage. We know that 'one' means 'a person', but the text itself does not supply a referent. We must identify, from our own experience (including literary experience), the category, the type of person, referred to; as we must in 'Old Man Travelling' and 'Resolution and Independence' (Trotter 1984, pp. 16–18).

We have to work hard at Stephen's vision, in the hope of an enriched effect. His elevated style constitutes a threshold: a threshold from which Joyce withdraws immediately, by reverting at the start of the next chapter to a plain style. What happens within a single paragraph in *Sons and Lovers* (see above, pp. 76–7), happens here in the gap between chapters. Except that Joyce reverts not so much to a social and literary norm as to a vertiginous nausea which abolishes norms of any kind. His thresholds are a good deal more volatile, both in their elevation and in their retraction, than Lawrence's. That volatility exhausts Stephen, and the reader. Its resolution was to require a more diversified, and even more demanding, novel.

NOSTOS

Jennifer Levine has suggested that there are three ways to read *Ulysses*: as a poem, as a novel and, in the wake of deconstruction, as a 'text'. The poetic model envisages 'a vast symbolic project whose logic is metaphorical and allusive rather than narrative' (1990, p. 139). Such a reading will not be troubled by the proliferation of styles from 'Sirens' onwards, because it never set much store by narrative evidence: how and when Bloom and Stephen meet, what they do together. It enables us to create patterns among words or phrases even while the pattern among events remains obscure. Its drawback is precisely that lack of interest in events.

If *Ulysses* is a novel, where events matter, then the odyssey of styles must reflect what is happening in the characters' minds. 'For, if the book seems for some hours temporarily adrift,' Kenner proposes, 'that reflects Bloom's state, adrift, too, putting in time, neither free to go home nor sure how long to stay away.' The stylistic complications are a veil drawn over events he won't want to discuss with Molly (1980, p. 101). This view is coherent and comprehensive, but it cannot cope with the extremity of the stylistic complications. Surely there are more economical ways to render avoidance?

It does at least remind us that *Ulysses* is not *all that* odd a book. Bloom's predicament resembles that of Waythorn, in Edith Wharton's 'The Other Two' (1904): a man revitalized by marriage, but increasingly disturbed by the continuing presence of his wife's two previous husbands. One of them has demanded access to his daughter, who lives with the Waythorns. On the day of the visit, Waythorn leaves for town earlier than normal. During the day he keeps bumping into, and having to avoid, the *other* previous husband, rather as Bloom just manages not to encounter Boylan. He delays his return home as long as possible, but cannot put off for ever the admission that his marriage is in trouble (Wharton 1968, I, pp. 380–96).

A 'textual' reading will suggest that the stylistic complications expose the limits not of Bloom's mind, or Stephen's, but of the symbolic order in and through which identity is constructed. The advantage of this view is that it does justice to the sheer scope of Joyce's interest in language, and its relation to subjectivity. However, I have already objected to its vagueness and inaccuracy as a theory of style. Its major shortcoming is that it drastically underestimates the strength of our desire for relevance, and Joyce's recognition of that desire. 'Textual' readings imagine a reader marvelling at, or ecstatically dispersed among, kaleidoscopic combinations and recombinations of language. I imagine a reader whose appetite for relevance is fed by the initial style, and frustrated by its successors. Joyce was as interested in the appetite as in the means by which it might be frustrated.

In a sense, *Ulysses* resumes normal (novelistic) business when Bloom returns home at the end of the day. In 'Eumaeus', he picks Stephen out of the gutter, escorts him to the cabman's shelter, and then back to Eccles Street. Stephen declines an invitation to stay the night, and departs, leaving the last words to Bloom ('Ithaca'), and Molly ('Penelope'). (Or: Odysseus and Telemachus rendezvous at Eumaeus's hut, before proceeding to the palace to slay the suitors.) There is also a return to consciousness, after the phantasmagoria of the brothel-scene in 'Circe'. For the first time in the book, the two central male characters talk at leisure. If we think of 'Circe' as a rite of passage, then the remainder is part aftermath, part convalescence, part forward planning. The relationship between Bloom and Stephen comes into focus. Bloom courts Stephen, as Aziz courts Fielding in Forster's *A Passage to India* (1924), out of mixed motives: curiosity, social advancement, compensation for a sexual and emotional deficit. Molly's belated entry into the book gives this and many other relationships a final spin.

From 'Sirens' to 'Circe', each new style is a threshold which raises the stakes either by suspending the Principle of Relevance or by reducing the contextual effects of interpretation to a modest reinforcement of existing knowledge. The last three episodes introduce yet more styles, and so cannot altogether be regarded as a resumption of normal business. But in 'Ithaca' and 'Penelope' at least, something changes. New information makes possible all sorts of inferences about the main characters. We learn a great deal more about them. Previous impressions are corrected or modified. These two episodes supply missing facts for any number of 'suspended patterns, momentous and trivial' (Kenner 1980, p. 79). The facts combine with already available contexts ('patterns') to alter our cognitive environment. These combinations make the book something else again: neither novel, nor poem, nor text, but encyclopaedia.

'EUMAEUS'

The ending of 'Circe' leaves Stephen in the gutter and Bloom hallucinating. By contrast, the beginning of 'Eumaeus' seems retributively, even mordantly, sober:

> Preparatory to anything else Mr Bloom brushed off the greater bulk of the shavings and handed Stephen the hat and ashplant and bucked him up generally in orthodox Samaritan fashion, which he very badly needed.
>
> (1960, p. 704)

'Preparatory to anything else' is itself, in a rather infuriating way, a syntactic preparation. We are witness to a new beginning: orderly, purposeful, prudent, Pooterish. But also a repetition. There is a faint echo of the first sentence of 'Telemachus': 'Stately, plump Buck Mulligan ...' (p. 1). Who has done more to buck Stephen up than Buck Mulligan? 'Eumaeus' mirrors 'Telemachus'. Mulligan's mockery finds its distorted reflection in Murphy's lurid tales, his masquerade in Murphy's mendacity (Mahaffey 1988, pp. 172–4).

Stylistically, however, there is a difference. The sentence describes the manner in which Bloom bucks Stephen up. Its focus is 'in orthodox Samaritan fashion'. But the information which ought to be new, or relevant in its own right, is in fact old, a cliché. To say that Bloom bucked Stephen up in orthodox Samaritan fashion is to say that he did what anyone (or 'Everyman') would have done. The sentence has none of the individualizing accuracy of observation which we have learnt to expect from the initial style. The redundancy of 'which he very badly needed' merely underlines the point. Bloom heads home. Stylistically, there is no way back.

We might say that the narrator of this episode wants to make it as easy as possible – insultingly easy – for us to understand what is going on. If we want to know how Bloom helped Stephen, we have only to draw upon the most easily accessible knowledge: the information stored in our memories at the conceptual address for 'Samaritan'. Several critics have suggested that 'Eumaeus' parodies the norms of good style proposed by such handbooks as W. B. Hodgson's *Errors in the Use of English* (1881) or H. W. Fowler's *Modern English Usage* (1926), or, unprescriptively, by recent 'text grammars' (Kenner 1980, p. 131; Stead 1982, pp. 150–1; Attridge 1988, p. 174). 'What the style of "Eumaeus" achieves, for all its attempts at propriety,' Attridge concludes, 'is a vivid demonstration of the impossibility of fixed boundaries and significations when the structures of language are permeated by the dissolving energies of erotic desire' (1988, p. 182). But it seems to me that in this episode literary style does something more radical than subvert or deviate from a norm, which is what we would expect it to do. Rather, it reinforces, or overstates, the norm. Any desire around is pretty much a spent force (if Bloom does think of offering Molly to Stephen, then surely he is renouncing desire). What prevails is the norm.

'So completely is the style of "Eumaeus" Bloom's,' Kenner writes, 'that when he speaks in the episode he speaks its very idiom; no one else does' (1980, p. 130). What matters, I think, is that the style is less easy to disown than, say, the interruptions in 'Cyclops'. Its flaccidity is not 'out there', the mechanical product of an institutional apparatus, but 'in here': congruent, at the very least, with the mental habits of the book's most sympathetic character. It is insidious because it colludes with our laziness, our tendency to deploy only that knowledge which is most easily accessible. Bloom decides that they should make their way to the cabman's shelter near Butt Bridge.

> But how to get there was the rub. For the nonce he was rather nonplussed but inasmuch as the duty plainly devolved upon him to take some measures on the subject he pondered suitable ways and means during which Stephen repeatedly yawned.
>
> (p. 704)

These sentences keep the cost of processing to the minimum by ensuring that we only have to access the most stereotyped knowledge about responsibility and decision-taking. The unscheduled internal assonance ('nonce'/'nonplussed') suggests that all other stylistic criteria have been subordinated to the painless transfer of information.

The yawns make us wonder whether Bloom, meaning to help, will only manage to patronize. Stephen's few contributions, cryptic and incisive, punctuate, and puncture, the flow of fatherly advice and reminiscence from Bloom. Stephen is sharp throughout the episode – with Corley (pp. 709–10), with the Italians (pp. 715–17) – as he would need to be in the company of so many impostors. He comes into his own. His sharpness serves as the standard against which Bloom's obligingness, and the style's obligingness, can be measured. This is particularly evident in the discussion of Parnell.

Joyce once congratulated the Irish for not throwing the fallen hero to the English wolves. 'They tore him to pieces themselves' (1959, p. 228). That complicity is explored throughout *Ulysses*; in 'Eumaeus', it touches Bloom himself. In 'Nestor', Stephen remains unimpressed by another older man, Mr Deasy, who speaks in a pompous conventional way. One of Deasy's themes is that a woman 'brought Parnell low' (1960, p. 43). In 'Hades' the mourners pay their respects to 'the chief', and consider rumours that he is not yet in his grave (pp. 142–3). In 'Cyclops' the Citizen repeats Deasy's claim (p. 420). These pieties merely conceal the fact that the Irish themselves destroyed Parnell, and that the damage done is irreparable.

When the men in the shelter begin to discuss rumours of the chief's return, Bloom is scornful (p. 753). But he can't help seeing parallels between Parnell's seduction of Kitty O'Shea and Boylan's seduction of Molly.

> Whereas the simple fact of the case was it was simply a case of the husband not being up to the scratch with nothing in common between them beyond the name and then a real man arriving on the scene, strong to the verge of weakness, falling a victim to her siren charms and forgetting home ties.
>
> (p. 756)

The style is perfectly judged. The internal repetitions alert us to Bloom's overriding aim: (self) pacification. The domestic parallel subordinates, or displaces, political understanding, muffling Parnell in a shroud of cliché (pp. 756–7). By spelling things out, by making events easily intelligible, the style has taken all the point, and all the individuality, out of them. Bloom is now free to identify himself – lazily – with Captain O'Shea, and Molly with Kitty O'Shea, who was, he can claim, 'Spanish too' (p. 757).

Stephen's irrelevant, and irreverent, answer is indeed the only proper response to all this relevance. Bloom, of course, has nothing to be ashamed of. But his domestic problems, as he nears home, and the obligingness mimicked by the style, draws him into the cabmen's world of self-deceptions, rumours and lies. By obeying one principle – to lower the cost of processing – the style has contravened another: to tell the truth. The encyclopaedia of cliché, of low-cost processing, alerts us to the fact that information is very much back on the agenda.

'ITHACA' AND 'PENELOPE'

'Ithaca' includes, among a great many other things, the last instalment of a miniature odyssey, as Bloom washes his hands with 'a partially consumed tablet of Barrington's lemonflavoured soap, to which paper still adhered (bought thirteen hours previously for fourpence and still unpaid for)' (1960, p. 785). For the first time, we are told the maker's name: Barrington. The significance of the maker's name is that it is there at all, a solid fact among many other solid facts. We have finally escaped from the treadmill of recapitulation.

A novelistic reading would suggest that the maker's name, like the description of the towel on which Bloom dries his hands, ensures by its randomness the authenticity of the scene: the absence of symbolic pattern. But a novel by, say, Arnold Bennett offers us only as much randomness as we would be likely, in normal circumstances, to 'take in'. Joyce, however, does not select. He offers us far more than we could ever take in (make sense of in one reading). By the same token, he offers in these concluding episodes more than the protagonists defined by the initial style could ever take in. The Bloom of 'Lotos-Eaters' selects for us. He notices the smell of the soap, and so do we. The Bloom of 'Ithaca' does not, as far as one can tell, notice the maker's name. The information lavished on us in the episode exceeds any novelistic requirement, whether for realism or for conformity to a character's point of view.

Stephen declines Bloom's invitation to wash; this evidence of his hydrophobia adds significantly to our knowledge of him; it confirms impressions that have been accumulating steadily for a long time. Kenner has rightly drawn attention to 'a governing rhythm of the book, whereby impression in the first half is modified by knowledge in the second, though only after resolute rereading has extracted the knowledge from a stylistic that tends to render it inconspicuous' (1980, p. 141). The catechistic method of 'Ithaca' makes available new information which does serve the purposes of a novel. Recognizing that Stephen's hydrophobia is no mere affectation, Bloom modifies his own behaviour.

> What impeded Bloom from giving Stephen counsels of hygiene and prophylactic to which should be added suggestions concerning a preliminary wetting of the head and contraction of the muscles with rapid splashing of the face and neck and thoracic and epigastric region in case of sea or river bathing, the parts of the human anatomy most sensitive to cold being the nape, stomach, and thenar or sole of foot?
>
> The incompatibility of aquacity with the erratic originality of genius.
>
> What additional didactic counsels did he similarly repress?
>
> Dietary: concerning the respective percentage of protein and caloric energy in bacon, salt ling and butter, the absence of the former in the lastnamed and the abundance of the latter in the firstnamed.
>
> (p. 786)

These passages at once demand and exceed a novelistic reading. They tell us about Bloom's prudential habits, about his stereotyped notion of genius, about his aspirations. They demonstrate his self-awareness: he realizes that he should not patronize Stephen by offering 'didactic counsels', as he had in 'Eumaeus'. We are back in the inference business. And yet the information offered us as the basis for inference is clearly surplus to requirements. The anatomical terminology insists on a degree of informativeness that would probably baffle Bloom himself. If we access that context – if we inform ourselves about the 'thenar' – we will have taken more trouble than the scene, strictly speaking, is worth. What would we *do* with that additional information? 'Ithaca', in short, delivers: impression is modified by knowledge. But this sudden, welcome generosity raises questions that cannot be answered if we think of the book as a novel, although they do identify and develop the novel the book subtends. Which data are valid? Which are relevant? What is the criterion of relevance?

What about the catalogue of Bloom's books (pp. 832–3), which pleases Kenner because no item is 'either incongruous or redundant' (1980, p. 143)? All of them reveal something about Bloom. But what does the abundant bibliographical detail tell us? We are invited to access, at some considerable expense of effort, a context of specialist knowledge which is remote from the business of the novel (that is to say, the book as novel). The point is to make us think about the business of relevance itself, a business conducted 'inside' the novel, as the relationship between Bloom and Stephen develops, but also 'outside' it, as readers sort and build upon information which they either possess already, or take steps to possess. 'Ithaca' is about the processes of decoding and inference which construct relationships of all kinds. Under its microscope, pinned by catechism, the blunderings of imagination, affect and power – the sketchy initiatives, the abrupt hostilities, the rapprochements – appear, momentarily, as cognitive sequences.

The randomness is never entirely random. The contents of Bloom's drawers reveal him in ways that even his interior monologues haven't, because Joyce sorts the information for us. The first drawer, which contains Martha Clifford's letters, erotic postcards and so on, reveal the night-town dimension of Bloom's temperament. The second reveals that he is a wealthier man than we might have thought (than his fellow Dubliners might have led us to believe), and a pious one. They include an insurance policy, a bank passbook and a certificate of possession of Canadian government stock; and mementoes of his father. The first drawer reinforces existing impressions of Bloom; the second contradicts existing impressions, and allows fresh inferences to be made. 'Ithaca' can scarcely be said to belong to a novel. But it tells us more than most novels do about how we know other people, and about the deceptiveness of that knowledge: the list of Molly's lovers (p. 863), for example, is lazily paranoid, the kind of thing the slack talk about adultery in 'Eumaeus' should have warned us against.

'Penelope' marks yet another threshold. Some critics have argued for its 'formal independence', its 'extramural' status (Cohn 1978, pp. 217–32). Joyce told Harriet Weaver that 'Ithaca' is really the end of the book, because 'Penelope' 'has no beginning, middle or end' (1957–76, I, p. 172). A famous letter to Frank Budgen emphasizes the latter's self-containment (I, p. 170). Molly 'reacts to virtually nothing but herself reacting to recollected experience on a sensual level' (Hayman 1982, p. 104). For the first time in the book, there is no overt arranging presence. Furthermore, unlikely as it might seem, Molly's 'sensitivity to the figurative dimension of words and names' makes her 'a poetic figure, a counterpart to Stephen, Echo to his Narcissus' (Mahaffey 1988, p. 178). Is this where the Dublin Sirens really come into their own, speak (sing) with their own voice?

The objection to this view is that the episode, for all its self-enclosure, conveys an enormous amount of information. Raleigh reckons that it supplied half the pages of his *Chronicle of Leopold and Molly Bloom* (1977, p. 9). A resolute enough reading will convert dozens of impressions into knowledge. The contexts provided by those impressions, and our impressions of the way the world is, enable us to break into the monologue, to use it as the basis for inferences about the novel it, too, subtends. Its most characteristic effect, the 'proliferation of pronouns' (Hayman 1982, p. 118), continually tests the Principle of Relevance, without ever frustrating it completely. We want to make sense of it, and we can make sense of it. The sense we make, either by identification or by voyeurism, is the most exuberant of the many regressive pleasures the book has to offer. Indeed, it is also a transgressive pleasure, since this is a man giving a woman the last word, his/her word. Modernism's double helix – the combination of 'raised' thresholds and 'lowered' subject-matter – had found its perfect expression.

This book has emphasized the extent to which the conditions of Modernist writing were already established by 1910, if not by 1900. It would be inappropriate for me to look forward beyond 1920, even though many of the writers I have discussed still had plenty of life left in them. I will conclude instead with a 'nostos' (a return) of my own, an anecdote which connects 1920 back to 1895. When he was a teenager, Joyce once sent his brother Stanislaus to the Capel Street lending library to procure a copy of *Jude the Obscure*. Stanislaus, confused by what he had heard of Hardy, asked the librarian for *Jude the Obscene*. Joyce liked the story so much that in later life he told it as though it had happened to him (Ellmann 1959, p. 54). His *Leopold the Obscure* (*Leopold the Obscene*) has quite a lot in common with Hardy's novel. Both caused offence. Both have proved hard to interpret. In both, a woman outlasts a man.

BIBLIOGRAPHY

PRIMARY SOURCES

Abbott, J. H. M. (1908) *Letters from Queer Street*, London: A. & C. Black.

Adams, Henry (1958) 'A letter to American teachers of history', in Brook Adams (ed.) *The Degradation of the Democratic Dogma*, New York: G. P. Putnam's Sons, pp. 137–263.

Allen, Grant (1889) 'Plain words on the woman question', *Fortnightly Review* 46, pp. 448–58.

—— (1894) 'The new hedonism', *Fortnightly Review*, 55, pp. 377–92.

—— (1895a) *The Woman Who Did*, Leipzig: Tauchnitz.

—— (1895b) *The British Barbarians*, London: John Lane.

Andrews, C. B. (1912) *An Introduction to the Study of Adolescent Education*, London: Rebman.

Angell, Norman (1930) *The Story of Money*, London: Cassell.

Anon. (1908) *Pleasure Bound 'Afloat'*, London: The 'Chatty' Club.

—— (1909a) *Maudie*, London: The 'Chatty' Club.

—— (1909b) *Pleasure Bound 'Ashore'*, London: The 'Chatty' Club.

—— (1911) 'The National Trust and public amenities', *Quarterly Review*, 214, pp. 157–78.

Anstey, F. (1895) *Lyre and Lancet*, London: Smith, Elder.

'A Peer' (1908) *The Hard Way*, London: John Long.

Arch, Joseph (1898) *The Story of My Life*, London: Hutchinson.

Arlen, Michael (1923) *These Charming People*, London: W. Collins.

—— (1924) *The Green Hat*, London: W. Collins.

Austin, Alfred (1902) *Haunts of Ancient Peace*, London: Macmillan.

Baden-Powell, Lord Robert Stephenson Smyth (1908) *Scouting for Boys*, London: Horace Cox.

—— (1915) *My Adventures as a Spy*, London: C. Arthur Pearson.

Bagnold, Enid (1918) *A Diary without Dates*, London: Heinemann.

—— (1920) *The Happy Foreigner*, London: Heinemann.

Baird, Mona (1916) *Matrimony*, London: Health Promotion.

—— (1923) *Girlhood*, London: Health Promotion.

Balfour, Arthur (1879) *A Defence of Philosophic Doubt*, London: Macmillan.

—— (1908) *Decadence*, Cambridge: Cambridge University Press.

304

Barclay, Florence (1922) *The Rosary*, New York: G. P. Putnam's Sons.

Barnes, William (1869) *Early England and the Saxon-English*, London: John Russell Smith.

—— (1878) *An Outline of English Speech-Craft*, London: C. Kegan Paul.

Becker, George (ed.) (1963) *Documents of Modern Literary Realism*, Princeton: Princeton University Press.

Bell, Lady Florence (1907) *At the Works*, London: Thomas Nelson.

Belloc, Hilaire (1904) *The Old Road*, London: Constable.

—— (1908) *Mr Clutterbuck's Election*, London: Eveleigh Nash.

—— (1909) *A Change in the Cabinet*, London: Methuen.

—— (1912) *The Servile State*, London: T. N. Foulis.

—— (1984) *The Four Men*, Oxford: Oxford University Press.

Bennett, Arnold (1898) *A Man from the North*, London: John Lane.

—— (1902) *The Grand Babylon Hotel*, London: Chatto & Windus.

—— (1903) *Leonora*, London: Chatto & Windus.

—— (1904) *A Great Man*, London: Chatto & Windus.

—— (1905) *Sacred and Profane Love*, London: Chatto & Windus.

—— (1906) *Whom God Hath Joined*, London: David Nutt.

—— (1908) *Buried Alive*, London: Methuen.

—— (1911) *Hilda Lessways*, London: Methuen.

—— (1913) 'The story teller's craft', *English Review*, 14, pp. 349–60.

—— (1916) *These Twain*, London: Methuen.

—— (1917) *Books and Persons*, London: Chatto & Windus.

—— (1922) *Mr Prohack*, London: Methuen.

—— (1923) *Riceyman Steps*, London: Cassell.

—— (1932) *Journals*, ed. Newman Flower, 2 vols, London: Cassell.

—— (1936) *Anna of the Five Towns*, Harmondsworth: Penguin Books.

—— (1954) *Clayhanger*, Harmondsworth: Penguin Books.

—— (1964) *The Old Wives' Tale*, London: Pan.

—— (1966–86) *Letters*, ed. James Hepburn, 4 vols, Oxford: Oxford University Press.

—— (1975) *The Card*, Harmondsworth: Penguin Books.

—— (1979) *Sketches for Autobiography*, ed. James Hepburn, London: Allen & Unwin.

—— (1987) *The Pretty Lady*, Gloucester: Alan Sutton.

Benson, E. F. (1894) *Dodo*, London: Methuen.

—— (1986) *The Luck of the Vails*, London: Hogarth Press.

Bentley, E. C. (1913) *Trent's Last Case*, London: Nelson.

Besant, Walter (1900) *The Fourth Generation*, London: Chatto & Windus.

Birrell, Olive (1900) *Love in a Mist*, London: Smith Elder.

Blount, Lady E. A. (1911) *Origin and Nature of Sex*, London: Health and Vim.

Bondfield, Margaret (1949) *A Life's Work*, London: Hutchinson.

Booth, Charles (1891–1902) *Life and Labour of the People in London*, 17 vols, London: Macmillan.

Bowen, Elizabeth (1983) *Collected Stories*, Harmondsworth: Penguin Books.

Braby, Maud Churton (1910a) *Modern Marriage and How to Bear It*, London: T. Werner Laurie.

—— (1910b) *Downward: A 'Slice of Life'*, London: T. Werner Laurie.

Braby, Maud Churton (1913) *The Love-Seeker. A Guide to Marriage*, 2nd edn, London: Herbert Jenkins.

Bramah, Ernest (1914) *Max Carrados*, London: Methuen.

Brooke, Emma (1894) *A Superfluous Woman*, London: Heinemann.

—— (1895) *Transition*, London: Heinemann.

Bryce, James (1899) *Impressions of South Africa*, 3rd edn, London: Macmillan.

Buchan, John (1900) *The Half-Hearted*, London: Isbister.

—— (1940) *Memory Hold-the-Door*, London: Hodder & Stoughton.

—— (1947) *The Thirty-Nine Steps*, London: Pan.

—— (1953) *The Three Hostages*, Harmondsworth: Penguin Books.

—— (1956a) *Greenmantle*, Harmondsworth: Penguin Books.

—— (1956b) *Mr Standfast*, Harmondsworth: Penguin Books.

Bullen, Rev. R. Ashington (1886) *Our Duty as Teachers*, London: Social Purity Alliance.

Bullock, Shan (1907) *Robert Thorne*, London: T. Werner Laurie.

Burnett, Frances Hodgson (1901) *The Making of a Marchioness*, London: Smith, Elder.

Burnett, John (ed.) (1974) *Useful Toil. Autobiographies of Working People from the 1820s to the 1920s*, London: Allen Lane.

Burroughs, Edgar Rice (1914) *Tarzan of the Apes*, London: A. L. Burt.

Bury, J. B. (1912) *A History of the Eastern Roman Empire*, London: Macmillan.

Butler, Samuel (1923) *The Way of All Flesh*, London: Page.

Caine, Hall (1891) *The Scapegoat*, 2 vols, London: Heinemann.

—— (1901) *The Eternal City*, London: Heinemann.

—— (1913) *The Woman Thou Gavest Me*, London: Heinemann.

Candler, Edmund (1924) *Youth and the East*, Edinburgh: Blackwood.

Cannan, Gilbert (1913) *Round the Corner*, London: Martin Secker.

Carrington (1979) *Letters*, ed. David Garnett, Oxford: Oxford University Press.

Chesney, George (1871) *The Battle of Dorking*, Edinburgh: Blackwood.

Chesser, Elizabeth Sloan (1913) *From Girlhood to Womanhood*, London: Cassell.

—— (1914) *Physiology and Hygiene*, London: G. Bell.

—— (1926) *The Woman Who Knows Herself*, London: Heinemann.

Chesterton, G. K. (1981) *The Complete Father Brown*, Harmondsworth: Penguin Books.

—— (1987) *The Essential G. K. Chesterton*, ed. P. J. Kavanagh, Oxford: Oxford University Press.

Chidell, E. F. (1904) *Africa and National Regeneration*, 2nd edn, London: Thomas Burleigh.

Childers, Erskine (1978) *The Riddle of the Sands*, Harmondsworth: Penguin Books.

Cholmondeley, Mary (1985) *Red Pottage*, London: Virago.

Chopin, Kate (1978) *The Awakening*, London: Women's Press.

Christie, Agatha (1989) *The Mysterious Affair at Styles*, London: Fontana.

Clifford, John (1885) *The Fight for Social Purity*, London: E. Marlborough.

Cody, William F. (1899) *Buffalo Bill's Wild West and Congress of Rough Riders of the World. Historical Sketches and Programme*, New York.

Colmore, G. (1911) *Suffragette Sally*, London: Stanley Paul.

Conrad, Joseph (1920) *The Rescue*, London: Dent.

—— (1957) *Under Western Eyes*, Harmondsworth: Penguin Books.

—— (1963) *Nostromo*, Harmondsworth: Penguin Books.

—— (1973) *Heart of Darkness*, Harmondsworth: Penguin Books.

—— (1975a) *An Outcast of the Islands*, Harmondsworth: Penguin Books.

—— (1975b) *Youth and The End of the Tether*, Harmondsworth: Penguin Books.

—— (1976) *Almayer's Folly*, Harmondsworth: Penguin Books.

—— (1977) *Tales of Unrest*, Harmondsworth: Penguin Books.

—— (1983–90) *Letters*, ed. Frederick Karl and Laurence Davies, 4 vols to date, Cambridge: Cambridge University Press.

—— (1986a) *Lord Jim*, ed. Robert Hampson and Cedric Watts, Harmondsworth: Penguin Books.

—— (1986b) *The Shadow-Line*, ed. Jacques Berthoud, Harmondsworth: Penguin Books.

—— (1989) *Victory*, ed. Robert Hampson, Harmondsworth: Penguin Books.

—— (1990) *The Secret Agent*, ed. Bruce Harkness and S. W. Reid, Cambridge: Cambridge University Press.

Conrad, Joseph and Hueffer, Ford Madox (1901) *The Inheritors*, London: Heinemann.

Coote, William (1902) 'Law and morality', in James Marchant (ed.) *Public Morals*, London: Morgan and Scott.

Corelli, Marie (1896a) *The Mighty Atom*, London: Hutchinson.

—— (1896b) *The Murder of Delicia*, London: Skeffington.

Crackanthorpe, Hubert (1893) *Wreckage*, London: Heinemann.

—— (1895) *Sentimental Studies and A Set of Village Tales*, London: Heinemann.

—— (1897) *Last Studies*, with an Appreciation by Henry James, London: Heinemann.

Crammond, Edgar (1908) 'Gold reserves', *Quarterly Review* 208, pp. 526–52.

Crane, Stephen (1983) *The Red Badge of Courage*, Harmondsworth: Penguin Books.

Cromie, Robert (1895) *The Crack of Doom*, 2nd edn, London: Digby, Long.

Crosland, T. W. H. (1905) *The Suburbans*, London: John Long.

Cross, J. W. (1907) 'Over Niagara – and after?', *Nineteenth-Century and After* 62, pp. 905–14.

Cross, Victoria (1907) *Life's Shop Window*, London: T. Werner Laurie.

—— (1914) *The Greater Law*, London: John Long.

Curzon, George, Marquess of Kedleston (1907) *Frontiers*, Oxford: Oxford University Press).

Danby, Frank (1889) *A Babe in Bohemia*, London: Spencer Blackett.

—— (1989) *Dr Phillips. A Maida Vale Idyll*, London: Keynes Press.

Darwin, Charles (1904) *The Expression of the Emotions in Man and Animals*, Popular Edition, London: John Murray.

Davies, W. H. (1980) *The Autobiography of a Super-Tramp*, Oxford: Oxford University Press.

Dehan, Richard (1910) *The Dop Doctor*, London: Heinemann.

Delafield, E. M. (1918) *The War-Workers*, London: Heinemann.

Dell, Ethel M. (1912) *The Way of an Eagle*, London: T. Fisher Unwin.

—— (1914) *The Desire of His Life*, London: Holden & Hardingham.

—— (1916) *The Bars of Iron*, London: Hutchinson.

Dickens, Charles (1966) *David Copperfield*, ed. Trevor Blount, Harmondsworth: Penguin Books.

Dickens, Charles (1968) *Martin Chuzzlewit*, ed. P. N. Furbank, Harmondsworth: Penguin Books.

—— (1972) *American Notes*, ed. Arnold Goldman and John Whitley, Harmondsworth: Penguin Books.

Dilke, Sir Charles (1868) *Greater Britain*, 2 vols, London: Macmillan.

Diver, Maud (1907) *Captain Desmond, V. C.*, Edinburgh: Blackwood.

—— (1908) *The Great Amulet*, Edinburgh: Blackwood.

—— (1916) *Desmond's Daughter*, Edinburgh: Blackwood.

Dixon, Ella Hepworth (1894) *The Story of a Modern Woman*, London: Heinemann.

Doughty, Charles (1906) *The Dawn in Britain*, 6 vols, London: Duckworth.

Douglas, George (1901) *The House with Green Shutters*, London: John Macqueen.

Douglas, Norman (1930) *South Wind*, London: Martin Secker.

Doyle, Arthur Conan (1898) *The Tragedy of the Korosko*, London: Smith, Elder.

—— (1912) *The Lost World*, London: Hodder & Stoughton.

—— (1981) *The Complete Sherlock Holmes*, Harmondsworth: Penguin Books.

Egerton, George (1901) *Rosa Amorosa*, London: Grant Richards.

—— (1983) *Keynotes & Discords*, London: Virago.

Eliot, George (1979) *The Mill on the Floss*, ed. A. S. Byatt, Harmondsworth: Penguin Books.

Eliot, T. S. (1932) *The Sacred Wood*, 3rd edn, London: Methuen.

Emerson, Ralph Waldo (1990) *Ralph Waldo Emerson*, ed. Richard Poirier, Oxford: Oxford University Press.

Ethelmer, Ellis (1895) *The Human Flower*, Congleton: Mrs W. Elmy.

Fairless, Michael (1931) *Complete Works*, London: Duckworth.

Faulkner, Peter (ed.) (1986) *A Modernist Reader*, London: Batsford.

Fenn, G. Manville (1907) *George Alfred Henty*, London: Blackie.

Findlater, Jane (1896) *The Green Graves of Balgowrie*, London: Methuen.

Findlater, Jane and Findlater, Mary (1908) *Crossriggs*, London: Smith, Elder.

Firbank, Ronald (1961) *Valmouth and Other Novels*, Harmondsworth: Penguin Books.

—— (1991) *The Early Firbank*, ed. Steven Moore, London: Quartet Books.

Fleming, Ian (1977) *From Russia, with Love* London: Granada.

Fletcher, Ian (ed.) (1987) *British Poetry and Prose, 1870–1905*, Oxford: Oxford University Press.

Forster, E .M. (1936) *A Passage to India*, Harmondsworth: Penguin Books.

—— (1941) *Howards End*, Harmondsworth: Penguin Books.

—— (1959) *Where Angels Fear to Tread*, Harmondsworth: Penguin Books.

—— (1960) *The Longest Journey*, Harmondsworth: Penguin Books.

—— (1972) *Maurice*, Harmondsworth: Penguin Books.

—— (1978) *A Room with a View*, Harmondsworth: Penguin Books.

Fowler, Ellen Thornycroft (1898) *Concerning Isabel Carnaby*, London: Hodder & Stoughton.

Fowler, Nathaniel C. (1897) *Fowler's Publicity*, New York: Publicity.

Frederic, Harold (1899) *The Market-Place*, London: Heinemann.

Freeman, Edward (1870) *The History of the Norman Conquest of England*, revised edn, 2 vols, Oxford: Oxford University Press.

Freeman, R. Austin (1911) *The Red Thumb Mark*, London: Hodder & Stoughton.

Freud, Sigmund (1953–74) *The Standard Edition of the Complete Psychological Works*, ed. James Strachey et al., 24 vols, London: Hogarth Press.

The Frontiersman (1910) n. s., 1.

Froude, J. A. (1886) *Oceana, or England and Her Colonies*, London: Longmans, Green.

Gallichan, Walter (1915) *How to Love*, London: C. Arthur Pearson.

—— (1920) *Youth and Maidenhood*, London: Health Promotion.

Galsworthy, John (1904) *The Island Pharisees*, London: Heinemann.

—— (1907) *The Country House*, London: Heinemann.

—— (1911) *The Patrician*, New York: Scribner's.

—— (1915) *The Little Man*, London: Heinemann.

—— (1922) *Fraternity*, Popular Edition, London: Heinemann

—— (1978) *The Forsyte Saga*, Harmondsworth: Penguin Books.

Galton, Francis (1905–6) *Eugenics*, 2 vols, London: Sociological Society.

Geddes, Patrick, and Thomson, J. Arthur (1914) *Sex*, London: Williams & Norgate.

Gissing, George (1961) *Letters of George Gissing to Eduard Bertz*, ed. Arthur Young, London: Constable.

—— (1974) *The Nether World*, ed. John Goode, Hassocks: Harvester Press.

—— (1978a) *The Crown of Life*, ed. Michel Ballard, Hassocks: Harvester Press.

—— (1978b) *London and the Life of Literature in Late Victorian England*, ed. Pierre Coustillas, Hassocks: Harvester Press.

—— (1980) *The Odd Women*, London: Virago.

—— (1982a) *Demos. A Story of English Socialism*, ed. Pierre Coustillas, Hassocks: Harvester Press.

—— (1982b) *In the Year of Jubilee*, New York: Dover.

—— (1987) *The Private Papers of Henry Ryecroft*, ed. Mark Storey, Oxford: Oxford University Press.

Glyn, E. (1900) *The Visits of Elizabeth*, London: Duckworth.

—— (1907) *Three Weeks*, London: Duckworth.

—— (1909) *Elizabeth Visits America*, London: Duckworth.

—— (1910) *His Hour*, London: Duckworth.

—— (1913) *The Sequence*, London: Duckworth.

Goldring, Douglas (1943) *South Lodge*, London: Constable.

Goodall, G. W. (1914) *Advertising. A Study of a Modern Business Power*, London: Constable.

Gosse, Edmund (1974) *Father and Son*, Oxford: Oxford University Press.

Gould, Frederick J. (1909) *On the Threshold of Sex*, London: C. W. Daniel.

—— (1912) *Our Empire*, London: Longman, Green.

—— (1929) *Moral Education*, London: privately printed.

Grand, Sarah (1889) *Ideala*, 3rd edn, London: Richard Bentley.

—— (1894a) *Our Manifold Nature*, London: Heinemann.

—— (1894b) *The Heavenly Twins*, 1-vol. edn, London: Heinemann.

—— (1898) *The Modern Man and Maid*, London: Horace Marshall.

—— (1980) *The Beth Book*, London: Virago.

Green, J. R. (1916) *A Short History of the English People*, revised edn, London: Macmillan.

Greenwood, Frederick (1893) *The Lover's Lexicon*, London: Macmillan.

Gribble, Francis (1906) *The Pillar of Cloud*, London: Chapman and Hall.

Griffith, George (1893) *Angel of the Revolution. A Tale of the Coming Terror*, London: Tower.

Haggard, Rider (1895) *Nada the Lily*, London: Longmans, Green.
—— (1902) *Rural England*, 2 vols, London: Longmans.
—— (1913) *Child of Storm*, London: Cassell.
—— (1914) *Nada the Lily*, London: Hodder & Stoughton.
—— (1917) *Elissa, or the Doom of Zimbabwe*, London: Hodder & Stoughton.
—— (1951) *Three Adventure Novels*, New York: Dover.
Haggard, Rider and Kipling, Rudyard (1963) *Rudyard Kipling to Rider Haggard. The Record of a Friendship*, ed. Morton Cohen, Rutherford: Fairleigh Dickinson University Press.
Hardy, F. E. (1962) *Life of Thomas Hardy*, London: Macmillan.
Hardy, Thomas (1967) *Personal Writings*, ed. H. Orel, London: Macmillan.
—— (1974) *Jude the Obscure*, ed. Terry Eagleton, London: Macmillan.
—— (1978a) *Tess of the D'Urbervilles*, ed. D. Skilton, Harmondsworth: Penguin Books.
—— (1978b) *Jude the Obscure*, ed. C. H. Sisson, Harmondsworth: Penguin Books.
—— (1981) *The Woodlanders*, ed. Ian Gregor, Harmondsworth: Penguin Books.
—— (1985) *Literary Notebooks*, ed. Lennart Bjork, New York: New York University Press.
Harraden, Beatrice (1899) *The Fowler*, Edinburgh: Blackwood.
—— (1903) *Katharine Frensham*, Edinburgh: Blackwood.
Hatton, Joseph (1890) *By Order of the Czar*, New York: John Lovell.
Hawtrey, R. G. (1927) *The Gold Standard in Theory and Practice*, London: Longmans, Green.
Hemingway, Ernest (1981) *Selected Letters*, ed. Carlos Baker, London: Granada.
Herbert, A. P. (1929) *The Secret Battle*, London: Methuen.
Hewlett, Maurice (1909) *The Forest Lovers*, Macmillan's 7d. Series, London: Macmillan.
Hichens, Robert (1894) *The Green Carnation*, London: Heinemann.
—— (1902) *Felix*, London: Methuen.
—— (1906) *The Call of the Blood*, London: Methuen.
—— (1911) *The Fruitful Vine*, London: T. Fisher Unwin.
—— (1930) *The Call of the Blood*, 13th edn, London: Methuen.
—— (1937) *The Garden of Allah*, 44th edn, London: Methuen.
Hill, Headon (1899) *The Spies of the Wight*, London: C. Arthur Pearson.
Hobbes, John Oliver (1906) *The Dream and the Business*, London: T. Fisher Unwin.
Hobson, J. A. (1901) *The Psychology of Jingoism*, London: Grant Richards.
Holdsworth, Annie (1894) *Joanna Traill, Spinster*, London: Heinemann.
—— (1904) *A Garden of Spinsters*, London: Walter Scott Publishing.
Holme, Constance (1919) *The Splendid Fairing*, London: Mills & Boon.
—— (1921) *The Trumpet in the Dust*, London: Mills & Boon.
Hope, Anthony (1894) *The Dolly Dialogues*, New York: Henry Holt.
—— (1966) *The Prisoner of Zenda*, London: Dent.
Hopkins, Ellice (1899) *The Power of Womanhood*, London: Wells Gardner.
Hopkins, Gerard Manley (1935) *Letters to Robert Bridges*, ed. C. C. Abbott, Oxford: Oxford University Press.
Horner, Joseph (1899) 'A mint of money', *Harmsworth Magazine* 3, pp. 589–94.
Hornung, E. W. (1992) *The Collected Raffles*, London: J. M. Dent.
Hudson, W. H. (1885) *The Purple Land*, 2 vols, London: Sampson, Low.
—— (1893) *Idle Days in Patagonia*, London: Chapmna and Hall.

—— (1900) *Nature in Downland*, London: Longmans.

—— (1903) *Hampshire Days*, London: Longmans.

—— (1904) *Green Mansions*, London: Duckworth.

—— (1908) 'Stone Henge', *English Review* 1: 60–8.

—— (1909) *Afoot in England*, London: Hutchinson.

—— (1910) *A Shepherd's Life*, London: Hutchinson.

Hueffer, Ford Madox (1905) *The Soul of London*, London: Alston Rivers.

—— (1906) *The Heart of the Country*, London: Alston Rivers.

—— (1907) *The Spirit of the People*, London: Alston Rivers.

—— (1913) *Mr Fleight*, London: Howard Latimer.

—— (1924) *Joseph Conrad. A Personal Remembrance*, London: Duckworth.

—— (1972) *The Good Soldier*, Harmondsworth: Penguin Books.

—— (1984) *A Call*, Manchester: Carcanet.

Hughes, M. V. (1978) *A London Home in the 1890s*, Oxford: Oxford University Press.

Hull, E. M. (1919) *The Sheik*, London: Eveleigh Nash.

Hume, Fergus (1898) *Hagar of the Pawn Shop*, London: Skeffington.

Hunt, Violet (1896) *A Hard Woman*, 2nd edn, London: Chapman and Hall.

—— (1906) *The Workaday Woman*, London: T. Werner Laurie.

—— (1908) *White Rose of Weary Leaf*, London: Heinemann.

—— (1911) *Tales of the Uneasy*, London: Heinemann.

Hunt, Mrs Alfred and Hunt, Violet (1912) *The Governess*, London: Chatto & Windus.

Hutchins, B. L. (1911) *The Working Life of Women*, London: Fabian Society.

—— (1915) *Women in Modern Industry*, London: G. Bell.

—— (1917) *Women in Industry after the War* (Social Reconstruction Pamphlets, No. 3), London: The Athenaeum.

Irwin, H. C. ('Mark Time') (1912) *A Derelict Empire*, Edinburgh: Blackwood.

James, Henry (1907–9) *The New York Edition of the Novels and Tales*, 24 vols, New York: Charles Scribner's Sons.

—— (1923) *The Sacred Fount*, London: Macmillan.

—— (1959) *Italian Hours*, New York: Grove Press.

—— (1962–4) *The Complete Tales*, ed. Leon Edel, 12 vols, London: Rupert Hart-Davis.

—— (1966a) *The Turn of the Screw*, ed. Robert Kimborough, New York: W. W. Norton.

—— (1966b) *The Golden Bowl*, Harmondsworth: Penguin Books.

—— (1974–84) *Letters*, ed. Leon Edel, 4 vols, Cambridge, Mass.: Harvard University Press.

—— (1983) *Autobiography*, ed. F. W. Dupee, Princeton: Princeton University Press.

—— (1984a) *Literary Criticism. Essays on Literature, American Writers, English Writers*, ed. Leon Edel and Mark Wilson, New York: Library of America.

—— (1984b) *Literary Criticism. French Writers, Other European Writers, the Prefaces to the New York Edition*, ed. Leon Edel and Mark Wilson, New York: Library of America.

—— (1987) *Complete Notebooks*, ed. Leon Edel and Lyall H. Powers, Oxford: Oxford University Press.

James, Henry and Wells, H. G. (1958) *Henry James and H. G. Wells*, ed. Leon Edel and Gordon Ray, Urbana: Illinois University Press.

James, M. R. (1984) *The Complete Ghost Stories*, Harmondsworth: Penguin Books.
James, William (1907) 'The energies of men', *Philosophical Review* 16, pp. 1–20.
—— (1967) *Writings*, ed. John J. McDermott, New York: Random House.
Jeffreys, Sheila (ed.) (1987) *The Sexuality Debates*, London: Routledge & Kegan Paul.
Jeune, Lady Mary (1895) 'The ethics of shopping', *Fortnightly Review*, 63, pp. 123–32.
Jevons, W. Stanley (1888) *The Theory of Political Economy*, 3rd edn, London: Macmillan.
Joyce, James (1957–66) *Letters*, 3 vols, ed. Stuart Gilbert (vol. I) and Richard Ellmann (vols II and III), London: Faber.
—— (1959) *Critical Writings*, ed. Ellsworth Mason and Richard Ellmann, London: Faber.
—— (1960) *Ulysses*, London: Bodley Head.
—— (1976a) *Dubliners*, ed. Robert Scholes, Harmondsworth: Penguin Books.
—— (1976b) *A Portrait of the Artist as a Young Man*, Harmondsworth: Penguin Books.
—— (1984) *Ulysses*, critical and synoptic edn, ed. Hans Walter Gabler, 3 vols, New York: Garland.
Keating, Joseph (1900) *Son of Judith*, London: George Allen.
—— (1916) *My Struggle for Life*, London: Simpkin.
Keating, P. J. (ed.) (1971a) *Working-Class Stories of the 1890s*, London: Routledge & Kegan Paul.
Ker, Alice (1884) *Lectures to Women*, London: John Heywood.
Kernahan, Coulson (1897) *Captain Shannon*, London: Ward, Lock.
Kidd, Benjamin (1898) *The Control of the Tropics*, London: Macmillan.
Kingsley, Charles (1875) *The Roman and the Teuton*, new edn, Oxford: Oxford University Press.
Kingsley, Mary H. (1901) *West African Studies*, 2nd edn, London: Macmillan.
Kipling, Rudyard (1940) *Kipling's Verse*, London: Hodder & Stoughton.
—— (1971) *Short Stories*, ed. Andrew Rutherford, 2 vols, Harmondsworth: Penguin Books.
—— (1978) *Kim*, ed. Mark Kincead-Weekes, London: Pan Books.
—— (1986) *Kipling's India. Uncollected Sketches 1884–8*, London: Macmillan.
—— (1987a) *Plain Tales from the Hills*, ed. H. R. Woudhuysen, Harmondsworth: Penguin Books.
—— (1987b) *Life's Handicap*, ed. P. N. Furbank, Harmondsworth: Penguin Books.
—— (1987c) *The Jungle Books*, ed. Daniel Karlin, Harmondsworth: Penguin Books.
—— (1987d) *Puck of Pook's Hill*, ed. Sarah Wintle, Harmondsworth: Penguin Books.
—— (1987e) *Rewards and Fairies*, ed. Roger Lewis, Harmondsworth: Penguin Books.
—— (1987f) *A Diversity of Creatures*, ed. Paul Driver, Harmondsworth: Penguin Books.
—— (1987g) *Something of Myself*, ed. Robert Hampson, Harmondsworth: Penguin Books.

—— (1988) *The Light That Failed*, ed. John Lyon, Harmondsworth: Penguin Books.

Kirk, E. B. (1905a) *A Talk with Boys about Themselves*, London: Simpkin Marshall.

—— (1905b) *A Talk with Girls about Themselves*, London: Simpkin Marshall.

Lankester, Edwin Ray (1880) *Degeneration. A Chapter in Darwinism*, London: Macmillan.

Law, Sir E. Fitzgerald (1906) 'The problem of the gold reserve', *National Review* 48, pp. 527–40.

Law, John (1888) *Out of Work*, London: Swan Sonnenschein.

—— (1890) *A Manchester Shirtmaker*, London: Authors' Co-operative Publishing Company.

—— (1984) *A City Girl*, New York: Garland.

Lawrence, D. H (1948) *Sons and Lovers*, Harmondsworth: Penguin Books.

—— (1955) *Selected Literary Criticism*, London: Heinemann.

—— (1960) *England, My England*, Harmondsworth: Penguin Books.

—— (1971) *The Mortal Coil*, ed. Keith Sugar, Harmondsworth: Penguin Books.

—— (1979–89) *Letters*, ed. James T. Boulton et al., 5 vols to date, Cambridge: Cambrige University Press.

—— (1982a) *The White Peacock*, Harmondsworth: Penguin Books.

—— (1982b) *Complete Short Novels*, Harmondsworth: Penguin Books.

—— (1983) *The Prussian Officer and Other Stories*, ed. John Worthen, Cambridge: Cambridge University Press.

—— (1987) *Women in Love*, ed. David Farmer, Lindeth Vasey and John Worthen, Cambridge: Cambridge University Press.

—— (1989) *The Rainbow*, ed. Mark Kinkead-Weekes, Cambridge: Cambridge University Press.

Lawrence, T. E. (1962) *Seven Pillars of Wisdom*, Harmondsworth: Penguin Books.

—— (1978) *The Mint*, Harmondsworth: Penguin Books.

Lea, Hermann (1977) *Thomas Hardy's Wessex*, London: Macmillan.

Le Queux, William (1894) *The Great War in England in 1897*, London: Tower.

—— (1896) *A Secret Service*, London: Ward, Lock & Bowden.

—— (1901) *Her Majesty's Minister*, London: Hodder & Stoughton.

—— (1903) *Secrets of the Foreign Office*, London: Hutchinson.

—— (1904) *The Man from Downing Street*, London: Hurst & Blackett.

—— (1906) *The Invasion of 1910*, London: Eveleigh Nash.

—— (1909) *Spies for the Kaiser*, London: Hurst & Blackett.

—— (1916) *Number 70, Berlin. A Story of Britain's Peril*, London: Hodder & Stoughton.

Leverson, Ada (1950) *Love's Shadow*, London: Chapman and Hall.

Levitt, Dorothy (1909) *The Woman and the Car*, London: John Lane.

Lewis, Percy Wyndham (1927a) *The Wild Body*, London: Chatto & Windus.

—— (1927b) *Time and Western Man*, London: Chatto & Windus.

—— (1973) *Tarr*, New York: Jubilee Books.

—— (1977) *Mrs Duke's Millions*, Toronto: Coach House Press.

—— (1979) *Collected Poems and Plays*, Manchester: Carcanet.

—— (1982) *The Complete Wild Body*, ed. Bernard Lafourcade, Santa Barbara: Black Sparrow Press.

—— (1984) *Rude Assignment*, ed. Toby Foshay, Santa Barbara: Black Sparrow Press.

Lyttelton, the Hon. E. (1900) *Training of the Young in Laws of Sex*, London: Longmans, Green.

MacGill, Patrick (1914) *Children of the Dead End*, London: Herbert Jenkins.

Mansfield, Katherine (1983) *Short Stories*, New York: Ecco Press.

Mansfield, Katherine and Murry, John Middleton (1988) *Letters between Katherine Mansfield and John Middleton Murry*, ed. Cherry A. Hankin, London: Virago.

March, Norah H. (1915) *Towards Racial Health*, London: George Routledge.

—— (1922) *Sex Knowledge*, London: W. Foulsham.

'Mark Time' (1912): *see* Irwin, H. C.

Mason, A. E. W. (1910) *At the Villa Rose*, London: Hodder & Stoughton.

—— (1924) *The House of the Arrow*, London: Hodder & Stoughton.

—— (1986) *The Four Feathers*, London: J. M. Dent.

Masterman, C. F. G. (1905) *In Peril of Change*, London: T. Fisher Unwin.

—— (ed.) (1909) *The Condition of England*, London: Methuen.

Maugham, Somerset (1934) *Liza of Lambeth*, Collected Edn, London: Heinemann.

—— (1990a) *Of Human Bondage*, London: Mandarin.

—— (1990b) *The Merry-Go-Round*, London: Mandarin.

—— (1990c) *On a Chinese Screen*, London: Mandarin.

—— (1991a) *The Magician*, London: Mandarin.

—— (1991b) *Mrs Craddock*, London: Mandarin.

Maxwell, W. B. (1913) *The Devil's Garden*, London: Hutchinson.

Mayor, F. M. (1913) *The Third Miss Symons*, London: Sidgwick & Jackson.

Meade, L. T. (1898) *The Siren*, London: F. V. White.

Mills, Eliot E. (1905) *The Decline and Fall of the British Empire*, Oxford: Oxford University Press.

Mitford, Bertram (1922) *The Gun-Runner*, Popular Edition, London: T. Fisher Unwin.

Moore, George (1903) *The Untilled Field*, London: T. Fisher Unwin.

—— (1914) *Impressions and Opinions*, 2nd edn, London: T. Werner Laurie.

—— (1936) *Esther Waters*, London: Dent.

Moore, T. Sturge (1910) *Art and Life*, London: Methuen.

Mordaunt, Elinor (1916) *The Park Wall*, London: Cassell.

Morrison, Arthur (1971) *Martin Hewitt: Investigator*, Philadelphia: Oswald Train.

—— (1982) *A Child of the Jago*, Woodbridge: Boydell Press.

Muller, Max (1861) *Lectures on the Science of Language*, first series, London: Longmans, Green.

National Home Reading Union (1909) *Report of the Council*.

Nesbit, Edith (1903) *The Red House*, London: Methuen.

Newbolt, Henry (1906) *The Old Country. A Romance*, London: Smith, Elder.

Nordau, Max (1920) *Degeneration*, Popular Edition, London: Heinemann.

Onions, Oliver (1913) *The Debit Account*, London: Martin Secker.

Oppenheim, E. Phillips (1898) *The Mysterious Mr Sabin*, London: Ward, Lock.

—— (1900) *A Millionaire of Yesterday*, London: Ward, Lock.

—— (1905) *A Maker of History*, London: Ward, Lock.

—— (1907) *The Secret*, London: Ward, Lock.

—— (1915) *The Double Traitor*, Boston: Little Brown.

—— (1920) *The Great Impersonation*, London: Hodder & Stoughton.

Orczy, Baroness (1905) *The Scarlet Pimpernel*, London: Greening.

BIBLIOGRAPHY

—— (1908) *The Old Man in the Corner*, London: Greening.

—— (1910) *Lady Molly of Scotland Yard*, London: Cassell.

Orwell, George (1962) *The Road to Wigan Pier*, Harmondsworth: Penguin Books.

Pain, Barry (1904) *Deals*, London: Hodder & Stoughton.

Parish, W. D. (1875) *A Dictionary of the Sussex Dialect*, 2nd edn, Lewes: Farncombe.

Paston, George (1898) *A Writer of Books*, London: Chapman and Hall.

Patten, Simon (1889) *The Consumption of Wealth* (Publications of the University of Pennsylvania, No. 4).

—— (1899) *The Development of English Thought*, New York: Macmillan.

—— (1968) *The New Basis of Civilization*, Cambridge, Mass.: Belknap Press.

Pearson, Karl (1905) *National Life from the Standpoint of Science*, 2nd edition, London: A. & C. Black.

Petrie, W. M. Flinders (1907) *Janus in Modern Life*, London: Constable.

Phillpotts, Eden (1898) *Children of the Mist*, London: A. D. Innes.

Pike, E. Royston (ed.) (1969) *Human Documents of the Age of the Forsytes*, London: Allen & Unwin.

—— (ed.) (1972) *Human Documents of the Lloyd George Era*, London: Allen & Unwin.

Pocock, Roger (1896) *Rottenness. A Study of America and England*, London: Neville Beeman.

—— (1904) *Curly*, London: Gay & Bird.

—— (1931) *Chorus to Adventurers*, London: John Lane.

Pound, Ezra (1983) *Pound/Ford*, ed. B. Lindberg-Seyersted, London: Faber.

Powell, Ellis T. (1915) *The Evolution of the Money-Market*, London: Financial News.

Proust, Marcel (1983) *Remembrance of Things Past*, trans. C. K. Scott-Moncrieff and Terence Kilmartin, 3 vols, Harmondsworth: Penguin Books.

Radford, George (1910) *The Faculty of Reading. The Coming of Age of the NHRU*, Cambridge: Cambridge University Press.

Raleigh, Walter (1906) *The English Voyages of the Sixteenth Century*, Glasgow: James MacLehose.

—— (1918) *England and the War*, Oxford: Oxford University Press.

Reid, Forrest (1911) *The Bracknels*, London: Edward Arnold.

Remington, Frederic and Wister, Owen (1972) *My Dear Wister. The Frederic Remington–Owen Wister Letters*, ed. B. M. Vorphal, Palo Alto: American West.

Richardson, Dorothy (1979) *Pilgrimage*, 4 vols, London: Virago.

Ridge, W. Pett (1895) *A Clever Wife*, London: R. Bentley.

—— (1910) *From Nine to Six-Thirty*, London: Methuen.

—— (1923) *A Story Teller*, London: Hodder & Stoughton.

Roberts, Morley (1897) *Maurice Quain*, London: Hutchinson.

—— (1899a) *The Colossus*, London: Edward Arnold.

—— (1899b) *A Son of Empire*, London: Hutchinson.

Robins, Elizabeth (1904) *The Magnetic North*, London: Heinemann.

—— (1913) *'Where Are You Going To . . .?'*, London: Heinemann.

Roosevelt, Theodore (ed.) (1909) *The Frontiersman's Pocket Book*, London: John Murray.

—— (1926) *Works*, National Edition, ed. H. Hagedorn, 20 vols, New York: Scribner's.

—— (1951) *Letters*, ed. E. Morison, 2 vols, Cambridge, Mass.: Harvard University Press.

Ruck, Berta (1918) *The Land-Girl's Love Story*, London: Hodder & Stoughton.

Ruskin, John (1903–12) *Collected Works*, ed. E. T. Cook and A. Wedderburn, 39 vols, London: George Allen.

Sabatini, Rafael (1915) *The Sea Hawk*, London: Hutchinson.

—— (1921) *Scaramouche*, London: Hutchinson.

St John, Christopher (1915) *Hungerheart*, London: Methuen.

Saki (1963) *The Bodley Head Saki*, ed. J. W. Lambert, London: Bodley Head.

Saleeby, C. W. (1911) *The Methods of Race-Regeneration*, London: Cassell.

Sayers, Dorothy L. (1989) *Whose Body?*, London: Coronet.

Saywell, Evelyn (1922) *The Growing Girl*, London: Methuen.

Scharlieb, Mary (1912) *Womanhood and Race-Regeneration*, London: Cassell.

—— (1915) *The Seven Ages of Woman*, London: Cassell.

Scharlieb, Mary and Sibly, F. Arthur (1912) *Youth and Sex*, London: T. C. and E. C. Jack.

Schreiner, Olive (1978) *Woman and Labour*, London: Virago.

—— (1982) *From Man to Man*, London: Virago.

—— (1987) *An Olive Schreiner Reader*, ed. Carol Barash, London: Virago.

Scott, Bonnie Kime (ed.) (1990) *The Gender of Modernism*, Bloomington: Indiana University Press.

Scott, Walter Dill (1909) *The Psychology of Advertising*, London: Sir Isaac Pitman.

Seeley, J. R. (1883) *The Expansion of England*, London: Macmillan.

Selfridge, H. Gordon (1918) *The Romance of Commerce*, London: John Lane.

Sergeant, Adeline (1902) *The Work of Oliver Byrd*, London: James Nisbet.

Sharp, Evelyn (1915) *Rebel Women*, new edn, with a preface by Elizabeth Robins, London: United Suffragists.

—— (1933) *Unfinished Business*, London: John Lane.

Shaw, Bernard (1946) *Plays Unpleasant*, Harmondsworth: Penguin Books.

Sinclair, May (1907) *The Helpmate*, London: Archibald Constable.

—— (1980a) *Life and Death of Harriet Frean*, London: Virago.

—— (1980b) *Mary Olivier: A Life*, London: Virago.

—— (1982) *The Three Sisters*, London: Virago.

Sokel, Walter (ed.) (1963) *Anthology of German Expressionist Drama*, revised edn, Ithaca, NY: Cornell University Press.

Somerville, E. Oe. and Ross, Martin (1897) *The Silver Fox*, London: Lawrence & Bullen.

—— (1911) *Dan Russel the Fox*, London: Methuen.

—— (1917) *Irish Memories*, London: Longmans, Green.

—— (1920) *Stray-Aways*, London: Longmans, Green.

—— (1970) *The Irish R. M.*, London: Sphere Books.

—— (1989) *Selected Letters*, ed. Gifford Lewis, London: Faber.

—— (1990) *The Real Charlotte*, London: Arrow Books.

Spiers, Ernest A. (1910) *The Art of Publicity*, London: T. Fisher Unwin.

Stacpoole, H. de Vere (1908) *The Blue Lagoon*, London: T. Fisher Unwin.

—— (1924) *Golden Ballast*, London: Hutchinson.

Stein, Aurel (1909) *Explorations in Central Asia, 1906–8*, London: Royal Geographical Society.

Stevenson, Robert Louis (1979a) *Dr Jekyll and Mr Hyde*, ed. Jenni Calder, Harmondsworth: Penguin Books.

316

—— (1979b) *Weir of Hermiston and Other Stories*, ed. Paul Binding, Harmondsworth: Penguin Books.

Stoker, Bram (1979) *Dracula*, Harmondsworth: Penguin Books.

Swan, Annie S. (1892) *The Guinea Stamp*, Edinburgh: Oliphant.

—— (1893) *Courtship and Marriage*, London: Hutchinson.

Swiney, Frances (1899) *The Awakening of Women*, London: William Reeves.

——(1907) *The Bar of Isis*, London: Open Road.

Swinnerton, Frank (1918) *Shops and Houses*, London: Methuen.

Thomas, Edward (1982) *The Heart of England*, Oxford: Oxford University Press.

—— (1984) *The South Country*, London: J. M. Dent.

Thompson, Charles (1917) *Manhood. The Facts of Life Presented to Men*, London: Health Promotion.

Thompson, Thea (ed.) (1981) *Edwardian Childhoods*, London: Routledge & Kegan Paul.

Thompson, Tierl (ed.) (1987) *Dear Girl. The Diaries and Letters of Two Working Women, 1897–1917*, London: Women's Press.

Thorburn, W. M. (1876) *The 'Great Game'. A Plea for a British Imperial Policy*, 3rd edn, London: Simpkin Marshall.

Thorne, Guy (1903) *When It Was Dark*, London: Greening

Tirebuck, W. E. (1895) *Miss Grace of All Souls'*, London: Heinemann.

Tourette, Gilles de la (1895) *Traité clinique et thérapeutique de l'hystérié*, Paris: E. Plon, Nourrit.

Townshend, Mrs (1912) *William Morris and the Communist Ideal*, London: Fabian Society.

Tressell. Robert (1965) *The Ragged Trousered Philanthropists*, London: Granada.

Trevelyan, G. M. (1901) 'The White Peril', *Nineteenth Century and After* 50, pp. 1043–55.

Tuke, D. Hack (ed.) (1892) *A Dictionary of Psychological Medicine*, 2 vols, London: J. and A. Churchill.

Turner, Frederick Jackson (1921) *The Frontier in American History*, New York: Henry Holt.

Tusser, Thomas (1878) *Five Hundred Pointes of Good Husbandrie*, London: English Dialect Society.

Tweedale, Violet (1917) *The Heart of a Woman*, London: Hurst & Blackett.

Veblen, Thorstein (1925) *The Theory of the Leisure Class*, London: Allen & Unwin.

Wales, Hubert (1906) *Mr and Mrs Villiers*, London: John Long.

—— (1907a) *Cynthia in the Wilderness*, London: John Long.

—— (1907b) *The Yoke*, London: John Long.

—— (1909) *Hilary Thornton*, London: John Long.

—— (1913) *The Purpose. Reflections and Digressions*, London: John Long.

—— (1917) *The Rationalist*, London: John Long.

Wallace, Edgar (1905) *The Four Just Men*, London: Tallis Press.

—— (1914) *Sanders of the River*, London: Ward, Lock.

Walpole, Hugh (1914) *The Duchess of Wrexe*, London: Macmillan.

—— (1918) *The Green Mirror*, London: Macmillan.

—— (1920) *The Captives*, London: Macmillan.

Ward, Mrs Humphry (1920) *Harvest*, London: W. Collins.

—— (1984) *Marcella*, London: Virago.

Waugh, Evelyn (1938) *Vile Bodies*, Harmondsworth: Penguin Books.

Waugh, Evelyn (1951) *A Handful of Dust*, Harmondsworth: Penguin Books.

Webb, Beatrice (1926) *My Apprenticeship*, London: Longmans.

—— (1986) *Diary*, ed. Norman and Jeanne Mackenzie, 2 vols, London: Virago.

Weigall, Arthur (1921) *The Dweller in the Desert*, London: T. Fisher Unwin.

Wells, H. G. (1896) *The Island of Doctor Moreau*, London: Heinemann.

—— (1922) *The Secret Places of the Heart*, London: Cassell.

—— (1941) *The War in the Air*, Harmondsworth: Penguin Books.

—— (1946) *The New Machiavelli*, Harmondsworth: Penguin Books.

—— (1964) *Tono-Bungay*, London: Pan Books.

—— (1980) *Ann Veronica*, London: Virago.

—— (1983) *Love and Mr Lewisham*, Oxford: Oxford University Press.

—— (1984a) *Kipps*, Oxford: Oxford University Press.

—— (1984b) *H. G. Wells in Love*, ed. G. P. Wells, London: Faber & Faber.

—— (1986a) *Marriage*, London: Hogarth Press.

—— (1986b) *The Passionate Friends*, London: Hogarth Press.

—— (1986c) *The Wife of Sir Isaac Harman*, London: Hogarth Press.

—— (1987) *The Time Machine*, ed. Harry M. Geduld, Bloomington: Indiana University Press.

Wentworth-James, Gertie de S. (1908a) *The Wild Widow*, London: T. Werner Laurie.

—— (1908b) *Red Love*, London: T. Werner Laurie.

—— (1910) *The Scarlet Kiss*, London: T. Werner Laurie.

—— (1915) *The Purple Passion*, London: T. Werner Laurie.

West, Rebecca (1982) *The Young Rebecca*, ed. Jane Marcus, London: Virago.

Weyman, Stanley (1893) *A Gentleman of France*, London: Longmans, Green.

—— (1894) *The Man in Black*, London: Cassell.

Wharton, Edith (1968) *Complete Short Stories*, ed. R. W. B. Lewis, 2 vols, New York: Charles Scribner's Sons.

Wheatley, Dennis and Links, J. G. (1936) *Murder Off Miami*, London: Hutchinson.

—— (1937) *Who Killed Robert Prentice?*, London: Hutchinson.

—— (1938) *The Malinsay Massacre*, London: Hutchinson.

—— (1939) *Herewith the Clues!*, London: Hutchinson.

Wilde, Oscar (1985) *The Picture of Dorian Gray*, ed. Peter Ackroyd, Harmondsworth: Penguin Books.

Wister, Owen (1930) *Roosevelt. The Story of a Friendship*, New York: Macmillan.

—— (1988) *The Virginian*, ed. John Seelye, Harmondsworth: Penguin Books.

Withers, Hartley (1909) *The Meaning of Money*, London: Smith, Elder.

Wodehouse, P. G. (1938) *The Man Upstairs and Other Stories*, Harmondsworth: Penguin Books.

—— (1961) *A Damsel in Distress*, Harmondsworth: Penguin Books.

—— (1969) *Piccadilly Jim*, Harmondsworth: Penguin Books.

—— (1970) *Psmith Journalist*, Harmondsworth: Penguin Books.

—— (1979) *Something Fresh*, Harmondsworth: Penguin Books.

Woolf, Virginia (1919) 'Modern fiction', in P. Faulkner (ed.) *A Modernist Reader*, London: Batsford, pp. 105–12.

—— (1924) 'Mr Bennett and Mrs Brown', in P. Faulkner (ed.) *A Modernist Reader*, London: Batsford, pp. 112–28.

—— (1985) *Moments of Being*, ed. Jeanne Schulkind, 2nd edn, London: Hogarth Press.

—— (1986–8) *Essays*, vols I–III, ed. Andrew McNeillie, London: Hogarth Press.

—— (1990) *A Passionate Apprentice. The Early Journals, 1897–1909*, ed. Mitchell A. Leask, London: Hogarth Press.

—— (1992a) *Jacob's Room*, ed. Kate Flint, Oxford: Oxford University Press.

—— (1992b) *Night and Day*, ed. Suzanne Raitt, Oxford: Oxford University Press.

—— (1977) *A Room of One's Own*, London: Granada.

—— (1992c) *The Voyage Out*, ed. Lorna Sage, Oxford: Oxford University Press.

Wordsworth, William (1979) *The Prelude*, ed. M. H. Abrams, Stephen Gill and Jonathan Wordsworth, New York: W. W. Norton.

Wyllarde, Dolf (1904) *Uriah the Hittite*, London: Heinemann.

—— (1906) *The Pathway of the Pioneer*, London: Methuen.

—— (1911) *Rose-White Youth*, London: Cassell.

Wyndham, George (1913) *Letters*, ed. Guy Wyndham, 2 vols, Edinburgh: T. and A. Constable.

Zola, Emile (1970) *L'Assommoir*, trans. L. Tancock, Harmondsworth: Penguin Books.

—— (1972) *Nana*, trans. George Holden, Harmondsworth: Penguin Books.

SECONDARY SOURCES

Abel, Elizabeth (ed.) (1982) *Writing and Sexual Difference*, Brighton: Harvester Press.

Ackroyd, Peter (1984) *T. S. Eliot*, London: Hamish Hamilton.

Adburgham, Alison (1989) *Shops and Shopping, 1800–1914*, 3rd edn, London: Barrie & Jenkins.

Althusser, Louis (1971) *Lenin and Philosophy*, trans. Ben Brewster, London: New Left Books.

Altick, Richard (1991) *The Presence of the Present*, Columbia: Ohio State University Press.

Anderson, Quentin (1988) 'The emergence of modernism', in Emory Elliott (ed.) *The Columbia Literary History of the United States*, New York: Columbia University Press, pp. 695–714.

Andrew, Christopher (1985) *Secret Service. The Making of the British Intelligence Community*, London: Heinemann.

Anesko, Michael (1986) *'Friction with the Market'. Henry James and the Profession of Authorship*, Oxford: Oxford University Press.

Armstrong, Paul (1987) *The Challenge of Bewilderment. Understanding and Representation in James, Conrad and Ford*, Ithaca, NY: Cornell University Press.

Ashcroft, Bill, Griffiths, Gareth and Tiffin, Helen (eds) (1989) *The Empire Writes Back. Theory and Practice in Post-Colonial Literatures*, London: Routledge.

Ashley, Bob (ed.) (1989) *The Study of Popular Fiction. A Source Book*, London: Pinter.

Atkins, John (1984) *The British Spy Novel*, London: John Calder.

Attridge, Derek (1988) *Peculiar Language. Language as Difference from the Renaissance to James Joyce*, London: Methuen.

—— (ed.) (1990) *The Cambridge Companion to James Joyce*, Cambridge: Cambridge University Press.

Attridge, Derek and Ferrer, Daniel (eds) (1984) *Post-Structuralist Joyce*, Cambridge: Cambridge University Press.

BIBLIOGRAPHY

Attridge, Derek, Bennington, Geoff and Young, Robert (eds) (1987) *Post-Structuralism and the Question of History*, Cambridge: Cambridge University Press.

Auden, W. H. (1948) 'The guilty vicarage', in *The Dyer's Hand*, London: Faber & Faber, pp. 146–58.

Baguley, David (1990) *Naturalist Fiction*, Cambridge: Cambridge University Press.

Baldick, Chris (1983) *The Social Mission of English Criticism 1842–1932*, Oxford: Oxford University Press.

—— (1987) *In Frankenstein's Shadow*, Oxford: Oxford University Press.

Barthes, Roland (1975) *The Pleasure of the Text*, trans. Richard Miller, New York: Hill & Wang.

—— (1977) *Image-Music-Text*, ed. and trans. Stephen Heath, London: Fontana.

Batchelor, John (1982) *The Edwardian Novelists*, London: Duckworth.

Beer, Gillian (1990) 'The island and the aeroplane: the case of Virginia Woolf', in H. Bhabha (ed.) *Nation and Narration*, London: Routledge, pp. 265–90.

Bell, Ian F. A. (ed.) (1984) *Henry James. Fiction as History*, London: Vision Press.

Bell, Millicent (1991) *Meaning in Henry James*, Cambridge, Mass.: Harvard University Press.

Belsey, Catherine (1980) *Critical Practice*, London: Methuen.

Benjamin, Andrew and Fletcher, John (eds) (1990) *Abjection, Melancholia and Love. The Work of Julia Kristeva*, London: Routledge.

Bennett, Tony (1990) *Popular Fiction*, London: Routledge.

Benstock, Bernard (1985) *James Joyce*, New York: Frederick Ungar.

—— (ed.) (1988) *James Joyce. The Augmented Ninth*, New York: Syracuse University Press.

—— (ed.) (1989) *Critical Essays on James Joyce's 'Ulysses'*, Boston: G. K. Hall.

Bergonzi, Bernard (1986) *The Myth of Modernism and Twentieth-Century Literature*, Brighton: Harvester Press.

Berridge, Virginia (1988) 'The origins of the English drug "scene" 1890–1930', *Medical History* 32, pp. 51–64.

Berthoud, Jacques (1978) *Joseph Conrad. The Major Phase*, Cambridge: Cambridge University Press.

Bhabha, Homi (1989) 'Signs taken for wonders: questions of ambivalence and authority under a tree outside Delhi, May 1817', in H. L. Gates (ed.) *'Race', Writing and Difference*, Chicago: Chicago University Press, pp. 163–84.

—— (ed.) (1990) *Nation and Narration*, London: Routledge.

Billington, Ray (1971) *The Genesis of the Frontier Thesis*, San Marino: Huntington Library Quarterly.

Birken, Lawrence (1988) *Consuming Desire*, Ithaca, NY: Cornell University Press.

Bjorhovde, Gerd (1987) *Rebellious Structures. Women Writers and the Crisis of the Novel, 1880–1900*, Oxford: Norwegian University Press.

Blackstone, Sarah (1986) *Buckskins, Bullets and Business. A History of Buffalo Bill's Wild West*, New York: Greenwood Press.

Blakemore, Diane (1987) *Semantic Constraints on Relevance*, Oxford: Blackwell.

Bloom, Clive (ed.) (1990a) *Twentieth-Century Suspense*, London: Macmillan.

—— (1990b) 'West is East: Nayland Smith's sinophobia and Sax Rohmer's bank balance', in Bloom (1990a), pp. 22–36.

Bloom, Harold (ed.) (1987) *Henry James's 'Daisy Miller', 'The Turn of the Screw,' and Other Tales*, New York: Chelsea House.

Bogardus, Ralph F. (1984) *Pictures and Texts. Henry James, A. L. Coburn, and New Ways of Seeing in Literary Culture*, Ann Arbor: UMI Research Press.

Boumelha, Penny (1982) *Thomas Hardy and Women*, Brighton: Harvester Press.

Bowlby, Rachel (1985) *Just Looking*, London: Methuen.

—— (1987) 'Promoting Dorian Gray', *Oxford Review* 9, pp. 147–62.

—— (1988) *Virginia Woolf. Feminist Destinations*, Oxford: Blackwell.

Bradbury, Malcolm (1971) *The Social Context of Modern English Literature*, Oxford: Blackwell.

Bradbury, Malcolm and McFarlane, James (eds) (1976) *Modernism*, Harmondsworth: Penguin Books.

Bradbury, Nicola (1979) *Henry James. The Later Novels*, Oxford: Clarendon Press.

—— (1984) ' "Nothing that is not there and the nothing that is": the celebration of absence in *The Wings of the Dove*', in I. F. A. Bell (ed.) *Henry James. Fiction as History*, London: Vision Press pp. 82–97.

Brandon, Ruth (1990) *The New Women and the Old Men*, London: Secker & Warburg.

Brantlinger, Patrick (1989) 'Victorians and Africans', in H. L. Gates (ed.) *'Race' Writing and Difference*, Chicago: Chicago University Press, pp. 185–222.

—— (1990) 'Mass media and culture in *fin-de-siècle* Europe', in R. Porter and M. Teich (eds) *Fin-de-Siècle and its Legacy*, Cambridge: Cambridge University Press. pp. 98–114.

Brewer, John and Porter, Roy (1992) 'Introduction', in *Consumption and the World of Goods*, London: Routledge.

Brewer, John, McKendrick, Neil and Plumb, J. H. (1982) *The Birth of Consumer Society. The Commercialization of Eighteenth-Century England*, Cambridge: Cambridge University Press.

Briggs, Asa (1988) *Victorian Things*, London: Batsford.

Bristow, Edward J. (1977) *Vice and Vigilance*, Dublin: Gill & Macmillan.

Brooks, Peter (1982) 'Freud's masterplot: questions of narrative', in S. Felman (ed.) *Literature and Psychoanalysis. The Question of Reading: Otherwise*, Baltimore: Johns Hopkins University Press, pp. 280–300.

——(1984) *Reading for the Plot* (Oxford: Clarendon Press).

Brown, Gillian and Yule, George (1983) *Discourse Analysis*, Cambridge: Cambridge University Press.

Brown, Keith (ed.) (1990) *Rethinking Lawrence*, Milton Keynes: Open University Press.

Brown, Richard (1985) *James Joyce and Sexuality*, Cambridge: Cambridge University Press.

Budgen, Frank (1934) *James Joyce and the Making of 'Ulysses'*, London: Grayson & Grayson.

Buitenhuis, Peter (1989) *The Great War of Words*, London: Batsford.

Bush, Ronald (1976) *The Genesis of Ezra Pound's Cantos*, Princeton, NJ: Princeton University Press.

Carroll, David (1982) 'The (dis)placement of the eye ("I"): point of view, voice, and the forms of fiction', in *The Subject in Question*, Chicago: Chicago University Press, pp. 51–87.

321

Cave, Richard (1978) *A Study of the Novels of George Moore*, Gerrards Cross: Colin Smythe.

Cave, Terence (1988) *Recognitions*, Oxford: Clarendon Press.

Cawelti, John G. and Rosenberg, Bruce A. (1987) *The Spy Story*, Chicago: Chicago University Press.

Caws, Mary Ann (1985) 'High Modernist framing: framing in the later James', in *Reading Frames in Modern Fiction*, Princeton, NJ: Princeton University Press, pp. 121–206.

Chandler, Alfred D. (1990) '*Fin-de-siècle*: industrial transformation', in R. Porter and M. Teich (eds) *Fin-de-Siècle and its Legacy*, Cambridge: Cambridge University Press, pp. 28–41.

Chapman, Sara S. (1990) *Henry James's Portrait of the Writer as Hero*, London: Macmillan.

Chase, Stuart (1971) *The Economy of Abundance*, Port Washington, NY: Kennikat Press.

Chatman, Seymour (1972) *The Later Style of Henry James*, Oxford: Blackwell.

Clark, Michael (1981) 'The rejection of psychological approaches to mental disorder in late nineteenth-century British psychiatry', in Andrew Scull (ed.) *Madhouses, Mad-Doctors, and Madmen*, London: Athlone Press, pp. 271–312.

Clarke, I. F. (1966) *Voices Prophesying War, 1763–1984*, Oxford: Oxford University Press.

Coggrave, John (1991) 'Behind the squirtscreen', *Times Literary Supplement* 5 April 1991, pp. 11–12.

Cohn, Dorrit (1978) *Transparent Minds. Narrative Modes for Presenting Consciousness in Fiction*, Princeton, NY: Princeton University Press.

Collier, Peter and Geyer-Ryan, Helga (eds) (1992) *Literary Theory Today*, Cambridge: Polity Press.

Collini, Stefan (1991) *Public Moralists*, Oxford: Clarendon Press.

Colls, Robert and Dodd, Philip (eds) (1986) *Englishness. Politics and Culture 1880–1920*, London: Croom Helm.

Colmer, John (1975) *E. M. Forster. The Private Voice*, London: Routledge & Kegan Paul.

Connor, Steven (1989) *Postmodernist Culture*, Oxford: Blackwell.

Coward, Rosalind and Ellis, John (1977) *Language and Materialism*, London: Routledge & Kegan Paul.

Cox, R. G. (1970) *Thomas Hardy: The Critical Heritage*, London: Longman.

Crackanthorpe, David (1977) *Hubert Crackanthorpe and English Realism in the 1890s*, Columbia: Missouri University Press.

Craig, Patricia and Cadogan, Mary (1986) *The Lady Investigates. Women Detectives and Spies in Fiction*, Oxford: Oxford University Press.

Cross, Nigel (1985) *The Common Writer. Life in Nineteenth-Century Grub Street*, Cambridge: Cambridge University Press.

Crossick, Geoffrey (ed.) (1977) *The Lower Middle Class in Britain*, London: Croom Helm.

—— (1984) 'Shopkeepers and the state in Britain, 1870–1914', in Crossick and Haupt (1984), pp. 239–69.

Crossick, Geoffrey and Haupt, Heinz-Gerhard (1984) *Shopkeepers and Master Artisans in Nineteenth-Century Europe*, London: Methuen.

BIBLIOGRAPHY

Crowley, Tony (1989) *The Politics of Discourse: The Standard Language Question in British Cultural Debates*, London: Macmillan.

Culler, Jonathan (1981) *The Pursuit of Signs*, London: Routledge & Kegan Paul.

Cunningham, A. R. (1973) 'The "New Woman fiction" of the 1890s', *Victorian Studies* 17, pp. 177–86.

Cunningham, Gail (1978) *The New Woman in Victorian Fiction*, London: Macmillan.

Cunningham, Valentine (1988) *British Writers of the Thirties*, Oxford: Oxford University Press.

Curtis, L. P. (1968) *Anglo-Saxons and Celts*, Hartford, Connecticut: Conference in British Studies.

Dasenbrock, Reed Way (1985) *The Literary Vorticism of Ezra Pound and Wyndham Lewis*, Baltimore: Johns Hopkins University Press.

Daugherty, Sarah B. (1981) *The Literary Criticism of Henry James*, Athens: Ohio University Press.

Davies, Alistair (1980) '*Tarr*: a Nietzchean novel', in J. Meyers (ed.) *Wyndham Lewis: a Revaluation*, London: Athlone Press, pp. 107–19.

Denning, Michael (1987) *Cover Stories. Narrative and Ideology in the British Spy Thriller*, London: Routledge & Kegan Paul.

Derrida, Jacques (1976) *Of Grammatology*, trans. Gayatri Chakravorty Spivak, Baltimore: Johns Hopkins University Press.

—— (1978) *Writing and Difference*, trans. Alan Bass, London: Routledge & Kegan Paul.

—— (1981a) *Dissemination*, trans. Barbara Johnson, London: Athlone Press.

—— (1981b) *Positions*, trans. Alan Bass, London: Athlone Press.

—— (1987) *The Post Card*, trans. Alan Bass, Chicago: Chicago University Press.

Douglas, Ann (1977) *The Feminization of American Culture*, New York: A. A. Knopf.

Douglas, Mary (1966) *Purity and Danger*, London: Routledge & Kegan Paul.

Dowbiggin, Ian (1985) 'Degeneration and hereditarianism in French mental medicine, 1840–90', in W. F. Bynum, Roy Porter and Michael Shepherd (eds) *The Anatomy of Madness. Essays in the History of Psychiatry*, London: Tavistock, pp. 188–232.

Doyle, Brian (1989) *English and Englishness*, London: Routledge.

Eagleton, Terry (1989) 'Modernism, myth and monopoly capitalism', *News from Nowhere* 7, pp. 19–24.

Edel, Leon (1969) *Henry James. The Treacherous Years 1895–1901*, Philadelphia: Lippincott, 1969.

—— (1972) *Henry James. The Master 1901–1916*, Philadelphia: Lippincott.

Ellmann, Maud (1982) 'Polytropic man', in MacCabe (ed.) *James Joyce: New Perspectives*, Brighton: Harvester Press pp. 73–104.

—— (1984) 'The intimate difference: power and representation in *The Ambassadors*', in I. F. A. Bell (ed.) *Henry James. Fiction as History*, London: Vision Press, pp. 98–113.

—— (1987) *The Poetics of Impersonality*, Brighton: Harvester Press.

Ellmann, Maud (1990) 'Eliot's abjection', in A. Benjamin and J. Fletcher (eds)

BIBLIOGRAPHY

Abjection, Melancholia and Love. The Work of Julia Kristeva, London: Routledge, pp. 178–200.

Ellmann, Richard (1959) *James Joyce*, Oxford: Oxford University Press.

—— (1987) *Oscar Wilde*, London: Hamish Hamilton.

Ellmann, Richard and Feidelson, Charles (1965) *The Modern Tradition. Backgrounds of Modern Literature*, Oxford: Oxford University Press.

Everett, Barbara (1991) 'Kipling's lightning-flash', *London Review of Books*, 10 January, pp. 12–15.

Fabb, Nigel (1988) 'Saussure and literary theory: from the perspective of linguistics', *Critical Quarterly* 30, pp. 58–72.

Faber, Richard (1966) *The Vision and the Need*, London: Faber & Faber.

Fahnestock, Jeanne (1981) 'The heroine of irregular features', *Victorian Studies* 24, pp. 325–50.

Felman, Shoshona (ed.) (1982a) *Literature and Psychoanalysis. The Question of Reading: Otherwise*, Baltimore: Johns Hopkins University Press.

—— (1982b) 'Turning the screw of interpretation', in Felman (1982a), pp. 94–207.

Fish, Stanley (1980) *Is There a Text in This Class?*, Cambridge, Mass.: Harvard University Press.

Fisher, Philip (1982) 'Acting, reading, Fortune's wheel: *Sister Carrie* and the life history of objects', in E. J. Sundquist (ed.) *American Realism. New Essays*, Baltimore: Johns Hopkins University Press, pp. 259–77.

Fleishman, Avrom (1990) 'Lawrence and Bakhtin', in K. Brown (ed.) *Rethinking Lawrence*, Milton Keynes: Open University Press.

Flint, Kate (1986) 'Fictional suburbia', in Humm et al. (eds) *Popular Fictions*, London: Methuen, pp. 111–26.

Fogel, Aaron (1985) *Coercion to Speak. Conrad's Poetics of Dialogue*, Cambridge, Mass.: Harvard University Press.

Fraser, W. Hamish (1981) *The Coming of the Mass Market, 1850–1914*, London: Macmillan.

Freedman, Jonathan (1990) *Professions of Taste. Henry James, British Aestheticism, and Commodity Culture*, Stanford, CA: Stanford University Press.

French, David (1978) 'Spy fever in Britain, 1900–1915', *Historical Journal* 21, pp. 355–70.

French, Marilyn (1982) *The Book as World*, London: Abacus.

Frow, Edmund and Frow, Ruth (1987) 'Ethel Carnie: writer, feminist and socialist', in H. G. Klaus (ed.) *The Rise of Socialist Fiction, 1880–1914*, Brighton: Harvester Press, pp. 251–66.

Fussell, Paul (1975) *The Great War and Modern Memory*, Oxford: Oxford University Press.

Gagnier, Regina (1987) *Idylls of the Marketplace*, London: Scolar Press.

Gallagher, Catherine (1985) *The Industrial Reformation of English Fiction*, Chicago: Chicago University Press.

Garnett, David (1954) *The Golden Echo*, London: Chatto & Windus.

Gates, Henry Louis (ed.) (1989) *'Race', Writing and Difference*, Chicago: Chicago University Press.

Giedion, Siegfried (1948) *Mechanization Takes Command*, New York: W. W. Norton.

Gilbert, Sandra (1982) 'Costumes of the mind: transvestism as metaphor in modern literature', in E. Abel (ed.) *Writing and Sexual Difference*, Brighton: Harvester Press, pp. 193–219.

Gilbert, Stuart (1952) *James Joyce's 'Ulysses'*, new edn, London: Faber & Faber.

Gilman, Sander (1989) 'Black bodies, white bodies', in H. L. Gates (ed.) *'Race', Writing and Difference*, Chicago: Chicago University Press, pp. 223–61.

Gloversmith, Frank (ed.) (1984) *The Theory of Reading*, Brighton: Harvester Press.

Goetz, William (1986) *Henry James and the Darkest Abyss of Romance*, Baton Rouge: Louisiana State University Press.

Gombrich, E. H. (1963) 'Psycho-analysis and the history of art' (1953), in *Meditations on a Hobby Horse*, London: Phaidon, pp. 30–44.

Gooch, John (1981) *The Prospect of War*, London: Cass.

Goode, John (1982) 'Margaret Harkness and the socialist novel', in H. G. Klaus, (ed.) *The Socialist Novel in Britain*, Brighton: Harvester Press, pp. 45–66.

Gordon, Lyndall (1984) *Virginia Woolf*, Oxford: Oxford University Press.

Gottfried, Roy K. (1980) *The Art of Joyce's Syntax*, London: Macmillan.

Grainger, J. H. (1986) *Patriotisms. Britain 1900–1939*, London: Routledge & Kegan Paul.

Green, Robert (1981) *Ford Madox Ford. Prose and Politics*, Cambridge: Cambridge University Press.

Greenbaum, Sidney and Quirke, Randolph (1990) *A Student's Grammar of the English Language*, London: Longman.

Greenslade, William (1982) 'The power of advertising: Chad Newsome and the meaning of Paris in *The Ambassadors*', *English Literary History*, 49, pp. 99–122.

Grice, H. P. (1975) 'Logic and conversation', in P. Cole and J. Morgan (eds) *Syntax and Semantics 3: Speech Acts*, New York: Academic Press, pp. 41–58.

Groden, Michael (1977) *Ulysses in Progress*, Princeton, NJ: Princeton University Press.

Halperin, John (1982) *Gissing. A Life in Books*, Oxford: Oxford University Press.

Hanscombe, Gillian (1982) *The Art of Life. Dorothy Richardson and the Development of Feminist Consciousness*, London: Peter Owen.

Hardwick, Joan (1991) *An Immodest Violet. The Life of Violet Hunt*, London: Deutsch.

Harrison, J. F. C. (1991) *Late Victorian Britain*, London: Routledge.

Hart, Clive and Knuth, Leo (1975) *A Topographical Guide to James Joyce's 'Ulysses'*, Colchester: Wake Newslitter Press.

Hart-Davis, Rupert (1952) *Hugh Walpole*, London: Macmillan.

Harvie, Christopher (1991) *The Centre of Things. Political Fiction in Britain from Disraeli to the Present*, London: Unwin Hyman.

Hawthorn, Jeremy (ed.) (1984) *The British Working-Class Novel in the Twentieth Century*, London: Edward Arnold.

—— (1990) 'Lawrence and working-class fiction', in K. Brown, (ed.) *Rethinking Lawrence*, Milton Keynes: Open University Press, pp. 67–78.

Hayman, David (1982) *'Ulysses'. The Mechanics of Meaning*, Madison: Wisconsin University Press.

Heath, Stephen (1982) *The Sexual Fix*, London: Macmillan.

—— (1986) 'Ambiviolences', in D. Attridge and D. Ferrer (eds) *Post-Structuralist Joyce*, Cambridge: Cambridge University Press, pp. 31–68.

Hennegan, Alison (1990) 'Personalities and principles: aspects of literature and life in *fin-de-siècle* England', in R. Porter and M. Teich (ed.) *Fin-de-Siècle and its Legacy*, Cambridge: Cambridge University Press, pp. 170–215.

Herr, Cheryl (1986) *Joyce's Anatomy of Culture*, Urbana: Illinois University Press.

Hewitt, Douglas (1988) *English Fiction of the Early Modern Period*, London: Longman.

Higham, John (1970) 'The reorientation of American culture in the 1890s', in *Writing American History*, Bloomington: Indiana University Press.

Hiley, Nicholas (1983) 'The failure of British espionage against Germany, 1907–1914', *Historical Journal* 26, pp. 867–89.

—— (1985) 'The failure of British counter-espionage against Germany, 1907–1914', *Historical Journal* 28, pp. 835–62.

—— (1990) 'Decoding German spies: British spy fiction, 1908–18', *Intelligence and National Security* 5, pp. 55–79.

Hobbs, Jerry (1990) *Literature and Cognition*, London: CSLI.

Hobsbawm, Eric (1969) *Industry and Empire*, Harmondsworth: Penguin Books.

Holcombe, Lee (1973) *Victorian Ladies at Work*, Hamden, Conn.: Archon Press.

Holderness, Graham (1984) 'Miners and the novel: from bourgeois to proletarian fiction', in J. Hawthorn (ed.) *The British Working-Class Novel in the Twentieth Century*, London: Edward Arnold, pp. 19–34.

Holroyd, Michael (1988–92) *Bernard Shaw*, 4 vols, London: Chatto & Windus.

Horne, Philip (1990) *Henry James and Revision*, Oxford: Clarendon Press.

Hough, Graham (1960) *Image and Experience. Studies in a Literary Revolution*, London: Duckworth.

Houston, John Porter (1989) *Joyce and Prose*, Lewisburg: Bucknell University Press.

Howkins, Alun (1986) 'The discovery of rural England', in R. Colls and P. Dodd (eds) *Englishness, Politics and Culture 1880–1920*, London: Croom Helm, pp. 62–88.

Humm, Peter, Stigant, Paul and Widdowson, Peter (eds) (1986) *Popular Fictions*, London: Methuen.

Hunter, Allan (1983) *Joseph Conrad and the Ethics of Darwinism*, London: Croom Helm.

Hunter, Jefferson (1982) *Edwardian Fiction*, Cambridge, Mass. : Harvard University Press.

Hutcheon, Linda (1985) *A Theory of Parody*, London: Methuen.

Huyssen, Andreas (1986) *After the Great Divide*, London: Macmillan, 1986.

Hynes, Samuel (1968) *The Edwardian Turn of Mind*, Princeton, NJ: Princeton University Press.

—— (1972) *Edwardian Occasions*, London: Routledge & Kegan Paul.

—— (1990) *A War Imagined*, London: The Bodley Head.

Irwin, Michael (1979) *Picturing. Description and Illusion in the Nineteenth-Century Novel*, London: Allen & Unwin.

Jacobson, Marcia (1983) *Henry James and the Mass Market*, Tuscaloosa, Alabama: Alabama University Press.

Jacobus, Mary (1975) 'Sue the Obscure', *Essays in Criticism* 25, pp. 304–28.

Jameson, Fredric (1979) *Fables of Aggression*, London: Routledge & Kegan Paul.

—— (1988a) *Modernism and Imperialism* (Field Day Pamphlet), Derry: Lawrence Hill.

—— (1988b) *The Ideologies of Theory*, 2 vols, London: Routledge.

—— (1990) *Signatures of the Visible*, London: Routledge.

Jauss, Hans (1982) *Towards an Aesthetic of Reception*, trans. T. Bahti, Brighton: Harvester Press.

Jefferson, George (1982) *Edward Garnett*, London: Jonathan Cape.

Jones, Gareth Stedman (1983) *Languages of Class*, Cambridge: Cambridge University Press.

Kaplan, Cora (1986) '*The Thorn Birds*: fiction, fantasy, femininity', in *Sea Changes. Culture and Feminism*, London: Verso, pp. 117–46.

Kappeler, Susanne (1980) *Writing and Reading in Henry James*, London: Macmillan.

Kearney, Patrick (1982) *A History of Erotic Literature*, London: Macmillan.

Keating, Peter (1971) *The Working Class in Victorian Fiction*, London: Routledge & Kegan Paul.

—— (1989) *The Haunted Study. A Social History of the English Novel 1875–1914*, London: Secker & Warburg.

Kelly, Dermot (1988) *Narrative Strategies in Joyce's 'Ulysses'*, Ann Arbor: UMI Research Press.

Kemp, Peter (1982) *H. G. Wells and the Culminating Ape*, London: Macmillan.

Kemp, Sandra (1990) 'But one isn't murdered: Elizabeth Bowen's *The Little Girls*' in C. Bloom (ed.) *Twentieth-Century Suspense*, London: Macmillan, pp. 130–42.

Kempson, Ruth (ed.) (1988) *Mental Representations*, Cambridge: Cambridge University Press.

Kennedy, Paul (1980) *The Rise of Anglo-German Antagonism, 1860–1914*, London: Allen & Unwin.

Kenner, Hugh (1972) *The Pound Era*, London: Faber & Faber.

—— (1980) *Ulysses*, London: Allen & Unwin.

Kent, Thomas (1986) *Interpretation and Genre*, Lewisburg: Bucknell University Press.

Kenwood, A. G. and Lougheed, A. L. (1983) *The Growth of the International Economy, 1820–1980*, London: Allen & Unwin.

Kermode, Frank (1966) *The Sense of an Ending*, Oxford: Oxford University Press.

—— (1983) *Essays on Fiction*, London: Routledge & Kegan Paul.

—— (1988) *History and Value*, Oxford: Oxford University Press.

Kershner, R. B. (1989) *Joyce, Bakhtin, and Popular Literature*, Chapel Hill: North Carolina University Press.

Kevles, Dan (1985) *In the Name of Eugenics*, New York: A. A. Knopf.

Klaus, H. Gustav (1982) *The Socialist Novel in Britain*, Brighton: Harvester Press.

—— (ed.) (1987a) *The Rise of Socialist Fiction, 1880–1914*, Brighton: Harvester Press.

—— (1987b) 'The strike novel in the 1890s', in Klaus (1987a), pp. 73–98.

Kohon, Gregorio (ed.) (1986) *The British School of Psychoanalysis*, London: Free Association Books.

Kristeva, Julia (1982) *Powers of Horror. An Essay on Abjection*, trans. Leon Roudiez, New York: Columbia University Press.

—— (1986) *The Kristeva Reader*, ed. Toril Moi, Oxford: Blackwell.

—— (1987) *Tales of Love*, trans. Leon Roudiez, New York: Columbia University Press.

BIBLIOGRAPHY

Leach, William R. (1984) 'Transformations in a culture of consumption: women and department stores, 1890–1925', *Journal of American History* 71, pp. 319–42.

Lee, Alan J. (1976) *The Origins of the Popular Press in England, 1855–1914*, London: Croom Helm.

Leech, Geoffrey N. (1983) *Principles of Pragmatics*, London: Longman.

Leech, Geoffrey N. and Short, Michael H. (1981) *Style in Fiction*, London: Longman.

Levine, George (1981) *The Realistic Imagination*, Chicago: Chicago University Press.

Levine, Jennifer (1990) '*Ulysses*', in D. Attridge (ed.) *The Cambridge Companion to James Joyce*, Cambridge: Cambridge University Press, pp. 131–59.

Levinson, S. (1983) *Pragmatics*, Cambridge: Cambridge University Press.

Lodge, David (1966) *The Language of Fiction*, London: Routledge & Kegan Paul.

—— (1977) *The Modes of Modern Writing*, London: Edward Arnold.

—— (1989) ' "Mrs Bathurst": indeterminacy in modern narrative', in P. Mallett (ed.) *Kipling Considered*, London: Macmillan, pp. 71–84.

—— (1990a) *After Bakhtin. Essays on Fiction and Criticism*, London: Routledge.

—— (1990b) 'Lawrence, Dostoevsky, Bakhtin: Lawrence and dialogic fiction', in K. Brown (ed.) *Rethinking Lawrence*, Milton Keynes : Open University Press, pp. 92–108.

Lowe, Donald M. (1988) *History of Bourgeois Perception*, Brighton: Harvester Press.

Lucas, John (1971) 'Conservatism and revolution in the 1880s', in Lucas (ed.) *Literature and Politics in the Nineteenth Century*, London: Methuen, pp. 173–221.

Lucie-Smith, Edward and Dars, Celestine (1977) *Work and Struggle. The Painter as Witness*, London: Paddington Press.

Lukacs, Georg (1963) *The Meaning of Contemporary Realism*, trans. John and Necke Mander, London: Merlin Press.

MacCabe, Colin (1978) *James Joyce and the Revolution of the Word*, London: Macmillan.

—— (ed.) (1982) *James Joyce: New Perspectives*, Brighton: Harvester Press.

McCormack, W.J. and Stead, Alistair (eds.) (1982) *James Joyce and Modern Literature*, London: Routledge & Kegan Paul.

McGee, Patrick (1988) *Paperspace. Style as Ideology in Joyce's 'Ulysses'*, Lincoln: Nebraska University Press.

Mackenzie, John (1984) *Propaganda and Empire*, Manchester: Manchester University Press.

—— (ed.) (1986) *Imperialism and Popular Culture*, Manchester: Manchester University Press.

McWhirter, David (1989) *Desire and Love in Henry James*, Cambridge: Cambridge University Press.

Mahaffey, Vicki (1988) *Reauthorizing Joyce*, Cambridge: Cambridge University Press.

Mallet, Philip (ed.) (1989) *Kipling Considered*, London: Macmillan.

Meisel, Perry (1987) *The Myth of the Modern*, New Haven: Yale University Press.

Melchiori, Barbara (1985) *Terrorism in the Late Victorian Novel*, London: Croom Helm.

Melman, Billie (1988) *Women and the Popular Imagination in the Twenties*, London: Macmillan.

Merry, Bruce (1977) *Anatomy of the Spy Thriller*, Montreal: Queen's University Press.

Meyers, Jeffrey (ed.) (1980) *Wyndham Lewis: a Revaluation*, London: Athlone Press.

Micale, Mark (1990) 'Charcot and the idea of hysteria in the male', *Medical History* 34, pp. 363–411.

Miles, Peter (1984) 'The painter's Bible and the British workman: Robert Tressell's literary activism', in J. Hawthorn (ed.) *The British Working-Class Novel in the Twentieth Century*, London: Edward Arnold, pp. 1–18.

Miller, Michael B. (1981) *The Bon Marché. Bourgeois Culture and the Department Store, 1869–1920*, Cambridge, Mass.: Harvard University Press.

Millgate, Michael (1982) *Thomas Hardy*, Oxford: Oxford University Press.

Mitchell, Jack (1987) 'Tendencies in narrative fiction in the London-based socialist press of the 1880s and 1890s', in H. G. Klaus (ed.) *The Rise of Socialist Fiction, 1880–1914*, Brighton: Harvester Press, pp. 49–72.

Mitchell, Juliet (1986) 'The question of feminity and the theory of psychoanalysis', in Kohon (ed.) *The British School of Psychoanalysis*, London: Free Association Books, pp. 381–98.

Mizener, Arthur (1972) *The Saddest Story*, London: The Bodley Head.

Modleski, Tania (1982) *Loving with a Vengeance. Mass-Produced Fantasies for Women*, Hamden, Conn.: Archon Press.

Moretti, Franco (1988) *Signs Taken for Wonders*, London: Verso.

Morgan, Rosemarie (1988) *Women and Sexuality in the Novels of Thomas Hardy*, London: Routledge.

Morris, A. J. A. (1984) *Scaremongers. The Advocacy of War and Rearmament, 1896–1914*, London: Routledge & Kegan Paul.

Morson, G. S. (ed.) (1986) *Bakhtin*, Chicago: Chicago University Press.

Mort, Frank (1987) *Dangerous Sexualities*, London: Routledge & Kegan Paul.

Nash, Walter (1980) *Design in Prose*, London: Longman.

Nehls, Edward (1958) *D. H. Lawrence. A Composite Biography*, 2 vols, Madison: Wisconsin University Press.

Newmeyer, Frederick J. (ed.) (1988) *Linguistics: the Cambridge Survey*, 4 vols, Cambridge: Cambridge University Press.

Norrman, Ralf (1982) *The Insecure World of Henry Jame's Fiction*, London: Macmillan.

Orel, Harold (1992) *Popular Fiction in England 1914–1918*, Hemel Hempstead: Harvester Wheatsheaf.

Overy, Richard (1990) 'Heralds of modernity: cars and planes from invention to necessity', in R. Porter and M. Teich (eds) *Fin-de-Siècle and its Legacy*, Cambridge, Cambridge University Press, pp. 54–79.

Page, Norman (1984) *A Kipling Companion*, London: Macmillan.

Parrinder, Patrick (1984) *James Joyce*, Cambridge: Cambridge University Press.

Parry, Benita (1987) 'Problems in current theories of colonial discourse', *Oxford Literary Review* 9, pp. 27–58.

Parssinen, Terry (1983) *Secret Passions, Secret Remedies*, Manchester: Manchester University Press.

Pick, Daniel (1989) *Faces of Degeneration*, Cambridge: Cambridge University Press.

Pinkney, Tony (1990) *D. H. Lawrence*, Hemel Hempstead: Harvester Wheatsheaf.

Pocock, J. G. A. (1975) *The Machiavellian Moment*, Princeton, NJ: Princeton University Press.

—— (1985) *Virtue, Commerce and History*, Cambridge: Cambridge University Press.

Pole, David (1983) *Aesthetics, Form and Emotion*, London: Duckworth.

Pool, Ithiel de Sola (1977) *The Social Impact of the Telephone*, Cambridge, Mass.: MIT Press.

Poole, Adrian (1989) 'Kipling's upper case', in P. Mallett (ed.) *Kipling Considered*, London: Macmillan, pp. 135–59.

—— (1991) *Henry James*, Hemel Hempstead: Harvester Wheatsheaf.

Porter, Bernard (1975) *The Lion's Share. A Short History of British Imperialism*, London: Longman.

—— (1982) 'The Edwardians and their empire', in D. Read (ed.) *Edwardian England*, London: Croom Helm.

—— (1987) *The Origins of the Vigilant State*, London: Weidenfeld & Nicholson.

Porter, Roy and Teich, Mikulas (eds) (1990) *Fin-de-Siècle and its Legacy*, Cambridge: Cambridge University Press.

Potter, David M. (1954) *People of Plenty. Economic Abundance and the American Character*, Chicago: Chicago University Press.

Radford, Jean (ed.) (1986) *The Progress of Romance. The Politics of Popular Fiction*, London: Routledge & Kegan Paul.

Radway, Janice (1984) *Reading the Romance. Women, Patriarchy and Popular Literature*, Chapel Hill: University of North Carolina Press.

Rainey, Lawrence (1989) 'The price of Modernism: reconsidering the publication of *The Waste Land*', *Critical Quarterly* 31, pp. 21–47.

Raleigh, John Henry (1977) *The Chronicle of Leopold and Molly Bloom*, Berkeley: California University Press.

Read, Donald (ed.) (1982) *Edwardian England*, London: Croom Helm.

Riquelme, John Paul (1990) '*Stephen Hero, Dubliners* and *A Portrait*', in D. Attridge (ed.) *The Cambridge Companion to James Joyce*, Cambridge: Cambridge University Press, pp. 103–30.

Rose, Jonathan (1986) *The Edwardian Temperament, 1895–1919*, Athens: Ohio University Press.

Rotman, Brian (1987) *Signifying Nothing*, London: Macmillan.

Rowe, John Carlos (1984) *The Theoretical Dimensions of Henry James*, London: Methuen.

Rubinstein, David (1986) *Before the Suffragettes. Women's Emancipation in the 1890s*, Brighton: Harvester Press.

Ryan, Kiernan (1987) 'Citizens of centuries to come: the ruling-class rebel in socialist fiction', in H. G. Klaus (ed.) *The Rise of Socialist Fiction, 1880–1914*, Brighton: Harvester Press, pp. 6–27.

Said, Edward (1975) *Beginnings. Intention and Method*, Baltimore: Johns Hopkins University Press.

—— (1978) *Orientalism*, London: Routledge & Kegan Paul.

Salveson, Paul (1987) 'Allen Clarke and the Lancashire school of working-class novelists', in H. G. Klaus (ed.) *The Rise of Socialist Fiction, 1880–1914*, Brighton: Harvester Press, pp. 172–202.

Sartre, Jean-Paul (1957) *Being and Nothingness*, trans. Hazel E. Barnes, London: Methuen.

Saveson, John (1974) 'Conrad, *Blackwood's*, and Lombroso', *Conradiana* 6, pp. 57–62.

Scarry, Elaine (1983) 'Work and the body in Hardy and other nineteenth-century novelists', *Representations* 3, pp. 90–123.

—— (1985) *The Body in Pain*, Oxford: Oxford University Press.

Schafer, Roy (1980) 'Narration in psychoanalytic dialogue', *Critical Inquiry* 7, pp. 29–53.

Searle, G. R. (1971) *The Quest for National Efficiency*, Oxford: Blackwell.

—— (1976) *Eugenics and Politics*, Leyden: Noordhoff International.

Sedgwick, Eve Kosofsky (1989) 'The beast in the closet: James and the writing of homosexual panic', in E. Showalter (ed.) *Speaking of Gender*, London: Routledge, pp. 243–68.

Seidel, Michael (1976) *Epic Geography. James Joyce's 'Ulysses'*, Princeton: Princeton University Press.

Seltzer, Mark (1984) *Henry James and the Art of Power*, Ithaca, NY: Cornell University Press.

Shell, Marc (1982) *Money, Language and Thought*, Berkeley: California University Press.

Shephard, Ben (1986) 'Showbiz imperialism', in J. Mackenzie (ed.) *Imperialism and Popular Culture*, Manchester: Manchester University Press, pp. 94–112.

Showalter, Elaine (1977) *A Literature of Their Own*, London: Virago.

—— (1987) *The Female Malady*, London: Virago.

—— (ed.) (1989) *Speaking of Gender*, London: Routledge.

—— (1991) *Sexual Anarchy: Gender and Culture at the Fin-de-Siècle*, London: Bloomsbury.

Simpson, David (1982) *Fetishism and Imagination*, Baltimore: Johns Hopkins University Press.

Smith, David C. (1986) *H. G. Wells*, New Haven: Yale University Press.

Smith, Neil (1989) *The Twitter Machine. Reflections on Language*, Oxford: Blackwell.

Sperber, Dan (1975) *Rethinking Symbolism*, trans. Alice Morton, Cambridge: Cambridge University Press.

Sperber, Dan and Wilson, Deirdre (1986) *Relevance. Communication and Cognition*, Oxford: Blackwell.

—— (1987) 'Précis of *Relevance*', in *Behavioral and Brain Sciences* 10, pp. 697–754.

Stafford, David (1981) 'Spies and gentlemen: the birth of the British spy novel, 1893–1914', *Victorian Studies* 24, pp. 489–509.

—— (1982) 'Conspiracy and xenophobia: the spy novels of William Le Queux, 1893–1914', *Europa* 3, pp. 163–85.

Stallybrass, Peter and White, Allon (1986) *The Politics and Poetics of Transgression*, London: Methuen.

Stead, Alistair (1982) 'Reflections on Eumaeus', in W. J. McCormack and A. Stead (eds) *James Joyce and Modern Literature*, London: Routledge & Kegan Paul, pp. 142–65.

Stubbs, Patricia (1980) *Women and Fiction*, Brighton: Harvester Press.

Sundquist, Eric J. (ed.) (1982) *American Realism. New Essays*, Baltimore: Johns Hopkins University Press.

Sutherland, John (1976) *Victorian Novelists and Publishers*, London: Athlone Press.

—— (1990) *Mrs Humphry Ward. Eminent Victorian, Preeminent Edwardian*, Oxford: Oxford University Press.

Tallack, Douglas (ed.) (1987) *Literary Theory at Work: Three Texts*, London: Batsford.

Tanner, Tony (1963) *Conrad: Lord Jim*, London: Edward Arnold.

Thompson, A. H. (1975) *Censorship in Public Libraries*, Epping: Bowker.

Thornton, Weldon (1968) *Allusions in 'Ulysses'*, new edn, Chapel Hill: North Carolina University Press.

Tickner, Lisa (1988) *The Spectacle of Women. Imagery of the Suffrage Campaign, 1907–1914*, Chicago: Chicago University Press.

Topia, André (1984) 'The matrix and the echo: intertextuality in *Ulysses*', in D. Attridge and D. Ferrer (eds) *Post-Structuralist Joyce*, Cambridge: Cambridge University Press, pp. 103–25.

Trotter, David (1984) *The Making of the Reader*, London: Macmillan.

—— (1986) 'Modernism and empire: reading *The Waste Land*', *Critical Quarterly* 28, pp. 143–52.

Tuchman, Gaye and Fortin, Nina E. (1989) *Edging Women Out*, New Haven: Yale University Press.

Turner, E. S. (1965) *The Shocking History of Advertising*, Harmondsworth: Penguin Books.

Vicinus, Martha (1985) *Independent Women. Work and Community for Single Women, 1850–1920*, London: Virago.

Vincent, David (1981) *Bread, Knowledge and Freedom. A Study of Nineteenth-Century Working-Class Autobiography*, London: Europa.

White, Allon (1981) *The Uses of Obscurity*, London: Routledge & Kegan Paul.

—— (1984) 'Bakhtin, sociolinguistics and deconstruction', in F. Gloversmith (ed.) *The Theory of Reading*, Brighton: Harvester Press, pp. 123–46.

Wicke, Jennifer (1988) *Advertising Fictions. Literature, Advertisement and Social Reading*, New York: Columbia University Press.

Wilde, Alan (1981) *Horizons of Assent. Modernism, Postmodernism, and the Ironic Imagination*, Baltimore: Johns Hopkins University Press.

Williams, Raymond (1982) 'Working-class, proletarian, socialist: problems in some Welsh novels', in H. G. Klaus (ed.) *The Socialist Novel in Britain*, Brighton: Harvester Press, pp. 110–21.

Williams, Rosalind H. (1982) *Dream Worlds. Mass Consumption in Late Nineteenth-Century France*, Berkeley: California University Press.

Wilson, Angus (1979) *The Strange Ride of Rudyard Kipling*, London: Granada.

Wilson, Deirdre and Sperber, Dan (1988) 'Representation and relevance', in R. Kempson (ed.) *Mental Representations*, Cambridge: Cambridge University Press, pp. 133–53.

Wilson, Edmund (1962) *The Triple Thinkers*, Harmondsworth: Penguin Books.

Winstanley, Michael J. (1983) *The Shopkeeper's World, 1830–1914*, Manchester: Manchester University Press.

Yeazell, Ruth Bernard (1976) *Language and Knowledge in the Late Novels of Henry James*, Chicago: Chicago University Press.

Yeo, Stephen (1977) 'A new life: the religion of socialism in Britain 1883–1896', *History Workshop Journal* 4, pp. 5–56.

INDEX